Architect's Handbook of Construction Project Management

Michael Murray and David Langford

2

RIBA Enterprises

© Michael Murray and David Langford 2004

Published by RIBA Enterprises Ltd, 15 Bonhill Street, London EC2P 2EA

ISBN 1 85946 123 9
Product Code 33066

British Library Cataloguing in Publication Data.
A catalogue record of this book is available from the British Library.

Publisher: Steven Cross
Commissioning Editor: Matthew Thompson
Editor: Christine Bury
Project Editor: Anna Walters
Typeset by Academic + Technical Typesetting, Bristol
Printed and bound by MPG, Cornwall

Contents

Contents continued

Contents continued

Foreword

The role of the architect has been seriously challenged over the last two decades. We have seen clients become more sophisticated, more demanding and prepared to take design and construction consultancy services from a much wider range of providers. The range of procurement routes available has widened and specialist trade contractors and managing contractors have, in different degrees, become engaged in the design process. Project managers have frequently been asked to undertake the duties of project administration formerly carried out by the architect.

Not only are the professional roles expected of the architect changing but the social position of the architect in relation to other team members is also under challenge. The once unilateral power of the architect has been dispersed to other members of the project team such that the construction project team is a much more democratic and pluralistic place.

These changes have challenged architects to re-engage with the other professionals in the construction team and stake a claim as managers of the overall construction process. The publication of this volume is but one step in the journey where architects, as much as any other profession, can manage the overall construction process as well as provide the creative input to the design.

The book takes its framework from the RIBA Plan of Work. As practitioners will know, this volume was updated in 2000 and still provides a valuable set of guidelines from which the architect can develop a project and determine how their responsibilities fit into the work of others in the construction team. The editors have successfully used this framework to evaluate the architect's role at each stage of the construction process. However, it is refreshing that the editors and the authors recognise that such linear models as the Plan of Work have their practical limitations, and the overwhelming message is that design and construction are not taken in discrete linear steps but as a reciprocating activity where design ideas iterate through the whole of the project process. The intention of the work is to present construction as an interactive activity where the best skills of designers, constructors and facility managers are employed to maximise user delight and function, and enhance the overall quality of the built environment. Whether the new ways of procurement and management of the construction process are enhancing or detracting from the quality of the built environment is a major question. It will presumably be answered by succeeding generations who will live with what is being built today for the rest of their lives. As Churchill pointed out: 'We make our buildings and then our buildings make us'. How we make our buildings is important today with a bearing upon tomorrow.

Finally, the editors have sought to integrate the best expertise drawn from the academic world and have commissioned authors from many countries – albeit the countries selected tend to use UK-based contractual systems and professional roles. More importantly than the provenance of the authors is the way that academics and practitioners have been harnessed together to produce chapters on each step in the Plan of Work: these chapters contain the very best theoretical analysis provided by the academic partner with case illustrations supplied by the practitioner. This combination of theory and practice provides ideas and applications to all steps in the architect's role.

This handbook should give invaluable support to all of us in architectural practice. I commend it to you.

George Ferguson

President, RIBA

January 2004

Contributor Biographies

Dr. Alex Amato is an assistant professor at the Dept of Architecture, University of Honk Kong where he teaches studio and construction technology. His research interests lie in the development of Life Cycle Assessment (LCA) methodology and modular prefabricated construction systems.

Previously he was a consultant architect to the Steel Construction Institute, UK for ten years. Here he initiated research in the LCA of steel intensive construction while at the same time running a one man architectural practice that specialised in tensile fabric and light-weight construction systems.

Before this, he was an associate at BDP working on large-scale shopping centres, and prior to this spent five years in a small practice in Islington working on public housing in the early 80's.

Dr John Anderson is an independent consulting engineer working with construction clients, designers, consulting engineers, contractors and others who wish to have expert advice on construction industry health and safety issues. He graduated in civil engineering and, following employment in industry, joined the UK Health and Safety Executive as a specialist inspector. During his 26 years with the HSE John helped investigate thousands of construction accidents and incidents and was involved in the drafting of both health and safety legislation and official guidance documents. He lectures at universities including Imperial College London on health, safety and risk management, and is regularly invited to speak at meetings and conferences on construction safety by the Institution of Civil Engineers. His published papers and articles on the subject have appeared in many parts of the world.

Professor Peter Barrett is Pro-vice Chancellor for Research at the University of Salford in the UK and a member, and past director, of the 6* rated Research Institute for the Built and Human Environment there. He is chairman of the Salford Centre for Research and Innovation, an innovative manufacturing research centre funded by the Engineering and Physical Sciences Research Council which focuses on the built and human environment.

A chartered surveyor by original training, Peter had nine years experience in practice before becoming an academic. His research covers organisational and management issues in construction and the built environment, including major research projects on quality management, innovation, facilities management and briefing. He is co-author of the Blackwell Science book *Towards Better Briefing*, which was based on extensive studies of live projects.

Peter Barrett is also co-ordinator of Working Commission 65 (Construction Organisation and Management) of the Conseil International du Bâtiment (CIB), which has around 150 members from some 40 countries.

Professor Philip Cox formed Philip Cox and Associates in 1967. The firm has grown to become The Cox Group Pty Ltd, a national practice in Australia comprising over 220 personnel. Philip received an Honorary Doctorate of Science in 2000 and is Professor of Architecture at the University of NSW. He has received numerous awards in recognition of his contribution to architecture, including the RAIA Gold Medal in 1984, Life Fellowship to the RAIA in 1987 and Honorary Fellowship of the American Institute of Architects in the same year. In 1988 he was awarded the Order of Australia for services to architecture. Five years later, in 1993 Philip received the inaugural award for sport and architecture from the International Olympic Committee, and was elected a Fellow of the Royal College of Humanities. He has published nine books on the history of Australia's towns and buildings.

Dr Branka Dimitrijevic is a Director of The Centre for the Built Environment, a joint initiative of the University of Strathclyde and Glasgow Caledonian University, which provides knowledge transfer between academia and the built environment sector. She has a BSc in Architecture (University of Sarajevo, Bosnia and Herzegovina), an MSc in Conservation of Architectural Heritage and a PhD in History of Architecture (University of Zagreb, Croatia). Branka has spent most of her career in higher education and research. Her research interests span from revitalisation of architectural and urban heritage in Bosnia and Herzegovina to a more recent focus on sustainable buildings, sustainable urban development and sustainable construction undertaken at the University of Strathclyde. She is a co-ordinator of CIB W102 commission on Information and Knowledge Management in Building and observer in the CIB's project 'Performance Based Building'.

John Easton BSc RIBA ARIAS SEDA is a senior architect working in private practice in Scotland. He obtained an Honours Degree in Architecture at Duncan of Jordanstone College of Art/University of Dundee in 1981. He practiced briefly in Dundee before moving on to work for major commercial practices in Edinburgh and Glasgow. John is an associate of the Royal Incorporation of Architects in Scotland and a member of the Royal Institute of British Architects.

His main professional role is as a project architect, leading a succession of design and construction teams, involving to-date over 90 projects and approaching £0.5 billion of construction. The breadth of John's experience extends from private houses, to shopping centres, schools, airports, and to offices and production facilities, many for global corporations. Experience of procurement methods has encompassed traditional contracts, partnering and private finance initiatives.

John has had a career-long interest in design and in the capture, distribution and application of technical knowledge to improve the design and construction processes. His own extensive technical knowledge has lead to contributions to the National Building Specification and to work with the UK Building Research Establishment. College studies sparked an interest in sustainability that has continued throughout his career, including a long-term involvement with the Scottish Ecological Design Association.

Professor Charles Egbu has been Professor of Construction and Project Management at the School of the Built and Natural Environment, Glasgow Caledonian University, since 2002. He was previously a reader in construction and project management at Leeds Metropolitan University; worked as a lecturer and senior research fellow at the University College London, UK and Before a successful career in academia he had been a project manager and senior research consultant at the Building Research Establishment, UK. He obtained his PhD in Construction Management from the University of Salford, UK. His first degree was in quantity surveying from Leeds, where he obtained First Class Honours, and won the *Building Magazine* award as the What? in Quantity Surveying. He is a corporate member of the Chartered Institute of Building and the Association for Project Management.

Currently, Charles is a grant holder of research on Knowledge Management for Sustained Construction Competitiveness and a Knowledge Management Approach for SMEs. He has contributed over 100 papers to various international journals and conferences, and was a contributory author to *Project Management Pathways* published by the Association for Project Management in 2002. He is a visiting Fellow to the Management, Knowledge and Innovation Research Unit (MKIRU) of the Open University Business School.

Charles is also a member of the W65 (Construction Organisation and Management), W102 (Information and Knowledge Management in Building) and TG47 (Innovation and Knowledge Broker) groups of the International Council for Research and Innovation in Building and Construction (CIB).

Dr Richard Fellows is an Associate Professor in the Department of Real Estate and Construction, University of Hong Kong. He graduated from the University of Aston and has worked as a quantity surveyor for several major contractors. He has a PhD from the University of Reading, was co-ordinator for research in construction management for the Engineering and Physical Sciences Research Council in the UK, and has extensive experience in research and teaching in many countries.

Dr Hildebrand Frey is Director of the Urban Design Studies Unit (UDSU) at the University of Strathclyde, Department of Architecture and Building Science. As such he is responsible for undergraduate teaching input in the department, for the Postgraduate Diploma/MSc Course in Urban Design, and for research into, and publications on, issues of urban design. Specifically, his research focuses on the investigation of the city and city region's structure – and with it the city and city region's social, economic, environmental, functional and formal properties – on the local, regional and global environment. UDSU is now a partner in the Engineering and Physical Sciences Research Council sponsored Sustainable Urban Design Consortium.

Research hypotheses generated by the Unit are generally tested in theoretical strategic and detailed urban design frameworks for urban areas in the City of Glasgow and the Glasgow conurbation. The objective is to explore approaches to urban regeneration and development that respond to sustainability indicators and target values while at the same time achieving a balance between all groups of interest. Specific importance is given to approaches that generate higher density development and achieve a mixture of uses, social inclusion and a balance of international and local economy. It is the pursuit of such interests that has led to the study of the Dublin Docklands Development in comparison to Glasgow's river front development at Broomielaw.

Michael Gilmour is a graduate of Dundee University. His initial experience was in private sector practice in the North of England where he was responsible for designing the practice offices which won a RIBA Regional Award and which, due to it's unusual design, was built by the practice using separate trades' contracts.

It was this experience that initiated a life-long interest in differing methods of procurement and their influence on design. After taking up a design tutor post at The Scott Sutherland School in Aberdeen he opened his own practice and was later joined by his partner, John Buchan. About 12 years ago they started a development company and this has grown to a medium size with a local property portfolio and developments across Scotland.

This experience encouraged him to approach the local university School of Architecture to found an internet-based Postgraduate Course in Development for Architects. This course is now up and running successfully. It is his eventual ambition to see the course integrated into the Under-Graduate course. As to the future, it appears that, having gained a reputation as both a design-led practice and a commercially aware developer, opportunities are opening to continue these roles in area regeneration and the health sector. An interesting and challenging period lies ahead.

Philip Graus graduated from the University of Sydney with first class honours in 1983 and a Master of Architecture from the University of Pennsylvania in 1985. He joined Philip Cox and Associates in 1992 and became a director in 1997. He was a member of the New South Wales Ministers Affordable Housing Advisory Group from 1999 to 2002. Philip undertook research into housing as part of a Byera Hadley Travelling Scholarship to the United States, Canada and UK in 1990.

Philip is primarily responsible for residential and master planning projects within the practice, including a range from high-density inner city projects to low rise residential communities. Significant project involvement includes the Sydney 2000 Olympic Village Master Plan, Victoria Park and Port Adelaide Master Plan.

David Greenwood is Associate Dean (Research & Consultancy) in the School of the Built Environment at Northumbria University. He worked for nearly ten years for a major contractor in a commercial role that involved tendering and planning for large building projects, and the subsequent management of their commercial and physical progress. For the last 20 years David has been a full-time academic at Northumbria University where he teaches and researches in the field of construction management and contract administration. During this time there he has maintained a close contact with the industry through consultancy and training work in related fields. Some of this work has been overseas, principally in the Far East and in France. David's primary research interests are the commercial relations between contracting organisations, including the way construction contracts are drafted. He has published and supervised research students in related subject areas.

Dr Joe Gunning is a chartered civil engineer and chartered builder, as well as a Fellow of the Institute of Quality Assurance. Following a career in managing the construction and design of projects in Canada, Ireland, the United Kingdom and the Channel Islands he entered the academic world at the University of Ulster and has directed its Masters Programme in Construction and Project Management since 1992. Joe also acts as a consultant to the construction industry, particularly the ready mixed concrete sector. He is a registered lead assessor of quality management systems with IRCA (International Register of Certified Auditors). Joe has published over 50 papers in academic and professional journals, and in the proceedings of national and international conferences. He has also published a textbook on Concrete Technology. His PhD thesis was on the enhancement of quality in construction project management, a topic upon which he has focused throughout his 35-year career in construction.

Frank Harkin MSc (Dist) MAPM, BIAT is a Construction Project Manager and Architectural Technologist with over 35 years experience working with award winning architects. The practice works throughout Ireland on a diverse range of architectural projects. He was awarded Best Graduate from the University of Ulster (MSc Construction Project Management) by the Association of Project Managers for his work on the relationship between aesthetic quality, architects, clients and their project managers

Dan Hobbs graduated from the University of Strathclyde in 1999 with a BEng (Hons) in Building Design Engineering (Structural Engineering Stream). After some time away from academia he has returned to undertake a PhD in the 'Implementation of Life Cycle Analysis into an Architectural Practice'. He is currently employed under the Government's *TCS Knowledge Transfer Scheme* working for the University of Strathclyde with his placement within a leading PFI/PPP Architects (HLM Design, Glasgow). The industrial experience has been invaluable to his research and he has experienced varied project work within a number of sectors, under differing procurement routes; from a £60m Hospital redevelopment and refurbishment under traditional contract to the £50m 'Glasgow Schools PPP', £1b SLAM Project, feasibility studies for sustainable procurement and design, and competition work. The nature of his research is in developing a Life Cycle Analysis methodology and a tool for use by designers throughout the design process, which will facilitate analysis of environmental impacts and life cycle costs of design decisions.

Professor John Kelly BSc MPhil MRICS is the Anglian Water Group (AWG) Professor of Construction Innovation at Glasgow Caledonian University. He trained with George Wimpey and Co Ltd and practised as a quantity surveyor with a small architectural practice before becoming an academic in 1976. John has researched, taught and practised in the field of value management for 25 years focusing on the investigation of value strategies at the inception of projects. He has published widely, conducted considerable funded research and undertaken consultancy in strategic and project briefing, partnering and procurement strategies with a wide spectrum of clients and projects varying from social housing to football stadia.

Professor Bimal Kumar is Professor of IT in Design and Construction in the School of Built and Natural Environment at Glasgow Caledonian University. He is well known for his work on the application of artificial intelligence/knowledge-based systems to structural design – this has resulted in two books and numerous publications. He is also the founding secretary/treasurer of the European Group for Structural Engineering Applications of Artificial Intelligence (EG-SEA-AI). Bimal sits on the editorial boards of two international journals – *AI in Engineering* and *Advances in Engineering Software* – and has chaired numerous international conferences on AI in Structural Engineering. He has regularly been invited to run courses and seminars on AI in Engineering in various countries including Portugal, Greece, Malta, Indonesia, Switzerland, USA and India. Bimal has held positions at Strathclyde, Sydney (Australia) and Heriot-Watt Universities not to mention Visiting Faculty positions at Malta and Stanford (USA) Universities. He is also a Professional Member of the British Computer Society and the American Society of Civil Engineers.

Professor Thomas Kvan MA, MArch, PhD, of the Department of Architecture, University of Hong Kong, has published over 60 papers in the areas of cognitive and computational aspects of collaborative design and professional practice management processes. His background includes the design of buildings and software as well as many years as a management consultant to design industry practices in Europe, Africa, North America and Asia. He is a member of several editorial boards, and a member of the Boards of CIB, CAAD (Computer Aided Architectural Design) Futures, IFMA (International Facility Management Association), among other international organisations.

Professor David Langford holds the Barr Chair at Strathclyde University, having had experience of working in the construction industry before taking up an academic appointment. During his academic career he has published, in conjunction with colleagues, several books and has contributed to many academic journals and conferences. He has taught and consulted throughout the world.

Professor Martin Loosemore is Chair of Construction Management and Associate Dean at the University of New South Wales, Sydney, Australia. He is a chartered surveyor and chartered builder and leads a consultancy specialising in risk and opportunity management, advising many government and private organisations around the world. In 2002 Martin was a consultant to the Australian Royal Commission into the Building Industry, advising on international workplace reform and productivity. He also lobbied the Australian government, on behalf of major contractors, in its recent OHS reforms. Martin has published over 100 articles and books on risk management, crisis management, occupational health and safety and human resource management. In 2000 he was awarded the American Society of Civil Engineers' Engineering Management – Outstanding Journal Paper Award for a peer-reviewed paper entitled 'The psychology of accident prevention in the construction industry'. Later, in 2002, he was awarded the UK Literati Club Highest Commendation Award for a paper entitled 'Customer focussed benchmarking in facilities management'.

Dr Steve McCabe is a senior lecturer and researcher in The Faculty of the Built Environment at The University of Central England in Birmingham. As well as teaching management to a wide range of courses at undergraduate and postgraduate level, he has carried out research into the use of quality management techniques in construction. As a consequence, he has published a number of articles which describe the experiences of organisations that have implemented QA (Quality Assurance), TQM (Total Quality Management) and Benchmarking for Best Practice. As well as this, Steve has given presentations to The Construction Best Practice Programme and written two books, *Quality Improvement Techniques in Construction* (Addison Wesley Longman, 1998) and *Benchmarking in Construction* (Blackwell Science, 2001).

Dr David Moore is currently a lecturer in The Scott Sutherland School at The Robert Gordon University in Aberdeen, and is also a visiting lecturer at University of Manchester Institute of Science and Technology (UMIST) for the MSc Project Management distance-learning programme. He has also delivered guest lectures as part of the University of Bath's MSc Construction Management summer school programme. David is involved in researching a number of areas including the nature of integrated teams in construction projects, behaviours differentiating between average and superior managers (receiving a research paper award from the Chartered Institute of Building for a co-authored paper on this subject), and factors in the perception and cognition of complex charts. To-date, he has produced over 50 journal and conference papers, along with three books. David has previously lectured at UMIST and De Montfort University, Leicester.

Dr Mike Murray is a lecturer in construction management within the Department of Architecture and Building Science at the University of Strathclyde. He completed his

PhD research in June 2003 and also holds a first class honours degree in Building Engineering & Management and an MSc in Construction Management. He has lectured at three Scottish universities (The Robert Gordon University, Heriot Watt and, currently, at Strathclyde) and has developed a pragmatic approach to both research and lecturing. He has delivered research papers to academics and practitioners at UK and overseas symposiums and workshops. Mike began his career in the construction industry with an apprenticeship in the building services sector and was later to lecture in this topic at several Further Education colleges. He is a member of the Chartered Institute of Building and is co-editor of *Construction Industry Reports 1944–1998* (2003) and co-author of a forthcoming textbook on Communication in Project Environments.

Margaret-Mary Nelson is a Research Fellow at the Centre for Facilities Management, in the 6* RAE rated School of Construction and Property Management, University of Salford. Her main areas of research are in the facilities management value chain including demand and supply chain management, performance measurement and process improvement. She is the lead researcher in the CFM Public Service Partnerships research programme, which includes Public Private Partnerships. She has a property management and development background, and over 12 years experience of working both in practice and academia.

Christopher Platt C.Arch, Dip.Arch (Mackintosh)_,RIBA, ARIAS, MILTHE held senior positions in architectural practices in Scotland, England, Germany and Ethiopia before establishing his current practice, studio KAP, in Glasgow. His built work is regularly peer reviewed in international journals and he is the recipient of several national architecture prizes including three RIBA Regional Awards. Chris combines practice-based research with a lectureship at Strathclyde University's Architecture Department and an involvement with other educational workshop initiatives at a national and international level. He is a regular guest lecturer at several UK Schools of Architecture and has taught and been external examiner in a number of European Schools. He has written and exhibited widely and his media appearances include radio and TV.

Professor Steve Rowlinson is a civil engineer by training, graduating from Nottingham University, and has worked for the past 17 years at the University of Hong Kong, first in the Department of Civil and Structural Engineering and (for the past 11 years) in the Department of Real Estate and Construction. During that time he has been engaged as a consultant and expert witness for a number of companies, including the Hong Kong Housing Authority and Hong Kong Government Works Bureau. Steve has researched into the Hong Kong construction industry and has written and co-authored four books on the subject. His areas of specialisation are construction site safety, IT and procurement systems. In the latter area he has been the co-ordinator of the CIB international working commission, W092, for ten years and has extensive experience of how construction projects are procured world-wide. Steve is currently an Adjunct Professor at the Queensland University of Technology in Brisbane, Australia and is a project participant in the project 'Value alignment in project delivery systems' and project leader on the project 'Value in project delivery systems: Facilitating a change in culture'. He has been an assessor for the professional examinations of both the HKIE and the Institution of Civil Engineers, UK, for a number of years.

Winston Shakantu has an MSc in Construction Management from the University of Reading. Currently, he is engaged in PhD research at Glasgow Caledonian University while also working as an academic in the Department of Construction Economics and Management at the University of Cape Town in South Africa.

Dr Danny Shiem-Shin Then is programme leader of the graduate programmes in Facility Management, Department of Building Services Engineering at The Hong Kong Polytechnic University. He led postgraduate programmes in Asset and Facilities Management in UK (Heriot-Watt University, Edinburgh, Scotland) and Australia (Queensland University of Technology, Brisbane) before joining the PolyU in Hong Kong in October 2001.

Danny has published and presented more than 50 papers internationally and is co-author of *Facilities Management and the Business of Space*. He has consulted and conducted in-house specialist training in areas of asset maintenance management, facilities management and workplace strategies in UK, Australia and Singapore. Danny is also Joint CIB Co-ordinator of Working Commission W70 on Facilities Management and Asset Maintenance.

Dr John Smallwood is an Associate Professor and Head, Department of Construction Management, University of Port Elizabeth, South Africa. Both his MSc and PhD (Construction Management) addressed aspects of construction health and safety (H&S). He specialises in construction H&S and ergonomics, and has conducted substantial research and authored numerous papers relative to the role of design in, and the influence thereof, on construction H&S.

He is a Past President of the South African Institute of Building, a Fellow of the Chartered Institute of Building (Southern Africa), and a member of both the Institute of Safety Management and the Ergonomics Society of South Africa. Other construction H&S experience includes contracting, consulting, contributions to the evolution of legislation, conference organising, judging, and chairing of committees and forums at regional and national level.

Dr John Tookey graduated in 1993 with BSc (Hons) in Technology and Management Science from the University of Bradford. Subsequently, he returned to the University of Bradford to continue his studies, graduating with a PhD in Industrial Engineering in 1998. His thesis was entitled 'Concurrent Engineering in the Aerospace Industry – A Comparative Study of the Exploitation of Concurrent Engineering within the UK and US Aerospace Industries'. This involved a wide-ranging study of the implementation and operation of a new methodology for the specification and delivery of complex engineering projects in a heavily sub-contracted operational environment. In 1998 John was recruited as post doctoral researcher in construction procurement processes in the School of the Built and Natural Environment, Glasgow Caledonian University. He was appointed lecturer in 2001, with research and particular teaching interests in construction logistics and marketing. John continues to publish regularly in the area of supply chain and logistics management in construction, whilst conducting active industry-based research and supervising several PhD students.

Peter Walker is a partner in the Newcastle office of DEWJOC Architects, a practice with offices in the North East and London. DEWJOC specialise in the design of education buildings, laboratories and clean rooms in the UK and abroad. Prior to this, he was a director of Conran Design Group, a multidisciplinary design consultancy. Peter teaches part time at the School of Architecture of Newcastle University and is variously an external examiner, on the advisory board and a visiting lecturer at Northumbria, Huddersfield and the Queen's University, Belfast. Peter has a particular interest in the way architects manage the design and procurement process, and in the education of architects in this area. He is a member of the Architects Registration Board Education and Practice Advisory Group, and is the co-author (with Dr David Greenwood) of the *Construction Companion to Risk and Value Management*.

Introduction

Introduction

Michael Murray and David Langford, Department of Architecture and Building Science, University of Strathclyde, Glasgow, UK

This book is intended for architects and other design professionals engaged in managing the construction process. Before declaring the contents of the book, it may be valuable to seek to define some of the terms which appear in the title. The central and active word is 'management' and here the editors see the designers' management role as facilitating effective performance of the temporary and multi-organisational system which constitutes a construction project. In all construction projects the designers will need to be decision makers and drivers of the actions necessary to realise the decisions made. These may be strategic decisions about form, aesthetics and how project objectives are to be satisfied. Supporting such high level decisions are those administrative decisions about how the work is to be planned and budgeted or operational decisions regarding what has to be done to ensure performance goals are realised. When construction was planned around the traditional sequential method of design–tender–build–occupy then many of these decisions could be made routine. One only has to look at work from a company called Guidelines (1986) who produced a tome called the *Construction Administration Manual* to realise that management for designs in this era was restricted to responding to a series of check lists. Somewhat later, Cairns (1992) argued:

> That in the past thirty years, the architect has allowed, through lack of interest, and subsequently been forced to allow through lack of knowledge, some of his roles in the fields of project and construction management to be assumed by others, losing control over their correct integration into the overall architectural process.

This continues to be a widely held view today and this predicament has acted as the catalyst for this textbook. Other more prescriptive texts, such as Green's *Architect's Guide to Running a Job* first published in 1962 and now in its sixth edition, are perhaps overly formal in their description of what is predominantly described as a rational design and construction process. This multi-contributor text is notably less prescriptive in its guidance and has been edited so as to encourage the reader to reflect on his or her own experience in practice. It should not be considered an A–Z of how architects can play a dominant role in the construction team. This would have been overly presumptuous and it is acknowledged that many expert designers will have little interest in the administration of a contract. Likewise, architects who have a flair for people management rather than innovative conceptual or detailed design may find this text particularly useful. It is however envisaged that all architects who perform a role within a construction project will find this book useful in navigating the path that leads to managing successful projects. Part of this will require the architect to set the objectives of the construction team, lead and develop it, linking it where necessary to the outer environment of the project.

In short the designer, especially the architect, needs to create a hierarchy of objectives of a construction project, full in the recognition that these objectives may, and are likely to, change during the course of the project process. These objectives must, of course, be realised if projects are seen to be a success and the management role of the architect is likely to involve them in developing ways and means of project realisation. These ways and means can be as diverse as selecting the procurement route, contract type, payment system, project organisation structure, integrated IT apparatus, and many other systems which enable the project to be delivered. The management process for designers will not only be a technical challenge but is as much a social skill. Here the organisational ecology of a project is changed to encourage a climate of opinion where the objectives are widely accepted and different interest groups in the project process can be aligned. Finally, the architect needs to measure the extent that objectives have been satisfied. In an era of Key Performance Indicators (KPI) the measurement of performance has been codified and the full range of KPIs can be used to evaluate projects. This theme is picked up in Section E of the book on project operations where performance and safety management are highlighted.

The second operative word in the book's title is 'construction'. Whilst for most practising architects the nature and shape of the construction industry will be known territory, for many students the character of the industry is less distinct. The management concepts and technologies referred to in the text are set in a construction industry context and this is set inside a 'feel' for the industry. Many of the chapters explicitly refer to the changing contours of the construction industry. This changing morphology of construction has been prompted by a procession of government reports in the 1990s (although Murray and Langford (2003) have noted that, in every government report on construction since 1944, a set of themes recur; procurement, professional relationships and performance being foremost amongst them).

The guiding documents of the 1990s have been the Latham (1994) and the Egan (1998) Reports. Both complained of the failure of the construction industry to innovate and adopt modern management methods. A core theme of both reports (and indeed most of them published since 1944) was the need to integrate the construction process to the benefit of clients; delivering greater value to clients by focusing attention on the need to meet functional business needs within a tighter budget was demanded of architects. To meet these new demands greater attention was placed upon the strategic actions at the start of the project and these are covered in Section B with some of the recipes for industry improvement referred to in Sections C, D, E and G (see contents' list for the titles of these sections). The construction context draws in contemporary issues such as partnering, supply chain management, lean construction, benchmarking, safety, knowledge management and post-occupancy evaluation. All have been recommended as providing the stimulants to a new construction industry. All are covered in the volume. Powell (1980) noted that the period 1940–1973 was a period when the construction industry moved from being a work horse to one which could canter. The promptings of Egan, Latham and others could develop the canterer into one which can run and possibly even challenge for the UK Derby, the USA Kentucky Derby or Australia's Melbourne Cup.

The third operative word in the title is 'handbook'. Here the editors' intention was to create a text which was sufficiently comprehensive for architectural and other design practices to use the book more for reference and information rather than inspiration. Our hope is that some of the contents do inspire readers to experiment with new ways of working or new roles in new relationships with others involved within the construction process. If it does, the editors would be pleased but our ambitions are to present a piece of work which informs architects of the change in direction of the construction industry and the processes or systems which are used to make buildings grow both in concept, physical reality and use. Each chapter can be considered as a 'stand alone'. The reader is free to dip into each chapter or read the text completely. It has not been structured as a desk-top guide but more as a prompt for readers to consider some of the issues which are driving the post-Egan construction industry.

We have spoken of the book's contents in the context of its title but we have not commented upon the framework we have used to structure the contents.

This framework is a professional one. Historically, the process of professionalism has ensured that common standards of practice are evident and the management process is more likely to be routine when compared to the design process. This drive to professionalisation is of itself not concerned with design or the design process but, as Lawson (1997) has argued, is more to do with the quest for status and power. Regularising this power through standard contracts which separated out the roles and responsibilities in the building process is one way in which managerial roles and functions are codified. This codification separated the designers' work from the task of building the design and, in the process, made the architect a conceived centrepiece of the building process with the building produced being perceived as the work of a single individual. So buildings are recognised and known as a Foster's building, a Rogers' or Gehry's building thus eliminating acknowledgement of others in the process of building. This consideration of the architects' work allowed a more artistic response to the needs of the built environment, but alongside this the architects required a well understood managerial framework within which to work. The tension between architect as individual artist and architect as professional designer is clearly evident. In the latter role, a profession increases collective control over the work of building design; in the former, it is perceived to encourage innovation in building design, often at the expense of smooth project administration. Nowhere is the tension more evident than in the managerial roles undertaken by architects.

In order to codify these managerial roles of architects, the RIBA published their first Plan of Work in 1963 with a revised edition appearing in 2000. The document created a logical structure for construction, starting with the brief and ending with post-occupancy evaluation. It will be recalled that the RIBA Plan of Work in its present format has 11 sequential steps (there is no step I). Despite its apparent linear nature, Chappell and Willis (2000) observe that there are many instances when two or more stages are combined and that it is not always transparent when a project is moving from one stage to another. As such, they conclude that it is an ideal tool, provided that it is conceptualised as providing the basic outline of the project process.

A. Appraisal

B. Strategic brief

C. Outline proposals

D. Detailed proposals

E. Final proposals

F. Production information

G. Tender documents

H. Tender action

J. Mobilisation

K. Construction to practical completion

L. After practical completion

The model established envisions a traditional construction process where a sequence of design–tender–build is the linear process of the art and science of building. Whilst the structure of the plan of work is under attack from more contemporary procurement methods, the management tasks identified still have to be undertaken. The issue is whether it is the architects who should do them. It may be observed that the newer procurement routes have displaced the architect from many of the managerial roles, especially those occurring after the construction has started, but it must be noted that they still have a strong managerial duty. Much of this managerial activity will take place outside the realm of the traditional architectural duties of design.

The book is broken down into seven sections, each one dealing with various stages of the RIBA Plan of Work. Section B covers the stages A, B and C (in part) of the plan of work. Section C concerns itself with design management and contains chapters on urban design through to detail design. The application of IT to the design process is also introduced in this section. Stages C (in part) – F are featured in Section C. In Section D the durable theme of procurement is tackled (an important part of stages B and C). How the role of the architect and others is changing under different procurement routes is considered along with different types of contract and conditions of engagement. Stages G and H are the relevant cross reference. Section E looks at construction operations and presents chapters on how a project organisation is built, how the various packages of work are broken down, how such work is monitored through the new regime of KPIs and, most importantly, how designers can design in a way which eliminates safety hazards during construction. Stages J and K map onto this section. Section F concerns post project evaluation and details how to close out a project, both physically and financially, along with a chapter which details how knowledge learned from the last project may be captured and used for the benefit of subsequent projects. Part of stage K will be covered by this section and some of stage L. Section G looks at how the architect can be engaged in facilities management. Whilst this section does not have a corresponding stage in the RIBA Plan of Work, it is a growing area for the architecture profession. Particular emphasis is placed upon the role of the designer in Private Finance Initiative (PFI) settings where the recurrent and operating costs over the life of a PFI concession will be very influential in allowing a project to proceed. Designers have to design in this new environment. Finally, Section H details the authors' conclusions on the future role of architects in the building process.

The purpose of the book is to provide architects and other designers with a helpful handbook in which they are able to draw upon the expertise of others and learn from the illustrative case studies which form part of each chapter.

References

Cairns, G. M., 'Education in the role of management', in M. P. Nicholson, *Architectural Management*, E&FN Spon, London (1992).

Chappell, D., and Willis, A., *The Architect in Practice*, 8th edn, Blackwell Publishing, Oxford (2000).

Egan, J., 'Rethinking Construction', Report of the Construction Task Force on the Scope for Improving Quality and Efficiency of UK Construction, Department of the Environment, Transport and the Regions (DETR) (1998).

Green, R., *The Architect's Guide to Running a Job*, Architectural Press, Oxford (2002).

Guidelines, *Construction Administration Manual*, Orinda Ca., USA (1986).

Latham, M., 'Constructing the Team', Joint Review of Procurement and Contractual Arrangements in the United Kingdom Construction Industry, Final Report, HMSO (1994).

Lawson, B., *How designers think: the design process demystified*, 3rd edn, Architectural Press, Oxford (1997).

Murray, M. and Langford, D., *Construction Reports 1944–98*, Blackwell, Oxford (2003).

Phillips, R., *The Architect's Plan of Work*, RIBA Enterprises, London (2000).

Powell, C. G., *An Economic History of the British Building Industry*, Methuen, Cambridge (1980).

Inception and Briefing

Briefing

Peter Barrett, Research Institute for the Built and Human Environment,
University of Salford, Manchester, UK

1.1 Introduction

This chapter considers the process of briefing, first emphasising the importance of it as a major communications channel between clients and their professional advisers, second summarising five major areas in which improvements can be sought in a progressive manner from whatever approach to briefing is currently used, third a case study is provided to illustrate how some of the ideas were used in a real-life situation with (realistically) mixed results, fourth good practice examples are provided in each of the five improvement areas and, lastly, a summary is provided with further reading suggestions.

Briefing can be seen as revolving around a document, the brief, or as a step early on in the construction process. In this section a broader perspective is taken, namely:

> Briefing is the process running throughout the construction project by which means the requirements of the client and other relevant stakeholders are progressively captured, developed and translated into effect.

This definition describes a creative process from which it is hoped good ideas will emerge as the pooled abilities and knowledge bases of the client, facilities manager, design team, contractor, etc. interact over time to find solutions that improve the built infrastructure provided to the client. The end result should be satisfied stakeholders, not only in terms of the end result, but also the process. What could be more critical than this?

Every organisation has its own particular approach to briefing and success can be achieved in many different ways. However, it has been found through in-depth research (Barrett and Stanley, 1999) that there are five common areas through which *improvement* can be sought, from whatever base. These are shown in Figure 1.1 and are described in more detail below. Empowering the client and managing the project dynamics are major areas; the first a relatively 'soft' area, the second really quite 'hard' and technical. Together, improvements in these areas are widely available and can make a huge impact. The other three areas underpin these two, but in these cases an appropriate level of effort is counselled, rather than arguing simply that more is better. Supporting appropriate user involvement links clearly to empowering the client, as does appropriate team building to managing the project dynamics. All are underpinned by the use of appropriate visualisation techniques, as a key communications issue.

Moving towards better briefing, from whatever approach is currently used, can be difficult owing to the systemically intertwined nature of construction activities.

Figure 1.1: Key solution areas

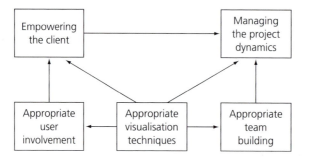

Various parties perform various roles typified by 'interdependence and uncertainty' (Tavistock, 1966), so that if one player wants to change what they do they have to be careful that the web of interrelationships is still effective. This was exemplified in the above quoted study, which found that the pragmatic, but effective approach used for implementation of improved briefing practices followed the pattern shown in Figure 1.2. This is, that briefing is done in a particular way (tacitly), usually because it has worked adequately in the past and that 'seeing' the problems, or

Figure 1.2: Practical change model

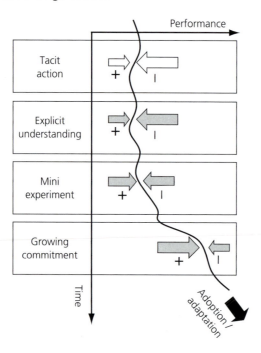

opportunities for improvement, takes time and even then it usually only makes practical sense to move forward via mini-experiments to begin with.

Interestingly, the strong linkages between the five improvement areas shown in Figure 1.1 do mean that organisations can latch onto any of the areas in the first place, maximising on the political imperatives of the particular situation, knowing that the initiative can naturally spread to include the other areas in due course.

1.2 Case study

1.2.1 Background

The project that is the subject of this case study involved moving or relocating around 110 academics, plus support staff and researchers. Time was very short, both to plan the project and to implement it during the Summer. The budget was very constrained. The project had a technical dimension, but beyond accommodating the numbers of people the project was very important as a symbolic, but also very tangible representation of the new structures. Thus the project went ahead against a background of raw feelings and emotions about the organisational restructuring and no great history of successful consultation with large groups of voluble academics!

1.2.2 Objectives

The project concerned accommodating new Schools in a new Faculty. The new Schools were made up of combinations of old departments or parts of departments. Thus a major objective was to represent this new organisational arrangement in the spaces and to emphasise interaction, meshing and a forward-looking feel. This last was important as the existing spaces were highly cellular, albeit rather lavish in size for two or three staff, with very long corridors and heavy 'institutional' feel.

The objectives for the office environment to be created by the project could be summarised at three levels:

- Organisational purpose
  - to reflect the new structure;
  - to be of higher quality, thus presenting a 'professional' image;
- Operational purpose
  - to engender integration through social spaces;
  - to facilitate flexible use of spaces;
- Individual purpose
  - to provide individual office spaces for academics;
  - to exceed minimum levels of light, heat, ventilation, etc.

Figure 1.3: Eliciting views

Questionnaire for Staff on Maxwell Space	Ref:	

Name: _____

School: _____

Position: _____   Date: _____

This questionnaire is to elicit your ideas and thoughts about the sort of space in Maxwell you ideally need to do your work effectively and efficiently in the future. Although significant improvements will be possible over the Summer, it will not be possible to meet all of your wishes, but at this stage you have a chance to dream and you will hopefully be pleasantly surprised with what can be achieved!

Your response will be treated in confidence, but aggregated to feed into the consultation workshops. Please send your completed questionnaire back to me in the post or as an attached file.

1.2.3   User consultation process

To get to the above statement of objectives all staff were consulted through a combination of questionnaires and workshops at which the aggregate results were discussed leading to a consensus on key variables. The invitation to comment at the start of the questionnaire is given in Figure 1.3 and includes an important combination of words that encouraged people to open up about what they really would like to see, whilst at the same time making it clear that it 'will not be possible to meet all your wishes'.

There was a good response to the questionnaire with a lot of views expressed. These were all orientated by 'prompts' to focus on the *activities* staff carried out and, from this perspective, what sort of spaces they needed. The findings were fed back to a workshop of 20 representative staff. Major issues were highlighted and illustrated with quotations from the questionnaires. For example, the overwhelming desire from academics for individual offices was twinned with the related view that 'it doesn't have to be big, but it has to be private'. This allowed the trade-off between privacy and large rooms to be explored, settling on a building block of a $10 \, m^2$ private study office in which one or two others could be accommodated for tutorials, etc. Photographs of different-sized offices were projected to reinforce the reality of what was being discussed. At the workshop other issues were fleshed out such as the desperate need for large, shared spaces for postgraduate researchers and the need for relaxing, social spaces for staff and students. Overall there was a strong call for 'style and flair' and a 'light and bright' feel.

This set of consensus views set some challenging design issues, but had successfully engaged the staff affected and empowered the internal client to then actively work with the designers to suggest an outline solution. This emerged as a broad concept exemplified in plan form in a particular leg of the building, but scalable to other areas as shown in Figure 1.4. This provided the basis for a second workshop that included some alternative layouts, but the one shown clearly met the set of objectives most closely and gained rapid acceptance as indicated by the questions moving onto practical issues, such as light to inner rooms.

From this point the detailed design, then construction, moved ahead apace with most communications going via the new Heads of Schools on issues such as colour schemes and the allocation of rooms to individual staff.

1.2.4 Design process

Some clear parameters had emerged out of the first user workshop. The key components were individual offices and shared social spaces, but in a building that was a difficult, deep configuration. Based on the quite simple challenge of these two types of spaces the designers quickly sketched the alternatives and the layout in Figure 1.4 stood out as 'breaking the mould' of the building by creating a very different, 'surprising' feel. The 'pods' of six relatively small offices and shared meeting spaces between became a module, which combined with large social spaces then defined the nature of the office layout proposed. Because of the obvious link between this and the users' requirements, acceptance of the layout was not problematic and it was flexible enough to be translated across various areas in the building. The design process had been a user-led progression from their needs to a module, then a generic layout, which had finally been applied across all the spaces concerned.

1.2.5 Assessment

The user consultation was successful and led to an efficient and effective design process up to the layout stage. The designers were not appointed early enough to attend the first workshop, but this was largely overcome through a detailed record being made followed by a face-to-face briefing.

As the project moved into detailed design there was some confusion over roles of the parts of the 'University client' in terms of the Faculty and the Estates Division, but also beyond this between the consultant project managers and the designers. This was then exacerbated by changes in personnel in several of the key players' teams. This led to a leakage of tacit knowledge and undermined some of the informal agreements or understandings between the parties. Being objective, the communications to users on more detailed design issues broke down. Anarchic, multi-channel communications began to build to an unacceptable level and momentum was lost until a really quite rigid protocol for briefing suggestions was imposed. This strict regime had unexpected implications much later. Towards the end of the refurbishment works there was significant pressure on the budget so that some of the furniture for social spaces, and planting more generally, were cut.

Figure 1.4: Broad concept

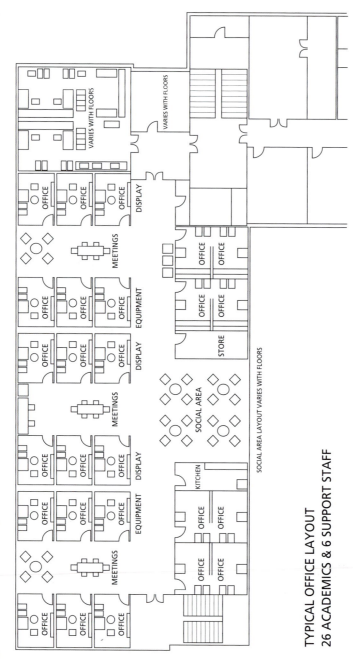

TYPICAL OFFICE LAYOUT
26 ACADEMICS & 6 SUPPORT STAFF

Overall the assessment of those involved was that the briefing process had been a lot better than usual, but fell down in terms of involvement at the more detailed design level. The project was finished on time and to budget.

1.2.6 Post-occupancy evaluation

Two years after completion the office space of one of the Schools was the subject of an independent post-occupancy evaluation (POE). The POE used a questionnaire, interviews and passive observation leading onto observing physical traces and focus group interviews using visual images as prompts.

Looking back at the objectives set out at the start of this case study it is clear from the POE that:

- Organisational purposes had been fully achieved. The School had a clear identity with a professional, modern feel.

- Operational purposes had been mainly achieved in that it was felt the layout had been important in the successful social meshing of the diverse groups in the School. However, the meeting and social spaces were not being heavily used.

- Individual purposes were achieved to an extent but staff did have concerns over ventilation, light and storage space.

The low use of meeting spaces seemed to be due to a lack of ownership and, behind this, an absence of norms within the School for *use* of the spaces. As the communications between the Faculty client and the users fragmented in the latter stages of the design process order was strictly enforced. In retrospect this appears to have led to the disempowerment of the users. So, for example, meetings tables set between the offices had never been moved in two years, despite being sectional to give flexibility! The missing element was a common ownership of the more detailed notions about how the spaces could be used. This had not really been discussed in the School so that, for example, it had not been revealed before the POE exercise that the meeting tables were in fact rather too big and so crowded the offices. The large social areas were used on more formal occasions, but much less so informally. This, it was thought, could be because of their very openness, which it had been intended to break up with planting so providing more personal spaces.

A discussion is now in process with the School so that experiments are underway in the use of different layouts in the meeting areas and planting in the social spaces. Responses of staff to different alternatives will be gathered and built on.

1.2.7 Case study conclusion

This real-life case study has illustrated the value of effective user involvement in creating a clear set of activity-orientated design objectives within which a creative solution was developed. It has also highlighted the nature of briefing as a continuing process, which demands well designed and resourced communications as the broad design moves to details and then to construction itself.

It is interesting that deficiencies in the briefing process created a legacy of problems in the 'use' phase of the building, even two years later. Behind this is a general point that the intended manner of use of the spaces needs to be shared, developed and, ultimately, owned organisationally by the user groups. This means that continuing discussion and evolution of the 'rules' or norms for use of the spaces can be expected if the full impact of the works is to be achieved. This is a long way from briefing as something that only happens at the start of a project. It reinforces the notion that briefing should be conceived of as an on-going dialogue between and with clients and users, in which their needs and aspirations are creatively given visibility and influence.

1.3 Good practice recommendations

The research that this chapter is primarily based upon clearly illustrated the illusory nature of 'best practice' as a notion. Good practice that has to be taken and adapted to lots of different and particular circumstances is a more realistic approach which stresses that taking up such ideas cannot be a passive process. As a result what follows are some relatively broadly drawn suggestions as to good practices in the five areas set out at the start of this chapter.

1.3.1 Empowering clients

Clients are not always expert in the area of construction and the built environment, but they are pivotal to a successful briefing process. To fully play their role clients need to be empowered and construction professionals can play an important part in this, either through consultancy advice or by acting as the 'expert client' of the organisation for which they work.

To be effective clients should:

- Be knowledgeable about their own organisation;
- Be aware of project constraints;
- Understand their roles and responsibilities;
- Maintain participation in the project;
- Gain the support of senior managers;
- Appoint an internal project manager;
- Integrate business strategy and building requirements.

Much of the knowledge about the organisation and its needs is available first hand within the client organisation, but this needs to be brought out through the lens of the project demands and twinned with a clear consensus with the client as to the technically driven project constraints and roles and responsibilities. It is essential that senior management support is obtained and maintained, together with a day-to-day project manager to act as a focus for stability in the relationship between the project-focused participants and the permanent staff of the organisation. This should all lead to an integration of the building requirements with the strategy of the client organisation.

Although this sort of activity can appear non-technical, off-line effort to construction professionals, in practice it is a vital investment towards a successful project outcome.

1.3.2 Appropriate user involvement

Various aspects of empowering clients involve the provision of a focus within the client organisation where the various views of the stakeholders that make up the client 'system' can be synthesised. A major stakeholder perspective that must be kept in focus is that of the user. This section focuses on users, but the same principles are likely to apply to other stakeholders.

It can be thought that more is better when it comes to user involvement. This is not so. It is quite easy to get together groups of users, involve them in consultation where the usual office status hierarchy skews the discussion and then disappointment sets in as it becomes clear that, in practice, involvement does not equate with influence.

Appropriate user involvement calls for:

- Understanding the benefits;
- An assessment relative to each situation or issue;
- Careful handling of group dynamics;
- User involvement which should be maintained throughout the project.

The benefits of user involvement should be the starting point, and these come in two broad forms. Firstly, there is a technical dimension where technical information about the needs and wants of the users can be obtained and, secondly, there is the social or political dimension of developing an acceptable solution. To achieve the first 'technical' aspect argues for specific groups of people brought together with particular knowledge to address a clearly focused issue. For an open discussion it is important to aim for groups that are of relatively equal power. To achieve a politically acceptable solution, active feedback to the groups is needed as to the impact of their contribution. This needs to be maintained throughout the project so that the transition from initial discussions to actually moving in is smoothed. As a little example, it could make sense for the technical designers working on finishes to meet with a group of cleaners specifically to discuss the floor/wall junction.

1.3.3 Managing the project dynamics

It is crucial to see briefing as a process, not as a document or an event. Seen like this, the dynamics of the process become very important and should run in parallel with the whole construction project, although, of course, the most intense activity will be towards the beginning and the process must include progressive fixity. What is required is a live record of the consensus; the shared vision held between the client, other stakeholders and the design team. This can then drive the design process, without constraining developments in the ideas.

To approach the dynamics in this way requires teams to give various aspects attention, namely:

- Establishing major project constraints early on, including critical dates;
- Agreeing procedures and methods of working;
- Allowing adequate time to assess client's needs;
- Careful validation of information with the client organisation;
- Feedback to all parties throughout the project.

It will seem obvious that it is important to establish major constraints, such as key dates, the overall budget, and the space and flexibility available. It is almost unbelievable, but projects have hit major problems over confusion as to whether VAT was included in the budget or because a key University committee was missed and a year was lost! A clear protocol for interacting throughout the project is rarely created, but is not difficult and this should allow adequate time at the early stages for the client's needs to be assessed. There is always pressure to move quickly, but time spent early on to allow ideas to grow is time well spent on all but the simplest projects. Construction professionals may very well have to argue for this space to be provided even though the client themselves simply want to get on. The communications must be interactive with extra efforts made to ensure that the client's apparent statements are clearly understood. This should link to additional efforts to make sure all are kept informed through feedback. The temptation is to short-circuit these efforts over and above simply getting an answer from the client and acting on it, but this will only lead to conflict and dissatisfaction later.

1.3.4 Appropriate team building

Many client organisations emphasise a hands-off, lowest price tendering approach to amassing the project team. This can result in superficial contractual arrangements between the organisations and a shifting mesh of participants as these organisations move staff from project to project to balance their internal demands. The result is that although the arrangements may look tight on paper, in practice the individuals involved keep building relationships and shared understanding and then breaking up so that the tacit understanding within the project team constantly erodes.

The result is not always optimal! Ideally:

- Selection should focus on assembling complementary skills, not simply on lowest price;

- Team members should approve and understand the management structure of the project and should, as far as possible, remain constant throughout the project.

These are areas where construction professionals may have to change ingrained habits, such as the consultant's partners setting a project off and then handing it over to someone more junior once it is well established. This may seem fine, but actually significant informal understandings can be lost leading to myriad problems. The suggestion is not that senior personnel necessarily have to remain involved throughout, but that there should be continuity in some of those in the team, or at least very carefully managed hand-overs. Taken positively, construction professionals can positively 'sell' the specific key individuals who are going to be dedicated to the project.

1.3.5   Using appropriate visualisation techniques

A key blocker to successful briefing is the failure of the communications used by the parties involved. This is particularly acute in the area of visualisation for the simple reason that the briefing process is a journey from a set of ideas in various people's heads to a single physical reality – a building or new space. Representing these ideas in terms of written specifications, two-dimensional drawings, etc. is not very reliable. Different people take different impressions from each of these mediums. For example, those in the construction industry are used to 'reading' drawings and assume that others can too. But in fact many people cannot imagine three-dimensional spaces from a flat drawing. They may never have been through that journey from plan to place before. Even within the construction industry silly things happen like colour-coded services drawings copied in black and white!

Getting to a shared consensus through these media is not easy or reliable. The consequence is that very often the built artefact that results is not what many of the participants expected, leading to confusion and disappointment or less often to a pleasant surprise. Unfortunately it is, more often than not, the client, maybe inexperienced in construction, who is least able to foresee what is going to result until it is too late. This can lead to problems of late re-design and severe inefficiencies.

Thus, using appropriate visualisation techniques is a major aspect of communications that, if successfully addressed, can make a huge difference to all other aspects of the briefing process. Again, the suggestion is not that more communication is better *per se*, but rather that appropriate techniques should be used.

This analysis has some simple implications:

- Basic techniques should be used carefully;

- Efforts should be made to help inexperienced construction participants visualise what is being proposed.

Many of the normal techniques used such as drawings and specifications can be very useful, but need to be used with care and sensitivity taking into account the experience of the participants. This may call for simply explaining to people some of the construction conventions used or orientating people so they know which way up the plan is, where the ground and first floors are, and so on.

Simple techniques that are not very commonly used can make a huge difference. For example, showing a variety of photographic images, taping out the size of the new office space on the floor or, more elaborately, mocking up an office space with some furniture, or visiting a similar building. This last can be very powerful especially if those involved make the visit(s) together and can discuss alternatives.

Construction professionals can have a key role in arguing for the importance of spending time and other resources in order to make sure that those who are not so experienced in construction are given a good chance of really knowing what is being proposed when they are asked to make serious, important decisions.

1.4 Conclusions

Briefing is not a document or an event, but rather it is an on-going process.

- It is essential for successful briefing that the client is empowered to perform their crucial role as the political driver for the project and a source of technical knowledge about the core activities being supported.

- The project dynamics in terms of key dates and deadlines, and major responsibilities and reporting lines is not especially complicated, but has to be handled carefully and made explicit to avoid confusion.

- Targeted consultation with users can be a key source of briefing information and at the same time briefing can provide a vital vehicle for the smooth transition of users into new spaces.

- Building and maintaining a team of individuals with complementary knowledge and skills is crucial.

- Using appropriate, often simple, visualisation techniques can make the difference between a successful briefing process and one built on misapprehensions and confusion.

- There is no one best way to do briefing and each organisation/project should take its current approach and progressively seek to improve their process focusing in at least one of the above areas.

- The quality of relationships and attitudes of the individuals involved in the briefing process are as important as the technical knowledge they have.
- Briefing can be thought of as an on-going dialogue, beyond any given construction project, through which the client and users work to better understand their needs and aspirations and then to maximise the value gained from their *use* (maybe through adaptation) of the built environment.

References

Barrett, P. S. and Stanley, C., *Better Construction Briefing,* Blackwell Science, Oxford (1999).
Tavistock Institute, *Interdependence and Uncertainty,* Tavistock, London (1966).

Key Reading

Barrett, P. S. and Stanley, C., *Better Construction Briefing,* Blackwell Science, Oxford (1999).
Construction Industry Board, *Briefing the Team – A guide to better briefing for clients,* Thomas Telford, London (1997).
Salisbury, F., *Briefing Your Architect,* Architectural Press, Oxford (1998).

Acknowledgements

Many individuals and companies contributed to the original work quoted from the *Better Construction Briefing* book and these are acknowledged there. More specifically, Sezgin Kaya, a PhD student in Salford University's Research Institute for the Built and Human Environment, carried out the POE that forms an important part of the case study, with valuable support and input from Dr John Ziesel of Alzheimer Hearthstone whilst he was at Salford on a visiting appointment.

Translating the brief into a design

2

Branka Dimitrijevic, The Centre for the Built Environment, Glasgow, UK

2.1 Introduction

Briefing is a communication process through which the client defines what building will satisfy the needs of their business or other end-users. Good interaction between the clients and designers in translating the brief into a design can contribute to a more sustainable construction and respond to the recent challenges of improving the industry's performance (Egan, 1998). How does this interaction happen? When does the briefing end, and the design begin? How is a complex set of ideas and requirements transformed into a building which embodies the client's needs and desires?

The experiences of two architects from two practices in Glasgow, interviewed for this chapter, show that approaches to translating the brief into a design depend on the external and internal work environment. The external work context is influenced by the client's experience and project management methods, the end-users' involvement, the level of architects' control of the final product in different procurement arrangements, and practicability and timing of evaluation methods such as value management (VM) and whole life costing (WLC). Management structure, project management procedures, information and knowledge management (including post-occupancy evaluation), and personal engagement of all team members influence the internal work environment. To address the problems identified by the two interviewed architects, this chapter indicates the guidance which can assist in influencing the external work environment and improving the management of an architectural practice.

2.2 Briefing in context

Two main managing aspects of translating the brief into a design emerge in every project as follows:

- Managing the external relationships, i.e. with the client/end-users;
- Managing the internal relationships within the architectural office, including the creative aspects of translating the brief into a design.

The external relationships are defined by the client's procurement strategy, which could be one of the following, as described by Blyth and Worthington (2001):

- *Traditional route* in which the design is completed before the start of the construction.
- *Construction management route* in which the client employs a design team and separately engages a construction manager who co-ordinates the design and

construction activities, and is able to inject construction expertise from the beginning and improve the buildability of the design.

- *Management contracting route* in which a management contractor is appointed by the client with responsibility for all construction work, and for providing construction advice to the design team. However, under this system, not all of the design work will be complete before the first trade contractors start work.

- *Design and build route* (D&B) in which the contractor has responsibility for designing and building the project.

- *Develop and construct route* in which the client appoints designers to prepare the concept design before the contractor assumes responsibility for completing the detailed design and construction, and in which the design team can be novated to the contractor to ensure continuity of design.

- *Build–own–operate–transfer (BOOT) route* in which a contracting organisation offers a package to provide and run a building for a number of years, and at the end of the period the ownership of the building reverts to the client.

- *Partnering route* in which the partners commit to agreed mutual objectives, an agreed method of problem resolution and continuous improvement throughout the relationship and throughout the supply chain, as initiated by the Egan Report (1998).

A chosen procurement route determines the architect's involvement in preparing the client's strategic brief, i.e. the brief which is developed at the pre-project stage, and the effect of this involvement on the project brief. During the work on the strategic and project briefs, architects have to ensure that the client/end-users' needs have been fully captured.

Many buildings can satisfy the needs of the client/end-users, but some can add value to the functions for which they are used. To examine how value can be added to a building design, the client/end-users can undertake a VM exercise. The use of VM is steadily increasing as clients seek better outcomes from their investment in buildings and structures. By bringing together the widest possible range of project stakeholders in the VM workshops, where different views and perspectives can be openly debated, many of the problems that typically arise in building projects can be avoided. The challenge is to determine how the client can achieve the best value from an investment in a building and how better buildings can result from a process that is based on good decision-making procedures being put in place before the design work actually commences (Seeley, 1996).

To the client, the costs to be incurred over the lifetime of a building are an important aspect of added value. WLC of an asset is defined as the present value of the total cost of the asset over its operating life including initial capital costs, occupation costs, operating costs, and the cost or benefit of the eventual disposal of the asset at the end of its life. WLC assists effective decision making, and thus helps satisfy the client's objective to achieve value for money. The relationship between life-costs and value for money is obvious: a client may pay more initially for the building but, over time, that extra investment generates savings that continue to accrue over the building's life. The challenge is to ensure that short-term financial considerations do not prevent the pursuit of long-term benefits.

However, the most common difficulties in using a WLC approach comprise forecasting accuracy, lack of historical data, professional accountability, technology changes, capital versus operating budgets, and the underpinning theory of discounting. The solution to the problem lies in the use of risk analysis, whereby the uncertainty of future events can be evaluated against the robustness of assumptions to add confidence levels to the final decisions. Although uncertainty may be high, particularly where long time horizons are involved, the risk of making a poor decision between various proposed courses of action may be quite low.

Since there is often a lack of historical data about maintenance, energy usage, operating costs and life expectancies of materials and systems, estimating operating costs from first principles is recommended, and context-specific databases will be formed from the routine comparison of predicted and actual performance. WLC should not be considered as an estimate of actual cost, rather as a framework within which effective cost management process can occur (Flanagan and Norman, 1983).

Apart from understanding the client/end-user's needs, which will be met by different functions of internal and external building spaces, communication with the client has to cover the areas of finance, time-scale and aesthetics.

The second management aspect of translating the brief into a design is related to the internal relationships within architectural practice. Members of the design team participate in the processes of managing external relationships outlined above. An effective design team includes specialists, from an architectural practice or outsourced, who can successfully manage each process. Most importantly, the team includes architects who tackle the creative aspects of translating the brief into a design. To ensure the firm's short-term competitiveness, as well as the long-term survival and growth, architectural practice aims to successfully manage the technical excellence, i.e. the firm's specialist technical knowledge and professional competence.

To achieve smooth project development, the project manager's focus is on the assets of a practice, that is people, information and business strategies. The project manager needs to know the key indicators with which to measure the performance of design activities. The project manager's tasks are facilitated if the internal relationships within the architectural practice are defined through decision-making procedures.

Project dynamics are very much influenced by changes in the project during the design process. The project manager needs to understand the reasons for, and sources of, change and the procedures that should be adopted in order to control and manage its impact.

Architects in the design team tackle creative aspects in translating the brief into a design. Creative leap, albeit a very personal and artistic process, draws upon the client/end-users' requirements within the cultural/social, technological, environmental, and economic context of the project, and the previous experience of the practice. The client/end-users' requirements, the main features of the project context, and the practice's experience can be captured by effective knowledge management, and further developed by updating the knowledge base. Starting from this common knowledge base, architects create original designs, drawing inspiration from very different sources. Their individual aesthetic imprint can be an asset which attracts future clients. However, aesthetics are only one element of a good building design.

Effective management of existing knowledge about the project context and the practice experience, and of new information on technological innovations can create a significant competitive advantage. Post-occupancy evaluation can contribute to the design of buildings which are memorable not only for their aesthetic attributes but are also valued by the client/end-users as buildings which can be used effectively and maintained in good condition at a low cost and for a long period of time.

2.3 Case study

The objectives of the interviews with the two architects[1] were to examine the real-life process of translating the brief into a design, to identify problems, and then to indicate guidance for solving them in the section on Key Reading. A series of questions which address the management of external and internal aspects of translating the brief into a design were prepared, and the architects provided the answers based on their personal experience. Similar interviews with other practices would probably reveal other nuances in the management and design aspects of briefing and design process.

Practice A has a total of 15 staff, with offices in Glasgow and Edinburgh. They are specialists in housing and have a strong reputation for participation and user involvement. Over the last ten years they have completed over 20 new build housing projects for association clients, many on 'brown field' sites. These projects have ranged in size from 10 to 71 units, several involving 'partnering' in various ways. Current topics in which they are actively involved include: sustainability issues, housing for varying needs, group heating, and wider issues such as opportunities for generating local employment, security, or any other issue on the agenda of local housing associations. They also offer planning, supervisor and energy consultant services.

Practice B has around 40 staff, with the main office in Glasgow and a smaller office in London. They have wide experience in the residential, industrial and commercial sectors, and have seen a significant expansion in the last five years mainly based on projects in the hotel sector. They are also one of the major designers in the health and care sector in Scotland. A new interior design department was formed in 2000, which adds to their design potential. Although in previous years they have run many traditional contracts, in the last few years most of the projects have been based on the design and build (D&B) type of contract, either being appointed by a contractor or novated by a client.

Practice A has been involved mainly in the traditional procurement route where the principal advantage appears to be maintaining control of the design process. They have been involved in a few partnering arrangements where some elements of risk appear to be transferred from client to contractor, principally cost uncertainty. In their limited experience, the advantage to the client was a 'lump sum contract', whilst the contractor had the advantage of control over the selection of many products/materials. This type of contract ran without a formal bill of quantities as a basis for pricing, making the cost of client-inspired variations difficult to measure. Frequently, contractors expect to gain control over elements of the design process, for example in the selection of products. In one case, the contractor insisted on using his own, locally produced UPVC windows and doors which have proven to be inferior to those preferred by the housing association. The housing association had (naively) accepted that the boost to local employment was a worthwhile trade-off.

Practice B has been involved in both traditional and D&B, and various other types of procurement. They have a continuous in-house debate on the advantages and disadvantages of D&B procurement because the role of the architect has changed. Architects work in a far more legally contentious and competitive environment. They have less control, yet they take higher risks and liabilities, and are being pushed to go down the D&B route by others.

Practice A is sometimes involved in preparing the client's strategic brief, i.e. the brief which is developed at the pre-project stage, usually as an integral part of a feasibility study. The process varies widely, in response to the needs and desires of the client group. Most frequently, the process involves meetings with the user groups as well as the funding bodies and/or building owner. These meetings build over time to a dialogue, with Practice A acting as enabler by, for example, illustrating options or arranging visits to similar facilities already built nearby. Their involvement in developing the brief tends to allow them to move through the outline design stage more speedily and can, therefore, bring forward the completion date.

Practice B has been involved in preparing the strategic brief on various occasions. The necessity for involvement usually occurs if the client has no previous experience in the sector or type of project. The practice uses its experience, researches into the subject, and proposes a brief, which is then 'shaped up' together with the client. Often a brief is developed in parallel with a proposal. Usually, the architects' involvement in the brief development does not help in speeding up the process. From the experience of Practice B, it is far more efficient to work with a client who has previous experience and has therefore already developed a brief, because time-consuming decisions have been taken in advance, and the architects can spend more time focusing on the proposal. The benefit for the practice to be involved at this stage is in securing a client and a job.

Practice A has never participated in VM, but frequently in cost saving exercises, which can often be the same thing. For example, the practice has entered into dialogue with clients as to whether high quality boundary treatments to front gardens are more important than additional thermal insulation or over-bath showers. Cost saving exercises are undertaken in most projects irrespective of size or risk. Cost saving lists are usually drawn up by the project architect and tabled at design team meetings, then discussed and ratified at management committee meetings. The quantity surveyor undertakes this at an early stage when the project is submitted for cost plan approval to the funding body – certainly by pre-planning application. The practice has a long experience with most client organisations and an even longer experience in designing the type of project, e.g. tenement rehab. Since the practice closely follows (and helps to shape) policy, both within the organisation and nationally, it has a strong understanding of the core project requirements.

Practice B applies VM as an integral part of design. With repeat clients and repeat building types, VM is based on a direct experience from the previous projects and is incorporated from the early stages of design. While a design team would incorporate VM into the design process in smaller projects, in larger projects and projects with early contractors' involvement, VM is applied with more definition. There are separate VM exercises/workshops that involve input from specialist and outside reviewers. The practice has, in the past, encountered various applications of VM, going from one extreme to another, depending on the size and type of project.

The whole design team usually takes part in an exercise. While the design team has a role in considering and evaluating the various proposals, often it is the client who decides on what final changes are to be applied. For instance, in a recent housing scheme, the internal partitions specification was changed from masonry to lightweight. The role of the architects and other consultants was to advise on the performance of both systems. Although the downside of the proposed system was losing some areas from the flats, the client decided to go ahead as advantages far outweighed this loss.

Value management has usually been undertaken within the first 30 percent of working design stages. Cost analysis plays a vital part in VM. Depending on the type of contract, and also the size and type of project, Practice B will have a different role as a consultant. Consequently, their role in implementation of VM will also vary. It is in the architects' interest to have VM applied as early in a project as possible. Unfortunately, in the D&B environment VM is usually driven by contractors and can be applied at any stage, often involving an enormous amount of revision work for consultants at their own cost.

Practice A rarely considers WLC, though it is often mentioned. It may affect the project's list, which is sometimes assessed by a maintenance officer within the client organisation. WLC is not used for several reasons; such as the lack of understanding of the principles of whole life costing, the view that this is an 'additional service' which many clients do not wish to pay for, and that even if whole life costing was applied, no additional capital funding would be made available.

The experience of Practice B is that WLC is client-driven and is not applied as a standard measure. It is more present in public related projects, and is enforced by either the client or end-user (often the same body). With private clients, WLC is directly related to ownership issues, and whether the owner is going to be involved in facilities management or not. Depending on the extent of the required changes, WLC can be a huge drawback for the design time-scale. It would be preferable to introduce a project evaluation exercise that would incorporate both VM and WLC at the very beginning of the project design process. This can definitely increase the quality of the building design. However, if introduced late in the process of design, it can jeopardise a design process time-scale, imposing a risk to project quality in other ways. It is necessary to programme WLC into the design process time-scale; architects as well as other consultants need to make sure that this is implemented and programmed up front.

Typically, housing association clients will hand over to Practice A a 'standard' design brief (tailored for new build or rehabilitation), developed by the development manager on behalf of the management committee incorporating best practice guidance from their governing bodies. The practice compares the brief with the recent experience of similar projects and meets with the design team to compare and contrast the brief with the consultancy's understanding of the opportunities presented. If there are any misunderstandings, they tend to arise when consultation with the end-users has been neglected. Practice A often anticipates user requirements by obtaining relevant feedback from occupiers of other recently built projects and tabling these at design team meetings for incorporation into the current project.

The vast majority of Practice A clients are community-based housing associations whose development sub-committees form policy. These are invariably based around best practice guidance issued by Communities Scotland and/or Scottish Federation of Housing Associations. Most projects require a series of decisions from the committee, ranging from the general (estate layouts, house plans) through to the specifics (kitchen/bathroom layouts, products lists) over a number of monthly committee meetings.

Practice A tries to ensure that the needs of the end-users are considered by encouraging their participation in the design process. The end-users are frequently represented on the Boards of Management Committees of Housing Associations. Whilst it is rare that the project proposals are in relation to their specific dwelling, as occupiers of similar housing they are well acquainted with the hazards and pitfalls of each dwelling type. The practice does not take specific steps when their refurbishment projects include owner/occupiers, where very full dialogue is maintained.

Practice A uses a number of visualisation techniques, from coloured plans to 3D CAD images. Their selection of techniques is usually determined by the time and money available for each specific stage of the project. As well as visualisation, they frequently promote site visits to recently completed similar projects or make models. They have also offered seminars on design topics, most recently on sustainability, to clients in order that they may have a more complete understanding of the issues.

The framework of Practice B's briefing process usually includes the following stages:

- Site finding (by the client or the practice).

- Basic brief (by client) – includes the type of building and the basic requirements. The majority of Practice B's projects involve repeat clients, and the brief does not have to be excessive.

- Feasibility study (by the practice) – shows the client the potential of the site, areas and provisions. This is usually speculative work.

- Planning stage (by the practice, based on the client's appointment). A scheme design in order to facilitate discussion with the planning department and to develop design in conjunction with the client. The brief is more detailed; it can evolve around the design.

- Building warrant stage and tender – working drawings. The brief expands into 'finishes' and is tightly related to cost.

- Contract and construction – production information and site coverage.

The briefing process takes place at various stages and goes into various depths depending on the stage. Practice B finds that repeat clients and work from the same sector is more efficient. However, introducing new clients and sectors is vital for the business, and the practice is often prepared to take a risk in order to secure future projects. Most of their clients are private developers and, in most of the cases, the priority is getting a product (building) within a budget. Practice B often has to make sure that quality is maintained throughout the project. It is very easy to fall for a 'cheap alternative' trap, especially in the D&B environment. A difference in priorities may be a problem; architects prioritise design whereas clients often prioritise the cost of the building.

Clients make decisions about the time-scale and design. The architect's role is to educate the clients about design at the early stages, and to explain the time-scale and consequences in delays. Problems often occur when clients take significant time to make some decisions, while architectural resources are left on hold or have to be transferred onto another project. When clients eventually make a decision, the architects are expected to act promptly in order to meet the desired deadlines. This is often very difficult and it involves a very dynamic human resourcing strategy. This, of course, often affects the continuity of the project.

All decisions have to be made relatively quickly. The experience of Practice B is that it is far more efficient to work with a private developer where one can talk directly to the person or body that makes these decisions. Problems usually arise when the practice is working for complex-structure clients, usually public bodies. In these cases, decision making goes through various stages and bodies, and needs lengthy presentations and meetings, signatures and approvals.

In order to meet the end-user's requirements, the practice consults various standards; technical or sector specific. Professional Codes of Conduct (RIBA, ARB, RIAS) require the provision of services that take the whole environment into consideration, from the end-users to the general public. Practice B often has to sign 'collateral warranties' which oblige the consultancy to provide services that take the end-user into consideration. Working for private clients means that the practice often works for an unknown or an anonymous end-user. However, when working for public clients, the practice is often required to attend public meetings and give public presentations. For presentations, the consultancy uses Computer 3D visualisation. At the early stages this is used to present massing and general design in a sketchy form; it then moves into a more detailed design, mostly to help obtain planning permission. The practice produces 3D images and occasionally films. In the past they have also prepared brochures, presentation boards and slide presentations.

In terms of the team within the office, Practice A has a flat management structure where the majority of designers are directors in the firm. The practice has a very low turnover; most of the employees have been working for more than 15 years. There are a predominance of senior architects who have worked together for many years. All architects act as Chair and Secretary for the design and construction teams, and encourage a free flow of ideas and opinions. Practice A does not usually brief the design team; this is carried out by the housing association development officer. The framework for interaction is usually effectively fixed by the client who usually opts to appoint each member of the design team separately, and therefore has direct control as employer over each individual member of the team (Figure 2.1). The design process is made more complex but more democratic because of this. Only one client's representative is present.

Practice A interacts with consultants in a positive way, making each feel at ease within the team. Areas of responsibility have usually been made clear through the interview/appointment process carried out by the client. The practice frequently works with the same consultants who are familiar with their style and method of working. The client engages directly with the consultants.

Figure 2.1: Client's relationship with the Practice A designers and external consultants

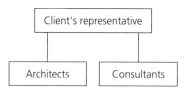

Practice A encourages the contractor to become part of the team and utilise the knowledge and skills that they have to benefit the project. This can sometimes mean the practice reassessing the products list or simplifying a detail, benefiting the contractor. For example, the practice frequently permits the contractor to substitute products which offer better value, with cost savings shared between contractor and client. The principal problem is tendering, both for consultants who sometimes find resourcing a project difficult because their fee bid may have been too low; equally, the contractor may have 'bought the job' and strives to minimise or avoid a loss by fabricating claims or cutting corners in the building/quality control process. Quality control is usually maintained by employing a clerk of works on a regular basis.

Practice B assigns a project architect at an early stage, and it is usually the same person who will see it through to completion. The team is then built around this person as appropriate, and depending on requirements. The team can be substantially increased for a short period of time to produce large information packages. It is more efficient and the practice prefers to have a smaller team on a project thereby allowing more time; often the design process is driven by a tight time-scale and this is not possible. A team can be increased either by the in-house employees or a temporary contract workforce.

A team structure consists of a partner and several associates. Every associate is in charge of a number of projects. A project architect has meetings with an associate or a partner on a regular basis where all the issues affecting both practice and project are discussed. In regular team meetings, the project architect then passes the information to the team. These meetings are carried out on a daily basis, but there are also team meetings with an associate and a partner as required. The usual structure of a team covering larger projects is presented in Figure 2.2.

Practice A does not manage project dynamics effectively. They use timesheets that record hours logged to each project. This, multiplied by hourly charge rates, lets them monitor expenditure against income. Income is measured by achieving stages from the RIBA Plan of Work. The practice fails to manage project dynamics effectively because they have not embraced change. They inherited the timesheet system from their early years when they were a research unit at the University of Strathclyde. The practice frequently overspends on projects, and tries to identify why. Often, the

Figure 2.2: Practice B team structure

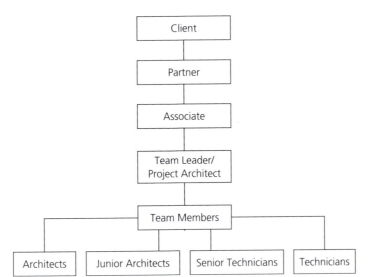

project architect ends up servicing the job in part from (free) overtime. Most over-spend is caused by tender prices being higher than budget costs. The practice often redesigns to reduce costs, without seeking extra fees. Planning building warrant applications frequently run in parallel and the billing process is well under way, or completed, prior to receipt of these. Contractor selection also runs in parallel with these activities. Billing would be better commenced after planning and building approvals.

The team leader in Practice B prepares a programme for a client, projecting the design stages from inception through to completion. It is often worked up from a desired completion date backwards. This emphasises potential milestones and raises the client's awareness of time-scale at earlier stages. A similar programme is then prepared for in-house purposes, mainly for the human resourcing and working out the fees and expenses. It is important for a practice to be able to keep resourcing fluent. Depending on the size of a project, the practice would assign a team to work on it. It is the team leader's role to maintain appropriate resourcing in proportion with information requirements. Practice B has a yearly programme for an upgrade of IT facilities. It is the IT manager's role to monitor day-to-day requirements and regularly report to the management team. If there is any urgent requirement for a facility that would be required on a project, the management decides whether it is feasible to invest in it.

The biggest problem is that clients do not appreciate the time required for certain stages of design. Clients take a long time to make their decisions but do not allow sufficient time for a design team to prepare follow up information. On a recent big project, a client spent five months on tendering and selecting the contractor. The contract value was reduced and, as a part of an exercise, some changes were made to specifications and building costs. The contractor started on site almost immediately, and there was virtually no time allowed for the design team to pick up on these changes. The design team were developing information packages in parallel with construction work. This is very risky and increases potential for making some costly mistakes.

Practice A tends to promote the idea of participatory design where dialogue is encouraged with the client and/or user. The practice develops options for the client to select, emphasising their 'green' credentials. These philosophies are apparent in the practice development material, and this is reinforced at interview. The practice gets many repeat commissions, so they tend not to 'hard sell' their services.

Design ideas tend to be developed in conjunction with the client. Typically, the design team may develop three alternative strategies for developing a site. These would all be drawn up, a presentation made to the Board of Management, offering commentary on the pros and cons, then they would take a decision, albeit Practice A and/or the development officer may make a recommendation as to which idea is most appropriate.

Innovation is identified as a goal in quite a number of projects. Funding, however, takes no account of the issue. Also, in risk management terms, housing associations, especially the smaller ones, cannot afford to innovate as any consequential remedial action would have to be funded from the rental income of their tenants. Nevertheless, Practice A strives to innovate, but pushes only a few short steps ahead of best practice. For example, the practice might introduce passive stack ventilation, which may require a lot of convincing of their client. The practice finds that aspects which address fuel poverty tend to be well received and they are currently looking at group heating within the tenement context. The designs always exceed the building regulation requirements for 'U' values within the building fabric.

Flexibility and adaptability tend to be a core requirement of Practice A's brief. For example, designers ply-plate the bathroom walls to receive grab-rails should they be required later. The practice configures the house layout so that the bathroom and bedroom can be interconnected at a later date.

Different design options are discussed first within Practice A's office, floated at design team meetings, and then offered to the committee. The design process can soak up an enormous number of design hours! The client tends to fine-tune or change their mind, especially if lead-in times are very long. Practice A mostly completes projects on time. Delays are usually down to weather or non-attendance of utilities.

Practice B's designs evolve within site constraints while also taking urban planning requirements into consideration. Efficient layouts have always been the main feature of their design, but in recent years a more contemporary design has been added as another priority to the practice's design strategy. In past years, their design was rather conservative, but since younger designers have entered into management, a more modern design has been introduced. This improvement has been recognised both by the clients and public, giving the practice a renewed confidence. Whilst retaining efficient layouts, designers are adding new elements that incorporate innovative materials, modern structures, and encourage sustainability. The key issue is to maintain the cost within established limits. Even some regular clients have moved forward with the practice's new design approach, accepting it with the belief that they will get a better building within the same budget.

Design for change has been addressed in Practice B's projects, mainly in residential buildings such as housing, and on a few occasions in health and care buildings. The practice has taken part in a national housing competition 'Accommodating Change', designing a standard unit with a flexible internal layout, which can be remodelled to adapt to new requirements. However, this approach is only applied if required by a client.

Problems within the design process occur mostly when a major change is necessary to an already fully developed design. This happens when a new piece of information is provided (for example, a pipe-way leave required within a site), or when the client changes the brief. Changes are often radical, and may result in a complete redesign and redraw. If all permissions have been acquired the problem is greater still because this can significantly affect the time-scale. To prevent this, the practice routinely seeks all necessary information at the beginning of a design process. Meetings are arranged with all the relevant bodies (planning department, roads department, etc.), and all public utilities information requested, including all maps and way leave zones.

Practice A conducts information searches in many ways, from mundane checking of technical matters through their reference library to attending 'cutting edge' seminars and workshops to bring ideas back for consideration by the team. Practice A 'buys in' the RIBA library service, including an electronic version, and a librarian regularly visits the office.

Concerning the performance requirements, the development officer checks that the design ideas meet the client's needs. Sometimes, as the practice tries to have direct dialogue, they get immediate, direct feedback.

Practice A does not undertake post-occupancy evaluation, except for anecdotal information picked up *ad hoc* from visits during defects inspections. It feels that post-occupancy evaluations could be very informative, but costs for this are not included as part of the practice's 'core' service. They attend the site every week as an integral part of their service, where they are frequently consulted over detailing. The practice has not yet developed a strategy for preventing the repetition of certain usual problems.

Practice B recognises the importance of information and knowledge management. The consultancy organises regular CPD (continuous professional development) lectures, either by inviting external lecturers or sharing in-house experience. A resource library has been established, and all members of staff have access to a range of architectural journals and magazines. Investments have been made in IT technology, allowing all the staff to access the latest information available from various sources. For example, the practice has Intranet access to the Barbour Index document database, which is updated quarterly with the latest publications. The practice also encourages accessing RIBA, RIAS, and similar websites.

Since Practice B mostly works on D&B projects, it is not involved in project construction, which is managed by a contractor. Post-occupancy evaluation is quite regular in some type of projects. In the hotels sector, the practice visits completed buildings and seeks comments from the operators. In other types of projects, where post-completion visits are not practicable, comments are invited from the clients, and outcomes applied in repeat projects.

2.4 Conclusions

Experience of the two architectural practices in translating the brief into a design shows that there are opportunities for solving or minimising the problems faced by adopting strategies for managing external relationships; i.e. the project's context (social, economic and environmental) and client/end-users involvement, and the strategies for improving the internal relationships within the architectural office, including the creative aspects of translating the brief into a design.

The issues that need to be considered are as follows:

Client procurement strategy

Client procurement strategy influences the briefing process. Early engagement in the briefing process is beneficial to both parties; with architects' assistance, clients gain deeper understanding of the end-user requirements and design options, whilst architects secure the job. Early engagement could speed up the outline design stage, and thus bring the completion date forward. Those architects interviewed appreciate having control of the design process in the traditional procurement route, in which the design is completed before the start of the construction. From their point of view, the design and build procurement route allows less control over the project, yet brings them higher risks and liabilities. In partnering arrangements, they perceive that some elements of risk are transferred from client to contractor, principally cost uncertainty. In this arrangement, architects are not always happy with the contractor's control over elements of the design process, for example in the selection of products. Architects' early engagement with clients provides the opportunity to discuss these concerns, establish a relationship which satisfies both parties, and develop appropriate decision-making procedures.

Capturing client requirements

It is vital that designers understand their clients' business/needs in order for them to provide what the client wants. Public clients often have a fully developed guidance for the design of their buildings. Repeat projects and communication with end-users make the briefing process easier. However, capturing the requirements for new types of building design and unknown end-users requires a structured approach. In this case, architects can facilitate the briefing process by using the guidance for capturing client requirements.

Value management

Architects' experience shows that it is in their interest to have VM applied as early in a project as possible. However, they caution that in the D&B procurement route contractors tend to apply VM at any stage, which often creates revision work for consultants at their own cost. This experience indicates that the cost of revisions due to VM needs to be discussed with clients at the outset.

Whole life costing

In addition to the problems in developing whole life costing that have been identified by researchers, both consultancies point out several difficulties in its use in practice. They include a lack of understanding of WLC; perceived extra cost for this exercise; doubts about provision of additional capital funding; and possible changes in the project that can affect the planned design time-scale. To achieve a regular use of WLC in practice, further research is needed to develop reliable and easy-to-use WLC methods. Educating owners and end-users about the benefits of WLC can help in increasing its use too. As far as the project time-scale is concerned, it is important to include WLC in the early stages of design to avoid later revisions and subsequent delays.

Communicating with the client

The two practices interviewed have worked regularly with their clients. Having experience of how the communication process usually develops, they feel comfortable in communicating with their clients. Thus Practice A, which often works with public bodies, does not object to the complexity of their decision making, while Practice B prefers one-to-one communication with a private developer. This indicates that each practice has developed its own procedure in communicating with clients with which both parties are satisfied. However, to improve their competitiveness when dealing with new clients, architects can use the guidance which shows how to communicate the design intent and overcome any physical, organisational and cultural barriers.

Building effective teams

Interviews with the two practices show that the relationship between the members of the team and external consultant, and between the design team and the client can vary from one architectural practice to another. These variations reflect the firms' evolution and the preferred working relationships in each practice. Architectural practices can examine how to manage their human resources effectively by consulting the guidance for better management and optimum productivity through successful team building.

Managing project dynamics and project change

Concerning the management of project dynamics, the two practices interviewed have some difficulties. They need some additional training in planning their financial and human resources, and resolving the impact of changes in the project on design time-scale, human resourcing and financing. Guidance in this area is also available.

Creative aspects of translating the brief into a design

The two practices interviewed strive to improve their design, to innovate, and to persuade clients of benefits of adaptable and more sustainable design. The available guidance related to these aspects of translating the brief into a design can assist architectural practices in achieving these goals more effectively.

Knowledge management and post-occupancy evaluation

Effective knowledge management, including the lessons learned from post-occupancy evaluation, assists in achieving competence and technical excellence. The available guidance on knowledge management and decision support techniques helps architects to exploit their knowledge as an asset.

The guidance related to tackling the issues in translating the brief into a design are listed in Key Reading.

References

Blyth, A. and Worthington, J., *Managing the Brief for Better Design*, Spon Press, London (2001).
Egan, J., 'Rethinking Construction', Report of the Construction Task Force on the Scope for Improving Quality and Efficiency of UK Construction, Department of the Environment, Transport and the Regions (DETR) (1998).
Flanagan, R. and Norman, G., *Life Cycle Costing for Construction*, RICS (1983).
Seeley, I. H., *Building Economics*, 4th edn, MacMillan Press, London (1996).

Key Reading

Brown, S. A., *Communication in the Design Process*, Spon Press (2000).

Building Research Establishment, *Value management: a series of four documents*, BRE, Watford (2000).

Edwards, S., Bartlett, E. and Dickie. I., *Whole life costing and life-cycle assessment for sustainable building design*, BRE (2000).

Emmitt, S., *Architectural Management in Practice: A competitive approach*, Pearson Education (1999).

Holti, R., Nicolini, D. and Smalley, M., *C546 – The handbook of supply chain management*, CIRIA Publication (2000).

Kamara, J. M., Anumba, C. J. and Evbuomwan, N. F. O., *Capturing client requirements in construction*, Thomas Telford (2002).

Oliver, G. M. B. (ed.), *SP088 – Quality management in construction – implementation in design services organisations*, CIRIA Publications (1992).

Endnotes

1 In order to preserve the anonymity of the two practices, they are named as Practice A and Practice B.

Project briefing: practice

John Kelly, School of the Built and Natural Environment,
Glasgow Caledonian University, UK

3.1 Introduction

Construction project briefing is the activity of taking from a client a clear, unambiguous and explicit performance specification of a project. The brief is the documentation that records the project performance specification. Briefing exists within an environment where a client wishes to introduce change within the organisation and being change focused the definition of the project is often prefixed by invest, refurbish, relocate, expand, replace, extend, consolidate, etc.

In order to undertake briefing effectively it is necessary to understand the strategic dimensions of the client's organisational change and to record and make explicit the client's strategy for the project through a project mission statement. In undertaking this activity it is also necessary to understand that the project is a separate, temporary activity for the client often unrelated in character to that of the client's core business. This implies an understanding of the concept of projects, project management and the importance of strategic fit within the client organisation.

The construction briefing process involves gathering, analysing and synthesising information needed in the building process in order to inform decision making and decision implementation. Further, the brief document should contain all the information used in the design process as a set of evaluation criteria to ensure an optimal solution to the building problem. It is a reference document against which audits can take place at any subsequent stage in the design, construction and use phases of the building process. It is recognised that people from a number of different roles undertake the collation of material that will become the brief. In this chapter the architectural programmer, architect, project manager, project sponsor surveyor, engineer or whomever is responsible for the collation of information and the production of the brief is collectively termed the 'brief writer'.

The aim of this chapter is to highlight those factors which determine the appropriate approach to briefing, the procedure best suited to the client and the client's project. The chapter is not a comprehensive 'how to' description of briefing, for this refer to authors such as Duerk (1993), Salisbury (1998) and Blyth and Worthington (2001); but rather a discussion of briefing as an investigation or as a facilitation of stakeholders within a distinct two stage process. Within this context the chapter introduces a technique to investigate the value system of the client. It is argued here that before undertaking briefing, a period of contemplation and prior planning is required in order to understand the client and the client's values, the change occurring within the client's organisation, the procurement environment, and the stakeholders involved with and affected by the project.

The material contained in this chapter has equal relevance to the service of Architectural Programming as defined by the American Institute of Architects and for the purposes of this chapter the terms 'briefing' and 'architectural programming' are assumed to be synonymous.

3.2 Client types

Projects for large owner-occupiers or frequent procurers of buildings are characterised by the identification of a need which has usually been revealed as a result of lengthy studies and forms an integral part of the client's long-term strategic plans. These clients frequently develop a project brief prior to approaching the construction industry and sometimes seek only a service that translates their stated requirements into a built solution. Many large and regular clients employ in-house project managers/facilities managers (although the precise meaning of this term varies from client to client) or call upon the services of outside consultants to act as project managers who, as well as providing the liaison between client and the design team, may also have responsibility for compiling the brief.

Small owner-occupiers and irregular clients are frequently characterised by an approach to the construction industry in response to unanticipated changes in the client organisation or in the environment that rendered existing facilities inadequate. Small clients generally have limited expertise available to them in-house, rarely undertake a strategic brief and rely more heavily on the design advice of a consultant architect at the project briefing stage. The way in which these clients present their requirements to the architect can vary considerably. Some clients have highly detailed preconceptions of the project, while others have only the vaguest notion of what they want, and consider it to be the architect's task to develop the project brief.

Public sector clients generally are analogous to large owner-occupiers. It is finance that distinguishes the public from the private sector. The public sector reports that their long-term building strategy is closely linked to the means of securing finance. However, private sector clients do not report the same concern over funding, and there appears to be an assumption that money can be found if it is needed. For developers, the decision to build is opportunistic and based on the availability of desirable sites. This distinction between the public and the private sector is important, the public sector will build what it can for a fixed budget, whereas to the private sector a specific rate of return generally determines success.

3.3 Including stakeholders in the briefing process

A stakeholder is someone trustworthy who holds a stake on behalf of others who invest a stake in a project or event and put that stake at risk. In the context of briefing, the stakeholder is the representative of groups within the client organisation, users of the project once it has been completed (who may not be the same as those within the client's team), members of the design team, the contractor's team, the contractor's supply chain, the local community, political or other lobby or interest groups. Within a briefing team some members will be stakeholders in the true sense of the word and others will be representing themselves. Woodhead and Downs (2001) identify that stakeholders within the briefing team will be of three decision types. These are:

1 Decision approvers are those who sign off, for example, drawings, budgets, etc. and are accountable for the investment of funds.

2 Decision takers are those who recommend actions to decision approvers.

3 Decisions shapers are those who are responsible for the development of proposals.

In addition there are:

- Decision influencers who represent individual or group views and lobby on behalf of those points of view.

In analysing the briefing team it is necessary to understand the role of the various stakeholders and the stake that they are holding on behalf of others. Difficulties arise where decision influencer stakeholders hold a significant political stake on behalf of a group or the public at large but have no stake in the financing of the project. In reality they see the risk of their stake as being incurring the wrath or losing the trust of those whom they represent. Political issues are often the most obscure factors to be included in the strategic and/or project brief but are significant factors in the client's value system.

3.4　Engaging the briefing team

Irrespective of how briefing is undertaken it is a team activity. The brief writer will engage with a finite team of people in collecting, collating and processing information that will lead to the performance specification of the project and the client's value system. The brief writer has a choice of either engaging with people in a workshop or series of workshops, or carrying out an exploration through interviews with all stakeholders. The two methods are referred to here as investigation or facilitation and the benefits and disadvantages of each method are considered below.

Investigation involves compiling the brief through a process of literature review, interviews and meetings with key client representatives, post-occupancy evaluation and existing facilities walk through. The data thereby gathered will be checked through presentations at team meetings.

The advantages of the investigation approach lie in the familiarity and skill of the brief writer in dealing with a particular client type and/or building type. A skilled brief writer will be able to logically collect data using proven techniques in an efficient manner, minimising client representative input. It is an often perplexing fact that because client representatives are focused wholly on the client's core business they sometimes show little sympathy for, or interest in, a new project until that too is absorbed into core business. If time is of the essence then more than one brief writer can be used on a project to gather data in the shortest possible time.

Using the investigation approach it is not necessary to identify all stakeholders at the commencement of briefing. If an important stakeholder comes to light during the process they can be interviewed in turn. Obtaining the honest views of those junior in the client organisational hierarchy and/or uncovering hidden agenda are more likely through a confidential interview on a one-to-one basis. Further, interviewing reveals the decision makers, in the types listed above, in situations where their identity is not clear.

Some disadvantages of interviewing are that points raised in later interviews may require re-visiting earlier interviewees to clarify issues, and sometimes checks need to be made to ensure that all interviewees are using language and terms in a common manner. In this respect, and where the brief writer is not knowledgeable in the client's business, it may be necessary to enlist the help of an expert to ensure that the right questions are asked. It is difficult to counter the 'wish list' syndrome, particularly where a forceful stakeholder puts over their requirements as a *fait accompli* and validation checks with the briefing team may not be possible until all of the interviews have been collated, and these may reveal discrepancies late in the briefing process.

In facilitation, a facilitator independent of the client and the design team will guide the whole team through a process of briefing using largely the techniques of value, risk and project management. It is still necessary to undertake literature review, interview, post-occupancy evaluation and existing facilities walk through as a means of providing information to the workshop to be supplemented and interpreted by the workshop team. The workshop team will comprise stakeholders appropriate to the stage of the briefing exercise, principally whether it is a strategic or project briefing exercise. Typically, a strategic briefing exercise will take between four and eight hours and involve between 6 and 20 stakeholders. A project briefing exercise will typically take one to three days and involve between 12 and 20 stakeholders.

A facilitated briefing exercise demands, concurrently, the presence of all stakeholders but will extract all of the information in the shortest time. The team contains all of the experts necessary to feed information into the project and ask appropriate questions of others; any misunderstandings and/or disagreements can be resolved immediately. This is particularly useful at a project briefing exercise which includes appropriate client representatives and the full design team. The facilitator or other members of the team can challenge 'wish lists'. The facilitator will summarise the data contributed by the team at stages during the team exercise, therefore the brief will largely comprise a collation of these conclusions. An intensive, focused, facilitated briefing exercise will encourage good team dynamics and effective team building, highlighted by some clients as the most important aspect of the process and the one least able to be replicated through the investigation process.

However, a facilitated strategic or project briefing exercise demands a skilled facilitator knowledgeable in briefing and, as stated above, drawing a facilitator from the design team should be avoided. It should be recognised by the facilitator that a representative client team would contain members from different levels in the client hierarchy, which may stifle contributions from junior members and also allow hidden agenda to remain hidden. The nature of a one-off workshop means that if a key stakeholder is missing then key information may be omitted. This may be difficult to incorporate subsequently and therefore considerable effort is required before the workshop in identifying all stakeholders. Further, it is impractical to undertake a facilitated team meeting without some prior interviewing which requires a measurable investment in terms of client team time. Finally, facilitated team meetings can challenge the authority of the architect or project manager, particularly in the role of brief writer, and therefore it is important to determine whether the facilitator becomes the brief writer or whether, for example, the architect takes the workshop report as feedstock for the brief, the architect remaining the brief writer.

3.5 Hazards in briefing

The literature on briefing (see especially Kelly *et al*, 1992) identify the following as hazards which can easily be overlooked in construction project briefing:

Correct representation of the client

The modern construction client is commonly not a single person with sole executive authority to brief. Even where there is a project sponsor it is important to realise the structure of stakeholders to whom the project sponsor is responsible. Mapping the client and the client organisation should be considered a primary briefing task.

Is a building the answer to the client's problem?

There is a tendency by the construction industry to assume that because of the client's approach the client has at least correctly identified that a building project of some kind is the correct solution to the problem. Clients are generally assumed to have investigated the need to build quite thoroughly but this may be a dangerous assumption to make and one that is the responsibility of the strategic brief writer.

Definition by solution

There is also a tendency by the construction industry to assume that if the client defines the project by solution, e.g. 'I need to extend my plant space by $1000\,m^2$', then the client will have considered all other options. A strategic briefing exercise might define the project's mission as 'to accommodate new machinery to increase production' which may lead to other solutions.

The wish list syndrome

It has been found that stakeholders tend to maximise their 'wish list' in anticipation of being bargained down from this. The problem confronting the brief writer is then to understand the priorities of the stakeholders such that high priority needs are not sacrificed for lower priority wants.

Mandatory design guides

Particularly in the public sector, but also amongst large corporate organisations, there are well defined design guides and standards that tend to be used by the design team without question. The design guides stand in place of the brief for large parts of the project. Outdated or irrelevant design guides can lead to incorrect design decisions.

Client change

A further difficulty facing the brief writer is the changes that can occur in the client organisation and the client environment during the briefing and design process. A brief can only reflect the needs (and anticipated future needs) of the client at a particular point in time, however these needs can change during the course of the project in a sudden and unpredictable manner. Further, Morris and Hough (1987) demonstrated that in larger projects history shows that the greater danger is the failure to recognise gradual changes which subtly alter the needs of the client organisation and render the project, as initially conceived, inappropriate. The brief writer should be aware of changes most likely to be implemented in the near future.

The less knowledgeable client

Clients with little experience of the construction industry often do not understand its structure, nor do they have an appreciation of the technicalities of buildings. Problems occur when this type of client is not led carefully through the strategic and project briefing process.

Lack of iteration in briefing

Briefing is not linear and regular summarising and checking should be a feature of the process. The brief writer should consider the audit role of the brief during its structuring and writing.

Hidden agendas

These are a feature of the inception stages of construction projects. Client representatives and the design team members can all withhold their agenda from the group.

Exposing hidden agenda by clear presentation and recording of project goals is a function of the brief writer.

3.6 Procurement systems and briefing

The anticipated procurement system will impact on the form and structure of the brief and therefore should be understood by the brief writer at the outset of briefing. In traditional procurement the brief is the means by which information is transferred from the client to the design team. In this context it is the briefing exercise that is important, indeed in many cases there is no specific document that can be called the brief (Barrett and Stanley, 1999). Briefing can be an iterative process in which the design team obtain information from the client, respond to this information through the production of the design and check back with the client that the design accurately reflects the client's intentions. Any changes can be agreed with the client and the drawings amended. In this way the brief is effectively the final approved set of drawings. It is important to realise that another system is in operation, albeit implicitly, concerning the client's value criteria. Through iteration the client's value criteria are drawn into the project such that the completed drawings incorporate and in many ways represent the client's value system. For example, if the client had a particular wish for the building to be low energy/environmentally friendly then this will be drawn into the design and the cost and time implications recognised. Thus the client will have incorporated a value formula for the factor environment. In traditional procurement the role of the contractor and the contractor's supply chain is to accurately reproduce the form represented on the drawings and thereby satisfy the client's requirements and value criteria.

Design, develop and construct is a hybrid form of procurement in which the designers operate in the traditional manner until the form of the building is accurately represented as floor plates, sections and elevations in sufficient detail to obtain detailed planning consent. After competitive tender the project is 'signed over' to a contractor for the completion of the detailed design and construction. Often the designers are also signed over to the contractor in a legal process known as 'novation'. If this is the case the client's value system has a greater chance of being reflected in the detailed design. If this does not occur then the client's value system is in danger of being lost unless made explicit. This hybrid form of procurement is often contracted on a standard design and build form of contract in which the client's requirements are explained in drawn form but the risk of design rests with the contractor.

Design and build is a form of procurement that requires a written brief often described as the client's requirements or the employer's requirements. The brief must capture the totality of the client requirements in performance specification form and the client's value system. The brief becomes a contract document. The design and build contractor will engage a design team who, usually in the absence of the client since the contractor will be developing a competitive bid, will interpret the written details and prepare designs for costing. The lack of interaction between designers and client is a reason why design, develop and construct appears to be more popular than design and build. The contract sum tendered by the contractor is based upon the designs developed by the contractor's design team and submitted as a part of the tender. Any change required by the client will be configured as a change to the brief resulting in revised drawings and a revised contract sum. For this reason design and build is often regarded as only suitable for straightforward projects which naturally attract straightforward and proven design solutions. However, the counter argument is that were the brief to be complete in every respect, including the client's value system, and be understood without question by the designers then design and build is suitable for every project. The Private Finance Initiative (PFI) generally adopts a design and build approach to the procurement and operation of a building for a stated period of time. PFI demands therefore a more complete brief than would normally be the case since the operation of the building has to be specified.

Recently, two government departments have introduced innovative procurement systems based upon framework agreements. These are the Prime Contracting Method introduced by Defence Estates and ProCure21 introduced by the NHS. Both procurement forms, being framework agreements, envisage the appointment of a contractor with a full supply chain (including design and design management) before the building project has been identified. Once a client has a project a framework contractor is appointed to the project and the brief is developed. Upon completion of the brief all parties sign it off as a statement of client requirements both understood and capable of implementation within an agreed guaranteed maximum price. This is an example of the project brief being written with the full team appointed and after the framework tender is completed.

In conclusion, it is important for the client to realise that within a design and build or PFI environment it is vital for the brief to be highly specific both in terms of the performance specification and the client's value system. Within traditional, design, develop and construct, Prime or ProCure21, the brief is an auditable record of facts understood by the whole team.

3.7 Briefing as a two stage process

Salisbury (1998) usefully summarises the briefing process in the context of the first four sections of the RIBA Plan of Work; inception, feasibility, outline proposals and scheme design.

Stage 1; the objective of the inception stage is to produce a general statement of the building project's requirements through an interaction between the client and the architect. Salisbury states: 'before producing drawings of any kind an architect expects to absorb a great deal of background'. The background encompasses information about the client's organisation, the project need, the site and its environment, and similar completed buildings. At feasibility the objective is to produce design options and financial and other appraisals. Sensitivity of the project to change to many variables is tested and a full understanding of the design team to the needs of the client and users is obtained.

Stage 2; at outline sketch design stage the main requirements of the project are firmed up and the briefing process focuses much more on an iterative process of appraisal between the emerging designs, the brief and the client's requirements. The end of the process is a consolidated brief including the specification of room data. The final step in the process is described as completing the brief and achieving scheme design. Salisbury describes the objective of this stage as being:

> To finalise all information and actions required to render the brief a firm and complete statement ... With the brief settled and the scheme design complete, no further changes should be entertained.

Kelly *et al* (1992) in an early review of the process of briefing identified a two step approach due to the nature of the early stage design problem, stating:

> First, it is the task of strategic management to identify the organisational needs and then to decide whether a building (or buildings) of a general type and in a certain location is the most effective solution to those needs. Next, there comes the tactical management decisions on the design of the building given the activities to be accommodated.

Kelly comments that the most striking feature about the two stage process is that the skills (and therefore the people) required at each stage are different. At the first stage, the decision making unit requires a broad understanding of the client organisation, and only the most general advice on matters which relate to the building industry. At the second stage, the decisions require a more detailed understanding of the operational characteristics of the proposed built facility and more detailed input as to their construction implications. This suggests that there should be two briefing teams, each composed of individuals with knowledge pertinent to the particular stage. This logic is the genesis of an argument for a briefing exercise comprising two distinct events.

The Construction Industry Board Working Group 1 document entitled *Briefing the Team* (1997) draws a distinction between a strategic brief and a project brief. The strategic brief sets the broad parameters of the project and includes such information as the project's mission statement, the context, the organisational structure and functions, and the overall scope and purpose of the project. The project brief converts the strategic brief into construction terms, puts initial sizes and quantities to the elements of construction and gives them a budget. The project brief includes the aim of the design, details of the site, the functional space requirements of the client and outline specifications.

The consensus from the above is that briefing is comprised of two distinct stages, strategic briefing and project briefing and that the team required for each stage may be different.

3.8 Briefing a project

A construction project is generally a reflection of a change within the client's organisation, a factor that must be considered at the strategic briefing stage. The concept of a change involves migrating from one state to another requiring the definition of objectives, the nature and scope of the change, and the performance measures used to determine a successful outcome. Therefore, a strategic brief must capture the nature of the change and, in so doing, define the project necessary to bring about the change.

The Oxford English Dictionary defines a project as being a plan, a scheme, or a course of action. Borjeson (1976) defines a project as 'a temporary activity with defined goals and resources of its own, delimited from but highly dependent upon the regular activity'. Morris and Hough (1987) define a project as 'an undertaking to achieve a specified objective, defined usually in terms of technical performance, budget and schedule'. Therefore, a project is the 'investment of resource by the client for a quantifiable return'. In this context investment is defined as being financial, manpower and/or material and the return, commercial or social. This is a useful definition, as it does not restrict the project to any particular industrial sector.

The essence of all of these definitions is the recognition that the investment in a project is undertaken to add value to the core business of a client. The project has by definition a start date, a completion date, resources for its undertaking, a method for its smooth integration into the core business and, ideally, performance indicators which allow its impact on the core business to be measured. The client is core-business focused and the client's team is likely to be a permanent team striving for long-term business success. This in some respects sits uneasily with the construction project team which is, by definition, a temporary team and is project focused striving for short-term success.

The client's core business will be governed by a set of value criteria which reflects the client's business culture. A significant danger of failure in respect of smooth integration and performance of the project becomes apparent when the project value system is allowed to develop independently of the client value system. The relationship of the project to the core business is illustrated in Figure 3.1. The client is only interested in the project from the perspective of increasing social or commercial well being.

In summary, a project is defined as an investment by a client organisation on a temporary activity to achieve a core business objective within a programmed time

Figure 3.1: The project in relation to client's core business

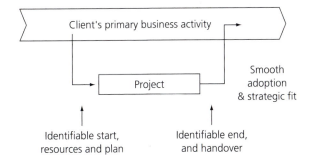

Client's primary business activity

Project

Smooth
adoption
& strategic fit

Identifiable start,
resources and plan

Identifiable end,
and handover

that, by reference to the client's value system, returns added value to the business activity of the organisation. The briefing process has to operate within this definition.

3.9 Strategic briefing methodology

Activity 1 – Discovery of the client's value system

The client's value system is a complex algorithm with variables related to time, cost and quality. It is those variables that define client quality, which are the most difficult to make explicit and which are the focus of this section of the chapter. It is vitally important for the client to understand that a project will absorb a value system through its development whether or not the client has chosen to make it explicit. It is obviously more satisfactory for all concerned that the project value system aligns or better still is driven by the client's value system.

In the analysis of architectural design, Vitruvius (100 BC: translated Morgan, 1960) stated that the value system for architecture depends on order, arrangement, eurhythmy, symmetry, propriety and economy. Pena *et al* (1987) state that the definition of a project for the purposes of an architectural programme (brief) can be arranged under the headings of function, form, economy and time.

Duerk (1993) states that design issues are processed through the filter of the values of the client, user and designer to yield goal statements about the qualities the design must have to ensure success. A goal is a concise statement of the designer's promise to the client about the quality of the design in relation to a particular issue. The quality is determined within the two extremes of a quality continuum and defined in terms of levels of performance. However, this has to be realised in context; for example, rooms in a Japanese house may be separated by paper walls because the cultural rules of polite behaviour require that sounds from other rooms be thoroughly ignored and therefore privacy is assured because sounds are unheard. Western culture has no such prohibition so one of the major complaints about hotels is that rooms are not private enough because the wall construction has not attenuated sufficient sound. In this context the public/private continuum is relative.

Kirk and Spreckelmeyer (1993) describe typical design objectives as being the aesthetic, esteem or image, the concept of the building and the way in which the building attracts attention to itself. Functional efficiency and flexibility are the degree to which the building is able to respond to the work process and flow of people, equipment and materials, be rearranged or expanded by the client to conform to revised processes and personnel changes with minimal disruption to existing building functions. Human performance is impacted by the physical and psychological comfort of the building as a place for working and living, supported by technical performance; how the building operates in terms of mechanical and electrical systems and industrial processes. Life-cycle costs are described as the economic sequence of building in terms of initial capital investment and then long-term operating costs. Good neighbour issues cover the impact on the community, energy conservation and security, addressing the degree to which the building can segregate sensitive functions from one another and prevent the entry of people to restricted areas. Kirk and Spreckelmeyer demonstrate the use of weighting design objectives as a methodology for highlighting the relative degrees of importance, or value priorities, of the various design objectives.

Best and De Valence (1999) highlight the complexity of quality by listing, for illustrative purposes, 15 factors that may be subjected to a quality continuum. Davies *et al* (1993) describe sets of scales for setting occupant requirements and rating of office buildings. These scales, published in a volume of over 300 pages, describe quality factors and performance attributes.

In a traditionally procured construction project the client value system becomes established through a process of trial and error on the part of the designers. It evolves slowly over time as the design team present and re-present schemes that reflect their current understanding of the client's value system. With each iteration, the designers take one step closer to full understanding. However, the newer procurement systems are not sympathetic to this slow iterative process. It is proposed here that the client's value system is made overt initially in a single operation, for later validation through a process of discovery using the technique described below.

For the client's value system to be meaningful the variables of time, cost and quality must be capable of description and measurement. The key to making the client's value system overt and therefore auditable, lies in understanding the description of quality. To derive a measurable statement of quality it needs to be uncovered and made explicit. A synthesis of the above leads to a conclusion that project quality can be represented by environment, exchange, politics/popularity, flexibility, esteem and comfort, each of which have their own continuum. The components of the full client value system become therefore:

Time – the time from the present until the completion of the project, the point when the project ends and is absorbed back into the core client business. Time can be assessed on a continuum from time is 'of the essence' to time is 'at large'. The former means that were the project to be delivered one day late then it would be of no value.

Capital cost (CAPEX) are all costs associated with the capital costs of the project, measured on a continuum from 'the budget cannot be exceeded' to 'there is flexibility in budgeting'. In many public sector situations capital cost might be substituted by space as a variable since the project has a fixed budget. In this situation it can be said that a finite amount space can be bought for a given budget. Each of the following attributes can have an influence on the amount of space that can be afforded. For example, to meet the requirements for user comfort and stay within budget then a certain amount of space might be sacrificed. In some situations the capital investment is subsumed within the operating cost and therefore the capital cost variable is omitted. This can occur, for example, where the cost of a building is rentalised within a total lease package, such as within a Private Finance Initiative project.

Operating cost (OPEX) refers to all costs associated with the operations and maintenance implications of the completed project as it moves to an operational product within the client's core business. In the context of a building this includes facilities management which may be limited to maintenance, repairs, utilities, cleaning, insurance, caretaker and security, but may be expanded to include the full operational backup such as catering, IT provision, photocopying, mail handling and other office services. The continuum is from 'OPEX must be at a controlled absolute minimum' to 'there is some flexibility in operating cost'.

Environment refers to the extent to which the project results in a sympathetic approach to the environment, measured by its local and global impact, its embodied energy, the energy consumed through use and other 'green' issues. The continuum is from 'maximum observance of Kyoto and Agenda 21 issues' to 'indiscriminate sourcing policies and solving every problem by adding more power'.

Exchange or resale is the monetary value of the project. This may be viewed as assets on the balance sheet, the increase in share value, capitalised rental or how much the project would realise were it to be sold. The continuum is from 'maximum return' to 'return is of no consequence'. If the physical asset is never to be sold, as in the case of co-operatively owned social housing, then this item would be scored as zero in the value system equation.

Flexibility represents the extent to which project parameters have to reflect a continually changing environment in the design. These value criteria are generally associated with changing technology or organisational processes or both. For example, medical practice is changing so rapidly that spaces in a hospital may need to accommodate a number of differing functions during the life of the building. The continuum is from 'being highly flexible to accommodate changing functions' to 'being unlikely to change to any extent'. If the project does not have to accommodate any flexibility then this variable is scored as zero.

Esteem is the extent to which the client wishes to commit resources for an aesthetic statement or portray the esteem of the organisation, internally and externally. The continuum is from 'we need to attract the admiration of the world' to 'esteem is of no significance'.

Comfort is the physical and psychological comfort of the building as a place for working and living, and will impact on human performance. Comfort is measured on a continuum from 'the support of the business in purely utilitarian terms' to 'a high degree of opulence'.

Politics is an external dimension that refers to the extent to which community, popularity and good neighbour issues are important to the client. The continuum ranges from 'must be popular with our local community or electorate' to 'we have no concerns towards our neighbours'.

To derive a client's value system, a Paired Comparison exercise is undertaken using the matrix shown in Figure 3.2. Only the client representatives may speak during this process, the design team, contractors' representatives and any other stakeholder not a part of the client body must keep silent and listen; for this is the client's value system. Each box represents a question phrased 'which is more important to you ...?' or 'would you be prepared to sacrifice ...?'. Either way the letter inserted in the box represents whichever factor is the more important. For example, the question may be posed – 'are you prepared to spend more now to offset costs in the future?'. If the answer is 'yes, I am prepared to spend more now to offset

Figure 3.2: Client's value system model

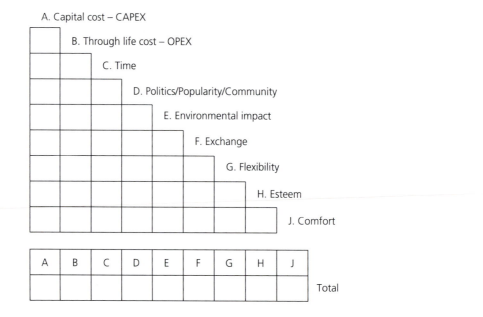

future costs', then obviously future costs are more important than capital costs and therefore the letter B is entered in the box. Conversely, if the answer is 'no, I must stay with the present budget even if it costs me more later', then future costs are less important than capital costs and therefore the letter A is entered in the box.

The number of times that A appears is entered in the total box and likewise for all of the other headings. The individual units of the value system can therefore be ranked to represent the overall client's value system. This may then be checked back against the client. The paired comparison method is useful when working with a number of client representatives as it allows discussion to occur at two levels, when discussing two variables only and, on completion, discussion can confirm the final result of the exercise.

The paired comparison approach is a particularly satisfactory method of deriving a client's value system in a workshop environment judged by the fact that clients generally agree with the summary when it is read back to them. For example, consider the sports centre shown in Figure 3.3. The summary of the paired comparison questioning is:

- It is equally primarily important that the project is delivered on budget and that it maximises internal comfort and satisfaction for the users.

Figure 3.3: An example of a client value system model used for a sports centre

A. Cost – CAPEX

B	B. Cost – OPEX							
A	B	C. Time						
A	D	D	D. Exchange income					
A	B	C	D	E. Esteem				
A	B	C	D	F	F. Environment			
A	G	G	G	G	G	G. Politics		
A	B	H	D	H	H	G	H. Flexibility	
A	I	I	I	I	I	I	I	I. Satisfaction/Comfort

A	B	C	D	E	F	G	H	I	
7	5	2	5	0	1	6	3	7	Total

- It is also of high importance that the sports centre is popular within the local community.

- Finally, it is important that operating costs are controlled and revenue opportunities maximised.

- Issues such as the timeliness of delivery of the project, environmental impact, flexibility in use, and architectural esteem are of lesser importance compared with the above.

Activity 2 – The issues surrounding the project: a checklist approach

The primary aim of the strategic brief is to make explicit the client's value system described above and also the goal or mission of the project with its primary associated functions. This section outlines those factors that have an impact on the understanding of the project goal, the client's value system being described in detail above. The factors which should be taken into account are:

Organisation – the identification of the client's business, the place of the project within the business, and the users of the project (who may not necessarily be a part of the client organisation). Under this heading there would be an investigation of the client's hierarchical organisational structure, and the client's key activities and processes that would impact upon the project. Included is information on the departments from which the client representatives will be drawn, the decision-making structures of the client and how these will interface with the project design and construction teams, and the communication networks anticipated for controlling the project. These decision-making structures become more important in situations where a single project sponsor or project manager represents the client team. The limits to the executive power of the project sponsor or project manager should be clearly defined. Information should be sought about the core and non-core business of the organisation and how they relate to space use if a building project is under study.

It must be recognised that most organisations are dynamic and that therefore any reorganisation, expansion or contraction anticipated within the life of the project or soon thereafter should be explored and recorded. Particularly important are such factors as health and safety and security, a change in the client's security environment could have a significant impact on the strategic requirements of the project.

Stakeholder analysis – following the discussion of the organisational structures it should be possible to identify all those who have a stake in the project. Stakeholders should be listed and their relative influence assessed.

Context – the context of the project should recognise such factors as culture, tradition or social aspects. Cultural aspects may include the relationship of one department with another, the fitting out and general quality of the environment, for example a law court. Tradition can cover such aspects as corporate identity that may be important in areas such as retailing. Social aspects will generally relate to the provisions made by the client for the workforce. For example, dining, recreation, sports and social club activities, crèche, etc.

Location – the location factors will relate to the current site, proposed sites or the characteristics of a preferred site where the site has not to-date been acquired. All projects, whether construction or service projects, will have a location.

Community – it is important to identify the community groups who may require to be consulted with respect to the proposed project. Some market research may need to be undertaken to ascertain local perceptions. The positioning of the project within the local community should also be completely understood.

Politics – the political situation in which the project is to be conceived should be fully investigated through the analyses of local and central government policies, and client organisational politics. The latter is often difficult to make overt at a workshop of representatives of different client departments however, client politics are a key driver behind any project. The political parties in power at national, regional and local levels, their views on the project, are there any changes in political persuasion anticipated over the project life-cycle and do these matter. In respect of client organisational politics it is useful to discover the powerful departments, the powerful individuals or groups, who are to be represented on the client's project team, from which departments do they come and how much power do they have to make decisions and influence project development.

Finance – the financial structuring of the project should be determined by considering the source of funding, the allocation of funding, and the effects of the project cash flow on the cash flow of the client organisation.

Time – under this heading are the general considerations regarding the timing of the project including a list of the chronological procedures which must be observed in order to correctly launch the project. In situations where the project is to be phased, time constraints for each stage of the project should be recorded.

Legal & Contractual issues – all factors, which have a legal bearing on the project, are listed under this heading including the extent to which the client is risk averse and also requires cost certainty. Also included here is data relating to the client's partnership agreements with suppliers and contractors.

Project parameters and constraints – a primary objective of the strategic briefing stage is to make explicit and fix the primary objectives of the project. Therefore, it is important that the team understand that the workshop is the end of one stage in the development of the project. Discussions must take place on the evolution of the project to the time of the workshop and to measure the extent to which key stakeholders believe that the project is still evolving. Any constraints surrounding the development of the project should be discussed and recorded.

Change management – the very fact that the client has launched a project means that a change process is under way which necessarily involves migrating from one state to another. The activities involved in change management are evaluating, planning and implementing, usually through education, training, communication, team and leadership development. As people are at the heart of any change process, communication and involvement are the keys to success. Recognising the change process, the organisation must be able to capture, record, process, structure, store, transform and access information. Change management involves more than just managing change within an organisation, it also involves managing risks and anticipating the effects of external factors.

Once the above information has been extracted and processed together with the client's value system, an exercise on the discovery of the mission or goal of the project can be undertaken.

Activity 3 – Discovery of the project mission: a function analysis approach

At this final stage of the strategic briefing process the aim of the brief writer is to make explicit the mission of the project, ideally in a short sentence that can be recognised as a project mission statement. The project mission statement should appear on the cover of the project brief and all other documents relating to the specification of the project. The mission statement will encapsulate the client values and project issues.

A method for deriving the project mission is through the facilitation of a workshop attended by the key stakeholders and, specifically, those members of the client organisation in executive control of the project and who have defined the client value system. The workshop starts with a review of the client value system and all project information available. This information will include those factors from the client's core business which have spawned the project. It should be emphasised that the objective of this exercise is to determine the mission of the project not to define a building. An outcome of correctly defining the project mission may be that no building is required or at least that the building is required in a different form. Examples from industry illustrate this point.

A manufacturer of alcoholic drink was failing to meet demand targets and instituted a project to increase the number of bottling lines which required a large extension to the bottling plant. An architect was engaged to take a brief for the new building. At a facilitated workshop the client stakeholders defined the project mission as 'the efficient bottling, labelling, packing, storage and distribution of alcoholic drink to meet peak demands'. In a review of the project mission a number of stakeholders questioned whether the problem was truly in the bottling area since the mission also included other activities, particularly storage and distribution. Further analysis revealed that a warehousing policy of minimising stock resulted in a large number of product changes on the bottling lines resulting in changes to carriers on the machines and labels, sometimes three or four one hour changes per day. The problem was therefore re-defined as inadequate warehousing and the technical project re-defined as a warehouse extension.

A bespoke furniture manufacturer had a workshop and showroom in a poor inner city location. The manufacturer had sufficient workshop capacity and a loyal workforce and was acknowledged by existing customers to be a reliable supplier of high quality products. However, it was apparent that tenders from new customers were not invited where that tender was preceded by a visit by the customer to the workshop and showroom. 'Lack of prestigious premises' was the problem identified by the marketing department. Reluctantly, the managing director sourced a plot for a replacement workshop on a prestigious out-of-town commercial park. An architect was engaged to take the brief. The mission of the project was confirmed as 'to enhance the image of the company through relocation to a prestigious building'. Further analysis of the mission highlighted that the problem lay in the prestigious location of the showroom alone and not the prestigious location of the showroom and workshop. The project was cancelled and the manufacturer rented showroom space in the central business district of the city. Subsequently, the existing showroom was demolished to make way for a workshop extension to meet increased demand.

To construct a project mission the facilitator of the client stakeholder team conducts a brainstorming of strategic functions. Commonly, the facilitator asks the team for strategic functions ideally expressed as an active verb and a descriptive noun, for example 'enhance image'. Having collected many strategic functions, usually on sticky repositionable notelets, the facilitator asks the team to order the notelets on a large sheet of paper with high order needs in the top left corner spread diagonally to low order wants in the bottom right corner. Usually the top three to six notelets can be word crafted into a mission statement. The remainder can be configured into a function tree diagram as illustrated in Figure 3.4. It is important to note that the sophistication of the mission statement is of less importance than its accuracy and the buy-in by all of the key stakeholders. In the exercise illustrated it was the health and fitness of the adult population that was of concern to the local community planning team. The construction of a swimming pool with all of the child attractions might have been an incorrect response.

A key question at this stage is: 'is it necessary to build to meet this goal?'. If the answer is 'yes' then the project brief is the next stage.

3.10 Project briefing methodology

The project brief follows the strategic brief and the decision to build, and is significantly influenced by the strategic brief. The project goal and the client's

Figure 3.4: A mission statement and function diagram

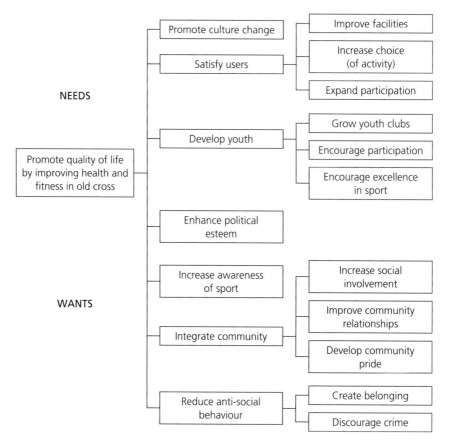

value system will infiltrate the content of the project brief and become embedded in the design. Project briefing methodology varies and is well described in the texts mentioned in the introduction. The techniques illustrated here are largely those that would be applicable to a facilitated project briefing exercise. It should be emphasised that the client team for the project briefing stage might be different to those who took part in the strategic briefing. At the project briefing stage it is important to involve client operational staff who can advise on how they might use the functional spaces contained within the building. It is also worth considering the involvement of the full design team and specialist contractors and suppliers.

Activity 4 – Post-occupancy studies

Not a team activity but one which feeds into the project brief are the results of a post-occupancy study of the client's last completed building of a similar type and function.

For example, at a recent design/build tender meeting for a new hotel project at the contractor's offices, the architect appointed by the contractor asked the assembled group how many of those present had stayed in one of the client's chain hotels and what did they think of them. Surprisingly, no-one had taken the initiative for even a weekend break. A properly conducted post-occupancy study including the questioning of staff will bring to light inefficiencies caused by the arrangement of the functional space and circulation, valuable information to feed into a project brief workshop.

Activity 5 – User flow patterns

User flow pattern diagrams represent both existing work patterns where these are available and the most efficient anticipated flow patterns in the proposed building. The first activity is to list all of the users of the building. This tends to be a long list and often includes subsets of the same users, i.e. disabled, accompanying children, etc. The diagram does not have to be complex and is often no more than a bubble diagram roughly drawn on a piece of flip chart paper. User flow diagrams are a good way of determining which users tend to use functional space in a similar way, setting up later opportunities for efficiency through timetabling. An example user flow diagram for a user of all sports facilities is shown in Figure 3.5.

In this example the team were of the opinion that all users undertaking whatever activity, e.g. swimming or basketball, would go through a process of change, activity, shower, change. This became a useful focus when considering the form and location of changing. The team considered that there were only two different requirements

Figure 3.5: Flow diagram for a public user

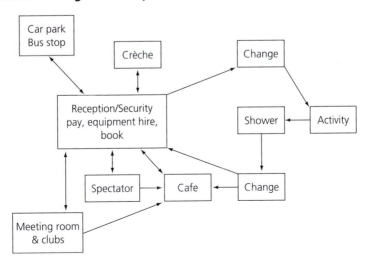

for changing, for outdoor sports such as football and for all indoor or court sports such as tennis.

Activity 6 – Functional space analysis

Functional space analysis specifications are taken from the user flow diagrams and represent, in outline terms, the space users require to carry out specific functions. The outline specifications will include, for example, size for function, an indicative description of the quality of finishings, the environmental controls necessary for the space and the IT support required by the space. This type of data will form the raw material for the room data sheets.

Activity 7 – Adjacency matrix

The adjacency matrix is a useful way of determining which spaces are required to be adjacent and which spaces should be remote from one another. A diagram similar to Figure 3.6 is drawn and the team asked to indicate the proximity of the various spaces one with another. Proximity is indicated on a scale of +5 to −5 where +5 is a high requirement for adjacency whereas −5 indicates that the spaces should be remote from one another. Zero indicates indifference. It should be noted that −5 does not mean that the spaces should be geometrically remote but that the spaces should

Figure 3.6: Adjacency matrix

Reception															
+4	Crèche														
+4	−5	Café/Pool/Snooker/Darts													
+3	0	0	Centre management												
+3	−5	+2	0	Changing (indoor)											
0	−5	0	0	+5	Swimming pool										
+3	−5	+3	0	0	+3	Casual swimming spectator									
+3	−5	+3	0	0	+2	0	Gala swimming spectator								
0	−5	0	0	+5	0	0	0	Technical sports (racket, gym, 5-a-side, etc.)							
+3	−5	+3	0	0	0	0	0	+2	Technical sports spectator						
+3	−5	+2	0	0	0	0	0	0	0	Changing for outdoor sports					
0	−5	0	0	0	0	0	0	0	0	+5	Outdoor sports				
0	−5	0	0	+5	0	0	0	0	0	0	0	Fitness suite			
+3	−5	+2	0	0	0	0	0	0	0	0	0	0	Meeting		
0	−5	0	0	+5	0	0	0	0	0	0	0	0	0	Dance	
0	−5	0	0	+5	+3	0	0	0	0	0	0	0	0	0	Life style

be inaccessible and insulated in terms of sight and sound. For example, two bedrooms in two semi-detached houses might only be separated by a 300 mm wall but to get from one to the other means leaving one house and entering another, the bedrooms are scored −5.

Activity 8 – Outline room data sheets

Completion of activities 4 to 7 will enable the completion of the room data sheets. At this stage they will describe only the room in terms of size, quality, environment and environmental controls, IT support required, position relative to other spaces and, where possible, timetabled use.

Activity 9 – Goal and systems modelling

Once completed the room data sheets should be analysed through a goal and systems model which describes on one side of a piece of paper the goal statements from the strategic brief and on the other side the systems now described to meet those goals. This is a useful check to ensure that all goals have been met and that space is not provided for a function which is not required.

Activity 10 – Sketch design

The taking away of all of the briefing material, the full functional specification by the architect and other designers confirms the end of the briefing process.

3.11 Conclusion

Construction project briefing is the activity of taking from a client a clear, unambiguous and explicit performance specification of a project. The brief is the documentation that records the project performance specification. This chapter has put forward the view that briefing is distinctly in two parts, the strategic briefing stage and the project briefing stage. Both are influenced by the client's value system and this too is described in detail and a method explained for its elucidation. The client's value system exists whether or not it is made explicit in the brief and whether or not briefing is undertaken by investigation or facilitation. These factors are the remit of the brief writer. The chapter has also included a debate on procurement since the making explicit of the client's value system becomes more important as the client moves from the traditional system to design and build, PFI, and frameworks such as Prime Contracting and ProCure21. However, the overriding conclusion of this chapter is that the strategic brief and, to a lesser extent, the project brief is a written document in performance specification terms which precedes design.

References

Barrett, P. S. and Stanley, C., *Better Construction Briefing*, Blackwell Science, Oxford (1999).

Best, R. and De Valence, G., *Building in Value: Pre-Design Issues*, Arnold (1999).

Blyth, A. and Worthington, J., *Managing the Brief for Better Design*, Spon Press (2001).

Borjeson, L., *Management of project work*, The Swedish Agency for Administrative Development, Satskontoret, Gotab, Stockholm (1976).

Construction Industry Board, *Briefing the Team – A guide to better briefing for clients*, Thomas Telford (1997).

Davies, G., Gray, J. and Sinclair, D., *Scales for Setting Occupant Requirements and Rating Buildings*, International Centre for Facilities (1993).

Duerk, D. P., *Architectural Programming: information management for design*, Wiley (1993).

Kelly, J., MacPherson, S. and Male, S., *The briefing process: a review and critique*, RICS (1992).

Kirk, S. J. and Spreckelmeyer, K. F., *Enhancing Value in Design Decisions*, Personal publication (1993).

Morgan, M. H., *Vitruvius: the ten books on architecture*, Dover (1960).

Morris, P. J. W. and Hough, G. H., *The Anatomy of Major Projects: A Study of the Reality of Project Management*, Wiley (1987).

Pena, W., Parshall, S. and Kelly, K., *Problem Seeking*, AIA Press, Washington (1987).

Salisbury, F., *Briefing Your Architect*, 2nd edn, Architectural Press (1998).

Woodhead, R. and Downs, C., *Value Management: improving capabilities*, Thomas Telford Publishing (2001).

Key Reading

Blyth, A. and Worthington, J., *Managing the Brief for Better Design*, Spon Press (2001).

Duerk, D. P., *Architectural Programming: information management for design*, Wiley (1993).

Pena, W., Parshall, S. and Kelly, K., *Problem Seeking*, AIA Press, Washington (1987).

Salisbury, F., *Briefing Your Architect*, 2nd edn, Architectural Press (1998).

Design Management

Managing sustainable urban development – contribution of mixed-use policies and urban design frameworks

4

Hildebrand Frey, Department of Architecture and Building Science, University of Strathclyde, Glasgow, UK

4.1 Introduction

This chapter investigates best practice in achieving and managing sustainable urban development. It sets out the key conditions for sustainable urban development and analyses the main reasons why it is so difficult to adhere to them, specifically in schemes involving large corporate developers and investors.

The main part of the chapter focuses on the development study of the Docklands Area in Dublin. Analysing the 1997 Master Plan for the Area, it becomes clear that the employed policies and development frameworks are based on the same key indicators of sustainable urban development summarised earlier in the study: a sufficient population density to sustain local services and facilities; a substantial increase in work places; a wide range of new housing to achieve social inclusion; training and education programmes to enable those currently marginalised to benefit from the new work places; mixed-use development to achieve vibrant public spaces; an integrated transport policy that promotes the extension of public transport; a civic design framework for the area at large and for its sectors that promotes mixed-use development and controls the nature and sequence of projects with the help of urban and architectural design guidelines.

At the end of the investigation which was kindly supported by Terry Durney, the Director of Planning and Technical Services of the Dublin Docklands Development Authority, it is evident that the policy of mixed-use development and urban and architectural design frameworks was not only accepted by investors and developers, but has resulted in well designed and landscaped, active and people-friendly public streets, squares and parks and urban areas with a place-specific character. There is no doubt that the project, which is still on-going, exemplifies best practice in the pursuit of socially, economically and environmentally sustainable urban development.

4.2 The strained relationship of contemporary buildings with their urban context

The traditional, i.e. the pre-modern, urban environment displays a clear distinction and delineation of public and private space, a visual–formal unity and harmony, an orchestrated juxtaposition of the ordinary as framework for the extraordinary, an integration of disparate activities in the same urban spaces and quarters, and a delightful mixture of architectural styles and details. It possesses a complexity and richness of space, form and activity patterns that today still attract millions of people, including many architects, to visit our old European cities (Brolin, 1980).

Today, with an ever growing majority of people living in an urban environment,[1] most contemporary architecture is designed for and constructed within an urban context. Whatever the architectural commissions are, one would expect that the same architectural and urban issues should be considered in the design and execution of buildings and also in relation to their wider urban context as in the past. This is not, however, the case. Looking at our contemporary cities, it is rather obvious that we have lost the ability to generate the quality of streetscapes and townscapes that our professional predecessors were capable of producing.

There are a number of reasons why it is so difficult today to generate a holistic, integrated urban environment:

- In the past those behind urban development were local people with an overall interest and pride in their city. Today, urban development is strongly influenced by the process of internationalisation, fuelled by a global economy and ever more sophisticated communication systems and networks. This process has led to the internationalisation of commercial and corporate architecture in our cities. More and more of their place-specific identity, which their unique historical development process generated, is lost. Cities are becoming increasingly everywhere and nowhere places (Commission of the European Communities, 1990; Urban Task Force, 1999).

- A major contributing factor to this development is that the system of procurement and development currently used focuses on large-scale profit distributing organisations who build large scale; the public realm for them is a lower priority then turning a profit. Response to the public realm is accordingly not a key part of the designer's brief and any design feature that increases cost will be eliminated.

- In a situation in which stakeholders behind city development no longer share urban values and a responsibility for the public realm, one would expect that the guidance, co-ordination and integration of disparate development projects would be dealt with by the planning system. In the UK, however, as the result of the segregation of planning, architecture and landscape architecture into different disciplines, our planning system is generally not design-based. Hence, with notable exceptions,[2] architects are still relatively rarely instructed by urban design guidelines or urban design frameworks (such as, for instance, the 'Projet Urbain' in France or the 'Bebauungsplan' in Germany).

- In view of the lack of design guidance through the planning system one would hope that urban designers and architects, who have to generate their own design rules, share the same or similar urban and architectural values; but when, for instance, comparing the comments on relatively recent commercial architecture in London published in the 21 & 28 December edition of the *Architects Journal* in 1988, there seems to be little agreement as to what constitutes a responsive urban environment and architecture. Furthermore, urban design frameworks and design guidelines, rather than being accepted as valuable tools to generate active, safe and secure public spaces, are frequently viewed by the planning system as counter-productive as they may deter development and by architects as unnecessary rules that constrain design freedom.

It is not astonishing that, without any shared design philosophy and urban design principles for the greater good of public space, the development of disparate buildings that form an urban area or space is unable to generate a 'growing whole', as Alexander *et al* (1987) puts it. Where design guidelines are not adequate or missing, it is up to the designers to face the responsibility of ensuring that best practice criteria are delivered; their power to procure best practice is, however, very small in comparison to that of investors and developers, and the frequently still rather reactive planning system.

4.3 The Dublin Docklands as case study

However, even though much of what is achieved by our urban development projects might be somewhat frustrating, there are examples throughout Europe that exemplify best practice in the pursuit of sustainable urban development. One of them is the Docklands Development in Dublin. It is the objective of this chapter to investigate how this project was set up, how it outlines and controls development, and what it has achieved to-date in partnership with local communities, large corporate investors and developers. The project clearly demonstrates that, as long as there is a strong will to do so, corporate architecture can not only be successfully integrated into mixed-use urban development but it can also achieve people-friendly streets and squares.

4.3.1 Evaluation criteria for the case study

For this investigation to become meaningful, evaluation criteria need to be established that respond to today's overriding goal of any urban and architectural project: sustainability. There is a large number of publications on sustainable urban development. Next to those of a more theoretical nature, there are some that can be directly used as designer manuals, for instance *A Pattern Language* by Alexander *et al* (1977) and *Responsive Environments* by Bentley *et al* (1985). The following sections will refer to these and other sources whose key issues help contribute 'by default' to the formation of well functioning, robust, well designed urban areas and public spaces. All sources used will be referenced so that the reader can consult the original publications.

4.3.2 The key conditions for SUSTAINABLE urban development

Today, the indicators of sustainable urban development are widely agreed upon (Jenks *et al*, 1996; Frey, 1999; Urban Task Force, 1999). These demand that urban development satisfies a number of key conditions:

4 Managing sustainable urban development – contribution of mixed-use
policies and urban design frameworks

Figure 4.1: Map 2 – the Dublin Docklands Area (from the DDA Master Plan 1997)

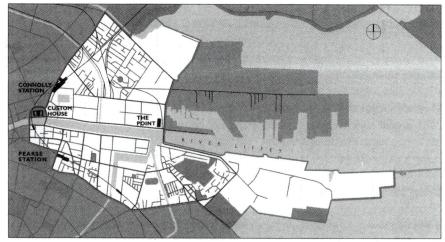

Source: Dublin Docklands Development Authority

- East Wall, North Strand and Seville Place are residential areas north of the North
  Quays with small-scale suburban housing, close-grain urban fabric and a strong
  sense of place, but include also some isolated, under-utilised and industrial land.
  The main problem of these areas is that they are segmented by raised railway

**Figure 4.2: Map 18 – Areas in the Dublin Docklands with distinct character
(from the DDA Master Plan 1997)**

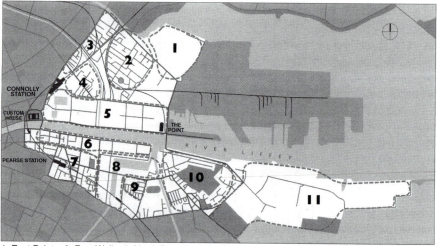

1 East Point   2 East Wall   3 North Strand   4 Seville Place   5 North Quays   6 South Quays
7 Pearse Street   8 Grand Canal Dock   9 South Lotts   10 Ringsend/Irishtown   11 Poolbeg

Source: Dublin Docklands Development Authority

tracks and extensive marshalling yards around Connolly Station which also compromise links to the city centre and central business district (compare DDA MP 1997, axonometric p. 122).

- The North Quays area, of specific interest to this study, is made up of large, impermeable industrial-scale urban blocks. The land use in the western part of the area is predominantly commercial, including the first phase of the International Financial Services Centre (IFSC 1) at the Custom House Docks, that of the eastern part is mostly low value warehousing, open storage, transport and some industrial and retail warehouses, interspersed with pockets of residential accommodation. There are some isolated buildings and structures of historical interest along the quays (compare DDA MP 1997, axonometric p. 128).

- The South Quays and Pearse Street areas consist of a mix of small to medium-scale urban fabric, unstructured and piecemeal development, but a vibrant mixture of residential and tertiary uses, long-established communities and associated facilities, established commercial enterprises and primarily small-scale cultural activities such as the City Art Centre. Problems are the raised railway line which constitutes a barrier, and the heavy through traffic in east–west direction (compare DDA MP 1997, axonometric p. 136).

- The Grand Canal Dock area is made up of large, impenetrable industrial-scale urban blocks; land use is predominantly industrial with disused and semi-derelict warehouses, grain silos and stores located at the dockside, and redundant and contaminated gas production sites. Much of the waterside of the dock is inaccessible (compare DDA MP 1997, axonometric p. 142).

- The Ringsend/Irishtown area has predominantly residential land use with attractive housing (two up, two down) and some larger-scale blocks and access deck flats. The area suffers from heavy through traffic. There are a number of large public open spaces, including a football and greyhound stadium (compare DDA MP 1997, axonometric p. 148).

This variety of different environments, from two-storey housing to large-scale industrial buildings, is considered to be one of the strengths of the Docklands. One of the Area's major disadvantages is the lack of permeability, specifically in the north–south direction, exacerbated by the lack of any river crossings between the Custom House and The Point at the eastern end of the North Quays (compare Map 18).

4.4.2   The Dublin Docklands Development Authority (DDDA)

Despite the decline of the Area during the last century, its location so close to the city centre and its considerable development potential causes its regeneration to be of considerable significance for the city at large. Consequently, the Government decided in January 1996 to set up an Authority with the responsibility of generating a vision statement for the Area and of preparing a Master Plan for its development. DDDA was established by the Minister of the Environment on 1 May 1997. The main task of the Authority is to achieve, within a time frame of 10 to 15 years, not only physical renewal of the Area but also in consultation and partnership with a wide range of interests – including residents and community groups, business and sectoral interests, environmental and cultural organisations, the statutory bodies and training and development agencies – a socially, economically and environmentally sustainable development of the Docklands. The Master Plan was adopted in November 1997.

4.4.3 *The 1997 Dublin Docklands Area Master Plan*

In Parts 2 and 3 of the Master Plan, the policies for economic and social consolidation and development, and for the creation of a wide range of employment opportunities are spelled out. The programmes outlined in these parts of the Plan are similar to those of urban regeneration projects elsewhere. However, when studying the following Parts of the Master Plan – Part 4 on land use, Part 5 on the transportation and infrastructural framework, Part 6 on the civic design framework and Part 7 containing the sectoral framework plans – one detects decisive differences to the 'normal' translation of policies into planning and design programmes. It is here that best practice in sustainable urban development becomes visible.

Economic and social framework (DDA MP 1997, Parts 2 & 3)

The key socio-economic objectives and policies contained in these parts of the Master Plan are formulated after intensive consultation with the five residential communities and the more than 100 community organisations and groups in the Area, and in response to submissions from a wide range of organisations and individuals (compare DDA MP 1997, p. 24).

The Master Plan pursues development policies aiming for socially and economically sustainable urban development: the consolidation and expansion of residential areas into what is now fashionably called 'urban villages'; the creation of a wide range of work places for different levels of education and skills; education and training programmes for the local population to develop skills which make them employable in the area; the development of disused sites; the improvement of transport links to, from and inside the Area, and the upgrading and expansion of the Area's infrastructure. The policy to develop the quays of the river and the canals into vibrant public spaces that attract local people as well as tourists and generate further employment responds to the development potential of the Docklands and their location close to the city centre. One statement, however, anticipates what is going to be elaborated in the following parts of the Plan: the physical development of larger state-owned sites in the Area for a mixture of uses.

Land use (DDA MP 1997, Part 4)

Mixed use is an important indicator of sustainable urban development and many regeneration programmes pay lip-service to it but rarely achieve it throughout project areas for the reasons outlined in the introduction to this chapter. All the more inter-esting therefore is the land use part of the Plan in which the policy of mixed-use development is expanded, but now with regard to the entire Area. The key statement regarding land uses is that the Authority will 'pursue a policy of mixed-use development in the Docklands Area which would achieve a sustainable environment integrating living, working and leisure' (DDA MP 1997, Part 4, p. 49).

The policy of a mixture of residential use, commercial offices including financial service, as well as enterprise and industrial uses in the North Wall Quay, the City Quay and Grand Canal Dock areas is clearly expressed in the Land Use Maps 11, 12 and 13, but one needs to read them in conjunction to see to what extent mixed use is proposed. A further policy seeks, in the same areas north and south of the River Liffey and along the Grand Canal Dock, the development of new cultural/tourist facilities, hotels and water-based activities to add to the already existing indoor sports, cultural and hotel facilities (Land Use Map 14). It is abundantly clear that there is a very strong wish to generate vibrant and attractive mixed-use areas along the water bodies, but specifically on either side of the River Liffey, i.e. to generate a similar quality of urban environment as already existing along the river in the central area of the city west of the Custom House. It is unquestionable that the pursuit of mixed use in the Docklands Area is one of the key policies that sets the Dublin project aside from many other docklands and riverfront schemes and contributes much to the project's success. Other key land-use policies expand the notion of mixed uses even further (compare DDA MP 1997, Part 4, pp. 47–70).

- A significant expansion of the population in the Area is being promoted. The target is an increase of up to 25,000 additional people over a 15 year period. New housing should be located in all parts of the Area (except in cases of incompatibility), and should include a minimum of 10 percent of social and affordable housing, but also sheltered housing and starter homes. The design of residential complexes should not articulate social difference. Here, too, is a refreshing deviation from the 'normal' practice of keeping public/social and private housing separate, a practice that must be regarded as being largely responsible for the lack of social inclusion in urban areas of our cities.

- As already indicated in Part 2 of the Plan, the Authority promotes a partnership with local communities and relevant bodies to generate action plans for community facilities, offices for Government services, and the consolidation and renewal of existing primary and secondary schools in the Area so that they can offer a full range of curricular activities. The objective of Part 2, to achieve better access to education and training for the local population, is translated into a policy for the development of training centres or other facilities to accommodate courses and programmes that help prepare local people for employment in the wide range of opportunities generated in the Area.

- The consolidation and expansion of the already well established International Financial Services Centre is promoted, together with the expansion of high-quality office building zones east of the existing central business district around major transport nodes, e.g. existing and planned railway stations. Major industries are encouraged to consolidate and expand, and suitable areas for small industry and workshops are retained while applying strong environmental management policies to alleviate any bad impact on adjacent residential areas. In appropriate locations light industry is encouraged in place of heavy or general industry, particularly in areas close to residential and commercial use. The physical development of under-utilised or open storage with buildings of appropriate scale, height and density areas is encouraged.

- The land use plan promotes significant tourist entertainment destinations, the development of a cluster of tourist facilities, including hotels, in the Grand Canal Dock area as well as hotels in Point Village and the North Wall Quay. The development of small guest houses, tourist hotels, and bed and breakfast activities in suitable locations is encouraged. Particularly in the waterfront areas, attractive restaurants, cafes, public houses and shops should be developed, also fishing, sailing and rowing facilities. A suitable location for a cruise liners' terminal within the Port area is sought. The strong objective of achieving animated public spaces specifically at waterfronts is apparent.

- Further plans are for the enhancement of existing leisure and sports facilities, specifically the development of Stack A, a listed warehouse at the Custom House Docks, as a major cultural visitor destination acting as an anchor project for the area. Existing cultural facilities are to be consolidated and expanded. A Government initiative should be facilitated to locate major cultural buildings in the waterfront area as part of a cultural corridor along the Liffey. The Plan calls for the provision of public art in appropriate locations through the Area at an early stage. The development of residential/workshop accommodation should attract artists and crafts people to live in the Area and help generate craft industries.

- The Plan includes a policy on the development of a district centre at 'Point Village' at the eastern end of the study area; the impact of the new retail outlets on neighbourhoods should be monitored. In residential and business areas local centres and/or corner shops should be developed, also shops on main pedestrian routes to achieve validity and security. The environment of existing neighbourhood centres should be improved through new paving, landscaping, street furniture and dedicated short-term parking bays.

- Regarding the improvement of the transportation and infrastructure framework, the Plan is based on the assumption that the light rail transport system (LUAS) and the Dublin Port Tunnel will be implemented. The penetration of the Area by private cars will be reduced by control, infrastructure and public transport measures; residential areas will be traffic-calmed. The Plan promotes the provision of an integrated transport infrastructure, specifically the early provision of an integrated public transport system with efficient interchanges between transport modes. The Plan promotes the provision of a dedicated and safe network of routes for cyclists and pedestrians. New bridge crossings should have lifting sections and should be of the highest visual and engineering standards.

Civic design framework (DDA MP 1997, Part 6)

The introduction to this section starts with a very clear statement of what the urban design framework is supposed to achieve but makes it also very clear that good urban and architectural design alone do not achieve animation of public spaces:

> Urban design deals with the ordering of physical development to create a three-dimensional articulation and form to the streets and open spaces that make up the city. The primary focus of this section of the Master Plan is on built form, but the Authority also recognises the critical dimension that use brings to the enlivening of streets and urban spaces (DDA MP 1997, Part 6.1.1, p. 90).

The importance of a link between use pattern and design is thus clearly recognised. The overriding objective of all urban design issues is to ensure that each project contributes to the socially and economically sustainable regeneration of the Area. The key design policies are summarised below.

- There is a group of policies that call designers to maintain the variety and diversity of development forms in the different areas of the Docklands and to conserve the existing street patterns where appropriate. The design of buildings should respond to the scale of their surroundings, and proposals for high buildings must be in line with the Dublin City Development Plan 1991. Major public buildings should form focal points to generate a particular character and identity to an area, particularly on waterfront locations. Recognising the lack of spatial links in parts of the Area, accessibility is to be increased; specifically, further bridges across the river should achieve closer psychological and pedestrian links between north and south.

- Regarding the scale and height of development, buildings close to the low-rise housing areas should take their cue from the scale of existing development and should not overshade or overlook their public spaces or deprive them from sun light. The height and scale of buildings on either side of the Liffey corridor are not so constrained, but a strategy is best achieved through Planning Schemes and Action Area Plans. As general guidelines, five and six storey development is preferred.

- There are policies on the retention and restoration of the best of the elements which have been inherited. Specifically highlighted is the retention and improvement of the original orthogonal street pattern; the open aspects of the Liffey quays; the buildings, features, structures and sites of historical, architectural or artistic interest. Existing residential and other Conservation Areas should be retained and extended. Older buildings should be rehabilitated, renovated and re-used in line with the policy on sustainability. Fiscal incentives are offered as means of achieving conservation and environmental objectives.

- Policies on high quality design of buildings and public spaces highlight that the quality of the design of the spaces between buildings, i.e. the streets, squares, parks and water spaces, is as important as that of the buildings themselves. The Plan encourages architectural and urban design competitions to achieve the highest standard of urban design for different areas. Streets and spaces should be linked together to exploit vistas and landmarks. Buildings on both sides of the Liffey and the Grand Canal Dock should have a coherent architectural expression so that these spaces can be read as coherent entities; regarding the use of materials, they should take their cue from Dublin's typical robust materials. A specific design response should be employed for sites of particular importance. The design of signage, street furniture and landscaping should be in a recognisable Docklands style. Incentives for development are linked with quality criteria, with particular focus on site utilisation and sustainability, and demonstration projects are promoted relating to sustainable building design.

- Policies on the definition and activation of public space call for a clear articulation of public, semi-public and private space through buildings to avoid any ambiguity and help generate a sense of security. Buildings should form a coherent enclosure to streets and public squares; fragmented building frontages should be avoided. Building functions, particularly on ground level, should contribute to the animation of the public realm.

- Policies on open spaces include: the transformation of the Liffeyside precincts into a public promenade and cycleway; the development of a linear park incorporating cycle and pedestrian routes along the Royal Canal; the enhancement of the banks of the river Dodder; opening up of the Grand Canal Docks to public amenity uses where possible; and the development of Pigeon House Harbour for recreational boating accommodation. Existing neighbourhood parks throughout the Area are to be rehabilitated through community participation in planning and managing their future development. There is a policy on the improvement of existing, and the development of new, pocket parks throughout the Area. Usable private and semi-private landscaped open space should be incorporated in new developments, particularly in residential apartment complexes. Existing streets and spaces are to be landscaped and furnished with new or improved street lighting and seating. The 'Community Greening Initiative' is promoted, and commercial enterprises are encouraged to plant and landscape their grounds.

Implementation

The Authority is required to prepare Planning Schemes for the Custom House Dock Area and any other areas specified by the Minister for that purpose. Two other areas are regarded as suitable: the Grand Canal Basin area and the Poolbeg Peninsula. Action areas are the Liffey Campshires (river quaysides), the Royal Canal Linear Park and the Urban Park, the Dodder River Linear Park, the 'Village Centre' of East Wall, the Ringsend/Irishtown 'Village Centre', the Townsend Street/Westland Row Precinct.

Regarding financial requirements, the Authority considers that tax incentives will be necessary in order to create sustainable development in the Area. Granting tax incentives provides the Authority with the mechanism to encourage and control the location, sequence and type of development in the Area.

What has been achieved so far?

In one of the Authority's publications there is an account of the history of planning for Dublin's Docklands and illustrations of schemes in the 1980s for the Spencer Dock and the IFSC 1 areas, made up of the symptomatic, out-of-scale and mono-use glass boxes of international corporate architecture in the 1980s that has nothing to do with Dublin and clashes abysmally with the form and fabric of the existing residential areas. This is the kind of commercial development, urban design and architecture so frequently produced still today in many of our cities; a visit to Glasgow's Broomielaw shows very recent examples right at the waterfront of the River Clyde (Figure 4.3). The streets and squares of such schemes are empty; there is nothing on

Figure 4.3: International corporate architecture at Glasgow's Broomielaw Development: there has been no attempt to activate the river front

Figure 4.4: Empty side street in Glasgow's Broomielaw area: note the failure of corporate architecture to produce attractive and secure urban spaces

offer for people that do not work there, and it is easy to imagine how utterly unsafe these public spaces must be at night after the offices have closed down. This is indeed the very best practice for unsustainable urban development (Figure 4.4).

Thankfully, with the exception of the IFSC 1 buildings which are rather bulky and do not contribute much to activate the public space around them, the 1980s projects did not materialise. The contrast between the 1980s and the contemporary buildings demonstrates vividly the change of circumstances and approaches to urban regeneration during the 1990s. Today's projects are guided by the 1997 Master Plan, by Planning Schemes and Action Area Plans all of which adhere to the principles of sustainability. The development of the area east of IFSC 1 is well advanced and demonstrates the impact of guidance and control through the Authority very vividly. Although in part an extension of the corporate installation of the IFSC 1, the area east of it has developed into a place with very remarkable characteristics:

- Although not complete yet, there is an astonishing juxtaposition and integration of office buildings, public and private housing schemes, hotels, restaurants/cafes, shops, etc. that generate lively streets and squares and a well activated river front (Figure 4.5).

- The form of the development is coherent yet with a refreshing variety of contemporary design both for housing and offices.

- Public spaces are clearly defined, well landscaped and well lit at night; the squares and the Liffey promenade are human-scale spaces despite their considerable size.

Figure 4.5: International corporate architecture at the northern Dublin Docklands Area river front, right next to hotels and housing

Figure 4.6: Market in a side street of the northern Dublin Docklands Area: an attractive and secure urban space

- People are attracted by the catering and entertainment uses, but also by the spaces themselves to stroll, sit, relax and watch others and cyclists passing by, while sculptures are reminders of historical events (Figure 4.6).

Here is evidence that uses as different as those accommodated in the Area blend well together, that international financial services can co-exist with housing. The result is a truly mixed-use urban area.

On questions of why investors accepted the mixture of uses, the Director of Planning and Technical Services explains that large corporate investors/developers did not have any problem in forming part of a mixed-use scheme provided they did not have horizontal mixing within their own buildings; they would not have accepted a shop next to their main entrance but did not mind if located beside a residential development with shops and restaurants on ground level. The strategy of a substantial increase in residential development, adopted by the Authority in order to generate a sufficiently high population to sustain the viability of retail in the evening and at weekends, seems to pay off. Again, on the question of why developers accepted mixed-use schemes, we are told that it was easy to persuade them to cater for shops, restaurants, etc. at ground level of housing schemes because this level is the least valuable for residential use. The reason why larger office users were located at the best sites is that this created the value that would allow the Authority to subsidise lesser value uses, in particular higher education facilities such as the National College of Ireland.

The usual argument that a mixture of uses will not be accepted by investors and developers has clearly been disproved in the Dublin Docklands. It is obviously feasible as long as there are no incompatibilities and if the mixture is of mutual benefit to all users. It is also quite clear that strong urban and architectural design frameworks and guidelines do not deter investors and developers. But mixed use needs to be planned for and the advantages of strong design guidance need to be promoted, not least by illustrating the quality of development that will be achieved which, next to incentives, must at least in parts have attracted investors and developers to form part of the scheme.

Needless to say that there is considerable progress on development in other areas of the Dublin Docklands, following much the same basic mix use strategy, planning, urban design and architectural guidance, and promising much the same success. The Authority is currently working on a project to link the Docklands along the riverside to the boardwalk west of O'Connell Street. To the south side of the Liffey, the Authority is developing schemes with horizontal layering of retail, offices and housing, with the office element confined to one or two floors for small lettings, and this appears to be acceptable to the market. So continued observation of the development of the Dublin Docklands Area is likely to demonstrate further the possibility of generating urban areas with characteristics that generally describe sustainable urban development and demonstrate best practice in achieving this.

4.5 Summary of the key issues that make the Dublin Docklands Development a success

The main reasons why the Dublin Docklands are so successful and deserve the distinction of best practice in sustainable urban development can now be summarised:

- There is a strong political will to use the development potential of the Docklands for the benefits of the Area and its communities and the City of Dublin.

- The DDD Authority has special planning power that promotes socially, economically and environmentally sustainable development. To achieve this it has developed policies and programmes for sustainable urban development.

- The Authority has generated, through these policies and programmes, and with the help of urban and architectural design competitions, urban design frameworks for the Docklands at large and for its constituent parts to consolidate, improve and expand individual areas, and to develop strong links between them and between the Docklands and the city centre.

- The Authority has the power to offer tax incentives to attract international, national and local companies to locate in the Area, while at the same time controlling the quality of urban and architectural design of projects.

- The Authority has adopted a partnership approach to ensure that the interests of all local communities, of multinational companies, employers, developers, investors and interest groups are defined and balanced to achieve an integrated whole that serves the benefits of all of them, including the city. To ensure that those currently disadvantaged and marginalised can benefit from the wide range of work places generated on the levels of international, national and local economy, the Authority has instigated a wide range of education and training programmes.

- The Authority has developed a Master Plan that responds to the key target values of sustainable urban development:

  - sufficient population density to afford local services and facilities and public transport;

  - mixed-use development, i.e. the integration throughout the Area of public/ social and private housing, offices, light industry and workshops, hotels, shops, restaurants/cafes, entertainment and cultural as well as recreation facilities, to achieve vibrant, safe, secure and attractive urban quarters as well as public streets, squares, promenades and parks;

  - social inclusion not only through a wide range of different types of public and private housing but also by the design of residential complexes with a mixture of dwelling and tenure types without manifesting the different social levels;

  - an integrated public transport system with a variety of modes from rail to light rail and bus which in turn will help reduce car dependency and road congestion;

  - a wide range of employment opportunities from international financial services to light industries and workshops, and community employment schemes, i.e. the development of a local economy in parallel to a national and global economy.

- The Authority has promoted a high quality of urban and architectural design:

  - the quality of public streets and squares, promenades and parks is achieved through an integrated design of hard and soft landscaping, lighting, seating, street furniture and art;

  - the quality of architecture is achieved through the co-ordination of the design of facades to achieve coherent public spaces without loss of the identity of individual architectural schemes.

References

Alexander, C., Ishikawa, S., Silverstein, M., *et al*, *A Pattern Language – Towns, Buildings, Construction*, Oxford University Press, New York (1977).

Alexander, C., Neis, H., Anninou, A., *et al*, *A New Theory of Urban Design*, Oxford University Press, New York & Oxford (1987), chapters 1 and 2.

Bentley, I., Alcock, A., Murrain, P., *et al*, *Responsive Environments – A manual for designers*, The Architecture Press, London (1985).

Brolin, B. C., *Architecture in Context – fitting new buildings with old,* Van Nostrand Reinhold, New York (1980) p. 19.

Buchanan, P., 'Facing up to Facades', *Architects Journal*, 21 & 28 Dec. 1988, Nos 51 & 52, Vol 188, pp. 22–57 and specifically 'Laying it Right on the Line – Eight Critics on Eight Facades', pp. 28–37.

Commission of the European Communities, Green Paper on the Urban Environment, European Commission, Brussels (1990).

Elkin, T. and McLaren, D. with Hillman, M., *Reviving the City: Towards Sustainable Urban Development*, Friends of the Earth, London (1991) p. 5.

Frey, H., *Designing the city – Towards a more sustainable urban form*, E&FN Spon, London/New York (1999) chapter 2, pp. 23–34.

Jenks, M., Burton, E. and Williams, K. (eds), *The Compact City – A Sustainable Urban Form?*, E&FN Spon, London (1996).

Urban Task Force, *Towards an Urban Renaissance, Department of the Environment, Transport and the Regions*, E&FN Spon, London (1999) Part One: The Sustainable City, pp. 25-107; pp. 251–54 and 258.

Endnotes

1 According to the World Resource Institute and the Institute for Environment and Development, in 1986 and 1988–9 the urban population of Europe was 71.6 percent and that of the UK 92.1 percent of the respective total population.

2 A complete list of urban design guided regeneration projects would be too long to be included here; projects stand as examples and represent with regard to their urban regeneration approach still the exception rather than the rule: The 1990 City Centre Design Strategy for the City of Birmingham by Tibbalds, Colbourne, Karski and Williams; the 1998 Urban Framework Plan for the Jewellery Quarter Urban Village, Birmingham, by EDAW Masterplanners & Urban Designers in conjunction with Hillier Parker and WSP Consulting Engineers; the 1996 Manchester City Council Supplementary Planning Guidance for the City Centre Bomb Damaged Area, including its planning and urban design guidelines for the area, also a masterplan framework by EDAW Masterplanners & Urban Designers from 1996; Hulme Regeneration Limited (1994) rebuilding the city – a guide to development in Hulme.

Managing the creative process

5

Christopher Platt, Department of Architecture and Building Science, University of Strathclyde, Glasgow, UK

5.1 Introduction

The location of this chapter in the early 'Design Management' section of the book suggests that its subject occurs at the early stages of a design project. The expression 'managing the creative process' itself implies that:

- There is a process to be studied;
- It is a creative process;
- This process can be managed.

This chapter will consider each of these presumptions.

In the present climate of professional project management culture many in the construction process will believe that the title could be expressed by concentrating solely on an examination of the demands of quality control, i.e. the delivery of a quality service and a quality product. A scan of the majority of practice statements in the RIBA/RIAS Directory of Practices shows that these twin goals underpin these statements. However, the questions are whether this is really what architects strive to achieve through any project; whether they simply seek to deliver something on time and at cost which satisfies the client's needs or whether they are driven by an additional set of values.

When architects talk about those aspects of their work which they find the least satisfying and what they miss the most, they often plead for more 'creative activity'. It is likely that the word 'creativity' in the context of a chapter dealing with the professional concerns of architects will raise the well worn spectre of the architect as an 'artistic dandy' who is unconcerned about practical matters and who is unreliable, delivering projects late, over-budget and technically flawed. But the profession has made a serious attempt to put its house in order both before and since the Louis Hellman cartoon which responded to the publication of *The Image of the Architect* in 1983. The view that design is creative, unlike management, is one that has been thoroughly debunked by Allinson (1993) who elegantly states:

> Design is not intrinsically a wild card, just as management is not intrinsically some philistine ogre substituting greed and conspicuous acquisition – both of these prejudices are misrepresentations, even if there is an element of truth in each.

Delivering any building is a highly complex task. Even the most humble house extension will involve a structural engineer, an architect and a building contractor, and will include several different structural systems and building products from

89

around the world, for example door furniture from Denmark and roof slates from Spain. In addition, there will be at least two local authority approval processes and risk assessments. At the other end of the spectrum, a major building project is likely to involve a dozen separate consultants and several building contractors dealing with sub-contractors from across the globe. Contemporary architectural practice is dominated by the need to cope with the effective and efficient management of product selection. The efficient and non-confrontational management of architecture is a major challenge and success in terms of budget and programme as well as professional relationships and the quality of the build should be celebrated whenever it is achieved.

The question is whether this is the process to which the chapter title refers. It is easy to become embroiled in the complexities of the building process and so forget what purposes those same processes are there to serve, thinking that they are self-serving. In order to understand the title of the chapter, it is necessary to take a careful look at the nature of creativity and at what architects do when they design.

A certain unease remains, both within and outwith the profession, around the idea that the architect is both a creative individual as well as a professional. This is surprising, since creativity and professionalism should not be mutually exclusive, but the belief that the architect works purely as an artist above, and separate from, grubby commercial concerns and material values retains its stubborn hold and has a malign influence on both debates within the profession and on how it is perceived by other parties to the construction process. Consequently, confusion and prejudice about the way architects work still remain; a confusion which may be based on a lack of understanding about the design process and a prejudice about the place of creative work within the construction industry. Therefore, this chapter looks at contemporary interpretations of the design process and of creativity with its psychological implications and then examines three case studies from architectural practice in the light of these interpretations. Each of the three practices has its own stated working method and the chapter investigates the extent to which these processes correspond with the interpretations of creativity.

5.2 The design process

In the present architectural climate it is not easy to explain the design process because the contemporary scene is so varied in its output that it is easy to conclude that there is no common ground among architects and that individual self-expression rules. The sheer volume of media coverage given over to 'signature buildings' and the media obsession with the cult of individual genius would leave any casual observer to conclude that the main objective of the creative architectural process was to deliver a landmark building conceived by a sole designer. At the same time there is, among architects, both a mistrust and a lack of interest expressed towards design methodology, almost as if the structure of a 'system' inhibits creativity by its inherent leanings towards rational management. Even so, some process is clearly at work when architects design because, in spite of a wide range of aesthetic positions, the result is often a completed building. Buchanan (2000) attempted to define design by stating that:

> The central theme of design is the conception and planning of the artificial... design provides the thought which guides the making of all products, whether by individual craftsmanship or mass-produced techniques.

However, this definition implies that design is a static process whereas the dynamic nature of design was described thus by Hirano (2000):

> The learning, creative–developmental process can be represented as a spiral. Viewed from the top, a spiral is a moving circle, constantly expanding in scope. Viewed from the side, upward movement is evident, representing the addition of experience and understanding.

Maguire (1980) takes these ideas further in a clear and succinct explanation of what architects do when they design. He expresses what he believes happens in the diagram given in Figure 5.1. He explains that this is neither a chronologically exact flow-chart nor a methodology but is simply an interpretation of what happens, whether this is acknowledged or not.

He proposes that there are three inputs into the design process:

1 The person of the architect/designer;

2 The problem as given;

3 The available data about the problem.

To consider each of these in turn:

The architects/designers bring their knowledge, skills, life-experience, developed sensibilities and prejudices to the design process and their faculties work on everything else to effect the transformation into a design.

The problem as given consists, on the one hand, of the people and their lives which are to be served and on the other, the surrounding physical, economic and political facts.

As Maguire says: 'these things will be partly bound up in a "brief", partly observable, and partly approachable only through living experience'.

The available data may be an unknown quantity (and of unknown quality). There could be a large amount of information relevant to the problem which could vary in terms of accessibility and relevance. For example, information on the conditions under which grants are awarded for upgrading homes or the latest government recommendations on avoiding condensation should be readily available but as

Figure 5.1: What architects do when they design

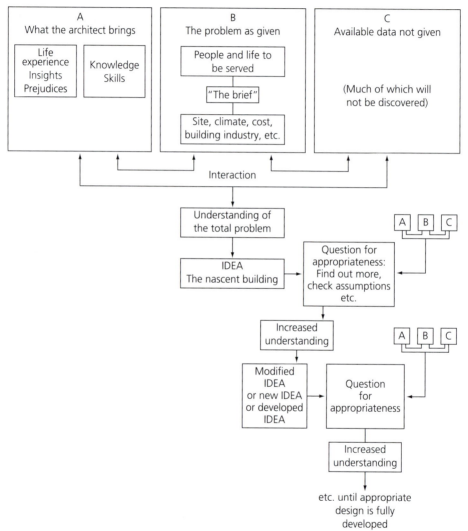

Source: Maguire, 1980

Maguire says: 'other important data may escape one forever. We live in an imperfect world.'

The diagram emphasises that ideas come rather from an understanding of the total situation than from knowledge or the manipulation of information. Furthermore, understanding may be enhanced by the rejection of those ideas which turn out to be inappropriate. This major understanding may occur quite late on in the design process and cause a major re-assessment of the design which has been developed. There may be a large number of these feedback operations which will continue until all the design details have been worked out. Consequently, the diagram is an imperfect and static representation of a complex dynamic process which may be grossly distorted by the recent attempt (in Britain) to divide drawings into those for the design stage and those for production information. Maguire is emphatic on this point, saying that:

> Working drawings were always, and so far as I know still are, the scene of detailed designing. This is untidy, and resists rational management, but is inevitable and necessary for good design.

5.3 Creativity

The subject of creativity is itself an entire field of psychology and there are between 50 and 60 recorded definitions of it, analysis of which is outwith the scope of this chapter. One example definition is that of Sternberg (2001):

> Creativity refers to the potential to produce novel ideas that are task-appropriate and high in quality.

Repucci (1988) divided the theories which were summarised in these definitions into six major groups, as follows:

1 *Gestalt* or Perception;

2 End Product or Innovation;

3 Aesthetic or Expressive;

4 Psychoanalytic or Dynamic;

5 Solution Thinking;

6 *Varia*.

One common characteristic of these theories is that they emphasised the central importance of talent but the theory used in this chapter is based on the componential model of Amabile (2001) which falls somewhere between the *Gestalt* and the End-Product groupings. According to the componential model, there are three basic components which are necessary for creativity, as follows:

1 Domain-relevant skills, competencies and talents which are applicable to the domain(s) in which the individual designers are working.

2 Intrinsic task motivation, i.e. an internally driven involvement in the current task which can be significantly influenced by the social environment.

3 Creativity-relevant processes, personality characteristics, cognitive styles and working habits which promote creativity in any domain.

Domain-relevant skills include all those things that individuals know or can do concerning their subject, drawing on their knowledge and experience. In the case of architects, their domain is, in the broadest sense, architectural design.

Intrinsic task motivation for many architects may be formed in the home but, more commonly, it is formed in schools of architecture and during the early years of architectural practice. Influential and inspirational teachers, the ethos of a particular school and university, and exposure to inspiring places can all open the eyes of students to the world outside their familiar environment.

A detailed examination of the creative process reveals that as well as being dynamic and demanding it also contains a number of stages which have their own psycho-logical consequences for the people involved. Evans and Russell (1985) saw the creative process as a reiterative one which has to address detailed as well as strategic issues. The process is characterised by the following five kinds of condition whose boundaries sometimes blurred and which could occur in different sequences.

Preparation

This takes place when the tasks at hand have been analysed and the necessary data gathered, then patterns are looked for, ideas are tried out and assumptions are questioned. Depending on the nature of the project and its problems, this part of the creative process can be either superficial or demanding; informal or requiring absorption in a large amount of data but it will always be reflective.

Frustration

This is the irritated, despondent and bored condition which arises when ambitions are in doubt and the issues appear to be insoluble. Although it can be dramatic, as in the case of Van Gogh, it is more often experienced as something insidious. This condition is one of feeling lost and suffering doubt and is a function of creative outputs being linked with ideas of self-worth. Because it is so psychologically loaded, frustration is possibly the key personal issue to be resolved in being creative, both through managing one's own creativity and in learning about it.

Incubation

This occurs when attempts to push through a solution are abandoned and the matter is left for the background subconscious to deal with. It may be momentary or it can last for much longer periods. Incubation relieves the conscious mind of the creative burden and is sometimes accompanied by the feeling that the sought-for solution cannot be forced. Even so, there may be much inner agitation and frustration arising from the realisation that anything less than a diligent search will not achieve the goal.

Insight

This is the 'aha!' moment which is usually associated with creativity; the result of all that has gone before. However, all that glitters is not gold and discrimination is required. Daring is needed too in order to let an idea be itself by beating the complex forms of self-censorship which permeate the mind. In other words, self-trust is required.

Working out

This involves testing insights followed by transforming them and then realising them. However, many good and creative ideas can become diluted in their execution or only realised as parodies of themselves so the very best good ideas are also robust ones. To avoid loss or dilution of good ideas it is very important to anticipate the issues which may arise during their unfolding, development and realisation.

There is clearly an overlap between this analysis of the psychological stages and Maguire's description of the design process, particularly in its reiterative character and the emphasis on the person involved. Maguire's analysis shows that there is not a clear end to the design process, although 'until appropriate design is fully developed' might appear open-ended enough to give the jitters to both clients and some members of the design team. It also does not imply that it reaches full development during this 'design stage'. There is an implication that it is professional judgement alone that is needed to decide when that development is complete or must be ended. Nor should the design process be unnaturally restructured into arbitrary divisions between scheme design and detail design. Where this happens, design can become compartmentalised between those who are concept architects and designers who work up the production drawings.

Architects have attempted to develop a creative influence over the detailed design phase of a project and have been willing to rethink a previously made and approved decision in the light of new information, whether it has been sought or not. Because of this, they have gained a reputation as poor project managers which has led to the swift rise of the profession of project management. Some, or perhaps most, of this criticism is justified although other members of the design team involved in the process are unlikely to appreciate its dynamic nature. In other words, there will be some who see thought and action as expressed in designing and drawing or in creativity and production as two separate, distinguishable and therefore manageable activities.

Underlying this are the assumptions that thought must be independent of action and that formulaic thinking must precede action. The concept of strategy formulation is characterised by thought, rationality, systematic analysis and control. Consequently, the exploration of alternative approaches and strategies is no longer possible once the formulation is complete. A more flexible approach to this problem was put forward by Mintzberg (1989) who drew an analogy between an emergent approach to forming a business strategy and the craft of pottery:

> Our potter is in the studio, rolling the clay to make a wafer-like structure. The clay sticks to the rolling pin and a round form appears. So, why not make a cylindrical vase? One idea leads to another until a new pattern forms. Action is driven by thinking; a strategy has emerged.

Mintzberg has suggested that just as potters must manage their craft, so managers should seek to craft their strategies. The outcome of this could be a mixture in the form of 'umbrella' or 'process strategies' which set out the main guidelines, so allowing the detail and content to gradually emerge.

This description is an example of how the inherent leanings of the creative process are used sympathetically in the making of decisions. In short, there are happy accidents which the practitioner wishes to exploit although this is increasingly difficult to manage in larger, more formally structured projects. Contemporary architectural practice now relies heavily on computer technology; the last ten years has seen an exponential growth in the role of computers in graphics, drafting, 3D, virtual reality and animation work. Even so, schools of architecture continue to develop the brain/hand relationship through traditional hand-generated media in addition to digital technology. The sketch done by hand is often the initiating graphic that begins the design discussion as well as the medium used to reflect on a design at some intermediate stage in its gestation. As Arnheim (2000) explains, the nature and function of sketches cannot be separated from the design that they serve. It is not possible to directly observe the creative process of designing which takes place in the mind although the sketches which are made for, and directed by, the eyes can render some of the design plans visible. Sketches not only supply designers with tangible images of the ideas they are trying out but also provide the onlooker with snapshots of the creative process.

5.4 The case studies (introduction)

If a practice's design credentials are confirmed by winning a single design award or publishing a project in an architectural journal, then there are many offices which would fit the bill. However, to continually do so by maintaining a consistent level of qualitative output is not common and marks out the three offices chosen for this study. Each represents a different size of practice; is located in a different city in the UK; is a regular recipient of national or international acknowledgements for their design output (awards and publications), and each exhibits a diversity of architecture in their built work.

Gareth Hoskins' practice is five years old. Since its inception, he has been the recipient of the Young Architectural Practice of the Year 2001 and Young Architect of the Year 2000, has won several awards and also published and exhibited widely in the UK. He previously worked for the London practice of Penoyre and Prasad after qualifying from the Mackintosh School of Architecture. His workload is almost exclusively UK-based and the practice has grown from 3 to 21 in the last three years. Hoskins is 35 and the office is based in Glasgow.

Sutherland Hussey is a four-strong practice founded in 1996 by Charlie Sutherland and Charlie Hussey, both of whom studied at the Mackintosh School of Architecture in Glasgow in the 1980s and went on to work for Sir James Stirling on a number of internationally acclaimed buildings. Charlie Hussey later worked with Renzo Piano and Charlie Sutherland became an associate at Stirling Wilford. In their independent practice, they have won 11 national awards, exhibited and published widely and their Barn House won The Architect's Journal 2002 Award for Best First Building. Despite being based in Edinburgh, the majority of their current work is located at opposite ends of the country in Tiree, Edinburgh, London and Truro.

Foster and Partners grew out of Foster Associates, and was established in 1967. Since then the practice has built an almost unrivalled reputation as one of the premier architectural practices in the world. Norman Foster was granted a knighthood in 1990; awarded the RIBA Gold Medal in 1993; the Pritzker Prize in 1999; was given a life peerage in 1999 and is the recipient of every major architectural citation. The practice has won a total of 290 design awards and is the subject of numerous books, publications and exhibitions. In the *Architects Journal* 100 survey his peers have consistently voted Norman Foster the most admired architect for the last eight years running. The practice's most notable buildings include The Reichstag, Berlin; Chek Lap Kok Airport, Hong Kong; Commerzbank, Frankfurt; The Hong Kong and Shanghai Bank. Foster himself is 67, has 4 partners, 12 directors and the practice totals 600 of which 580 are located in the Foster studio in London.

All the practices have distinctive and different characteristics at this particular moment in their history. Sutherland Hussey is presently a small practice building modestly-sized but architecturally ambitious projects geographically distant from their Edinburgh office base. Gareth Hoskins' practice has grown rapidly on the back of a series of medium size projects all about to begin on site at the same time. Foster and Partners is a large international practice, with its founder at the helm, and is still capable of carrying out any type of project of any size in any location. Each practice therefore is grappling with certain particular problems related to its own profile and history as well as the general pressures common to all architectural practices. Each of them is also associated with a different architectural product related to their way of working.

This chapter is based on several hours of personal interviews over two sessions with senior members of each practice carried out over a period of several months. In Gareth Hoskins and Sutherland Hussey's case, the interview was conducted both times with Hoskins, Sutherland and Hussey respectively. In Foster's case, the first interview was carried out with director, Andy Bow, and the second with project director, Charles Rich. The aim of the interviews was to ascertain what the driving

at this stage should revolve around broad issues such as environmental impact, heritage, development density, traditional land ownership rights and zoning issues. Engineering input is also significant at this stage and consultations should occur with important authorities relating to water supplies, drainage, roads, footpaths, traffic control and services such as electricity, gas and telecommunications. Initial sketch plans of alternative concepts are then prepared based on survey data regarding contours, shape, vegetation, surface water and climate. This assists in narrowing down options and providing more information about the economic feasibility of the proposed development. Reference to national and local government authority planning policies, guidelines and development plans would also receive special attention at this stage.

The end result of the above process, if the development continues to appear viable, is a concept plan which depicts the overall scheme with designated land-use areas, development density and sub-division details, infrastructure and transportation arrangements, landscaping and general arrangements relating to built forms such as heights, character, building materials, colours and textures, etc. The concept plan should communicate a clear vision of the proposed development, define how the proposed development adds value to the interests of key stakeholders and provide a valuable document for further testing of the development's financial feasibility.

At this point in the development process, more detailed testing of financial feasibility occurs involving comparisons of total revenues and costs, and the rates at which these will flow. Development costs are usually calculated on a cost per floor or cost per lot basis and sale prices will have to be estimated from marketing intelligence and considerations of location, floor/lot sizes, rental or price trends, development quality standards and infrastructure support, and economic and political events which may impact upon business or personal prosperity, etc. However, at this early stage, the accuracy of such data is often lacking, meaning that 'gut feeling' and significant contingency allowances form part of this early estimating process. Since expenditures will have already occurred in developing the concept plan and will continue to accumulate well before any revenue flows, the break-even point of the development also needs to be calculated. This will determine the period over which financing is required and its associated costs. Estimates of finance costs can be made from interest rate predications and through continued negotiations with financers, which at this stage would still be tentative in nature. Although informal discussions with potential financers are likely to have taken place, a formal approach to acquire finance would not normally occur until a final decision to proceed is made, which itself rests on a more detailed analysis of future costs and revenues. Before approaching financers, it will be important to plan the development's completion to ensure that revenues are brought forward at the earliest possible time.

Another consideration, if the development vehicle is a joint venture, is the distribution of risks for cost and revenue flows between the various partners. Potential financers

Embarking on a project – the role of architects in promoting urban
design as the foundation of effective project management

6

will want to know that a thorough risk analysis of the development has been conducted, that systems are in place to manage those risks and that risks are distributed in an appropriate way. As Arnold (1991) points out, many developers who finance a development with debt assume far too much risk which leads to many projects encountering major set backs. Therefore, a critical part of capital budgeting should be worst-case and sensitivity analyses which assess the validity of underlying assumptions made about risks and test the sensitivity of the projected cash flows to changes in circumstances. In larger, longer-term developments, a full dynamic cash flow forecast will be needed which considers changes in the value of future revenue and cost flows and discounts them back to a 'Net Present Value' (NPV). The discount rate is normally the required interest return and if the NPV when using this rate is negative then the assumptions underlying the development would be reconsidered. This kind of analyses clarify the investment decision and raise questions which might otherwise go unasked. For example, if the overall NPV is negative, the focus of development could shift to a second project where the NPV is positive.

When such calculations have been conducted, the development proposal is presented to selected lending institutions and subjected to a credit proposal evaluation. In effect, these institutions make the decision to proceed with a development or not and, thereafter, become the 'real' clients of the development for any subsequent contributors.

6.4 The importance and potential of good urban design

The traditional development process, as described above, focuses very much on the economics of development, at the expense of social and environmental issues. This is not surprising given the difficulties in effectively engaging the public in such emotive debates. Furthermore, the traditional analytical tools of developers are grounded in accountancy and are not suited to assessing the value of social amenity. For example, while NPV calculations are valuable in assessing financial viability, they are of little value in assessing the social benefits of a development (Barwise et al, 1991). A good investment from a social perspective can often have a negative NPV.

What is missing from the traditional development process is a thorough assessment of the wider social context in which development occurs, so that it becomes part of an integrated and considered social system where people can live in happiness, harmony, health and prosperity. Although financial analysis is a necessary part of project management, there is a need to inject greater public interest into the development process. This means considering the wider social, political and environmental context in which a development takes place in order to balance the needs of all stakeholders in the built environment. This is the practice of urban design which involves generating sound design guidelines that encompass physical and symbolic elements to ensure the effectiveness, efficiency, health and vitality of the physical settings in which society, commerce and industry exist.

Urban design is an important area of study that has received little attention in the field of project management and there are many reasons to give it more attention. For example, with the emergence of corporate responsibility, businesses will be increasingly required to consider their ethical and moral responsibilities towards the community as well as to their shareholders. Furthermore, the rapid pace of modernisation, globalisation and population growth around the world will place enormous threats on the integrity of the urban environment and fabric. In many developing countries, the rush to satisfy these needs, often by insensitive external developers, is compromising the quality of the urban environment in which people live. This is resulting in the destruction of important natural and heritage environments and, more significantly, the cultural capital invested in them, which provide people with a sense of community memory, identity and history.

These problems are not confined to developing countries. For example, in the UK, the social and economic degradation resulting from insensitive urban design has reached crisis proportions and has been elevated to the top of the political agenda (Crewe, 2002; Spring, 2002). Indeed, in April 2002, Lord Rogers, former Chair of the UK Government's Urban Taskforce, criticised the Government's 'short sighted' and fragmented approach to development arguing that the money will be wasted if individual developments are not integrated within the wider infrastructure of the city, which is currently 'run down' (Richards, 2002). It is clear that good urban design must be underpinned by a broader regional understanding of land use, social and cultural issues, environmental impacts and employment, etc.

Good urban design has the potential to redress these complex and inter-related problems and counteract the damaging and unsustainable trends which shape contemporary development activity. It is a field of study which offers much potential to ensure that the products produced by the construction industry enrich society, the environment and the economy, rather than destroy it. More selfishly, it also offers the architectural profession an opportunity to regain their respect and their lead role in the development process.

The following case study illustrates how these goals can be achieved. It shows how architects can take a lead role in the development process and create a built environment which balances the needs of developers with those of the government and the community.

6.4.1   Case study – Victoria Park Master Plan, Sydney, Australia

In December 1997 Landcom acquired a former, under-utilised, 25 hectare industrial site from the Department of Defence in order to transform it into a high quality living and working environment. Landcom is the New South Wales' Government's land release agency which sets benchmarks for good urban design and is responsible for developing and implementing the current policy of consolidating brown field development around the Sydney metropolitan area. The site, known as Victoria

Embarking on a project – the role of architects in promoting urban design as the foundation of effective project management

6

Park, is located three kilometres south of the Sydney Central Business District (CBD) and is part of the larger 'Green Square' development area. It is one of the largest single development parcels in South Sydney and lies within a strong urban setting which is the result of over 150 years of development, featuring vestiges of 19th century housing, pre- and post-second world war housing and extensive areas of large scale industrialisation. The site was originally low lying swamps, which were drained and filled in the late 19th century for market gardens. In 1907 a racecourse was built on the site, which operated until 1945 when it was developed as industrial land. Existing structures on the site date from its use as the Nuffield/Leyland motor vehicle plant and Department of Defence storage area.

The site was bought by Landcom in 1997 and the development of new rail and road links to Sydney's south will herald fundamental changes in the area and locate the site strategically on a regional expressway network that will extend from Sydney's north to the airport in the south. The site, with its close proximity to the airport, CBD, universities, technology parks and regional leisure attractions such as beaches and parks, has been identified by the State Government as one of significant economic importance in terms of future employment and wealth generation. An aerial photo of the site is illustrated in Figure 6.1.

Figure 6.1: Aerial photo of the Victoria Park site

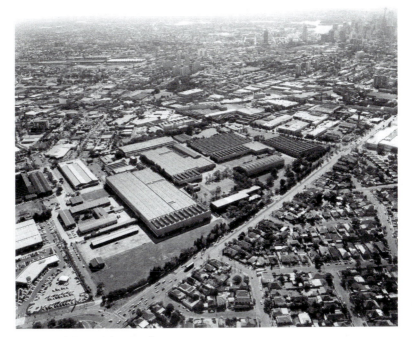

Source: Cox Architects and Planners, Sydney, Australia

Figure 6.2: The urban design process

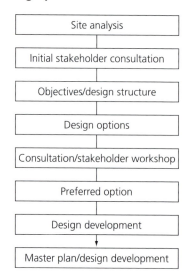

The vision for the redevelopment of Victoria Park was that of a vibrant mixed-use community with a distinctive and memorable character that integrates into the existing fabric of South Sydney and acts as a catalyst for the transformation of the Green Square area. The main stages in the design process are summarised in Figure 6.2.

The Master Plan was developed in consultation with the State Government's Urban Design Advisory Service, the South Sydney Development Corporation, members of the local community, the Roads and Traffic Authority and South Sydney Council. This was achieved through a major design workshop where consultants and stakeholders could present options, constraints and discuss issues; weekly liaison meetings with major stakeholders; and peer assistance from prominent Sydney academics and Government Architects. In addition, market information was collected during focus group meetings with real estate agents and potential purchasers. The main issues to emerge from the consultation process are shown in Table 6.1.

The final Master Plan, that emerged from the extensive consultation processes, was a flexible document which recognised that the design process is not static. Rather than presenting a definitive solution, it was structured to respond to the changing needs of stakeholders, significant local infrastructure developments and the dynamic framework on on-going regional planning initiatives. The main aims and objectives of the Master Plan are listed in Table 6.2 and were translated into the master plan framework depicted in Figure 6.3.

The master plan framework was translated into a detailed Master Plan document with more detailed guidance and plans relating to issues such as land-use parcelling,

Embarking on a project – the role of architects in promoting urban design as the foundation of effective project management

6

Table 6.1: Main consultation issues and responses

Issue	*Response*
Urban form – the final form must integrate into the existing local and regional context and contribute a unifying structure to the larger Green Square development area.	The preferred form must acknowledge the existing circulation structure, create a memorable urban gesture which resolves circulation desire lines, over land flow constraints and the creation of a clear identity within the overall renewal of Green Square.
Land use – employment generation and the maintenance of Sydney's south as an economic gateway is a major concern of the State Government.	The introduction of active uses to enliven the commercial sector beyond working hours is important in maintaining safety and preserving the quality of the area.
Traffic – the north–south link through the site became a critical issue, especially to potential residents.	The removal of north–south through traffic from the residential precinct allowed flexibility in the road network, as did the creation of a commercial road in the east of the site.
Open space – a range of active and passive uses to create options for users.	The open space ($12 \, m^2$ per person) should be broken down into a series of more accessible spaces, which should be linked into a network.
Permeability – perceived privatisation of major open spaces in the centre of the site was agreed to be avoided.	The network of roads and open spaces should link to space at the centre of the site to allow pedestrian permeability, local traffic accessibility and reduce car dependence.
Storm water – the efficient and environmentally appropriate management of storm water is an important issue for South Sydney. Safety and amenity concerns were raised about the proposed system of open channels in the Green Square Master Plan.	On site detention during 5 yr, 20 yr and 100 yr storm events will reduce pressure on the existing storm water network. Consideration was given to an ornamental feature which can be fully charged with water all year round.
Community facilities – community facilities must comply with the South Sydney Council's social infrastructure plan.	Preference is for a facility on the southern boundary of the site which may be incorporated into a future district park.
Density – a 2.5 to 1 floor space ratio is difficult to achieve without reducing resident amenity.	The likely maximum development scenario is 1.5 to 1. However, lower densities may be likely which would impact upon population estimates for the site.

precinct designations, open space distribution, landscaping, traffic and access, infrastructure and built form (set backs, maximum heights, densities, materials and architectural style, etc.). One of these detailed plans relating to the landscape network is illustrated in Figure 6.4.

The eventual result was an indicative Master Plan accompanied by concept sketches from various elevations, some of which are illustrated in Figures 6.5 and 6.6.

Table 6.2: Main objectives and aims of the Master Plan

Objective	Aims
Provide a responsive land-use strategy.	Encourage business, employment and residential opportunities.
	Create an integrated mixed-use community which responds to aspirations of existing and future residents.
	Create distinctive and identifiable neighbourhoods with a strong social infrastructure.
Create integrated and legible open space networks.	Create recognisable gateways to the main entry points.
	Respond to the NE–SW pedestrian desire line within the site, which links other local areas.
	Integrate, if feasible, the canal theme with the open space links.
	Provide a range of publicly accessible open spaces suitable for a range of uses.
Guide built form.	Define streets and public open space with built form.
	Reinforce the Green Square Master Plan principles of increased height from west to east.
	Minimise built form overshadowing of public domain.
	Ensure high residential and commercial amenity.
Ensure efficient access and movement within the site.	Provide safe and secure streets with high pedestrian amenity.
	Develop a street hierarchy to allow efficient movement and minimise car use.
	Discourage through traffic but create legible links to surrounding streets and neighbourhoods.
	Manage traffic to minimise impact on surrounding communities.
Develop a flexible infrastructure strategy.	Provide services reticulation to maximise development flexibility and opportunity.
Enhance heritage.	Retain fig trees within the site.
	Retain and enhance the existing historic Totalisator building.
	Maintain a built edge to local communities.
Promote environmentally sustainable development.	Re-establish biodiversity through site remediation.
	Ensure high quality water management within the site.
	Develop efficient transport links.
	Optimise solar orientation and building energy performance.
	Promote use of renewable source materials.
Manage site development and staging.	Ensure stages have individual and complete identity.
	Provide for future flexibility by allowing potential extension and expansion of street grid with changes in context and density.
	Accommodate future links to the south and allow grid to be continued.

Figure 6.3: Master plan framework

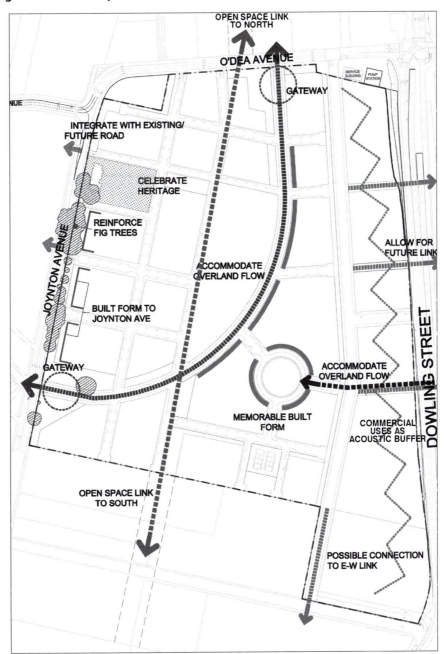

Source: Cox Architects and Planners, Sydney, Australia

Figure 6.4: Landscape network

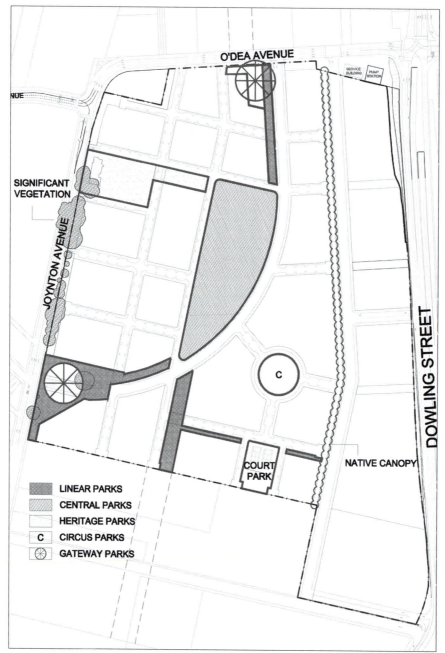

Source: Cox Architects and Planners, Sydney, Australia

Embarking on a project – the role of architects in promoting urban design as the foundation of effective project management

6

Figure 6.5: Indicative Master Plan

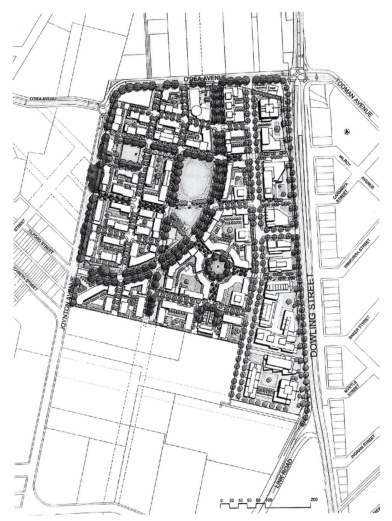

Source: Cox Architects and Planners, Sydney, Australia

Having approved the Master Plan, Landcom has now proceeded to develop the public domain and essential infrastructure in successive stages. The private sector, in conjunction with Landcom, is developing the built form within the flexibility provided by the Master Plan. As development applications are prepared and submitted, detailed provisions, which are within the overall framework of the Master Plan, will be developed subject to the market conditions and development context at that time.

Figure 6.6: View of central park looking south east

Source: Cox Architects and Planners, Sydney, Australia

6.5 Best practice in urban design

The above case study illustrates that, like all design, the urban design process is undertaken within economic, social, environmental and political constraints. Undertaken rigorously, it involves rigorous and extensive consultation with many stakeholders with widely varying values, interests and power relationships. This makes the urban design process a difficult and complex consideration of inter-related issues and considerations that are much wider than the physical organisation of built form which is the end result (Hamid, 1985). In essence, urban design brings together a broad range of disciplines associated with the spatial configuration, construction and management of the built environment to enable urban environments to function effectively. Like all design, the urban design process is an organic process that emerges in response to the political, social, physical, natural, economic and cultural environment of the development setting. It is difficult and overly simplistic to reduce the process to a series of neat, prescriptive and systematic steps. Nevertheless, Lang (1994) argues that there is considerable agreement over the key phases of the urban design process and that it is possible to identify these in the above case study. Broadly speaking, these are the intelligence phase, the design phase, the choice phase, the implementation phase, the operational phase and the post-occupancy evaluation phase. These are discussed below in more detail and in reference to contemporary urban design practice and theory.

6.5.1 *The intelligence phase*

The built environment has an enormous impact upon society and is constantly being scanned by the multitude of interest groups it affects. For example, developers look for development opportunities, environmentalists look for impacts upon the natural environment, the general public look for issues that affect their personal quality of life and local governments may look for potential employment opportunities, tax revenues, etc. Inevitably, with so many competing interests focused on the built environment, the urban designer must become a manager who has to positively manage the conflicts and pressures from the varied constituencies wanting to influence the design.

Traditionally, many architects have isolated themselves from this difficult process, carrying out their design in isolation, uncontaminated by the politics of participation and guided by pure design ideologies and philosophies. While this could be attributed to the neglect of management theory and practice in traditional architectural education, it is an approach which cannot continue since society is becoming more knowledgeable about the built environment and more empowered to do something about it. The case study shows that contemporary urban design is increasingly requiring designers to work openly in the community with full public participation in the process. In this egalitarian environment, intelligence gathering from the multitude of stakeholder groups about their expectations of buildings is a critical part of the design process. However, many architects are not equipped to embrace this challenge and it is a problem which continues to contribute to the demise of their profession.

For example, Lang (1992) pointed to an increasing gap between the self-image of architects and reality, arguing that there is much that falls within the domain of the discipline of architecture which has little to do with contemporary architectural education. More recently, Duffy and Hutton (1998) argued that there continues to be 'no connection between what happens in architectural practice and what is taught in the schools, except the bitter tears of those tens of thousands of people who have suffered from a misdirected system'.

6.5.2 *The design phase*

The design phase involves collaboration with a range of different designers to produce a series of alternative concept plans for evaluation during the next phase of the urban design process (the choice phase). Intellectually, the process of creating these concept (or sketch) plans involves a combination of habitual and original solutions, the ultimate goal being to generate a number of alternative design solutions (Lawson, 1990). These early designs are very important documents, which should show an overall plan of the development within the broader context of designated land-use areas, development density and sub-division details, infrastructure and transportation arrangements, landscaping and proximity to other areas and developments (Clark and Tinsley, 1991). Conceptually, these elements can be designed using a rationalist or empiricist design philosophy or, more normally, a combination of both. A rationalist philosophy is guided by the development of geometric, modular systems while an empiricist philosophy is concerned with the development of behaviourally cognitive coherence with no externally imposed organising system or principle (Lang, 1994). Whichever philosophy underpins a scheme, the concept plan is a very important document since it will shape initial public perceptions of the development's impact on the surrounding community and often determines whether a development proceeds with ease or difficulty.

The case study shows that the best concept plans locate the proposed development within the regional, sub-regional and district context with supporting arguments as to how the proposed development adds value to the community and is a sustainable aspect of the urban environment. It should include quantitative impact statements on existing and future planned roads, pedestrian and other transport facilities; supporting infrastructure such as services, schools, community and health facilities, and population holding capacities, density, and age and gender distributions. It should also clarify the urban design qualities and themes, which underpin the proposed development, and general details relating to built forms such as heights, character, building materials, colours and textures, etc. should be communicated to create a clear vision of the proposal and its impact on, and within, the existing environment. As well as providing a key political document for communication with planners and the general public, the concept plan also provides a valuable economic document for further testing of the development's financial feasibility (Clark and Tinsley, 1991).

To achieve the above objectives, the case study shows that urban designers must work carefully within the significant amount of planning legislation and strategic planning initiatives that exist in most developed countries. For example, Australia has a hierarchy of State, Regional and Local Development Plans which define a series of evaluative criteria against which urban designs are assessed. In essence, State Plans deal with important statewide issues such as protecting important forests, ensuring equity in development for all social groups and encouraging development which creates jobs. They may also plan important infrastructure projects or major developments in specific locations such as special development or economic zones. Regional Plans deal with issues peculiar to a region but generally those that go beyond local areas. This may include protecting river catchments and coastal environments, providing public transport systems, infrastructure development for industry and housing, etc. Finally, Local Plans are prepared by councils and guide planning decisions for local developments in the council electorate. Through zoning

Embarking on a project – the role of architects in promoting urban design as the foundation of effective project management

6

and development control plans, they allow councils to determine and supervise how land is used to ensure that local economic, social, heritage and environmental assets are nurtured and preserved.

6.5.3   The choice phase

During this phase, alternative concept (sketch) designs are evaluated and one chosen for implementation into a fully detailed working design. Alternatively, if no schemes are satisfactory, the whole project might be abandoned or the design process returned to earlier phases to better understand and define the problem and produce other design solutions.

It is difficult to evaluate designs before they are implemented and, traditionally, the evaluation process has been a subjective one carried out by a jury. Juries normally comprise representatives of major stakeholder groups who collectively attempt to predict the performance of each scheme in practice. This may be on the basis of presentations from urban designers or simply on submitted documentary evidence. The two main criteria used to assess an urban design are: how the design will function when implemented, and how it will impact upon the environment when implemented. Predicting how a design will function is difficult, although computer and physical models can help to communicate the visual appearance of a scheme. Indeed, computer modelling can now simulate certain performance features such as traffic flows, pollution and noise control, sunlight shading, wind effects, energy efficiency and consumption, and circulation distances and routes, etc. However, it is much more difficult to assess the social and psychological impact of a design, and it is in this area that much of the debate revolves. This is because people tend to evaluate a design from the biased context of their own value systems. So to overcome the difficulties in this area, urban designers trying to sell their scheme might often use case studies of similar developments in the past, or use analogies to predict what the outcome will be.

While these types of techniques have formed part of the traditional design assessment toolkit, juries are becoming increasingly uneasy about committing to schemes on the basis of such qualitative evidence. Unfortunately, in an increasingly risky, numerate and legalistic world, they have satisfied their desire for certainty by turning to science and the well established measurement techniques of finance, economics and risk analysis where the return on capital invested can be predicted with apparent precision. As Duffy and Hutton (1998) have noted, the result is that continuity is lost in projects, aims are readily diverted by political expediency, and social objectives are too frequently subordinated, fragmented, sub-optimised and inadequately co-ordinated. While science and finance inevitably have a part to play in assessing any urban design, an over reliance on it can create a dangerous illusion of control and sterilise the development process of its emotional and social context. The challenge for architects is to recapture this early part of the development process from the scientists and developers and return it to those who will work and live in the spaces and urban environment it creates and affects.

6.5.4 The implementation phase

Assuming the choice phase produces a decision, the implementation phase begins. The aim of this phase is to produce a completed urban design and management plan which can realistically bring the selected design into physical reality in an economically, politically, environmentally and socially sensitive manner. The challenge is to obtain firm commitments from stakeholders that their promises of support – financial, political or otherwise – secured during the intelligence phase will manifest themselves. For example, promises of potential building purchases, physical leasing from potential tenants, financial support from banks and adoption of services by regulatory authorities will have to be confirmed and secured. Guidelines will also have to be accepted as official policy by local government authorities that are responsible for managing development in an area.

Once the design has been accepted as policy by local governments and commitments of support secured from various stakeholders, design guidelines are produced for individual sites in the total urban design and development proposals sought from potential developers. These proposals will include specific building designs for individual sites and where the urban design process has not involved the pre-securing of tenants or building purchasers, developers may also cover such issues and may even suggest changes to proposed building design concepts required by their proposed tenants. These are evaluated against criteria set down in the design programme established during the intelligence phase and, once accepted, individual development designs are converted by developers into working drawings, programmes and specifications to enable construction to begin. Construction normally commences once further requirements established by building regulations and other statutory service boards have been met.

6.5.5 The post-occupancy evaluation phase

As urban designs come to life and are used, they will be assessed by a multitude of different groups against a vast array of different needs, expectations and value systems. Faced with such an enormous volume of complex feedback information over such a long period of time, few designers have the time and inclination to collect it and learn from it. As Lang (1994) points out, the majority of lessons learnt in urban design result from studies commissioned by users experiencing problems and academics who are often isolated from the practitioners who could benefit from their ideas. Coupled with the newsworthiness of failures compared to successes, and the assistance of some very prominent, if not poorly-informed, amateurs, the public's perception is of an incompetent architectural profession. While there are many wonderful examples of good urban design that have gone unnoticed, architects

Embarking on a project – the role of architects in promoting urban
design as the foundation of effective project management

6

must expect to be held accountable for their designs and it is essential that lessons are learnt so that a better understanding of urban design principles can be built to inform better future decisions.

6.6 Conclusion

This chapter has attempted to integrate the principles of urban design and project management in order to make the development process more effective and efficient. In doing so, it has extended forward the traditional perception of the procurement process as beginning in briefing, to beginning in urban planning. It has been argued that nowadays more and more projects are being created out of a business need, often by developers whose primary objective is to produce a quick financial return. This is not conducive to effective development. Neither is it good for the poor public image of the construction industry because the inevitable result is increasing disquiet among the public about a lack of consultation in the development process and the negative impact of building development upon the environment in which they live.

A case study has been presented to demonstrate that the best projects are socially-driven in an economic framework rather than economically-driven outside a social framework. That is, that efficient and effective development must be based on an understanding of urban design and that development led by design, rather than the opposite, is more likely to result in effective project management outcomes. It promotes effective urban design as the foundation of effective project management in clarifying and integrating the values, philosophy and vision underlying a development from a variety of stakeholder perspectives. Urban design is portrayed as a consultative and socially responsible way of embarking on a project and one whose results contribute most value to the wide variety of stakeholders whose economic and social interests are affected by the development process. This contemporary approach to development can help to ensure that our buildings add enduring quality and value to the lives of those who are affected by them. It is in stark contrast to the current trend where development is dominated by minimum cost without regard to other attributes.

It is a principle which architects are uniquely positioned to advocate and there has probably been no better time to do so, with the emergence of developing countries, of corporate responsibility and accountability, and the increasing sensitivity of people to the impact of the urban environment on their day-to-day lives. As Duffy and Hutton (1998) argue:

> It is essential to reverse these trends and to renew in the built environment a reaffirmation of the roles of the professional architect, planner and engineer. These professionals ought to act as interpreters of requirements, guides towards means, seers for future change and coordinators of other elements for success, and organizers of consequential projects. It can hardly be claimed that they are currently fulfilling these roles successfully.

6 Embarking on a project – the role of architects in promoting urban design as the foundation of effective project management

References

Akintoye, A., Beck, M., Hardcastle, C., *et al*, *Framework for risk assessment and management of Private Finance Initiative Projects*, Glasgow Caledonian University (2001).

Arnold III, J. H., 'Assessing capital risk: you can't be too conservative', in Project Management, *Harvard Business Review*, Harvard College, Harvard, USA, 1991, pp. 17–29.

Barwise, P., Marsh, P. R. and Wensley, R., 'Must finance and strategy clash?', in Project Management, *Harvard Business Review*, Harvard College, Harvard, USA, 1991, pp. 3–9.

Clarke, M. and Tinsley, M., 'Project finance', in C. Foster (ed.) *Guidelines for the management of major construction projects*, NEDC Construction Industry Sector Group, London, HMSO (1991) pp. 23–29.

Conway, H. and Roenisch, R., *Understanding architecture*, Routledge (1997).

Crewe, D., 'Housing forum: Build new towns', *Building*, 17 May, 2002, p. 16.

Duffy, F. and Hutton, L., *The idea of a profession; architectural knowledge*, E&FN Spon, London and New York (1998).

Hamid, S., *The urban design process*, Van Nostrand Reinhold, New York (1985).

Lang, J., 'Architectural education – under pressure for change', *Architectural Bulletin*, Feb. 1992, pp. 14–15.

Lang, J., *Urban design: The American experience*, Van Nostrand Reinhold, New York (1994).

Lawson, B., *How designers think: The design process demystified*, 2nd edn, Butterworth Architecture, Oxford (1990).

Reynolds, H. and Solomon, P. L., *The property development process: Western Australia*, Victor Publishing, Perth, Western Australia (1998).

Richards, M., 'Rogers attacks Brown's "short-sighted" budget', *Building*, 26 April, 2002, p. 11.

Spring, M., 'A man with a plan', *Building*, 28 June, 2002, pp. 20–21.

Key Reading

Resource for Urban Design Information (RUDI), www.rudi.net

Urban Design Group (UDG), www.udg.org.uk

Sustainable Urban Design and Climate, (See 'How Climate Affects Us') www.bom.gov.au/climate/

Information technologies in design management ***7***

Bimal Kumar, School of the Built and Natural Environment, Glasgow Caledonian University, and
Daniel Hobbs, TCS Associate, HLM Design, Glasgow, UK

7.1 Introduction

We live in an Information Age. In this day and age, managing design efficiently without the aid of information and communication technologies (ICTs) seems unthinkable. Man has been involved in the act of design since times immemorial (Coyne *et al*, 1989). However, the tools and techniques at the designer's disposal have undergone considerable change. The single most important development that can be attributed to have influenced the designer's toolbox has to be the information and communication technologies. The digital computer initially provided a major *amplification* of designer's speed. With more developments in the different ways computers could be used, designers were able to *amplify* human intellect in the act of designing.

On a commercial level, the use of IT at the design stage is hard to over-emphasise if the industry is ever going to achieve significant performance gains.

A recent influential report by Sir John Egan (Egan, 1998) underlines the importance of IT in design:

> One area in which we know new technology to be a very useful tool is in the design of buildings and their components, and in the exchange of design information throughout the construction team. There are enormous benefits to be gained, in terms of eliminating waste and rework for example, from using modern CAD technology to prototype buildings and by rapidly exchanging information on design changes. Redesign should take place on computer, not on the construction site.

ICTs can help gain a better understanding of the client's requirements through the use of visualisation techniques and by using specification software applications to create project documentation. This could radically improve the process of tendering. Clients want better information to run their buildings once they are built, but they will only get this economically if it is provided at the start of the construction process, by the designers and amended during the building process. Any major project begins with an interaction between designers from various fields like architecture, structural engineering, building services and so on. Modern developments in IT are proving a real boon in facilitating this interaction, saving enormous amounts of time and money on the projects.

Over past years, there have been various research projects that have shed light on all kinds of ICT applications in design. We present some of these here in the following paragraphs.

7.1.1 Collaborative design/concurrent engineering

One area of intense activity in recent years has been in the development of frameworks and systems for collaborative design. A related (but not the same) area is concurrent engineering. Zaneldin *et al* (2001) describe recent advances in information technology and computer collaboration tools to improve co-ordination and increase productivity in the design of building projects. Based on a structured information model, presented in a companion paper, a collaborative design system is developed incorporating a client–server environment for representing building data, recording design rationale and effectively managing design changes; and Internet-based collaboration tools for sharing documents, reviewing changes and conferencing among remote design participants. Implementation issues and the perceived changes imposed on the traditional design process are discussed, and an example application is worked to demonstrate the applicability and features of the developed prototype. The developments explained in this chapter provide guidelines for modelling complex information-dependent processes in the construction domain. See Anumba *et al* (1998) for more details.

7.1.2 Representation for conceptual design of buildings

This is another area which preoccupies a number of researchers around the world. Most of the bottlenecks that hinder the progress of efficient and useful applications of ICT in design, centre around the inability of the systems used by different *actors* in the project to *talk* to each other. One of the first steps in resolving these issues is the development of standard representations of designed artifacts. Rivard and Fenves (2000) describe a particular way of representing buildings for their conceptual design in a system called SEED-Config. The building representation for storing design solutions adopted in SEED-Config consists of two levels of abstraction models defined on top of the object-oriented data model. The first level is an information model, called the building entity and technology model, which stores design data as they are generated during conceptual design, supports case-based reasoning, and shares data among all design participants. This model represents each building entity as a generic container that encompasses its properties, taxonomy, geometry, composition, relationships, and design knowledge applied in generating it. The second level is a conceptual model that defines the types of objects, relationships and data needed to fully represent the information in a given design domain. The conceptual model specifies the semantics of the design information for the domain using the syntax defined in the information model. The proposed representation also includes a faceted classification scheme to define the controlled vocabulary from which indexes are obtained. The representation has the following advantages: it integrates multiple views, supports design evolution, supports design exploration and is extensible.

7.2   ICT in design practice

Broadly speaking, the use of IT in applied design can be classified into the following categories (Information Technology Construction Best Practice [ITCBP] website):

- 2D Computer Aided Drawing (CAD);

- 3D CAD;

- Integrated Building Modelling;

- Structural modelling.

7.2.1   *Two-dimensional modelling*

The use of this technology is now well established in large parts of the industry. Since the launch of AutoCAD many years ago, adoption of computer-based drafting systems has become increasingly popular. Other systems like the Intergraph and Bentley systems also hold a quite substantial market share. Two-dimensional modelling can be seen as replacements of drawing boards, pen and paper (ITCBP website) and CAD technicians as replacements of draftsmen. However, they clearly bring enormous advantages in terms of speed once the initial learning curve is achieved.

7.2.2   *Three-dimensional CAD*

3D CAD allows you to create and print three-dimensional drawings on a computer and is, therefore, the electronic equivalent of the project-scale model (ITCBP website). Some of these systems also include facilities to import and export bills of quantities and materials directly in and out of them. More advanced systems exist which utilise visualisation technologies to give a user more *feel* for the structure.

3D CAD systems arrived on the market a number of years after the 2D systems and quickly became very popular. These systems are gaining more ground in terms of being the central representation of the structure from which all of its other *views* can be derived and manipulated. Coupled with advanced rendering techniques, these systems are also used as presentation tools.

7.2.3   *Integrated Building Modelling*

As mentioned above, a further extension of 3D modelling is its use as a central, all encompassing representation of a structure. This is exactly what is meant by 'Integrated Building Modelling'. In theory, this approach should allow easy inter-change of information for all parties in a project, which can be drawn from this integrated model. However, major obstacles remain in achieving this goal. Common information exchange standards need to be in place before this can be achieved.

Various groups are working towards developing such standards like International Alliance of Interoperability (IAI) and Centre of E-Business in Construction (CITE).

7.2.4 Structural modelling and analysis

A structural engineer's life has never been the same since the digital computer took over the mundane repetitive calculations required to analyse a structure. There are now a large number of structural analysis programs on the market and they are in vogue amongst even the smallest of engineering practices. These systems also include relevant portions of BS Codes of Practice for checking the conformance of designs. More modern systems exist which exploit non-numerical programming techniques as well as spreadsheets to facilitate what-if scenarios (Tedds, TK-Solver). Some of these programs also provide seamless interfaces with CAD packages so that inputs to the program in terms of a structure's geometry, topology, etc. can be fed in directly.

7.2.5 Other IT usage in design

In addition to the above-mentioned categories of IT usage in design, there are some other applications of IT which are becoming increasingly popular.

Visualisation

Visualisation techniques like 'Virtual Reality' and 'Augmented Reality' are now increasingly popular at the early conceptual design stage. 'Walkthrough' systems enable a designer to demonstrate various aspects of a design to the client which makes it far easier for anyone to get a *feel* for the building.

Extranets

Extranets are those Intranets that allow selected external parties to access them from outside. These are mostly used at the project execution stage but do have implications for design as well. Extranets can make any change to a design and its communication a lot easier to manage. The case study from HLM Design includes a discussion on this.

7.3 Some futuristic thoughts

We live in extraordinary times. The Internet and related technologies have caused the costs of certain kinds of interactions and transactions to plummet. As a consequence, new ways of communicating and trading have been opened up. As with any dramatic technological change, the most obvious effects are incremental: we find easier and less costly ways of doing the things we used to do anyway. Over time, however, there are changes that are non-incremental. We discover that we can do entirely new things, or completely restructure the ways in which we do the things we used to do. The current technological change will have a non-incremental impact on business transactions. Entire supply chains are being re-engineered and so too are the industries that participate in them.

7.3.1 E-Governance – some thoughts and issues

As e-government projects expand and diversify, the distinction between consumer and business-focused applications becomes more evident. The e-government industry is developing into two worlds: consumer-to-government (C2G) and business-to-government (B2G). Each class of applications has unique characteristics that enable new vertical markets to flourish and determine an evolutionary pathway toward commercial success.

The differences between the consumer and business e-government applications include the depth of functionality; the level of information available; the extent of integration between legacy and enterprise resource planning (ERP) systems; the capacity to handle high-volume transactions; the duration of transactional relationships and the ability to improve workflow, not just provide a convenient service.

A significant B2G application sector emerging in e-government is online planning permission and inspections for the construction industry. As construction forms a significant part of the gross domestic product in any industrialised country, an acceleration of the planning permission process has the power to make a solid economic impact while greatly improving the convenience to builders and operational efficiency of government agencies. Yet to address this challenge, the unique B2G attributes must be used as the performance standard and serve as a framework for a new vertical market.

There are seven major attributes that must be present for a successful online planning permission process. A true B2G web application for permits must:

1 Include a complete integration of systems, not just a front-end interface;

2 Parallel existing processes as extensions, not replacements, of workflow;

3 Support multi-disciplinary cross-functionality to stimulate teamwork;

4 Support interdependencies so that critical-path work is not impeded;

5 Enable real-time communications between team members for speed;

6 Provide access to multiple databases and database types for flexible operations;

7 Include action and management steps that offer greater project control.

Future implications of this new vertical market go beyond eliminating the need to stand in line or wait on the phone for a planning permission. The operational efficiencies for government and the economy will continue to grow with the advent of wireless technologies that push computing power to the edge of the

'Net, and by connecting planning approvals to ERP and procurement to increase project deployment velocity.

7.4 Case study – HLM Design

The following section highlights issues raised by architects when using particular types of software on design projects. The software tools that are discussed are Codebook, ADB, MicroGDS and BuildOnline.

The use of CAD and database tools is pervasive on HLM Design's hospital projects. This case study highlights, in addition to the general issues, particular issues with IT use on one project. The project discussed is a community hospital in Lochgilphead, Scotland that is being procured using the PPP/PFI procurement route, the construction cost of this project is £10 m, and the current stage of the project is post Financial Close. The key services that will be included are out-patient services, acute in-patient accommodation, obstetrics, accident and emergency, and x-ray facilities.

The application of the tools that were used and the issues discussed have been obtained through discussions with the project architect.

7.4.1 CAD

The core CAD software within the practice is MicroGDS although other software such as AutoCAD is available. MicroGDS is object-based allowing graphical databases to be set up and queried which aids functionality in a number of ways that will be discussed later. The CAD software is linked to a bespoke database system (Codebook) that contains a library of commonly used components.

Throughout all projects that use CAD, a naming convention is imposed to facilitate additional functionality. The naming convention, based on the CI/SfB code, is adopted and built into the default interface through internal development applications.

Applications developed internally, also control the naming procedure for drawing layers, again based on the CI/SfB code, where '21:' refers to external walls, or '74:' refers to sanitary ware.

The graphical database has many benefits including automatic generation of equipment schedules, internal layouts and internal elevations. Recently, work has been undertaken to utilise this system for facility management, where components within the building can be identified through queries and highlighted on relevant drawings.

Finally, one other benefit of using MicroGDS is that it operates in a multi-user environment in which it is possible for many team members to work on the same drawing at the same time.

7.4.2 Codebook

Codebook is a suite of tools that interface with a database of components used on typical hospital projects to produce room layouts, schedules and other themed information. The components stored are based on the NHS's ADB database, which is a database of equipment and preferred room layouts. Codebook, within HLM Design, is used predominantly on hospital projects but there exists scope to use the software on any building type; the issue is one of creating and managing of the building-specific library of components.

The use of Codebook significantly improves the productivity on hospital projects through reducing time in developing 'C-sheets' which are equipment schedules, room layouts and internal elevations, combined on a single drawing. This information is generated automatically. C-sheets are crucial drawings that are used within the design process to discuss room layouts/functions with the key user groups.

The use of Codebook in practice, however, requires significant levels of control for the additional functionality that the software offers to be exploited.

The control that needs to occur for successful use includes:

- Drawing convention;

- Attribution convention.

Specific issues where functionality has been inhibited within the Lochgilphead community hospital project are discussed in the remainder of this section.

Untrained users can cause a myriad of problems with respect to the automatic generation of C-sheets and area schedules. Particularly, on this project, certain users moved the equipment graphic (object) away from its original reference point (hook point in MicroGDS terminology) which led to the internal elevations on the C-sheets showing the equipment in the wrong place when generated automatically.

Following the initial concept design, the project model had to be redrawn completely. This was to correct the mistakes made in building the project graphic model and to remove redundant elements from the database. The greater the redundancy, the slower the database works; redundancy is due to the initial library being generic rather than project specific, i.e. the generic database contains all components available at that time; not all components will be used on one particular project.

The most recent project undertaken within the practice has the most up-to-date data within the Codebook database; however, if components are not used, or have not been specified within brief, there is redundancy within the database that affects speed of regeneration. Components that may be needed within any project can be inserted into the project database from the generic database if needed.

The components in the database are linked to graphical representations on screen. Through this link certain tasks can be automated such as when an area polygon is drawn, the text indicating the floor area is drawn automatically, however, the regeneration function is slow: the user must delete any existing text and then synchronise with the database, rather than immediate regeneration of the text and graphics being made dependant upon changes made automatically.

The graphical database of components is under continual development to ensure that it corresponds with equipment that is actually available. The generic library of equipment is based upon ADB, the generic database developed by the NHS: any change to availability of components can be slow to incorporate into either ADB or Codebook.

Specifically, within the Lochgilphead hospital project, a graphic for radio diagnostic equipment was required, but did not exist within the Codebook database. The ADB database had data for radio diagnostic equipment but not the graphic for it. In this situation the architect was able to use a graphic from a specialist contractor's drawing, but this may not represent the actual equipment that will be used which will impact on the spatial organisation.

The link between the CAD model and the database is only 'live' at the point when the C-sheet is generated. The elevations and schedules are produced when Codebook scans the plan information to establish which elevational graphics and descriptions it requires. In the event of irregularities in the resultant C-sheet drawing, minor alterations can be made manually but care must be taken when regenerating the C-sheet that these alterations are not overwritten.

In the case of C-sheet creation, change control is not efficiently automated within the current system; the changes are not automatically recorded, although within the project a PDF file of the C-sheet drawing is kept to show pre-changes.

The scheduling that is done in Codebook does not allow for reports to be created with bespoke templates (to include corporate data) i.e. the output from the report has to be transferred to a spreadsheet that contains the corporate template for a schedule. However, once the link between the Codebook report and the corporate template has been made, it should remain intact throughout the scheduling process.

7.4.3 Extranets

BuildOnline is the Extranet system used on the Lochgilphead hospital project and is considered quite user-friendly.

Certain problems, however, did occur with other consultants who are using slower connections to the Internet.

The red-lining facility is not considered a sufficient record of changes for HLM Design's insurers and, therefore, additional hardcopies of the drawings are required for each change.

The Extranet's facility to red-line the drawing online has only been used by one out of 20 of the Trust's staff with regard to room layouts and departmental changes. This may indicate that further training is required for the users of the system. The ability for each hospital department to red-line changes online is considered extremely useful, however, managing and recording of those changes is of crucial importance, which has not been fully considered within the Lochgilphead project.

The BuildOnline system of issuing drawings is considered preferable to the traditional method; as only one copy is necessary for internal records and one PDF version for uploading to the Extranet site. Previously, it may have been that 25 hardcopies were required which could mean a day for printing and collating of that one issue. Significant time-savings can now be made.

Revisions are made easy through the use of a shared database of the drawings, which is also auditable, and was considered by HLM Design to be beneficial.

The notification function of the system has been successful, and has enhanced the speed of information transfer between parties.

However, problems occurred in one instance where notification of a drawing revision was sent to the client by mistake. The Hospital Trust had no access to the folder in which the drawing was kept. This meant that trust was broken down, due to the client being informed that they could not access this particular folder.

In this case, the changes to the drawings that were needed for a couple of departments had to occur through a particular communication route specified contractually and not directly with the architect, which would be the quickest and easiest way for the client to make a change!

7.4.4   Case study summary

The use of IT within HLM Design is crucial for efficient working procedures, particularly with hospitals, due to the complexity, scale and time-constraints of these particular types of projects.

The Lochgilphead project raised certain issues with regard to the functionality of Codebook and of the data management of the component library.

There existed a non-optimised communication/information transfer route on the Lochgilphead project with respect to the use of the Extranet system. This occurred because of the prescribed communication route that was agreed contractually.

However, the system was generally well received by the project stakeholders and some time-saving benefits were realised by HLM Design.

7.5 Summary and conclusions

This chapter presents a brief overview of different kinds of ICT applications in design. Whilst there are many ICT applications in design now well established, some obstacles remain in terms of information exchange and collaborative design systems are still being developed. Some overview of research in this area is provided. Based on case studies carried out by ITCBP and Movement for Innovation (M4I), here are some important points to bear in mind as pointers to best practice in relation to applications of ICT in design (ITCBP and M4I websites):

- Ensure the commitment of all partners.

- Ensure that the ICT infrastructure, both in terms of hardware as well as software for all partners concerned, can support the kind of tools to be used on a project.

- Do not be over-ambitious in expecting hugely different benefits accruing out of ICT. Expect incremental improvement and benefits.

- Assign ample resources dedicated to the ICT activities. Consider it as a mainstream activity with due respect accorded to any such activity.

- Introduction of a new tool should be gradual and an on-going training programme for the staff using it must be in place.

References

Anumba, C. J. and Newnham, L. N., 'Towards the Use of Distributed Artificial Intelligence in Collaborative Building Design', *Proc., 1st Intl Conf. on New Information Technologies for Decision Making in Civil Engineering*, E. T. Miresco (ed.), Sheraton Hotel, Montreal, Canada, 11–13 Oct. 1998, pp. 413–24.
Coyne R., Rosenman M., Balachandran B., *et al, Knowledge-based Design Systems*, Addison–Wesley (1989).
Egan J., 'Rethinking Construction', Report of the Construction Task Force on the Scope for Improving the Quality and Efficiency of UK Construction, Department of the Environment, Transport and the Regions (DETR) (1998).
Rivard H. and Fenves S. J., 'Representation for Conceptual Design of Buildings', *ASCE Journal of Computing in Civil Engineering*, Vol. 14, No. 3, July 2000, pp. 151–59.
BuildOnline, www.buildonline.com
ITCBP (Information Technology Construction Best Practice), www.itcbp.org.uk
M4I (Movement for Innovation), www.m4i.org.uk

Key Reading

Kamara, J. M., Anumba, C. J. and Evbuomwan N. F. O., *Capturing client requirements in construction projects*, Thomas Telford (2002).

Phiri, P., *IT in Construction Design*, Thomas Telford (1999).

Platt, D. G., 'Building Process Models for Design Management', *ASCE Journal of Computing in Civil Engineering*, Vol. 10, No. 3, July 1996, pp. 194–203.

Retik, A. and Langford, D., *Computer Integrated Planning and Design for Construction*, Thomas Telford (2001).

Procurement

Procurement systems

Steve Rowlinson, Department of Real Estate and Construction,
University of Hong Kong, and
Tom Kvan, Department of Architecture, University of Hong Kong, Hong Kong

8.1 Introduction

Procurement concerns the acquisition of project resources, and contract strategy is the strategic decision concerning how these project resources are put together and the structure of the project team is governed. The authors set out a clear definition of the variables that must be considered in selecting a contract strategy but then go on to discuss the roles that individuals play in the project team (actually project coalition). Key issues such as integration and co-ordination are introduced and the parallel between these and the co-operative and collaborative approaches espoused in relational contracting is drawn out.

8.2 What is procurement?

Procurement is about the acquisition of project resources for the realisation of a constructed facility. This is illustrated conceptually in Figure 8.1 which has been adapted from the International Labour Office (Austen and Neale, 1984). The figure clearly illustrates the construction project as the focal point at which a whole series of resources coalesce. For the purposes of this chapter, the following definition is proposed: 'Procurement is a strategy to satisfy the client's (owner's) development and/or operational needs with respect to the provision of constructed facilities for a discrete life-cycle' (adopted by CIB W92 in 1998). This emphasises that the procurement strategy must cover all of the processes in which the owner has an interest, perhaps the whole span of the life of the building.

At the simplest level the client can be regarded as the sponsor of the building process; the organisation that initiates the building process and appoints the building team. Newcombe (1994) identified a change in the nature of the client from an individual to a corporation, from a unitary body or single person to a series of stakeholders. Walker and Kalinowski (1994) give a good example of the complexity of the client organisation in their description of the construction of the Convention and Exhibition Centre extension in Hong Kong.

8.3 Contract strategy – procurement systems

Previously, in periods of buoyant demand, the traditional approach to contract strategy has dominated the industry. This approach is characterised by the appointment of a principal adviser, normally an architect, who leads the design team which is assembled through recommendation. The building project is designed and detailed up to a point where the various elements of the design can be taken-off and worked-up into a bill of quantities. At this stage the builder is invited to bid for

Figure 8.1: Procurement: the acquisition of project resources

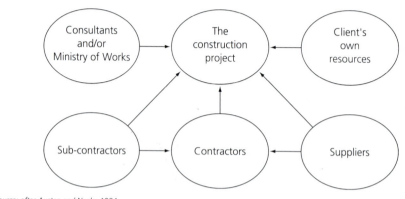

Source: after Austen and Neale, 1984

the construction work and, if successful, is expected to start on-site within a few days with very little knowledge or understanding of the building to be constructed and, probably, having made no acquaintance with the owner for whom the building is to be produced. The traditional method has been criticised for its slowness, due to the sequential nature of the work, and the incidence of time and cost overruns, attributed in part to the lack of input by the builder during the design phase. Its advocates point to its flexibility in allowing a wide choice of consultants and builders, and to the fact that it has flourished for most of the 20th century.

The alternatives to this approach fall into two main categories, the design-build approach and the management (or consultant builder) approach. Design-build methods offer single point responsibility for the owner with one organisation, generally a building company, contracting to fulfil all the design and construction responsibilities for the project. This approach has been criticised on two counts: firstly, architects have denigrated the architectural quality of buildings produced thus; secondly, the quantity surveying profession has cast doubts on the value for money obtained by entering into such contracts which are commonly assumed to be let by negotiation. These criticisms are countered by design-builders claiming to build more quickly and more efficiently. Management approaches allow the builder to have an input into the design phase without disturbing the principle of divided responsibility. They are believed to lead to rapid and efficient construction but may reduce price competition or add an extra consultant to the team, and so fee, to the bill.

At the simplest level the owner can be regarded as the sponsor of the building process; the organisation that initiates the building process and appoints the building team. This owner has an identified need for a project but, generally, its business is not construction but some other process; be that manufacturing, sale or rental of property, commerce, retail, services or other productive processes. Central to the

Figure 8.2: Contract strategy

Traditional approach
Accelerated traditional
Management contracting   Increasing
Construction management   integration
Project management   of design
Design and build/turnkey   and
Build operate transfer   construction

International Labour Office model is the owner's own resources that are supplemented by the construction industry participants; that is, the consultants and the contractors along with the suppliers and sub-contractors. The model clearly illustrates the need for the acquisition of resources in order to realise the project. This acquisition of resources is part of the procurement system – note, only a part of the system. This part of the system can be referred to as the contract strategy; that is, the process of combining these necessary resources together. The contract strategy is not the procurement system but only a part of it: the rationale behind this definition is that the procurement system involves other features such as culture, management, economics, environment and political issues.

Conventionally, contract strategies have been described as, for example, the traditional approach, construction management or build-operate-transfer. However, writers such as Ireland (1984) and Walker (1994) indicated that there is little difference between many of these supposedly alternative strategies. This situation has occurred due to a reluctance by many writers to clearly delineate the various variables which make up a contract strategy. The list given in Figure 8.2 indicates an increasing integration of design and construction expertise within the one organisation as one works down the list. However, to assume that these labels will uniquely define a contract strategy is a false supposition. What is needed is a set of key variables which can uniquely define a contract strategy rather than the arbitrary list of definitions given in the figure.

Why has this range of contract strategies developed within the construction industry? One of the reasons is illustrated in Figure 8.3, the vicious circles in the construction procurement process. The logic behind the model is that each participant wishes to obtain as much as possible from the process in terms of its own financial rewards. Given the fact that the process takes place in a competitive market there is a cycle of fluctuating pressure on prices at all times. A downward pressure thus forces the contracting participant to look to alternative means to recoup its profit. This leads to claims of conscious behaviour and can also stimulate reductions in quality and functional performance. As a consequence, the owner and its advisers are forced into the position of exerting greater surveillance over the contractor in order to minimise the effects of this behaviour. As can be seen from the figure this results

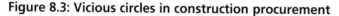

Figure 8.3: Vicious circles in construction procurement

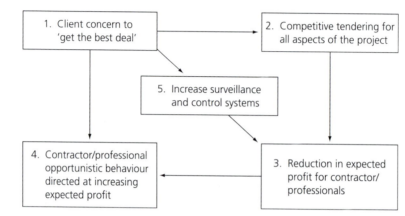

Source: Reproduced by kind permission of CIRIA

in a vicious cycle of negative behaviours. One way of avoiding this model, which is based around the traditional contract strategy, is to adopt alternative contract strategies.

Factors have combined to force the construction industry into the position where it has to change to survive.

8.3.1 Relational contracting

In recent years relational contracting, which embraces and underpins various approaches, such as partnering, alliancing, joint venturing, and other collaborative working arrangements, and better risk sharing mechanisms has become a popular mechanism for avoiding this vicious circle. Relational contracts are usually long-term, develop and change over time, and involve substantial relations between the parties.

Partnering is defined as a structured management approach to facilitate team working across contractual boundaries. Partnering is primarily concerned with 'maximising effectiveness' and partnering has three essential components:

1 Establishment of agreed and understood mutual objectives;

2 A methodology for quick and co-operative problem resolution;

3 A culture of continuous, measured improvement.

Strategic alliances enable organisations to speed up the market-entry process and increase their responsiveness to consumer markets. A project alliance (strategic alliance) is a business strategy where sponsor and commercial participants' objectives (client's objectives) are aligned to:

- Maximise performance;
- Reduce cost;
- Achieve outstanding results in the sponsor's key project objective.

As for partnering and relational contracting, trust between strategic alliance partners is important because it creates an opportunity and willingness for further alignment, reduces the need for partners to continually monitor one another's behaviour, reduces the need for formal controls, and reduces the tensions created by short-term inequities. Hamel (1989) suggests that organisations that enter into collaborative alliances (short-term) are aware that their partners are capable of disarming them. Parties to these alliances have clear objectives and understand that their partner's objectives will affect their success. Co-operative alliances (long-term) encourage alliance partners to commit their resources to the relationship to generate mutual learning (Love and Gunasekaran, 1999). Ketelholm (1993) suggests that co-operative strategic alliances can create a competitive advantage.

8.4 Organisation theory and the project process

8.4.1 Interdependence

A theme which for many years has come out of the procurement systems literature is interdependence. This interdependence is both in terms of the construction process and also the organisational structure. It is typical of project-based organisations and is a key consideration in the analysis and design of the organisation structures, and the relationships in the construction project team. In analysing and designing contract strategies this interdependence of both the organisations in the project team and the tasks in the construction process present special problems which most owners have not faced before. (Owners of constructed facilities are generally not singular entities but organisations, within which exist different departments, interests, objectives and viewpoints. It is these client organisations which have to be managed in the procurement process.) As a consequence of this factor, the design of the project organisation presents unique problems for many construction owner bodies and this, in part, can be seen as a cause of the discontent expressed with the performance of the construction industry by many owners. In this context, the choice of an appropriate contract strategy takes on great significance.

8.4.2 Differentiation and specialisation

The construction industry is also characterised by high degrees of specialisation, as evidenced by the many independent professions represented on a typical construction project and this specialisation inevitably leads to high degrees of differentiation. Walker (2002) discusses this in the context of organisational design and identifies four levels of differentiation operating in the industry, namely, time, territory, task and sentient differentiation. This neatly sums up, in theoretical terms, the nature of the construction project team which is characterised by small groups of professionals working in different locations on specialist tasks that are all interdependent. The differentiation of the contractor from the rest of the team is most apparent and is highlighted by the different process of contractor appointment and payment compared with the consultants. Conventionally, the design and construction process, when broken down into its constituent parts, is seen as sequential and leading to the smooth flow of individual contributions through a project life-cycle. This view is, of course, unrealistic and what happens in reality is that contributions are refined and revised and the new information is passed backwards for further analysis and re-design. This recycling of work is a source of frustration and friction to participants who are working to the conventional model.

8.4.3 Integration and co-ordination

The necessary corollary to this specialisation of the contributors to the construction project is the process of integration and co-ordination. Integration may be achieved by adapting the organisation structure to fit the degree of differentiation present in the team. Examples of this in the construction industry are the appointment of a project manager who acts as an integrating device linking team members together or the use of design-build methods. Each of these is seen as a method of drawing the separate specialist functions of the construction process together and bringing down the barriers that exist between the separate organisations in the project team.

8.4.4 Universal versus contingency approaches

The search for the best contract strategy has been the topic of many articles and papers over the years. However, if one adopts a contingency theory view of procurement systems then it is possible to identify a range of contingency factors which will impinge upon the effectiveness of the strategy chosen. Many researchers (for instance, Ireland, 1984; Walker 1994) have identified contingency factors on construction projects and assessed their impact on project performance. Others have attempted to develop from such research a methodology for choosing a best contract strategy (e.g. Skitmore and Marsden, 1988). Liu (1995) has identified the fact that perceptions of project performance vary amongst members of the project team and within the client body. Hence, the problem of choosing a best contract strategy becomes almost impossible as each participant will bring to the debate their own views and values rendering the choice of a best system impossible. This raises the issue of expectations and perceptions – systems often fail, not because of inherent system weaknesses, but because people do not get what they thought they were due.

8.5 Generic strategies

Much of the literature in this area uses terminology such as the traditional approach, design and build, build-operate-transfer, management contracting, etc. In order to

Figure 8.4: The traditional approach

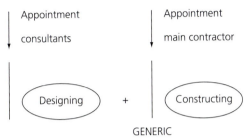

GENERIC

Source: after Austen and Neale, 1984

clearly define the parameters being considered in this book, a generic taxonomy of organisational forms is given below. The function of this taxonomy is to provide a clear and simple description of construction project organisation forms which, when taken with other contract strategy variables, uniquely define a strategy which is further clarified when put in the context of the overall procurement system.

8.5.1 Traditional

The traditional (or conventional) approach is shown diagrammatically in Figure 8.4 and its key characteristic is the separation of the design and construction processes and the lack of integration across this boundary, along with the employment of a whole series of separate consultants to design the project and an independent contractor to take charge of the construction process. Typically, the project team will be led by an architect charged with the responsibility for both designing and project managing the project. Other consultants will join the design and administration team (such as structural engineers and quantity surveyors) through the life of the project and the contractor will be selected from a competitive tendering process on a fixed price bid. The contractor's input to the design process will be minimal, often nil, and in many countries most of the production work on-site will be sub-contracted to other organisations. The design and construction processes and their sub-tasks are seen as sequential and independent.

8.5.2 Design-build

⇒ QUALITY of DESIGN NOT AS GOOD.

The design-build approach is characterised by the single point responsibility offered to the client by the contractor and the opportunity for overlapping the design and construction phases which stems from this unitary approach. As with the traditional approach, there are many variants on the basic theme of design and build. Of particular interest are the variants which include project financing and which go under the headings of build-operate-transfer, build-own-operate-transfer, build-own-manage and the like. The organisation of a design and build project is more complex than the traditional project at the tender stage as the situation will often

---

Figure 8.5: The design-and-construct approach

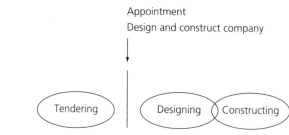

Source: after Austen and Neale, 1984

occur where different priced bids with different design solutions are competing for the same project (Figure 8.5). The adjudication of such bids is a complex process and requires, to be fair to all bidders, some assessment scheme to be put in place before bids are submitted.

The underlying principle behind the design-build system is that the client body contracts with one organisation for the whole of the design and construction process; the concept of single point responsibility exists. This and the overlapping of the design and construction phases, are the underlying principles behind design-build systems. Hence, this can be considered as one of the three generic types of organisation forms in contract strategy and each form of design-build can be uniquely defined by addressing the status of the other contract strategy variables, such as leadership, selection process, payment systems, etc.

For a detailed discussion of design-build forms, see chapters 2 and 12 of Rowlinson and McDermott (1999).

8.5.3 *Divided contract approach*

The divided contract approach is illustrated diagrammatically in Figure 8.6. The key principle in this form is the separation of the managing and operating systems. It can be clearly seen that the project organisation is over-arched by a managing system. This managing system is generally provided by a management contractor or a construction manager or a project manager. The tasks of design and construction are undertaken by separate organisations which specialise in the technical aspects of the process and their inputs are integrated and co-ordinated by the management organisation. The high degree of specialisation allows for the fast-tracking of the project which is the fundamental characteristic of this type of organisation form.

The nature of this type of project organisation, and the underlying goal of providing a specialist management role, necessitates that the managing organisation is appointed at the outset of the project and the role of the contractor is one of consultant builder rather than constructor. This change in role leads to a reshaping

Figure 8.6: The divided contract approach

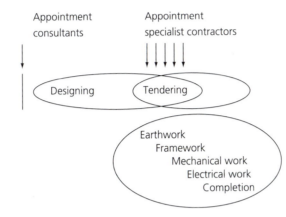

Source: after Austen and Neale, 1984

of the roles that all of the other professionals play and so there is scope for role ambiguity and conflict to arise. Hence, it is essential that roles and reporting relationships are clearly defined at the outset and that those consultants providing technical services are fully aware of the limits of their authority and responsibility. This management role is increasingly being undertaken by management consultants and is a threat to the traditional construction industry participants who may find themselves distanced from their client base if this trend continues.

8.6 Contract strategy variables

It should now be clear from the foregoing discussion that the organisation form adopted cannot uniquely define the contract strategy being used. This takes us back to Ireland's (1984) concept of 'virtually meaningless distinctions between nominally different procurement forms'. In order to more clearly define contract strategy, a minimum of eight separate variables must be considered. These are identified as follows:

Organisation form

This variable has been discussed in detail above and it defines the responsibilities of each of the disciplines in the project life-cycle.

Payment methods

Payment methods, particularly for contractors, are either cost-based or price-based. The latter places more risk in the hands of the contractor, whilst the former places more risk at the feet of the client. Veld and Peeters (1989) in their paper 'Keeping large projects under control: the importance of contract type selection' discuss seven different payment methods and indicate the advantages and disadvantages of each.

Overlap of project phases

This variable defines the degree of acceleration or fast tracking that is desired within the construction process. In most instances it would be true to say that the traditional process is difficult to fast track and little overlap occurs with this organisation form, but varying degrees of overlap occur with both the design-build and the divided contract approaches.

Selection process

Contractors may be selected by open competition, select competition among an unlimited number of pre-qualified contractors or by negotiation in one or more stages.

Source of project finance

The source of project finance can have a significant impact on the contract strategy and procurement system chosen. If the client body provides finance then it essentially has a free hand in the choice of strategy, but if third parties or the contractor organisation provides part or all of the finance then strings will be attached.

Contract documents

The contract documents used in construction projects are, in the main, drafted by the clients or industry bodies with representatives from all parties. Most important is the appropriateness of the documents to the type of contract strategy being used. Issues such as the degree of completion of drawings at commencement of construction and the use, or not, of bills of quantities or schedules of rates are important considerations.

Leadership

An important strategic decision is the choice of project team leader. Any of the project participants, including the client, can take up this role. The choice of leader should be based on a number of factors including personality, expertise and experience, and an analysis of the roles and responsibilities to be allocated to the participants.

Authority and responsibility

The distribution of authority and responsibility are important issues in any organisation and the design of the distribution of these is of paramount importance in project organisations, which have the characteristics of temporary multi-organisations.

Table 8.1: Hypothesised performance of 'organisation forms'

	Traditional	*Design & Build*	*Divided Contract*
Speed	Low	High	High
Cost	Medium	Low	High
Potential for incorporating variations	High	Low	High
Cost certainty	Medium	Medium	Low
Occupational Health & Safety management	Low	High	High

8.7 Performance

The performance of different organisation forms, and indeed contract strategies, has been the subject of much research over the past 20 years. No definitive outcome has stemmed from this research but a series of commonly held beliefs can be presented in Table 8.1 above. The reader should be aware that comparison of the performance of the different organisation forms is fraught with difficulty and the opinion expressed below cannot be relied upon in all circumstances.

8.7.1 The fallacy of cost certainty

Adopting the traditional approach based on full drawings and bills of quantities should give the client a firm, fixed price for construction but, in practice, very few projects are actually completed within the tendered price. Indeed, the crux of the matter is that full drawings and a complete bill are often not available when the project goes to tender.

8.8 Case study

The client, an airport authority, was seeking to expand their capacity and attractiveness as a hub. Already one of the busiest airports in the nation and operating at capacity, the airport had been approached by a major airline tenant to double capacity on their terminal. The project cost was estimated in the realm of several hundred million pounds.

The airport management went through the traditional procedures to secure a design team and to bring in a contractor. The owner, as client, took on the role of project manager, providing leadership to the project. The airline assigned one person to be the user representative, especially to monitor the progress since airline schedules were being changed to take advantage of the greater passenger capacity of the expanded terminal. Since time was of the essence, the project was fast-tracked; the contractor was brought on board soon after design started such that the completion time could be accelerated.

One year into the process, the building was under construction. The architect had designed the building form and basic layout, the engineers had analysed the structure. Detailed design of the interiors was underway. The contractor had started to prepare the site, ordered the structural frame and expected to start erecting the main structure before long. Soon, however, the contractor found himself at logger-heads with the design consultants and started to inform the owner that requests for extra costs would be forthcoming arising from inadequate communication with the design consultants; delays were also threatened. Since this was early in the process, the owner interpreted this as a harbinger of a strife-laden future for the project and wished to minimise possible problems. Coming from a corporate culture of trust, it did not want the team hiding behind contractual barriers in an antagonistic manner. The owner therefore turned its attention to the relationships between the parties and examined what might be done to facilitate the project process.

With the help of a consultant, the owner explored alternative methods to improve the process. After the consultant interviewed the participants, it was discovered that the core problem arose from the conflicts of expectations from the project. Project roles, contributions and deliverables had all been spelled out in the contracts the owner had placed with each participant, but the participants had no agreement between them as to their responsibilities and obligations to each other. The model of responsibilities, therefore, was radial, with the owner at the hub. In a fast-track context, this radial model of responsibility was failing to work. The procurement relationships and forms failed to support the complex network of responsibilities that a fast-tracked project had accentuated.

To address this difficulty, the owner realised that the problem was not in the contracts and records of formal relationships, but lay in the informal obligations implied in the contracts. What was hindering communication was a failure to understand the roles of each participant and the obligations they brought to others within their firms but not present in the project at hand. The team was brought together to review the situation, stated in terms of 'increasing *teamsmanship*'. Agreement was reached that the problem was indeed the divergence of goals, and hence priorities in decision making, and a remedial process started. In the course of the first meeting, concerns of each party were identified as 'pressure points' that reflected the key aspects of each parties' world. The strategy used was not to change the contractual arrangements but to build group support for the divergent goals with a mechanism to accommodate the various pressure points. The various parties came to greater understanding of each other's perspectives of the project, in particular of the problems in the design activities of such a complex project. A process was established for collective decision making when major problems threatened progress, hence sharing responsibility for solving problems and avoiding assignment of blame as the first reaction. This process followed the partnering model and changed the project process without contractual changes being needed. Procurement documents alone were inadequate to provide the framework for the project.

8.9 Roles

With the foregoing case study in mind it is now appropriate to discuss the concept of role and its relation to the building team. Kast and Rosenweig (1974) defined the concept of role as:

> ... relating to the activities of an individual in a particular position. It describes the behaviour he/she is expected to exhibit when occupying a given position in the societal or organisational system.

Specialists (or professionals) operating in conjunction with other specialists from different domains are faced with role conflict, ambiguity and inter-group conflict. Klauss and Bass (1982), in a study of inter-personal communications, argue that the literature indicates that role clarity (lack of ambiguity) leads to organisation effectiveness. Katz and Kahn (1978) use the concept of role as the linking pin between the individual and the organisation (and others within the organisation). The roles played by the actors in the building team have their origin and development in history and, until recently, had atrophied into the frozen roles of the traditional system. New interpretations of old lines (of demarcation) lead to new procurement forms; a different view of the process, a paradigm shift. Each actor has certain expectations when playing their role and the formal and informal controls in the process allow them to fulfil these, but only if they are aware of how the director is interpreting the play.

Hersey and Blanchard (1972) discuss the process of change using the phases of unfreezing, change, refreezing. Unfreezing is the breaking down of old ways of doing things so that an individual is ready to accept new alternatives; the driving forces for change are increased. In construction, the introduction of new methods of procurement, the push for change by clients, exposure to foreign competition and the downturn in workload can be seen as media bringing about unfreezing. Hersey and Blanchard argue that change occurs through learning new patterns of behaviour and this comes about through internalisation (new behaviours are persistently demanded of the individual) and identification (behaviour is learnt by identification with the presented models).

If one attempts to extend this concept and relate it to building teams one might propose that individuals in specialist design-build and construction management organisations change and adapt to their new roles by internalisation whilst those who work with such organisations on an irregular basis change by identification. Schein (1961) contends that internalisation 'automatically facilitated refreezing' into the new role whereas identification 'persists only so long as the ... original influence model persists'. Thus, such propositions indicate that individuals and teams engaged in the same procurement form regularly (or who have an established relationship) are likely to have their new roles constantly reinforced and so refrozen.

8.9.1 Relationships

A major factor in the smooth running of the building process is the relationship between the resource controllers and stakeholders in the various professions represented in the construction team. As the Tavistock report (Higgin, 1965) points out:

> The central problem arises from the fact that the basic relationship which exists among resource controllers has the character of interdependent autonomy. There is a lack of match between the technical interdependence of the resources and the organisational independence of those who control them.

Thus, Tavistock viewed the social system, the relationships between resource controllers, as a major problem. Why is this social system a problem? The answer lies in the people involved, they have their own reasons for being involved in the project and a set of needs to be fulfilled from the project. These are almost certainly going to conflict with other team members and so the client's objective, a successful project, may not be top of anyone else's list of objectives. As Cyert and March (1963) pointed out: organisations do not have objectives, only people have objectives. Thus, the client's objective of a successful project is subsumed into the social system which is characterised by:

> Participants... excessively concerned with their roles *vis a vis* each other. Participants are insufficiently responsive to the needs of the manufacturing industry (Graves, 1978).

The coalition

It is clear that what is thought to be a team is really a coalition, 'a temporary combination for special ends between parties that retain distinctive principles'.

The characteristics of the coalition (Cyert and March, 1963) are as follows:

- It has shifting and multiple goals.

- Management time is spent more on controlling the coalition and so less on controlling the environment in which the coalition operates.

- Its objectives vary between members and over time, thus requiring a consensus to be reached by a satisfying technique.

- Uncertainties will exist due to professional and organisational barriers which are manifested in communication problems.

- The worst scenario is for conflicting objectives to generate dissent and so the need for members to leave the coalition.

The coalition needs to be managed so that dissenting views are avoided and roles are harmonised. This can be done by modifying the expectations of the participants to fit the particular process and by operating the coalition in a controlled environment –

this implies using tested, well known and understood methods and so is an inhibitor to innovation. Even so, claims, contingencies and crisis management are inevitable consequences of the coalition as described: the side payments referred to by Cyert and March (1963) which 'represent the central process of goal specification . . . policy commitments'.

If the above view of the people and relationships in the building process is accepted, its implication for contract strategies is manifest. Any system which moves away from the conflicting goals of a coalition and towards the unified effort of a team is likely to be more efficient and effective. The problem of individuals having their own peculiar goals within any organisation will always exist but a system which allows organisations to co-operate with one another is obviously advantageous. This probably explains the current trend towards relational contracting in a complex, changing world.

8.10 Conclusions

In devising and implementing an appropriate contract strategy the following key points are important to bear in mind:

- Vicious circles exist in the construction procurement process.

- A strategic alliance is a business strategy where sponsor and commercial participants' objectives are aligned and can create a competitive advantage.

- Interdependence and specialisation have to be balanced by integration and co-ordination.

- A set of key variables exist which can uniquely define a contract strategy.

- A contingency view should be adopted in making the strategic decision on choice of contract strategy (which involves at least eight different variables).

- The roles played by the participants have to be unfrozen and changed, by internalisation and identification, depending on the strategy chosen.

- The interdependent autonomy of the resource controllers in the project team has to be recognised and managed (as the construction team is essentially a coalition).

- The principles behind relational contracting potentially provide the environment to address these issues.

References

Austen, A. D. and Neale, R. H. (eds) *Managing Construction Projects – A Guide to Processes and Procedures*, International Labour Office (ILO), Geneva (1984).
Cyert, R. M. and March, J. G., *A Behavioural Theory of the Firm*, Prentice-Hall, New Jersey, USA (1963).

Graves, F., *Construction for Industrial Recovery*, NEDO, London (1978) p. 7.

Hamel, G. 'Collaborate with your competitors – and win', *Harvard Business Review*, Jan.–Feb. 1989, pp. 133–39.

Hersey, P. and Blanchard, K. H., 'The Management of Change: Part 3 – Planning and Implementing Change', *Training and Development Journal*, Mar. 1972, pp. 28–33.

Higgin, G. and Jessop, N., *Communications in the Building Industry*, Tavistock, London (1965) p. 77.

Ireland, V., 'Virtually meaningless distinctions between nominally different procurement forms', in *CIB W65 Proc. of the 4th Intl Symp. on Organization and Management of Construction*, University of Waterloo, Canada, Vol. 1, pp. 203–12 (1984).

Kast, F. E. and Rosenweig, J. E., *Organization and Management: A Systems Approach*, McGraw-Hill, New York, USA, (1974), p. 261.

Katz, D. and Kahn, R. L., *The Social Psychology of Organizations*, Wiley, New York (1978).

Ketelholm, W., 'What do we mean by cooperative advantage?', *European Management Journal*, 11(1), 1993, pp. 30–7.

Klauss, R. and Bass, B. M., *Interpersonal Communication in Organizations*, Academic Press, New York (1982) p. 43.

Liu, A. M. M., *Analysis of Organizational Structures in Building Projects*, PhD thesis, Department of Surveying, The University of Hong Kong, Hong Kong (1995).

Love, P. E. D. and Gunasekaran, A., 'Learning Alliances: a Customer-Supplier Focus for Continuous Improvement in Manufacturing', *Industrial and Commercial Training*, 31(3), 1999, pp. 88–96.

Newcombe, R. 'Procurement paths – A power paradigm', in S. M. Rowlinson (ed.) *East Meets West, Proc. of CIB W92 Procurement Systems Symp.*, Department of Surveying, The University of Hong Kong, Hong Kong, Dec. 1994, pp. 243–50.

Rowlinson, S. and McDermott, P. (eds), *Procurement Systems: A Guide to Good Practice*, E&FN Spon, London (1999).

Schein, E. H. 'Management Development as a Process of Influence', *Industrial Management Review*, Vol. II, No. 2, May 1961, pp. 59–77, quoted in Hersey and Blanchard, 1972.

Skitmore, R. M. and Marsden, D. E. 'Which procurement system? Towards a universal procurement selection technique', *Construction Management and Economics*, **6**, 1988, pp. 71–89.

Veld, J. and Peeters, W. A. 'Keeping large projects under control: The importance of contract type selection', in *Project Management*, Butterworth & Co. (Publishers) Ltd., 7, **3**, Aug. 1989.

Walker, A., *Project Management in Construction*, 4th edn, Blackwell Science, Oxford (2002).

Walker, A. and Kalinowski, M., 'An anatomy of a Hong Kong project – organisation, environment and leadership', *Construction Management and Economics*, 12, 1994, pp. 191–202.

Walker, D. H. T., *An Investigation into Factors that Determine Building Construction Time Performance*, PhD thesis, Department of Building and Construction Economics, RMIT University, Melbourne, Australia (1994).

Key Reading

Bennett, J. and Jayes, S. *The Seven Pillars of Partnering: A Guide to Second Generation Partnering*, Reading Construction Forum, Thomas Telford Publications, London (1998).

Rowlinson, S. and McDermott, P. (eds), *Procurement Systems: A Guide to Good Practice*, E&FN Spon, London (1999).

Walker, A., *Project Management in Construction,* 4th edn, Blackwell Science, Oxford (2002).

Procurement, contracts and conditions of engagement

David Greenwood, School of the Built Environment, Northumbria University, Newcastle-upon-Tyne, UK, and
Peter Walker, School of Architecture, Planning and Landscape, University of Newcastle, and DEWJOC Architects, Newcastle-upon-Tyne, UK

9.1 Introduction

The selection of appropriate procurement and contractual arrangements for a project requires the consideration of a number of criteria that vary with projects and with project clients.

The case study illustrates how a procurement strategy was developed for a project with specific needs, and the way in which a relatively innovative system emerged from the criteria that were set. A different approach was used towards the design consultants and construction contractors, although ultimately both had to work and both had to be merged. Both elements of the combined approach involved the service-suppliers (the design consultants and the contractor) in entering non-traditional 'territory', offering the potential for each group to increase their knowledge-base 'upstream'.

9.2 The key concepts

Definitions are notoriously difficult to establish, but for the sake of simplicity we will refer to the entire nexus of a project's procurement and contractual arrangements (including the engagement of consultants) by the term 'procurement system'. A project's procurement system can have important implications for its cost, gestation period and function, as well as for how the participants come together, interact, communicate and are motivated. In short, the procurement system can have a critical effect on a project's success. The overall concept – *procurement system* – can, in fact, be thought of as comprising at least four distinguishable elements: the *organisation of inputs* for the project; the *relationships of the participants*; the *reimbursement regimes* for these participants, and the *contractual arrangements* that bind all of them together. The four are inter-linked, but initially it is useful to consider them separately. It is also useful to make an occasional 'artificial' split between the way these elements relate to the project's consultancy services and to its physical construction. The two are, of course, inter-related and, indeed, the trend in the UK construction industry is toward their evermore intimate linking. It will also be seen from the case study of The Devonshire Building that a key objective of the procurement system adopted was to bridge the design and construction gap. For all four elements of the procurement system the criteria for choice, typically, include:

- Time and cost constraints;

- Requirement for certainty, single point responsibility and the overall risk attitude of the client;

- The required level of client commitment and involvement;

- Requirements for functionality, design quality and innovation;

- The need for flexibility; and, particularly in the public sector,

- Rules of public accountability and procurement.[1]

Criteria such as these will be evident in the case study. It must be remembered, however, that projects differ: there is no magic formula, single set of choices or perfect procurement system to suit all.

9.2.1 Organisation of the inputs

Projects involve a range of different inputs, including finance, design, management, installation, provision of materials and plant, and sometimes the maintenance and running of the facility. Because of the structure of the industry's supply-side these project inputs often come from a multiplicity of sources in a variety of combinations. Economic, political and technical influences tend to push one or another delivery method to the fore, and sometimes cause new methods to emerge. These methods are often classified as 'separated', 'integrated' and 'management systems' (e.g. by Masterman, 1992).

Separated systems: traditional general contracting

Traditionally, design and other consultancy services are provided by independent or in-house designers (architect, engineer) in direct contract with the building promoter, while a separate contract for the construction of the project is placed with a contractor. The consultant team see the project through the various stages from establishing the feasibility and financial viability of the project, through the design (including negotiating and securing statutory approvals); preparing the production information – the specifications and drawings for the building; assembling the tender and contract documents; and inspecting and supervising the works on site. The system is characterised by a nexus of contracts between the employer, their agents, designers, and a main contractor, whose involvement and responsibility is limited to the construction phase of the project. For the client, the advantages of this system lie in the fact that design is retained by its appointed designers, affording the possibility of close control of the specification and realisation of product. Advantages to the supply-side (main-, sub-contractors and suppliers) include limited liability and relatively low bidding costs. The system is tried and tested and well understood by most parties. The perceived disadvantages lie in the separation of the design, procurement and construction phases. This adds time to the process. It also limits opportunities for early and direct communication between designers, contractors and (in particular) their specialist suppliers: the project may therefore miss out on the benefit of their specialised knowledge, particularly concerning buildability and value for money. The arrangement is normally combined with lump-sum reimbursement and selective tendering (see below) to form the full procurement system described as 'traditional'.

Integrated systems: design and build, design & construct and package deals

These methods became increasingly popular during the 1980s and 1990s (Franks, 1984). The contracting organisation undertakes both the design and construction of a project. The greatest impact is on the way in which consultancy services are delivered: there being various possible levels of employer-involvement, ranging from 'pure' design and build (where the contractor has the opportunity to control a substantial part of the project's design) to extreme situations where the entire design control is retained by the employer, but the ultimate liability for the design is passed to a contractor. The most popular variant involves the novation – or switch – of the design team from the building promoter to the building contractor (Chappell, 1997). Typically, the design team prepare the scheme design – general arrangement plans, elevations, sections and outline or performance specifications – on behalf of the building promoter. These form the basis of the tender documentation (the Employer's Requirements) on which the tendering contractors base their offer (the Contractor's Proposal). Once the contract is let, the design team (but normally not the quantity surveyor) is novated to the building contractor; is retained by the contractor until the conclusion of the project, and produces the production information on the instructions of the contractor. The service delivered for the contractor differs fundamentally from that which would have been delivered for the employer, in that the function of the drawings and the specifications is simply to describe what is to be built. They are not contract documents. For this reason, the drawings are always simpler and therefore cheaper for the consultant team to produce. Package deals or turnkey projects and integrated design and build – where the design and build functions are carried out within the same firm – are rare in the UK.

A number of advantages are claimed for integrated systems. For the client, there will be less up-front expenditure on contract documentation and the likelihood of a more economic design for construction (although savings may not necessarily be passed on to the client). There will be single point responsibility, with the possibility of passing all major risks (including those of maintaining cost and time certainty) to the supply-side. Perhaps most importantly, the integration of design and construction within the same team permits much shorter overall project time periods. Despite the disadvantages of higher bidding costs and risks, the system offers the contractor almost total control of all aspects from design to commissioning. This offers scope for 'value engineering' and 'buildability', and an enhanced opportunity to manage risk in return for reward. The disadvantages to the client are in the loss of direct control at the point at which design responsibility is transferred to the contractor. The contractor's commercial objective will invariably be economy of design, although appropriate output specifications, in the form of a considered and effective set of Employer's Requirements, should guard against quality being compromised. The system also demands earlier and firmer commitment to these requirements. The client may not enjoy the luxury of flexibility, since giving up control of the design may mean that any post-award changes in client's requirements will be difficult, or at best expensive. These integrated systems readily lend themselves to a guaranteed maximum price reimbursement (see below) to reinforce the client's certainty of cost and time.

Management systems: management contracting, construction management and design & management

The concept of procuring a project's management input separately is based on the fact that most of the construction and, indeed, much of the design is procurable from specialist 'works' or 'trade' contractors, leaving the traditional main contractor free to engage in a consultant–managerial role. Management Contracting (MC) is often preferred where time is of major importance or the project is complex. Construction Management (CM) is a variant that originated in the USA and is common in many other countries. Its most significant feature is the direct contractual link between the client and the 'trade contractors'. There are a number of other variants within the management systems, the most prominent of which is Design & Management (D&M). This is, in fact, a hybrid of design and build and management contracting where design and construction overlap, and the construction work is packaged and procured progressively.

The main advantage of the management methods is their speed. There are two reasons for this. Firstly, the relatively 'open' nature of its commercial relationship with the client means that the management organisation (whether MC, CM or D&M) needs little lead-in time as a prelude to its involvement in the project and can thus work at an early stage with client consultants. Secondly, the fact that construction is carried out in specialist works or trade packages (overseen by the management organisation) means that their design, procurement and construction periods can be overlapped. As with the traditional procurement approach, the client retains control of the design team, thus avoiding compromise on quality, while maintaining flexibility in terms of managing and incorporating change. The management organisation itself carries little or no financial risk for the project and, consequently, can assume a more independent and 'professional' role in the project. Moreover, in business there is normally an association between risk and reward: the management role attracts relatively low fees in line with its low associated risks. The main disadvantage for the client is in regard to cost-certainty. Management systems have historically been associated with cost-plus methods of reimbursement, and choosing a conventional management system has been considered as precluding the client from the comfort of a either a lump sum or guaranteed price (see section 9.2.3 on methods of reimbursement). The same openness, speed and flexibility that characterises the relationship brings with it a lack of financial certainty prior to the commitment to build, and a lack of 'single point responsibility'. Attempts to overcome this have resulted in some interesting hybrid procurement systems, one of which is described in the case study.

9.2.2 Relationships of the participants

A project's inputs can come from a multiplicity of organisations, but there is also a variety of ways in which these organisations define their commercial relationships with one another. In fact there are two distinct dimensions: one relates to the continuity that parties ascribe to their relationship (whether it is specific to the one project, or extends beyond) while the other concerns the basis of the relationship (whether it is founded in competition or co-operation). However, these choices are not entirely at the discretion of the parties themselves: when projects are procured there are, in many cases, public policy requirements to be satisfied, and national or international procurement rules may constrain choice.

Continuity of relationship

The conventional view that construction projects are sets of one-off, discrete, contractual deals is not always the correct one. Looking at local building projects in Massachusetts, Eccles (1981) found they were more than just separate transactions and identified coalitions[2] of main- and sub-contractors that worked regularly together. In the UK, writers like Cox and Thompson (1998) have described the trend to longer-term arrangements such as framework agreements and 'serial' or 'strategic' partnering which involve long-term relationships over programmes of work rather than an individual project.[3] The advantages lie in saving the costs of re-bidding each individual project, the prospects of continuous improvement from one project to the next, and a more predictable workflow for the supply-side. Disadvantages include the chance of relationships becoming too comfortable, and the client's loss of access to 'market value' that comes with abandoning repetitive tendering. To offset these, such deals often include incentives or performance improvement regimes. In some of these longer-term agreements[4] a competitive element is retained. Each agreement must be advertised and competed for in accordance with the UK Public Procurement Regulations, implementing EC rules.

Basis of relationship

Whether relationships are extended or one-off, they need to be formed in the first place, and this is accomplished with a greater emphasis on either competition or co-operation. At the competitive end of the spectrum open and selective tendering rely on price competition as their main or only criterion.[5] However, some clients adopt a more co-operative outlook and favour negotiation, where non-price criteria play a significant part. Many decision makers use 'weighted scorecards' to achieve the balance between price and quality that is appropriate for their project. Paradoxically, as client–contractor relationships have become closer, the client–consultant relationship has become more competitive. The traditions of mandatory fees and standing relationships have given way to competition and formality. The advantages and disadvantages of the various approaches are fairly self-evident: it is often argued that 'lowest tender does not equal best value'. Since 1999 this philosophy has dominated public-sector procurement in the UK.[6] However, the benefits of 'taking the lowest bid' can be very persuasive, especially in terms of demonstrating financial probity. This philosophy is at the heart of European public procurement rules.

Two-stage tendering is a popular hybrid approach that seeks to exploit the advantages of negotiation and competition. It also accelerates the process by permitting the overlap of design and procurement. The appointment of a contractor is carried out in two stages: Stage 1 is competitive, and based on costs for preliminaries, overheads and profit; the Stage 2 appointment is made after a satisfactory open-book negotiation of the final price. Co-operation at this stage can also help bring significant value improvements, not least through the early involvement of specialist contractors.

Project-specific partnering,[7] as the term suggests, relates only to a project, and is based on a change of attitudes of the participants, sometimes involving 'open-book' costing. However, it is misleading to assume that a more co-operative procurement has taken place as the co-operation may be entirely post-award and follow an intensely competitive tendering process.

9.2.3 Methods of reimbursement

There are two basic approaches to paying for any service or supply, namely a price-based, or a cost-based approach. The former typically involves a price (often, though not necessarily, submitted in competition) for a given output, while in the case of the latter, the provider is reimbursed for its inputs (for example, the costs of the time and materials expended). In the case of price-based reimbursement, the risks of process inefficiency lie with the supplier, whereas the purchaser is at more risk with a cost-based system. For this reason, cost-based systems are not common for construction work; they are reserved for special circumstances and specific services. The various reimbursement regimes are underpinned by the delivery methods adopted: in other words, the method of setting the price is influenced by the method of delivery and vice-versa.

Paying for the construction work: price-based systems

Price-based systems include lump-sum arrangements that range from Guaranteed (Maximum) Price (GMP) to remeasurable. A guaranteed price is a common feature of projects where design control is exercised by the contractor, which is typical with a design-build delivery mode. Effectively, the contractor contracts to deliver the project within a maximum price; the impact of design changes will be absorbed within the price unless they are instigated by a change of project scope. Remeasurable contracts are characterised by the contract bill of quantities (or schedule of rates) which permit unforeseen work to be valued at prices similar to those tendered. Under this arrangement, risks of unforeseen work are shared: the contractor is protected by the re-valuation, and the employer by the fact that prices can be referenced to the original tender. This payment method is typical of traditional general contracting.

Paying for the construction work: cost-based systems

Cost-based reimbursement methods include cost-plus and target-cost. Cost-plus contracts effectively remove the risk of variable production costs from the supplier, who is reimbursed on the basis of time spent and materials used rather than on the basis of a tendered price. The employer is therefore at risk of being exploited. Management contracts are often carried out on a 'fee and expenses' basis, and there may be an incentive incorporated to ensure maximum efficiency from the management contractor. Target-cost contracts are a variant of cost-plus designed to limit the employer's risk exposure. Although the reimbursement is made, as before, on the basis of time and materials used rather than on the basis of a tendered price, a target-cost is established at the outset (usually in competition). When the out-turn cost is within the agreed target there is a sharing of the savings between the employer and the contractor; when the out-turn cost exceeds the agreed target there is a sharing of the extra cost. The precise proportions of these shares are a matter for individual negotiation.

Traditionally, the timing of payments has been based on interim (usually monthly) systems of measurement, valuation (by the quantity surveyor) and certification (by the architect) but these rely on contract bills of quantity. In the absence of these – with a design and build project, for example – payment is usually linked to pre-agreed events called 'milestones' or 'stages' which attract payments that are also pre-agreed in a schedule.

Paying for the consultancy service

There are a number of ways in which construction consultants may be reimbursed for their services. Reimbursable fees (payment based on the hours worked multiplied by pre-agreed hourly rates) are common in many professions but have been relatively unusual in construction up until the advent of open-book partnering arrangements, where the consultant's fee may be arrived at by adding an agreed overhead recovery and profit mark-up[8] to the basic hourly cost (i.e. the salary and direct on-costs of individual staff). Percentage fees are based on a percentage multiplier applied to the construction cost, thus presuming a direct relationship between this and design complexity. It is a method that has clear shortcomings for both parties: for the designer, it fails to recognise the time and ingenuity involved in producing an economic design; and to the client, it appears to reward the consultant for an extravagant design. Lump sum fees, possibly fixed to be effectively a 'guaranteed maximum price', will potentially limit the designer's efforts when they have reached a certain level.

In some cases the form of reimbursement may be mixed – for example, the early feasibility study may be paid for on a reimbursable basis and converted to a percentage fee or lump sum once the brief for the building is finalised.

Less common methods of payment include contingency fees, where payment is made dependent on some condition or performance: for example, a developer may agree to pay the consultant fees only if planning permission or land purchase is secured. Fees based on value added are extremely rare in the construction industry, although it is easy to imagine how these could be arrived at. For example, a commercial property developer may pay an enhanced fee for a building designed in such a way that it achieves a more dense site coverage, or for a building that lets quicker or on better commercial terms. Occasionally, consultants may be employed on a regular retainer – often paid on a monthly basis. This would be appropriate where a consultancy service is provided on an intermittent but regular basis; for example, an architect providing a consultant architect service to a local planning authority. Payment of royalties is common in the private housing sector where a house builder pays architects for the use of a standard house design when it is used. What all these fee arrangements share is payment based on the input value, i.e. the time spent on doing the task, rather than payment based on the value added by the service or the value added to the finished product.

Fees for longer-term arrangements such as framework agreements are typically paid as a pre-agreed percentage of the construction contract sum (like the traditional method described above) but linked to productivity improvements over time. For example, the consultants could agree that their fee percentages will reduce annually over the life of the agreement – effectively giving back a share of the financial benefit they gain from being a consultant panel member.

Traditionally, the timing of the payment of consultants fees for construction projects is linked to pre-agreed events – for example, the application for planning permission, the start on site or practical completion. The obvious disadvantage of this is the absence of any relationship to the firms outgoings (salaries, rent, etc.). This has cash flow implications and may mean that the consultant will need to tie up capital to fund outgoings. In recent years consultants have increasingly moved from this form of reimbursement to monthly payments, although many client organisations see the obvious positive benefits in reducing risk and delaying payments that arise from the stage payment system.

9.2.4 Contractual arrangements

The approach to contractual arrangements for building in post-war Britain has been characterised by a period of stability, during which standard building and consultancy contracts have been built around established procedures and traditions. These standard contracts have been extensively documented in various texts (e.g.

Chappell and Powell-Smith, 1997; Cox and Thompson, 1998; Murdoch and Hughes, 2000) and are generally well understood by the participants, although the recent tendency towards amended or experimental forms has made the situation more complicated.

Construction contracts

Of the many standard forms of contract available, the most familiar is that published by the Joint Contracts Tribunal (JCT, 1998). The changes in procurement outlined earlier have encouraged the JCT to include variant forms for Management Contracting and Design and Build. Increasingly, the JCT competes with other standard forms – for example, the New Engineering Contract (NEC) suite of contracts – and there is also a marked tendency for non-standard contracts, or amended versions of standard forms to be drafted. Essentially though, construction contracts contain terms relating to:

- Details of the parties and description of the Works;
- Employer's representative and their powers of instruction;
- Obligations (of Contractor and Employer) and sanctions for non-fulfilment;
- Time, Payment and claims for extra time and payment;
- Liabilities and Insurance;
- Quality of materials and workmanship (and, where appropriate, Design);
- Health and Safety;
- Disputes and Termination.

Typically, other contract clauses might cover topics such as ownership of materials, bonds, sub-contracting and responsibilities to third parties.

Consultancy contracts: conditions of engagement

For many years the professional institutions (RIBA, RICS, ACE) have produced model standard contracts for engagement, although a current trend appears to be for clients to prefer their own bespoke form of agreement.[9] Furthermore, forms have been published recently that aim to integrate design and construction services more closely; for example, the NEC suite of contracts now includes a form of consultant agreement (NEC, 2002). These changes have arisen, of course, as a result of demand – in recognition of the new ways in which construction procurement is organised.

However, new, standard and bespoke forms all tend to follow a similar format. Typically, the agreement covers the following matters:

- The parties;

- Consultant's Obligations – in which the consultant undertakes to discharge their duties using reasonable skill and care;[10]

- Fees – including periods for payment, variations, rights of set-off, deductions, additional payments;

- Intellectual property – copyright usually remains with the consultant who grants the client a licence to use it for defined purposes;

- Insurance – an undertaking that the consultant has, and will maintain, a defined level of professional indemnity cover;

- Assignment – usually forbidding assignment on the part of the consultant and restricting the employer's right;

- Dispute resolution – there is a statutory right to adjudication, as most agreements fall within the scope of the Housing Grants Construction and Regeneration Act, 1996;

- Deleterious materials – an undertaking not to specify or approve the same;

- Suspension and determination – circumstances, procedures and payment;

- Jurisdiction – the 'nationality' of the courts and the legal system.

Other matters might include defining the key people to work on the project, confidentiality, special safety arrangements and an undertaking at some point in the future to enter into a collateral warranty.

The scope of the service is normally set down in a separate schedule. This is of fundamental importance as this is effectively what the consultant has priced for doing.

Novation

Where it is intended that the responsibility for the project's consultants will switch from the employer to the contractor there will also be a Novation Agreement. This is a relatively simple document that sets out the terms of such a switch.

Warranties

It is also normal for clients to require collateral warranties that extend consultants' duties of care to third parties with an interest in the project: for example, funders, tenants or purchasers.[11] The need for such warranties arises for a number of reasons such as English Law[12] rules of privity of contract and the limited ability to recover economic loss in tort. Understandably, collateral warranties were initially resisted and remain unpopular with consultants and their underwriters (who in many ways take the greater burden),[13] although they are ubiquitous and accepted as the way of the world.

9.3 Case study: The Devonshire Building at Newcastle University

9.3.1 Introduction

The Devonshire Building is an Environmental Research Facility for the University of Newcastle that provides laboratory and office space for traditional, environmental and E-sciences. The building's fabric and M&E services were designed to reduce energy consumption and to achieve an 'excellent' environmental assessment rating.[14] The principle consultants were DEWJOC (architects), Turner and Townsend (cost consultants and client's representative), White, Young, Green, W.S.P. and Battle McCarthy (engineering consultants) and the contractors were HBG Construction (North East).

9.3.2 Constraints, requirements and criteria for choice

A procurement strategy was produced by the client's adviser early in 2002.[15] A number of constraints were identified that in turn presented criteria upon which to model the procurement system.

Time constraints

The building was to be fully operational within 26 months. It was subject to EC procurement rules, local planning permissions, required a site investigation, and extensive 'fit out' works. Thus, the criteria for the choice of procurement included:

- The early completeness of the design;

- A relatively short construction period.

Cost constraints

The project's budget was not to be exceeded. The client, as end-user, wanted an energy efficient design and low maintenance costs, and the basis of funding had included environmental considerations. For these reasons, criteria for the choice of procurement included:

- The requirement for early and strict cost certainty;

- An innovative design that was energy efficient and low maintenance.

Functional and other design requirements

The future users of the building, who were to be consulted and involved throughout the design process, came from a number of academic specialisms but the common theme was the requirement for high quality architecture and facilities. As a result, the criteria for the choice of procurement included:

- An innovative design solution;

- Flexible functional provision;
- The early involvement of specialist contractors.[16]

9.3.3 Choice of procurement systems and contractual arrangements

In terms of the organisation of inputs, the client and its adviser concluded that a design and management procurement method would best serve the project.

The method seeks to capture the main advantages of design and build and management methods. The overlapping of design with construction and the progressive procurement and completion of work packages offered major advantages in terms of programme; while the novation of the entire[17] design team to the design and management contractor allowed it to take on control of (as well as liability for) the design. The consequent degree of design control inherent in the arrangement made it commercially viable for the contractor to provide the client with cost-certainty in the form of a guaranteed maximum price.

The way that the various parties 'arrived at' the project was, however, quite different. Well before the start of The Devonshire Building project, there was already in existence a consultant panel agreement between the client and key members of the design team. The advantages of such arrangements have been discussed above and, in this instance, they included the availability for the project of a ready-made design team at short notice. The Newcastle University consultant panel agreement terms follow very closely the typical format of a consultancy agreement for construction works. The fees are pre-agreed across a range of project types and costs, and there are minor modifications to recognise that it is a contract for more than one project. The basic idea is that it allows the university to call-off the appropriate consultant and to select the appropriate services and fee from the pre-agreed menu. The method of reimbursing the designers (pre-agreed percentage fees that altered to reflect productivity improvements over the life of the agreement) had already been agreed, as was the fact that they would expect to be novated at a later stage to the project contractor. A form of collateral warranty and a novation agreement were established and agreed by the parties at the outset of the agreement period.

The contractor's appointment, however, was by two-stage tender. The first stage was competitive (based on costs for management fees, preliminaries, overheads and profit) and resulted in the identification of a preferred contractor to progress to Stage 2. This involved the preferred contractor with the design team in the parallel task of developing the design and the open-book negotiation (including risk and value management, and the involvement of the contractor's preferred supply chain) of the project's guaranteed maximum price. Once this had been agreed, the contract was executed as normal.

This procurement profile necessitated some ingenuity regarding the form of contract, since there is, as yet, no two-stage standard form available in the industry. However, the client's advisers, Turner & Townsend, had experience of managing similar hybrid procurement systems using their own contract based on a modified version of the NEC Engineering & Construction Contract with incorporated provisions for contractor's risk management and performance measurement. This bespoke 'DMC contract' was suitable for management contracting or construction management, and was also able to accommodate the novation of design consultants. The contractual arrangements thus supported the objectives of speed, flexibility, early contractor involvement and cost-certainty, and permitted the setting of financial incentives with a 'pain share, gain share' approach.

9.4   Reflections on the case study

The case study project illustrates how the choice of a project's procurement and contractual arrangements can be influenced by a number of key criteria. There were two distinct aspects in this example.

9.4.1   The consultant panel agreement

The construction project itself was pre-dated by the consultant panel agreement. There are a number of benefits for the consultants within this arrangement. These could arise from the volume of work, the regular flow of work or increased efficiency arising from a better understanding of the clients' business and their building needs. Construction is generally a project-based cyclical industry: the balancing of capital and resources to cope with unpredictable fluctuations in demand can create real business difficulties for consultants. Against this backdrop the attraction of a longer-term agreement, with regular payments and a greater degree of predictability and certainty in workflow, can be clearly seen.

The benefits to the consultants are clear, but why do clients enter into these longer-term agreements? The process of placing advertisements, sifting through the applicants, short-listing, interviewing and eventually agreeing terms with the successful firms is time-consuming and costly; so why bother? The answer, as with almost all business processes, is that the return justifies the investment. The investment is easy to identify (and, indeed, relatively easy to quantify), it is the management time and expense that the promoter goes to in establishing the preferred contractor; but the identifying and quantifying the return requires a little more effort. It is the case, of course, that for different promoters in different businesses the benefits will vary, but many will consistently occur. Some of these are:

Quality improvements: This has two distinct components. Firstly, a better quality product: buildings that perform better as a result of the better understanding of the promoter's business needs, aspirations and functional requirements. And secondly, a better quality process: a way of working together that adds value by eliminating the problems that arise in temporary project teams. These problems include a lack of common management procedures and compatible systems; a lack of inter-personal understanding (usually accompanied by a high degree of inter-personal conflict!); a lack of common goals and culture or at least a lack of understanding of what these might be.

Reduced transaction costs: It could be argued that the initial costs involved in setting up the agreement are higher than those incurred for a single project. However, this is a one-off cost with a payback that improves with each new commission placed during the life of the agreement. The total costs are therefore considerably lower. Savings arise in many ways: savings in time arising from a reduced mobilisation period; savings in fees, for example, lawyers fees in preparing and agreeing forms of appointment for each new project; savings in management time, for example, in the briefing and induction of new consultants.

Value improvements: The ability to expand learning from one project to another will increase the value delivered in the end product. The greater the global knowledge of the consultant team the greater their ability to eliminate non-value adding processes. This can manifest itself in many ways. For example, if the consultant panel architects understand the local authority planning constraints on the promoter's land, they will avoid exploring options that are unlikely to obtain planning approval. Similarly, if the engineers have developed a good understanding of the ground conditions they can very quickly arrive at a realistic foundation design without the need to embark on very detailed investigations too early in the project.

Project cost savings: A better understanding of the client's budget will allow the design and cost consultant to develop solutions that spend the money wisely. For example, the client may have modest funds for the capital cost of building but may have access to grants and other income to support the running costs. This can be an important informer of the design and budgetary strategy.

A greater motivation to success: It is inevitably true that companies, like individuals, will invest more personal capital in relationships that have a long-term future. Companies will have a strong commercial incentive to work to the success of such an agreement to ensure that they get a good volume of work. Also relevant will be (a) the fact that the consultant has invested in resources and established these at a level that recognises the consultant panel workload, (b) the saving in marketing and bidding costs that the consultant makes from repeat business rather than pursuing new contracts, and (c) the ultimate incentive of renewing or maintain a place on the consultant panel. The consultant will also inevitably be closely identified with the consultant panel client by the public and by peers and therefore the kudos and PR value of successful projects will be high.

Framework or consultant panel agreements may be attractive in providing security and greater certainty but they do not represent a panacea to the problems that beset consultants in the construction industry. The difficulty of managing the upstream design process, of dealing with late changes to the client requirements and the inherent difficulty of each new development being effectively a prototype remain. However, the ability to better forward plan the business cost and resources potentially reduces business management time and allows more design and project management time – time that potentially adds more value to the finished product.

9.4.2 *The construction project*

It is clear that the approach taken to procuring The Devonshire Building project and organising its construction was dictated by a number of carefully considered criteria. The solution – a two-stage, design and management contract, with guaranteed maximum price and cost-saving incentives – was designed to provide speed (avoiding the traditional need for extensive tender documentation), flexibility (prolonging the ability to incorporate change) and 'inclusivity' (in terms of incorporating the preferred contractor's design, programme, buildability and cost advice) whilst at the same time being partly competitive, and offering the comfort of a guaranteed maximum price.

Two-stage tenders are considered to be popular with contractors: the competitive element (Stage 1) involves a minimum of risk, since the Stage 1 tender is based only on management fees and preliminary costs, with overheads and profit addition. There is then the opportunity to negotiate the more risk-laden construction work phase. It is true that in this example a guaranteed maximum price is required to be agreed, but this figure is not 'bottomed-out' before a period of negotiation, during which the contractor has control over the designers, and access to its preferred supply-chain while completing the parallel tasks of design development and value management.

9.5 Conclusions

The project that has been considered as a case study faced some of the perennial problems that surround the procurement of construction services, namely:

- The resolution of the (often conflicting) demands of time, cost and quality;

- The successful creation of a temporary multi-organisational project team.

In doing this, the client utilised two very different solutions for bringing together the design consultants and the constructors. Where successful projects result from these novel approaches to project procurement more clients will be prompted to experiment with such non-traditional methods.

It is possible to speculate upon another effect of this combination of a consultants' consultant panel agreement with a two-stage tendered design and managed construction project. Both elements (the consultancy and the construction) have enabled the suppliers to increase their knowledge-base into non-traditional areas. Through operating within the consultant panel, the consultant designers experienced the longer-term 'upstream' concerns (e.g. master-planning) of a regular promoter of buildings who also owns a considerable property portfolio. The contractor, by involvement as a design and construct manager and at an earlier stage than is traditional, has itself shared in the solution of 'upstream' problems – in this case those normally reserved for the design and consultancy teams.

References

Chappell, D. and Powell-Smith, V., *The JCT Design and Build Contract*, 2nd edn, Blackwell Scientific Publications (1997).

Cox, A. and Thompson, I., *Contracting for Business Success*, Thomas Telford Publishing, London (1998).

Eccles, R. G., 'The Quasifirm in the Construction Industry' *Journal of Economic Behavior and Organization*, 2, 1981, pp. 335–57.

Franks, J., *Building Procurement Systems*, The Chartered Institute of Building, Ascot (1984).

Masterman, J. W. E., *An Introduction to Building Procurement Systems*, E&FN Spon, London (1992).

Murdoch, J. and Hughes, W. P., *Construction Contracts: Law and Management*, 3rd edn, E&FN Spon, London (2000).

Key Reading

Cox, A. and Thompson, I., *Contracting for Business Success*, Thomas Telford Publishing, London (1998).

Murdoch, J. and Hughes, W. P., *Construction Contracts: Law and Management*, 3rd edn, E&FN Spon, London (2000).

Endnotes

1 See, for example, the Office of Government Commerce guidelines, PROCUREMENT GUIDANCE No: 2, *Value for Money in Construction Procurement* (Supersedes CUP guidance, Nos 33 (Revised) and 41).

2 Eccles referred to these coalitions as 'quasifirms'.

3 As opposed to 'project specific partnering'.

4 As in the BAA 'consultant panel' systems, for example.

5 With selected tendering there is a requirement for applicants to pre-qualify for a short-list of tenderers.

6 Following the abandonment of Compulsory Competitive Tendering in the Local Government Act 1999, and its replacement with a requirement to obtain Best Value.

7 As opposed to serial partnering.

8 Difficulties can arise in defining what is meant by profit in the context of a business partnership. It would generally be necessary to make an adjustment to allocate a notional salary to the equity partners.

9 It is interesting to speculate on the reason for this. On the face of it, it is understandable that clients may be sceptical regarding the equitable nature of agreements prepared by a particular professional body for its members. The RIBA Standard Form of Agreement published in 1992 came in for considerable criticism due to a perceived bias in favour of the architect. That it was little used is perhaps no surprise.

10 The normal standard for professional services (as distinct from the building contract standard of fitness for purpose).

11 Their identity is often not known at the time the consultant is appointed.

12 It was at one time thought that the introduction of The Contracts (Rights of Third Parties) Act 1999 would remove the need for collateral warranties. In fact, most subsequent consultant agreements, as the law allows, have specifically excluded the application of the act. Understandably, consultants and their underwriters are reluctant to give blanket contractual rights to all third parties, whoever they might be!

13 The warranties are backed by professional indemnity insurance.

14 BREEAM (Building Research Establishment's Environmental Assessment Method).

15 Turner & Townsend.

16 Including sub-structure, frame, cladding, engineering services and laboratory furniture.

17 With the exception of Battle McCarthy, whose input was at a very early stage in the design.

Roles and responsibilities of architects within differing procurement routes

10

David Moore, Scott Sutherland School, Robert Gordon University, Aberdeen, and Michael Gilmour, Gilmour Associates, Aberdeen, UK

10.1 Introduction

The traditional approach to the management of construction projects in the UK has been one that can fairly be described as Newtonian or transactional. This has relied on the assertion that fear + greed = result (or $x + y = z$, in Newtonian terms). Standard forms of contract have enshrined this assertion through legitimising authority as flowing from an individual's position within a hierarchy. An individual positioned in the higher levels of a hierarchy can therefore use reward (greed) and coercion (fear) to extract the required result from an individual lower down the hierarchy. This approach is starting to be questioned and new forms of relationships are being considered. These are based on an Einsteinian, or transformational, approach to management that is driven more by the need to achieve a consensus and recognition of the importance of the psychological contract.

The Newtonian approach to the role of architect as project leader is argued to be at odds with the architect's responsibility to practice design creativity. A more congruent approach is suggested as being the Einsteinian, with its willingness to allow for creativity in the management process. The extent to which this approach can be implemented is constrained, however, by the degree of contingency within the standard form for a specific project. High levels of contingency within a standard form are evidence of a transactional approach to management in which creativity is given little value. Low levels of contingency evidence a more transformational approach, within which creativity is given a high value.

10.2 Procurement and the role of architects

Throughout the history of architecture as a profession, the role and responsibilities of the architect have undergone a process of change. Both the rate and extent of change have varied, but it is arguable that the modern-day architect is faced with greater and faster changes than in any period since the Renaissance. During that period, the architect emerged as a professional distinct from the established master masons whose approach to procurement was, by and large, firmly rooted in the mechanics of the construction process. The architect emerged as a new role with a position of authority that also came with new responsibilities. Their designs were regarded as being perhaps more 'creative' than those of the masons and this attracted (and continues to attract) clients who wished to make bold and/or fashionable statements about themselves. On this basis, architects were able to move themselves into an authoritative role as leaders of construction projects.

Within the context of a society where a relatively small number of people were in a position to resist orders from those at the top of the hierarchy, architects could perhaps rely on the authority of clients such as bishops and princes to pressure masons into accepting a diminished (in terms of authority and prestige) role. Such a situation is a good example of what can be referred to as transactional management, the basis of which is the power to reward or punish. Many managers still rely upon the transactional approach, although its relevance is increasingly being questioned. Transactional management is enshrined in procurement routes that are defined in terms of standard forms of contract which distribute authority and responsibility. They also distribute risk, but this will be covered in the section dealing with contingency thinking. As leader of the project, the architect is at the top of the hierarchy (excluding the client, who can, in this context, be argued to exist outside of the project team boundary) and therefore their authority flows from the conditions of contract that allow them to reward or punish others lower down the hierarchy. Those towards the bottom of the hierarchy generally have to work within contract terms that arguably place greater emphasis on punishment than on reward. This may all seem a very feudal approach to management, but it has worked quite well for quite some time, albeit with a few tweaks along the way.

One particular tweak worth considering is that the basic theory was dressed up to appear to have a basis somewhat more scientific than the application of fear and greed. This resulted in an alternative name for transactional management: Newtonian management. As Newton and other scientific thinkers began to more rigidly define the laws of nature and the universe, a form of thinking that seems an anathema to the stereotypical architect emerged. This is referred to as linearity and is essentially a case of $x + y = z$. The Newtonian perspective on management is basically one of fear + greed = result. While Newtonian management has worked well for several hundred years, its relevance is increasingly being questioned and a new perspective on management is starting to emerge: Einsteinian or transformational. This will be discussed further at a later point of this section, but is worth noting here in that it adds to the complexity of the environment in which management has to be exercised.

The modern architect can rarely rely on their client's authority in the same manner as their Renaissance counterpart, and so there is a need to consider a more rounded approach to management issues. Typically, these will include teambuilding and the soft, people skills within the management of projects. It has been argued that there is therefore a perceived need to achieve balance between creativity in design and technical expertise in project management. But is this actually the case? Is construction project management in reality a purely technical process? This chapter will try to show that the skills required for construction project management are, by and large, simply another manifestation of creativity. Unfortunately, project management creativity is constrained by a very Newtonian concept: the standard form of contract. Architects are faced therefore with the requirement to be creative in their 'day job' of design, but then find themselves constrained in the implementation of that design by the manifestation of contingency thinking that is the standard form of contract. This situation is arguably the result of the client adopting double standards: one standard of creativity for the design process and a different standard (focused on minimising the risks inherent in implementing a creative design) for the construction process.

In management terms the situation becomes further complicated in that managers need not only to consider the requirements and constraints of the standard form of contract. They also need to consider the requirements of their team members with regard to a second type of contract, that of the psychological contract. Team members all have their own needs that they seek to achieve through what is referred to as the psychological contract; the unwritten agreement between them and the organisation that they work for. A project manager who is focused solely on the transactional management approach will be unconcerned with soft issues such as the psychological contract. The Einsteinian manager will, however, seek to use such issues to the advantage of the project. By accepting that $x + y$ does not always equal z, the constraints of linearity can be moved to one side and the benefits of non-linearity achieved. The extent to which such benefits can be achieved is determined largely by the constraints of the standard form being used. Figure 10.1 illustrates the relationship between the objectives of standard forms and the extent

Figure 10.1: Constraints imposed through contract types

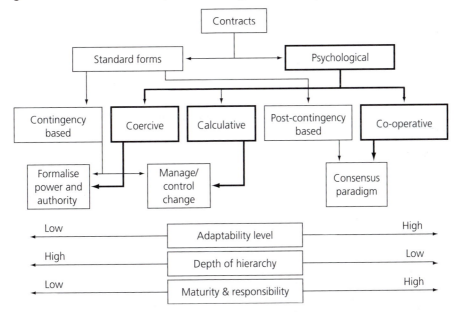

Source: after Moore, 2002

to which they constrain the ability to meet the requirements of psychological contracts and achieve non-linearity.

A contingency-based contract such as JCT 80 imposes a high level of formalised power and authority (exhibited through its depth of hierarchy) and, consequently, is slow to adapt/respond to change. It also rates maturity and responsibility amongst team members lowly. It is then a good example of a Newtonian standard form, which is possibly why it has been widely adopted in the UK construction environment. The reason for suggesting this is that the UK construction industry is generally perceived as being a bastion of contingency thinking. This is particularly so in comparison to say the Danish construction industry, whose AB72 standard form was a prime example of post-contingency (or Einsteinian) thinking, with an emphasis on seeking consensus. What though is contingency thinking?

Moore (2002) suggests contingency thinking is a product of the need to reduce risk through imposing control on a project. This style of management began to emerge during the industrial revolution and went hand-in-hand with the increasing degree of specialism that manufacturing industries required. The basic concept is one of breaking a process down into increasingly narrowly-defined tasks, thereby allowing individuals to gain greater expertise in each task. Contingency thinking then asserts that once increased skill has been developed, there will be decreased risk of poor quality work resulting. This is fine up to a point – there were certainly benefits to be had from implementing this approach to managing the production processes typical of the industrial period. However, we are now arguably exiting the industrial period and the relevance of contingency thinking to manufacturing industries is increasingly questioned. Unfortunately, the UK construction industry has never been one that has sought to embrace management methodologies which have not been proven elsewhere (another characteristic of contingency thinking), and has yet to seriously attempt full-blown, post-contingency approaches to the management of projects. There remains, by and large, a reliance on the transfer of risk through the application of hierarchical authority enshrined within contingency-based forms of contract. This situation is changing slowly, as will be discussed further in the case studies later in the chapter, but it is worth noting at this point that the post-contingency mindset is generally seen as resulting in a more creative approach to problem solving. Therefore, it should be more congruent with the architect's perspective on the need for creativity, and may present an approach to construction project management that helps to address the earlier assertion that the architect is being called upon to work to two different standards within the procurement.

The previous paragraphs have introduced some terminology, and associated concepts that may well be unfamiliar to the majority of architects. Management may well be a creative process, but it, along with just about every other specialism, has its own terminology and concepts. A good general source of reference is the APM (Association of Project Management) glossary of project management terms. Within this chapter the emphasis will be on some of the key management terminology and concepts of relevance to those who wish to develop creative construction project management skills. The discussion will, however, be within the context of the boundaries defined by the RIBA, an example of which can be found in a consideration of the procurement process. The construction industry is a complex environment and the proliferation of standard forms of contract within the industry works, for many architects, against the opportunity to develop expertise in a single procurement route as represented by a given standard form. The RIBA note several general categories of procurement route, namely:

- Single stage tender;
- Multistage tender;
- Negotiation with preferred parties;
- Management contracting;
- Design & Build;
- Construction management;
- Design, construct & maintain/maintain & operate;
- Design, build, finance and operate;
- Prime contracting;
- Project team partnering.

Each of these contains specific unique requirements of the architect. However, they also contain generic requirements in that an architect is generally expected to exhibit certain behaviours (design competence, etc.) that fit the perception by others of what an architect does. When an architect behaves 'out of role', as when they take on the 'role' of developer, this can cause others (particularly those deeply wedded to contingency thinking) within the procurement process some confusion and discomfort. This point will be developed further, at a later point in the chapter, but is worth noting that the real role, as opposed to the expected role, of an architect may vary between projects – they are not always behaving as architects! However, this represents a slight digression and so back to the issue of management terminology.

The above example of categorisation in the procurement route is an example of several management concepts. Firstly, it is an example of the old problem generally referred to as fragmentation (the more optimistic members of the management community may refer to this as diversity) in that each standard form tends to result in the development of specialists. These are usually from a quantity surveying background and will be happy to advise on the minutiae of contract clause interpretation. While this skill is an excellent attribute within a confrontational environment of claim and counterclaim, it tends not to promote good teambuilding or a management style based on consensus. It is very much Newtonian rather than Einsteinian. The development of a specialism tends to result in a barrier being placed around it in a way that allows differentiation between that specialism and every other one. Once a barrier is erected, it can become difficult to achieve a cohesive working environment. In other words, fragmentation, where each specialism competes against others, results. For a further exam[...], simply consider the number of specialists that are required to [...]ly-sized project team. Each is defined in terms of their own [...]s and this can be argued to be both a result of, and a [...]ngency thinking. In such environments project management [...]eking to maintain communication between the interfaces [...] boundaries meet another's. Consequently, the project [...] used in a positive manner, as evidenced by one definition [...] being a charismatic fire-fighter!

[...]tive that project management is a specialism, what are its [...] and how may they differ from those of the architect? [...]agers have experience, knowledge and competence of? [...]tions have developed a formalised Body of Knowledge [...]ession. The project management BoK, for example, outlines [...] groups them in terms of six types of knowledge: strategic, [...]cial, organisational and people (APM, 2000). These can be [...] to the creativity and technical expertise requirements for [...] an architect is responsible in that they are seen from the perspective of the [...] role. Reference to the APM BoK is suggested as a useful additional activity after having completed this chapter.

A further facet of the fragmentation problem is that architects may find themselves working within practices that have significantly different characteristics and areas of activity. Within one practice an architect may encounter a wide range of procurement routes while another practice may expose its architects to very few procurement routes. Each procurement route may place the architect in a different role (leader of the project team, leader of the design team only, single provider of part or whole of the design, etc.), and impose different responsibilities. The situation is complicated further in that a single procurement route may have several variations thereby allowing further permutations of role and responsibility. The design and build (D&B) procurement route, for example, has developed a number of variations. This is evidenced by the difference between 'true' D&B, where the architect is claimed to be a part of an integrated design and build team, and novated, where the architect is separate from the team. It is perhaps appropriate therefore to consider the possibility of generic (common to all procurement routes) roles and responsibilities. Such an approach will be more readily appreciated if placed in the context of the functioning of an actual architecture practice, in this case Michael Gilmour Associates.

10.3 Cases

10.3.1 Study 1

The type of work handled by Michael Gilmour Associates (MGA) is largely a combination of industrial and commercial, with a reasonable stream of housing projects. MGA carry out both housing association and private work. One example project involves the construction of ten luxury flats. There is also a start-up company dealing with the development of medical buildings for medical practices, and it is anticipated that the area is going to become a strong part of the practice. There is also an increasing amount of work being undertaken by a smaller development arm. MGA are also in the process of setting up, in conjunction with Robert Gordon University (RGU), an Internet-based programme for the training of architects. This is partially funded by an architecture/development practice based in Edinburgh. The programme springs from the belief that the profession has, to some degree, become disenfranchised and the intention is to give architects back greater control of the built environment. This can be achieved through architects operating as clients. Even if architects are not going to become developers, MGA believes that the omission, from the educational process, of the financial generators of the built environment is an omission that handicaps architects.

The type of work undertaken by MGA can be characterised in terms of three or four strands. Throughout the life of the practice (23 years), the main stream of its work has tended to be oil-related, commercial, industrial work, which is perhaps not surprising given the practice's location. However, this type of work is important from the perspective of roles and responsibilities because the oil industry has, in some ways, led the way in terms of writing their own forms of contract. The industry has not been afraid of addressing partnering and other such issues. As the construction industry itself has begun to increasingly consider partnering and so on as part of the procurement process, in some respects it has not been an issue for MGA in that the oil industry forms of contract have proved to be more innovative than some of the newer forms of contract within the construction industry.

MGA's interest in the development and financial generators in the built environment has resulted in them carrying out area studies for local authorities. While MGA's primary perspective in these is from the architectural and design viewpoint, the practice has also taken what may be viewed as the next logical step and actually demonstrated that the development is commercially possible. Part of this has been to examine how it could be funded, particularly with regard to the balance of public and private finance that would be required. This has led to a level of recognition by others that, while the practice views itself as being primarily design-led, it is also developing a strong commercial expertise. However, the mixed nature of the work undertaken by MGA has also led to an awareness that it is possible for a development which is successful commercially to be somewhat less than successful architecturally; a problem that they seek to avoid. One current project of the practice that illustrates this awareness is an evaluation of the sea front area in Aberdeen. The proposal is primarily design-led in an effort to raise the perceived quality of the sea front and to reverse the trend of recent developments which, whilst commercially successful, have turned away from the sea. MGA are also showing how such a development could be financially funded with very little, if any, public funding thus proving that good design principles can be married to financial viability.

MGA have a limited number of staff and experience a common problem in that they do not view themselves as being a large enough practice to justify total specialism. Anybody within the practice could end up working on any of the projects at any point in time – there are not, as yet, any specific boundaries, largely because there is not a sufficiently regular stream of work in any one area to allow it. Architects within the practice therefore have to be very flexible, with the result that they must also be prepared to fulfil varying requirements and possibly even roles.

Two relevant points to end this section on are that all procurement routes have a common feature in that they seek to apportion risk between the parties covered by whichever is the standard form of contract used. Procurement routes also, to varying extents, seek to allow opportunities to control the change process, in as much as all projects can be argued to be concerned with achieving that change which has been planned for. The change process has traditionally been regarded as being composed of two essentially separate processes: design and construction. Change control within the construction process is normally dealt with through project management, an area of expertise of which architects increasingly need to be aware.

Clients, along with perhaps the majority of people, tend to structure their relationships with others on the basis of their perception of an individual's role. It is arguable that people tend to have a primary role – the one with which they identify themselves, or are identified by others, most closely. They may well have other, secondary roles but it is the primary role that is of most importance, particularly in relationships with others. Consequently, it can be important that the primary role is not confused, as can happen when an individual may be operating one project as an architect, but on another project as a developer. However, in both cases the use of project management skills can be of assistance in reducing the potential for role confusion. Earlier in the chapter mention was made of the APM Body of Knowledge (BoK) and its six sections, with expertise in each providing an individual with the basis for successfully managing any project. One of the BoK sections is entitled 'People'. This is composed of several sub-sections: Communication, Teamwork, Leadership, Conflict Management, Negotiation and Personnel Management. As far as role confusion, or ambiguity (Moore, 1996) is concerned, the sub-section on conflict management is of relevance, and MGA have experienced some of the problems arising from role ambiguity, and developed a means of managing that particular form of conflict.

MGA have noted that some clients experience difficulty when dealing with a representative of the practice (when the practice is a partner with them in a development) if the representative moves between the roles of development partner and professional architect. Some clients seem to have a certain grasp of the relationships involved, and that they should be equal in both cases. But when a person changes hats (moves from one role to another) suddenly, it can cause them to become very uneasy and they are usually uncertain as to how to handle the situation. It seems that such clients find role ambiguity confusing and they appear to be concerned that perhaps they cannot get the service that they would expect architects to be responsible for providing. MGA have found that it is better to provide a clear separation of roles, so that when attending a meeting an individual is there in either an architect's role or a developer's role, but not as both. MGA ensure that a second individual attends the meeting to carry out that role. In so doing they find that it seems to remove any potential conflict arising out of one person's wish to relate to another person in a specific and single role. Experience has suggested that once a client (or any other member of the project) perceives an individual as an architect they find it very difficult if that individual then appears and acts as a developer. The response, in many cases, is along the lines of 'you can't do that!' MGA have realised that some clients and potential partners have narrowly conceived ideas of what an architect does and is capable of, and it certainly does not include in their eyes the development role. This seems to suggest that one responsibility of an architect is to clearly communicate the role they are acting in on a particular development, particularly given that the current proliferation of standard forms of contract can result in an architect carrying out their role within a range of contexts.

10.3.2 Study 2

It is arguable that an architect, along with other members of a construction project team, has a responsibility to contribute to the reduction of risk and uncertainty in the procurement process. The reduction of uncertainty may come about, however, as a result of other professions exhibiting creativity that then places the architect role under some pressure. One example development in west London illustrates this point, in that both client and contractor exhibited creativity in the procurement of a £86 m package within an overall regeneration project valued at £350 m (Leitch, 2001). The regeneration project is focused on the redevelopment of the area around Paddington Station in west London, and will result in over 730,000 m^2 of new development. The £86 m Phase 1 package contains two office buildings with over 32,000 m^2 between them, a leisure unit of almost 4,000 m^2, over 6,000 m^2 of retail units, 210 residential units, and a landscaped public area, all of which had to be designed and constructed within a relatively short project duration.

The client for this project took the unusual step of asking the four tendering and pre-qualified contractors to suggest the most appropriate form of contract to use. Not surprisingly, each came up with a different procurement route, ranging from traditional construction management through to design and build. This diversity of response has been interpreted as evidence of a marketplace willing to take a wide variety of risk (some forms place more risk on the contractor than others), but that the product would be priced according to the risk accepted (Leitch, 2001). Bovis Lend Lease were awarded the project, with the form of contract being an amalgam of several different ideas about the nature of the project and how that related to their recent experiences on other complex projects. Essentially, the form of contract is closest to a traditional construction management procurement route, but has a number of significant differences formalised through the use of a modified JCT 98 (without quantities) standard form. The modifications include:

- Inclusion of a detailed work packages cost plan;

- Contract sum based on cost plan, plus an agreed contingency figure to represent the risk remaining in the project;

- A 'bonus' clause allowing Bovis Lend Lease to receive up to 50 percent of any savings on the contract sum;

- A 'penalty' clause requiring Bovis Lend Lease to contribute up to 50 percent of their agreed fee towards any cost overrun on the contract sum;

- Inclusion of a mechanism to adjust the contract sum in response to variations.

The progress of the project has been such that there has been a call for the modified form to become a standard form in its own right, with a proposed name of Paddington Central Building Contract. All of this seems to have met one of the initial desires of the client; to create a working environment in which everyone worked together to sort out problems arising during construction (which are inevitable?), rather than being forced by the form of contract into defensive positions from day one. What is interesting in this study is that the form of contract used appears to have strong contingency-based characteristics such as the penalty clause. However, the detail of the changes actually evidence a move (albeit slight) towards a post-contingency approach. The inclusion of a detailed work packages cost plan is very much a Newtonian feature that, in a traditional form of contract, would have been deemed to be the contractor's response to reducing risk and uncertainty. Nonetheless, in this form of contract the client was willing to allow for the fact that not all risk and uncertainty can be identified and/or eliminated, and accepted the suggestion that an additional contingency figure should be included. The evidence may be slight, but Paddington Central does appear to be a move towards a post-contingency form of contract. This may well be a factor in its success.

Irrespective of any moves towards post-contingency based contracts, as MGA argue, the architect must always remember that they are, for the present at least, functioning within what is essentially a master–servant relationship. That does not mean that the detail of the relationship should not be open to negotiation, as evidenced by MGA's use on a project in Glasgow of a similar approach to that used at Paddington Central. What remains a constant is that the architect is being paid to offer a service and because of that some clients will talk about design, with a proportion taking the architect's advice while others will ignore it. That is their right to do so, but it is also an architect's responsibility to communicate while being aware that many clients are not particularly sophisticated when it comes to language in the design context.

10.4 Best practice

Communication is definitely an important part of the relationship between architects and clients (under certain standard forms) and between architects and other members of the project team (under other standard forms). As MGA have noted, clients vary in their ability to communicate. The way they use language and the sort of language they use, particularly in terms of terminology, can make a considerable difference to the relationship. Such a situation is to be expected within the context of an industry with a high level of fragmentation and resultant specialist use of language. For clients who go to an architect for a service, language can be a significant problem. The architect may frequently have to second-guess their needs because they do not always use language correctly, particularly in the context of design, and communication suffers. However, clients who go to an architect for a product can be easier to deal with because there is no real need to communicate about the aesthetic. They have already accepted that component of the process, and that is why they go to see a specific architect who can concentrate on the context of the product. In both cases the nature of both the form of contract and the nature of the psychological contract may differ considerably. The product-focused client is willing to trust the architect and adopt a contractual relationship oriented toward the post-contingency model. In contrast, the service-focused client needs to exert control in a typical contingency manner and would not feel able to proceed without a suitable contract in place.

It is arguable that the architect has a responsibility to be aware of, and respond to, a given client's level of sophistication and need. In some cases the client may appear to be saying that they cannot trust the architect to do what they are supposed to be good at and may seek to impose a highly contingency-based transactional form of contract. The architect must be aware of what such an approach by the client is actually evidencing: a deep feeling of being at risk. When MGA operates in the development role, they try to create an environment in which risk transfer is replaced by trust. But this has to be in conjunction with the realisation that there has to be a clearly defined responsibility – if MGA get it wrong, they know what the results will be in terms of costs to them, and to the project as a whole.

The RIBA clearly encourage architects to form some sort of contract for the allocation of their expertise. However, MGA have found that the nature of this contract has to be tempered by an acceptance that many clients can be horrified when they are faced with a formal contract letter because they imagine that in some way it will limit the service that an architect is offering, which, of course, it does to some extent. The situation may be worsened by the production of a multiple-page document that goes into huge detail about exactly what the architect should be doing for them. The client starts to worry about extra sets of drawings, other extras and, in the event of a problem, that there may be an extra fee.

10.5 Conclusion

In the present rapidly changing environment of fragmentation within the context of procurement routes it is perhaps unrealistic to seek to identify all of the responsibilities of the architect for each standard form of contract available. Beyond the fact that such an approach would result in a book for that subject alone, the rate of change would inevitably add apparently new responsibilities quite rapidly. The word 'apparent' is important in that any given procurement route should not place anyone operating in the role of architect in a situation whereby they need to deal with responsibilities out-with those identified by RIBA. Doing so would represent an unrealistic distribution of risk in that the architect would be trying to deal with issues outside of their education, training and experience as an architect. It is arguable therefore that procurement routes should only vary insofar as they place a different number and mix of responsibilities on the architect, but all of them should be within the recognised palette of responsibilities for an architect.

In a situation where an architect chooses to move (or allows themselves to be moved) into a different role, such as a developer, then the above argument no longer holds. The palette of responsibilities for a developer differs from that of an architect, although there are still some responsibilities that are generic to a range of roles. In such a situation, the 'new' role of the architect must be clearly communicated to all relevant members of the project team so as to avoid problems arising from role ambiguity. Clear communication will also help in building up trust in the architect as they operate in their new role – project team members may well have trusted the architect when operating as an architect, but such trust may have little or no currency when they move into a new role.

Best practice guidelines summarised.

- Be aware of the constraints imposed by the standard form of contract with regard to the soft issues within construction project management.

- Clients who insist on highly contingency-based standard (or bespoke) forms of contract are actually also making a statement regarding their psychological contract needs.

- Be aware of the language problems that can result from the UK industry's high level of fragmentation and specialisation. Communication can be badly affected by 'noise' resulting from differing meanings for individual words and terms. This can occur when moving between design and management functions.

- Seek to reduce role ambiguity wherever possible. A communication process that revolves around mixed signals will not engender trust.

- Post-contingency approaches to management will provide opportunities for improved performance, but individuals may take time to become comfortable with this. Be responsive to the psychological contract needs of other project team members.

- An element of risk and uncertainty will always be present in any project. Seeking to engender a high level of maturity in project team members and clients with regard to addressing this will be more productive than imposing risk transfer to others based on authority.

References

APM, *The Project Management Body of Knowledge*, 4th edn (2000). www.apm.org.uk/
Leitch, J., 'Hybrid forms take shape', *Contract Journal*, 24 Oct. 2001, Reed Business International.
Moore, D. R., 'The Renaissance: the beginning of the end for implicit buildability', *Building Research Information*, 24, 5, Sep.–Oct. 1996, pp. 259–69.
Moore, D. R., *Project Management: Designing Effective Organisational Structures in Construction*, Blackwell Science Publishing, Oxford (2002).

Key Reading

Hughes, W. and Murdoch, J., 'Roles in Construction Projects: Analysis & Terminology', a research report undertaken for the Joint Contracts Tribunal Ltd (2001).

Construction Operations

Building a project organisation

11

Joe Gunning, School of the Built Environment, University of Ulster, Northern Ireland, and Frank Harkin of Mary Kerrigan and Frank Harkin, Chartered Architects, Londonderry, Northern Ireland

11.1 Introduction

This chapter examines the characteristics of an effective project organisation and sets out recommendations as to how the architect can build and maintain a successful project team. It discusses the essential elements such as unity of purpose, shared interests, mutual support and a culture of flexibility. A sense of urgency is seen as the driving force throughout the realisation of the project.

Requirements for an effectively-led team are reviewed, along with the major influences upon a project leader. A conservation project is used as a case study to illustrate some of the problems encountered on projects. Sources of leader power are examined, and the lessons to be learned from the partnering philosophy are discussed. Suggestions are put forward on developing the project team as a 'learning organisation'. Project structures are briefly considered, and the concept of linear responsibility analysis is introduced. The chapter ends with a series of tips on leadership skills and on the maintenance of an effective project team, followed by a list of key readings on the topic.

11.2 Project organisations

Every construction requires to be organised, and every project needs its own unique project organisation (often referred to as TMO – temporary multi-organisation) which is made-up of individuals drawn from a range of parent organisations. It is clear that a successful project must have an effective project organisation, and that these organisations do not merely arise by chance – they must be built and managed throughout their limited existence.

A textbook definition of an organisation is 'a structured process within which persons interact to achieve objectives'. In other words, it is the framework within which individuals behave and work. There are, in effect, two co-existent structures within every organisation: one is the formal organisation, largely dictated by the procurement arrangement which has been selected and the parent organisations who supply the staff; the second is the informal structure which will inevitably arise as a result of the personal interaction of individuals within the TMO.

This informal organisation may mirror or, more commonly, may vary considerably from the formal structure as set out by the chosen procurement system. It will be very much dictated by the personalities of the contributing individuals, and can operate to greatly enhance or hinder the effectiveness of the formal organisation. There may be little that an architect can do to influence the design of the formal

193

organisation structure once the client has chosen a preferred procurement method. However, there is much that the architect can do to promote an effective informal organisation, which encourages active participation and team spirit within an integrated project team.

This, in essence, requires team-building and team maintenance, the former being the ability to gather together the best available people to join a project team, and to get them working together for the benefit of a project, regardless of their own company or individual objectives. The development and maintenance of this team needs active encouragement and stimulation through the sharing of experiences and creation of a 'learning' organisation within some degree of partnering.

Unlike most sporting teams, the object of a project team is not to defeat the opposition, but to achieve a 'win–win' solution by overcoming the obstacles and completing the project to the satisfaction of all concerned. The role of the project leader can be compared to that of a composer trying to convert ideas into reality.

At a world conference on project management, 72.6 percent of several hundred delegates affirmed that the most crucial area of interest was 'educating the project team in the human aspects of project management'. The 'hardware' and technical/contractual/financial systems are important, but professional members of the construction project organisation will already possess skills in these. Establishing and applying the ground rules for personal behaviour and inter-relationships during the project represents the real challenge for the project leader ('software').

As a project leader, the architect should add to their primary discipline the role of generating and maintaining a sense of unity of purpose and shared interest in success among a group of construction professionals with varying perspectives and priorities. They must be brought together quickly, with a tolerance of uncertainty in the project environment of incomplete or changing information. A culture of flexibility and mutual support under decisive leadership needs to replace one which is characterised by excessive objectivity, reactivity and over-analysis. Effective communication must replace undue reliance on order and hierarchy. In particular, the communication of the design concepts and details is vital. The project environment created must be one of mutual respect and trust, with a common purpose in successful project completion.

Design ability is not enough. The architectural concept, idea or vision is primary in overall design terms and must guide and inform all other decisions. But the vision must be communicated first to the client and then to the rest of the team. Good interpersonal relations and effective communication is the starting point. Drucker (1995) suggests that communications are most effective when they speak to the motivation of the recipients. He refers to members of the professions as 'knowledge professionals' whom, he says, cannot be motivated. They must motivate themselves. Drucker says:

> They are the guardians of their own standards, performance, and objectives. They can be productive only if they are responsible for their own job.

Setting high but attainable standards for these people and letting communications flow upwards from them will ensure that they maintain high expectation for the project. Quality will only come from people who have a sense of personal excitement. A sense of urgency is the starting point. By letting their perceptions and expectations be the driving force good communications will be fostered.

There is little then that the team leader can do to motivate the team whose members must motivate themselves. However, assembling the right team is vital for success. There must be a 'fit' between architectural philosophy and the motivation of all other team members.

An important role in building and maintaining a project organisation is in leading by inspiration, as well as by example – accepting responsibility and removing obstacles which might impede the team. Controlled risks may be required, and people must be encouraged to learn from each other whilst displaying innovation and optimising their individual contributions to the project. They should willingly share information rather than remain gatekeepers of it. It is also essential to note that the role of the architect, like those of most of the team, will change with varying phases of the project.

According to Adair (1986), the key roles of a team leader are as follows:

- Initiating action by the team;
- Regulating the pace and direction of developments;
- Informing the group;
- Supporting team members 'emotionally';
- Evaluating goals, decisions, performance and procedures.

11.3 Designing the team

The requirement for an effectively designed team have been summarised by Hastings et al (1986) as:

- Clearly defined roles and responsibilities;
- Effective channels of communications – both formal and informal;
- Flexible but detailed planning;
- Negotiated success criteria and bonding;
- Well managed factors external to the project.

Whilst the formal organisation structure plays an obvious but static part in achieving some of these, team-building is a much more dynamic form of behaviour which requires effective leadership. Leadership can be thought of as the process of influencing others to work willingly towards an organisation's goals to the best of their abilities. The essence of effective leadership is 'followership' – the willingness of people to follow is what makes someone a leader.

Architects may long have considered themselves to be the natural leaders of the building team. The traditional procurement arrangement reinforced this view, and many project teams have felt themselves to be led by an architect who had not earned the title of 'leader'. In other words, it is the failure of some architects as project managers and leaders in the past which gave rise to the demands for 'modern' procurement systems. Many architects remain relatively unskilled in the tasks of leadership and project management, despite their intensive training in creative design. Most architects would benefit from improving their ability to lead and manage projects, with particular emphasis on the social skills of team-building.

The four major influences upon a leader of a project are as follows:

1 Their own personality characteristics (relatively fixed);

2 The attitudes and needs of the rest of the team (variable);

3 The nature of the project organisation, as dictated by the procurement arrangement (relatively fixed);

4 The external environment beyond the project (relatively fixed).

In effect, the primary responsibility of the leader/team builder is to influence or change the attitudes of team members so that they subjugate their personal and parent organisations' goals to those of realising the project. Team-building exercises, such as assignments, discussion groups or workshops (not necessarily project-related) help to weld a cohesive and effective team.

11.4 Example: Conservation project

Conservation is a specialist area within the construction industry with many differences in approach. Views on pastiche vary and how modern interventions – whether adaptations or extensions – should be treated is central to the design philosophy.

In this example an old school with a B1 listing is to be renovated and adapted for use as a community arts centre. The client is concerned about preserving our heritage and wishes to see as much of the original building retained as possible.

The architectural appointment was secured by the client approaching The Society for the Protection of Ancient Buildings (SPAB) who supplied a list of architects who were SPAB scholars. The chosen architect discussed his and the SPAB philosophy for the treatment of old historic buildings and agreed on a design approach. This can be summarised as follows:

The basis of the SPAB approach to conservation is rooted in a deep respect for the workmanship, skills and materials of past generations and their societies, and a belief that all buildings must be allowed to adapt to change in a manner that respects and understands their traditional technology, but which also reflects the technologies, society and architecture of today in any interventions and changes that become necessary to meet today's needs.

In working with old buildings of all ages and types the architect aims to allow the building to tell its story to future generations by conserving the historic fabric as much as possible and by using traditional materials for repair to slow down the rate of decay. The architect seeks to allow that story to continue unfolding by incorporating sensitively the best contemporary design and technology in situations where alterations and new insertions are required.

To incorporate this philosophy into a design solution the architects will be looking to assemble a team of professionals who can empathise with this outlook. All design problems are subject to subjective interpretation. What is crucial is how each of the different disciplines perceives the design problem. Sensitivity towards traditional construction techniques and the philosophy of conservation and repair rather than renewal is required.

An engineer – whether structural or M&E – who is likely to fall into the 'category trap', i.e. identifying the problem by the category of solution most commonly found is unlikely to bring much to work on historic buildings. The transfer of solutions previously seen in new buildings to the conservation of historic buildings is seldom the answer.

The structural engineer will need to be experienced in the refurbishment of old buildings. Many engineers are well versed in modern techniques of reinforced concrete, structural steel and brick structures. An understanding of old buildings with load-bearing stone walls built with lime mortars is not so common. Where repair rather than renewal is called for by the architect, an engineer who can think outside the 'box' of concrete and steel will be able to make a considerable contribution to the design. There will be a 'fit' between the aspirations of the architect and engineer and a solution that is not in conflict with the stated design aims.

The problems for M&E engineers are that historic buildings will have solid stone walls and single glazed sash windows. The design philosophy will not allow any improvement in the insulation values through the use of dry lining to increase 'U' values (to comply with current building regulations, the building will need to be listed to adopt this approach). Most old buildings relied on very good ventilation to maintain the fabric from penetrating damp and dry rot. Draught proofing to conserve energy and the installation of central heating can disturb the environmental balance that has kept the building sound and encourage the growth of dry rot. Sensitivity towards these types of issues, and an understanding that there are few service voids for new services and that historic detail must be maintained, is important.

The quantity surveyor will have to understand that the repair and conservation of old buildings is the protection of our heritage and that ripping out and replacement is not an option with a listed building – even though in many cases it may be the cheapest. It must also be understood that the cost implications of using lime mortars and renders are not the same as using sand and cement plasters and renders.

Much of the knowledge of traditional trades used to construct building for centuries has been unlearnt over the years. A demand for more and bigger buildings that are energy efficient and respond to new requirements has found this traditional knowledge of little use. But it must now be re-learnt – by designers and engineers as much as by craftsmen – and disseminated to gain greater acceptance and understanding for use on future historic building projects.

Design in the context of conservation projects is an investigative process and a form of research. The historical context of the building and the techniques used must inform the design solution whether structural or M&E as much as architectural.

11.5 Power in teams

This demands that leaders possess a degree of power, from some or all of the following categories:

1 Legitimacy, from the authority vested in their official role;

2 Reward, based on the capacity to control and reward others;

3 Coercion, based on the capacity to penalise undesired behaviour;

4 Expertise, which is valued by others;

5 Information, the distribution of which is within their control (including design concepts and details);

6 Reference, resulting from being admired or liked by others.

Architects on a traditional project are particularly strong in numbers 1 and 5. Well respected architects may rate highly on several of the others, but their greatest challenge is in gaining the respect of the rest of the project team for their powers of leadership and team-building. Leaders must balance a concern for production with a concern for people: they are not running either a prison camp (chain gang) or a holiday camp. They must not allow their concern for the aesthetics of design or for strict adherence to contract conditions to override their focus on effective interpersonal relationships, and on fair treatment of all stakeholders in order to realise the design. A supportive style, displaying personal commitment to the project objectives and loyalty to the project team, should result in improved teamwork, with consequent reductions in grievances, conflict and dysfunctional behaviour.

Given that most projects operate in a moderately favourable situation, (where leader–member relations, task structure and position power are neither very strong nor very weak) management theory indicates that interpersonal-orientated leaders are most effective. This is where the emerging concepts of partnering may assist the architect in developing the most appropriate type of leader behaviour, from the range of directive, supportive, participative and achievement-orientated styles. Leaders should display inspiration, intellectual stimulation and personal consideration, coupled with whatever charisma they can muster. They need to offer a sense of mission/vision and instil respect and trust in themselves and in their design by the rest of the team if they are to be fully effective.

11.6 Lessons from partnering

Partnering represents more than just another project procurement technique, although any appropriate procurement system can be used to activate good practice, to bring about a change of team culture and to create a more cohesive group. Formal partnering is where there is an explicit arrangement between parties, although informal partnering, like informal organisational structures, will exist regardless of the formalities: partners should be selected using quality-based criteria and previous experience rather than on price alone.

The stage of a project at which partners are brought together will depend upon the selected method of procurement, with the chances of successful partnering increasing with earlier involvement of the parties. The primary function of project partnering is to enthuse the team with the challenges of the project, developing trust and mutual co-operation with a view to optimising project performance. This generally includes completing on or before programme, at or below budget, with a reasonable profit margin for all participants and with zero accidents and zero quality defects. Designs will be primary, and of course remain the prerogative of the architect.

Even in informal partnering arrangements, where the term partnering is not actually used, it makes sense to bring the project team together at the earliest possible stage and to spend some time in a neutral venue in a workshop which will develop team spirit and open communications, agree specific goals and plans, and foster commitment to the success of the project. It should be remembered that there is no such thing as an 'optimum' design, so the architect's design concepts must remain paramount. Whilst a formally signed partnering agreement or charter will strengthen the partnering culture, even informal arrangements can use the workshop approach to promote co-operation. Occasional follow-up workshops may adopt a similar format to the initial one, with a view to reinforcing co-operation and encouraging a win–win outcome.

The Royal Commission into Productivity in the Building Industry in New South Wales has developed a ten point partnering effectiveness monitor which might usefully be adopted by architects in managing their projects.

1 Quality achieved in the completed project;

2 Cost controlled;

3 Time performance;

4 Teamwork;

5 Safety;

6 Avoidance of industrial disputes;

7 Avoidance of litigation;

8 Satisfactory cash flow;

9 Environmental impact contained;

10 High morale and job satisfaction.

The first three factors were rated as three times as important as the last three, with the middle four being rated as twice as important as those last three.

There is a risk in formal partnering if performance is unsatisfactory, but partnering of any description has several critical success factors.

- The team should have no 'weak links' in its membership.

- Clients must be properly and actively represented, and guided throughout the project.

- The team should remain stable throughout the project (if possible).

- Partnering should commence at the design stage; there should be a team leader or project 'champion' to maintain the partnering ethos and principles.

- Major sub-contractors, suppliers and specialist trade contractors should be included.

Of course, partnering may involve additional expense (for example, the cost of 'workshops') and there are other risks relating to risk of over-dependency, loss of confidentiality, possible corrupt practices and risk of loss investment in partnered developments. The 'workshop' sessions may be extremely informal, and their key aim, other than team-building, should be to allow communication of design concepts. However, it is considered that the concept of partnering has much to offer the architect and the rest of the project team in providing guidelines for the development and maintenance of trust and commitment, irrespective of the degree of formality adopted for a particular project.

A final feature of the partnering approach is the completion workshop where the entire project is evaluated and, hopefully, the lessons learnt are disseminated. This is similar to a post-completion audit, and should benefit all participants in the future. It should represent the culmination of the work of the project team as a 'learning organisation' which learns from the past. These lessons can be put into practice effectively if the team as a unit is reused for future projects – otherwise much of the learning may be dissipated.

11.7 The project team as learning organisation

There has been much written about the concept of the learning organisation, based on the academic theories of learning such as that of Kolb (1984). Kolb's learning cycle consists of a four-part loop of Planning/Hands-on experience/Reflection/Abstract Conceptualisation, with multiple cycles (i.e. Plan/Do/Check/Act repeated).

Architects are often regarded as preferring the active experimentation phase, whilst engineers are considered to choose the hands-on experience phase. Reflection, resulting in abstract concepts, is less commonly implemented, but this represents the true learning part of the cycle – learning from experience. Where architects, as project managers, can benefit from Kolb's theory is in the promotion of reflection and subsequent improvement by team members. As leaders of project teams they should encourage constructive discussion of project developments and the suggestion of innovative solutions to problems as they arise. Feedback to all team members can only benefit their performance on existing and future projects.

A learning organisation can be identified as one which promotes communication and collaboration so that it may continuously experiment, improve and increase its capability through its members' problem-solving activities. The memory of the learning organisation exists both in the recollections of its human resources and in its record-keeping/archiving. Each of these may be an imperfect source of memory, and it is up to the project leader to manage the output of the creative problem-solving process as well as to stimulate effective engagement with the learning process. Action research, as advocated by Revans (1971), is an excellent method by which team members can develop their technical and personal skills.

Aesthetics and architectural expression are always to the fore in the architects' mind but some modern buildings are fundamentally efficient utilitarian sheds. Their design is more of a partnership with process engineers who understand the production line flow and the specialist equipment required. The production process is paramount. Efficiency in terms of layout and cost is crucial. A basic understanding of each other's discipline is crucial for good communication – all decisions are interdependent and close teamwork is essential. Assembling a new team for every new project is just not efficient. The solutions and techniques learnt on past projects must be carried over and reused. For example, the service requirements for food processing buildings can be very different to most buildings, with refrigeration rather than heating being the focus. The building envelope must keep the heat out – not in. Cost is vital and a structural engineer who can design economical and efficient steelwork is necessary. Where relationships built up on previous projects have worked successfully they must be used again. Working together over several projects allows for the development of standard solutions to recurring design problems.

In summary, there is benefit for all in creating a learning organisation out of a project team. The resultant culture of excitement and innovation will be easier to bring about if team members have confidence in each other's competence and integrity. However, the main influence will be that of the team leader, whose primary role should be to encourage creative thinking, constructive criticism and effective learning from the problem-solving experiences throughout the project.

11.8 Project structures

Organisational structures dictate the allocation of tasks and responsibilities, reporting formats, levels of authority and groupings of individuals. They play an important part in the performance and morale of a project, and need to be appropriately designed for a particular project and the parties to it.

Among the principles of organisational design are clarification of objectives, specialisation into functions, defined levels of authority and responsibility, with an effective open control. Whilst a badly designed structure can lead to inefficiency, delay, conflict, rising costs and low motivation, a well chosen framework can be of major benefit in achieving the goals of the project, with satisfaction for all team members.

Other than for very major projects with staff fully dedicated to a single contract, (known as a pure project structure) most construction developments use a matrix-type of organisation structure. This tries to combine the advantages of a pure project structure with those of functional organisations which operate within most non-project based businesses. It is recognised that staff from a multitude of backgrounds and parent organisations have come together, often on a part-time basis, for the purpose of executing one single project, before moving on to other projects or back to their parent organisations. The multi-disciplinary nature of project teams, made up of staff with varying loyalties and directions, makes the task of team-building a challenging one. The harmonising of a multiplicity of motivations to produce a focus on the needs of the project and its client represents the most difficult part of the role of the project manager.

An important factor is the degree to which the project manager is able to exercise executive power, rather than merely act as a co-ordinator. The essential form of the structure is likely to have been dictated by the selected procurement system, and by the construction experience of the client themselves, but the team leader retains some discretion as to the detailed shape of the structure. The most variable factor will be the means by which the contractor is appointed and the stage at which this happens.

Regardless of the above, the manager of the project team may find it helpful to compile and issue a linear responsibility chart as shown in Figure 11.1. This is a device which lists the major tasks of the project team and clearly identifies the level of responsibility (if any) that each team member has for every activity. This has the benefit of allocating tasks and of clarifying for all team members the duties of every other member. Symbols can be devised to summarise the relationship between each

Figure 11.1: Linear responsibility chart

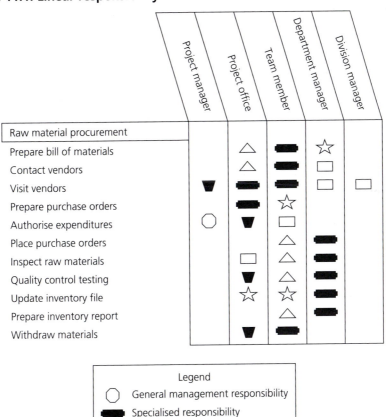

task; one matrix can summarise the array of duties and responsibilities, integrating the contribution of each party to the project. Analysing the responsibilities of each member at the start of a project in order to produce such a chart is an excellent discipline for the team leader, compelling them to plan in detail for all aspects of the future management of the project and the connections between the parties to it.

11.9 Developing the team

Root cause analysis of problems and effective development of solutions in an open, proactive and positive environment can develop an effective project organisation without the need for formal training. Most construction projects are of a nature and duration that there is inbuilt training and learning by the participants. Additional training programmed should be simple and flexible, promoting open discussion and reducing the perceived risk of possible rejection by participants. Realistic team-building objectives are required, with appropriate set-up, approaches and administration which focus on enhancing participation by all involved. The types of team-building exercises adopted will depend on the project, the individual team members and their stage of development as a group. They may include questionnaires, interviews, syndicate discussions and responsibility charting.

A construction project tends to operate on the border of stability and instability, on the knife-edge of order and disorder; hence, building a project team cannot be regarded as a straightforward collecting of appropriate individuals, telling them what to do, and leaving them to it. People must be trained in how to co-operate fully with the rest of the team, and be allowed to participate fully in developing the best means of achieving the project objectives, even if these targets have necessarily been dictated by the client and the brief.

Effective leaders of project teams may require training in the behavioural skills necessary to perform this role effectively, regardless of technical expertise and depth of experience. They should attend relevant courses and study relevant texts (listed at the end of this chapter in the reference and key reading sections). They should also develop themselves by studying the performance of other effective project leaders and by having discussions with them. The newer skills which are increasingly being recognised as necessary include:

- The timing of interventions (neither too early nor too late);
- Asking the correct questions, in a challenging but non-critical fashion;
- Using the appropriate language, without excessive jargon, analysis or intellectualising the team-building and management process;
- Saying nothing and remaining invisible when appropriate;
- Following several processes within the project simultaneously;
- Making statements truthfully in a way which will be of maximum benefit.

These skills may be used to foster an 'action learning' culture within which trust, confidence and harmony will lead to more successful projects, with all of their attendant benefits. The team needs to simultaneously break through the two barriers of uncertainty and the need to share information. It is not enough to be open merely for the sake of being open, particularly in the uncertain conditions of construction projects. One must break down any practice of 'gate keeping' (keeping one's knowledge to oneself so far as possible) whilst balancing this with progressive reduction of uncertainty through agreed specific targets.

11.10 Maintaining the team

Building and maintaining an effective project organisation represents the most important role of the leader of a building project: they should promote the 'teamthink' approach and maximise the focused creativity of participants in balancing divergent and convergent thinking. 'Groupthink' is where individuals spend an inordinate amount of time in seeking agreement with each other, to the exclusion of alternative solutions to problems. This self-censorship may obviously result in defective or sub-optimal decisions. Teamthink, where members engage in synergistic thinking, encouraging divergent views whilst being aware of both uniqueness and limitations of each party, is widely considered to enhance decision making and team performance.

Teams are often considered as developing through four stages, from forming, through storming (early disagreements) and 'norming' (developing effective ways of working together) towards performing as an effective mature group. Unfortunately, project teams rarely have the luxury of this natural evolution, but the variations in effectiveness of a team during a project will follow a pattern such as illustrated by Moore (2002):

COLLECTION → ENTRENCHMENT → RESOLUTION → SYNERGY(PEAK) →
DECLINE → BREAKUP

Because of the nature of the typical construction project, there may be justification for having different project leaders at particular phases of the work. This requires a flexible, transformational organisation which relies on participants' disinterested vision of the needs of the project as a whole rather than a transaction–action structure which operates on the basis of exchange of services for remuneration. However, few projects or parties to them appear to be fully prepared to introduce this open-system concept and the traditional, closed-system paradigm remains the dominant approach.

Managing a project, like managing a meeting, operates on two levels; the 'content' (what should be done, when, by whom, at what cost, requiring what information) and the 'process' (managing peoples' interactions and satisfying their ego needs, ensuring productive rather than passive agreement, and controlling digressions to achieve decisions). It must be remembered that whilst individuals exercise control, the role of the organisation structure is to mediate between the conflicting demands of team members and harness these in pursuit of the project objectives.

If an effective project team has been established, it can be identified by many of the following characteristics:

- People smile, naturally and genuinely;
- People display confidence and a 'can do' attitude;
- People show loyalty to the team and the project, rather than attempting to denigrate or criticise their colleagues;

- People are relaxed and friendly rather than tense and hostile;

- People are open to outsiders, and to new ideas;

- People are energetic, lively and active, with energies directed towards the 'project' rather than towards self-protection or justification;

- People are enterprising and proactive rather than reactive;

- People listen attentively to each other without interruptions;

- Peoples' efforts match, complement and augment each other, producing a team energy which exceeds that of the sum of the individuals' energy;

- People communicate effectively, using image, metaphor and analogy for complex concepts, as well as the usual speaking and writing skills;

- People maintain enthusiasm and optimism regardless of set backs.

The effective manager of the project team will continually monitor team behaviour and encourage this to be as outlined above, taking speedy action to correct any situations where there are signs of the opposite occurring. However, team maintenance should not require undue energy to be diverted from task achievement.

11.11 Conclusion

This chapter has tried to illustrate the ways in which successful project team-building can learn from partnering, learning organisation concepts, the theory of organisational structures, and traditional and modern team-building techniques. Readers must judge what aspects of these are relevant to their own particular role or project and act accordingly. They must remember that, despite the advent of e-commerce and computerised project information, teams which meet face-to-face on a regular basis generally operate more effectively than the 'virtual' teams currently being created as a result of the 'information explosion'. Other factors being equal, most people still prefer to do business on a personal basis, within an encouraging, constructive environment. Combining concern for the individual and the group with consideration of the needs of the project and its client, they will have built the basis of a successful project organisation.

Best practice bullet points which summarise the chapter are as follows:

- High performance teams do not arise spontaneously, but must be selected, developed and maintained proactively.

- Teams must be led, gently but decisively, with a firm focus upon the client and the project.

- Effective leaders are supportive, flexible, are people-orientated, creating environments where members motivate themselves.

- Teams need clearly defined roles, responsibilities, procedures and communication channels.

- Leaders should exercise their power very carefully, and recognise the value of informal groups within the team.

- Team members should be treated as equal partners, with emphasis on the critical success factors of partnering arrangements.

- The project should be treated as a learning opportunity for all team members, with periodic review of lessons learned (feedback).

- The principles of organisation theory should be followed in choosing an organisation structure and monitoring its performance.

- Teams must be developed and maintained through continuous efforts by the project leader, preferably face-to-face.

References

Adair, J., *Effective Team-building*, Pan Books Ltd (1986).

Drucker, P. F., *Managing in Time of Great Change*, Butterworth Heinemann (1995).

Hastings, C., Bixby, P. and Chaudry-Lawton, R., *Superteams*, Fontana Paperbacks (1986).

Kolb, D. A., *Experimental learning-experience as a source of learning and development*, Prentice Hall, New Jersey, USA (1984).

Moore, D. R., *Project Management, Designing Effective Organisational Structures in Construction*, Blackwell Science Publishing, Oxford (2002).

Revans, R. W., *Developing Effective Managers – A New Approach to Business Education*, Longman, London (1971).

Key Reading

Adair, J., *Effective Team-building*, Pan Books Ltd (1986).

Belbin, R. M., *Management Teams: Why They Succeed or Fail*, Heinemann (1981).

Fryer, B., *The Practice of Construction Management*, 3rd edn, Granada (1999).

Garrett, R., *The Learning Organisation*, Fontana Books (1987).

Garrett, R., *Learning to Lead*, Fontana Books (1990).

Glass, N., *Management Masterclass – A Practical Guide to the New Realities of Business*, Nicholas Brealey, London (1996).

Handy, C., *Understanding Organisations*, 4th edn, Penguin Books Ltd (1999).

Hastings, C., Bixby, P. and Chaudry-Lawton, R., *Superteams*, Fontana Paperbacks (1986).

Lawson, B., *How Designers Think*, Architectural Press Ltd (1986).

Mackay, I., *40 Checklists for Managers and Team Leaders*, Gower Publishing Ltd (1993).

Moore, D. R., *Project Management, Designing Effective Organisational Structures in Construction*, Blackwell Science Publishing, Oxford (2002).

Moxon, P., *Building a Better Team*, Gaver Press, Hampshire (1993).

Newcombe, R., Langford, D. and Fellows, R., *Construction Management; Organisational Systems*, Mitchell Ltd, London (1990).

Nolan, V., *Teamwork*, Sphere Books Ltd, London (1987).

Reiss, G., *Project Management Demystified*, E&FN Spon (1993).

Revans, R. W., *Developing Effective Managers – A New Approach to Business Education*, Longman, London (1971).

Scott, J. and Rochester, A., *Effective Management Skills; Managing People*, Sphere Books Ltd, London (1984).

Walker, A., *Project Management in Construction*, 4th edn, Blackwell Science Publishing, Oxford (2002).

Effective construction sub-contracting management

John Tookey, School of the Built and Natural Environment,
Glasgow Caledonian University, UK, and
Winston Shakantu, Department of Construction Economics and Management,
University of Cape Town, South Africa

12.1 Introduction

In the modern construction industry, an effective approach to the management of sub-contractors is a prerequisite for overall success on a project. This has never been more critical from the point of view of today's architect. The tendency towards an increasing use of sub-contractor designed elements within the construction process means that a project can rapidly get 'out of control' from a design standpoint. A problem magnified by the lack of any single point of contact with which to deal, since sub-contractors may have been employed at the behest of the main contractor, or by any one of a number of other project stakeholders. Consequently, this chapter attempts to set out the main criteria for successful sub-contractor management through the vehicle of a case study of a large international construction project with a total of some 200 sub-contractors. The bulk of the chapter, therefore, focuses on the development of the Cape Town International Conference Centre (CTICC), within the metropolitan Cape Town area.

The site, as well as the project as a whole, has various interesting features making the management of both the construction process and sub-contractors a particular challenge. The approaches utilised by both architects and contractor in order to manage sub-contractors are analysed and assessed within the context of the challenges of the project. The relative merits of each approach or technique are then critically assessed according to the degree of success that was achieved. The chapter concludes with recommended methods of dealing with sub-contractor management from the point of view of the architect. Whilst it is recognised that the methods recommended do have particular regional and cultural biases, the general and generic nature of best practice from a South African case study offer lessons to both UK and international architects.

12.2 The evolution of the construction process

During the early decades of the 20th century it was common for contractors to undertake all of the construction work on a building project. Overseeing the work of the dedicated multi-functional contractor, the architect controlled the design and construction process from initial stages all the way through to completion. Procurement tended to take place over a considerable period of time which, in turn, allowed the architect to develop fully the design of the building. Since that time, many factors have colluded to cause an increasingly rapid shift away from this paradigm.

Time, or more precisely the lack of it, has become a dominant factor in the construction industry. Less and less time is available to develop more and more complex project solutions. This applies equally to all the stakeholders in the process, from both a design and an engineering perspective. Since procurement time is at a premium, contractors have to quote for work based on incomplete designs. This significantly increases the risk factors associated with the development of a project. As a means of mitigating that risk, contractors increasingly take the pre-eminent position in many contracts – thus, the degree of control enjoyed by architects of both design and process has been gradually eroded.

Another crucial factor in the changing face of construction has been technology and its advancement within the construction industry. Technology has changed tremendously, and so has the knowledge of its application. Historically the industry has been hallmarked by its conservatism with regard to the adoption of new technologies. The application of new materials and technologies represent particular challenges to architects, engineers and contractors, and consequently needs to be addressed by the professional bodies within the industry.

The combination of these rapidly evolving operating conditions has created significant changes in the approaches and principles adopted by industry as a whole. Contractors have tended to be at the focus of these changes, since they are effectively required to take on significantly more risk and design responsibility than ever before. Contractors have responded by adopting more flexible, responsive business strategies designed to minimise risk. Various reports have been published which have sought to restructure and refocus the industry to one more in line with the needs of the economy and the government in general. Numerous personalities, Emmerson (1962), Banwell (1964), Latham (1994) and, most recently, Egan (1998) have all had an input into the on-going debate as to how to best run the construction process. Arguably, many of the main points raised by each of these reports are raised in each successive report. The seminal montage from Murray and Langford (2003) investigates these issues and provides an essential backdrop to both current and historic concepts and policies within the industry.

12.3 Origins of sub-contracting

Sub-contracting can therefore be seen as the reality and, indeed, future of the construction industry. In order for architects to be in a position to better influence the decisions routinely taken in relation to sub-contracting, it is essential for the architect to understand the philosophical construct in which sub-contracting is extant. There are in general three different origins of specialist and trade contractors: sub-letting of labour content by main contractors, replacement of main contractors' craft operatives by trade contractors and the proliferation of technologically advanced firms.

12.3.1 Sub-letting of labour content by main contractors

This has been an on-going process, which has accelerated in recent years as contractors have downsized to a point of being mainly shell administrative organisations. In essence the risks, costs and overheads associated with maintaining substantial numbers of personnel 'on the books' cannot be sustained in the context of the microscopic margins 'enjoyed' by contractors. Contractors know well that they can hire and fire labour with ease by employing a labour-only sub-contractor. This, in turn, means that contractors do not have to maintain the substantial infrastructure associated with the recruitment and administration of such workers.

In general terms this does not have a significant impact from the point of view of the architect since direct (i.e. unskilled or, at best, semi-skilled) labour normally does not have direct impact on quality or aesthetics. The use of this type of labour has no impact at all on the control of that labour. Arguably, it could be said that such labour is much easier to control since there is much greater financial control that can be afforded to the project team.

12.3.2 Replacement of main contractors' craft operatives by trade contractors

Craft workers have also become a commodity much like the unskilled types of labour. Again, the issue revolves around the costs and overheads associated with their continuous employment by a contractor. It is well known that certain types of skilled worker can command significant salaries through a combination of high piece rates and an ability to 'moonlight' by doing private jobs concurrently with their input to substantial projects. In spite of the high costs associated with employing skilled craft operatives on a short-term basis it is more cost effective than to hire their services continually.

Potentially this approach has a significant impact on the role of the architect and the delivery of a high quality product. Craft operatives are largely responsible for finishes on any construction project, particularly such elements as joinery, plasterwork, electricals, etc. Since finishes are the element of the construction process most visible to the client, potentially the use of 'fly by night' sub-contractors brought in by a main contractor on a short-term basis with no long-term 'ownership' of the project may present some not inconsequential problems for the commissioning of a building. However, although the operational and quality issues raised by contractors not using directly employed skilled tradesmen do cause concern, they do not represent a problem for control of the design of a building. Largely, it can be reported that the 'good' contractors in the industry today try to build up a reasonable number of directly employed (or at least retained) craftsmen as a means of ameliorating the problems highlighted here.

12.3.3 Proliferation of technologically advanced firms

Recent years have also seen a substantial increase in the technological complexity of the construction process. As materials and system solutions have evolved so the construction industry has had to rapidly ramp-up its technological proficiency. Consequently, substantial numbers of technical specialist contractors have begun to permeate the mainstream construction industry.

The preponderance of technical specialists presents significant difficulties of design control for the architect of today. Specialist contractors are bought in for the purpose of contributing a technical capability in areas of engineering or production of which the architect may have very limited knowledge. Architects have traditionally exercised control in the construction process through a superior knowledge of both the process itself and on the techniques of construction. The change in the technical ascendancy of the various contractors and sub-contractors, therefore, inhibits the architect in the exercise of design control. In a very real sense, this trend can be seen as an analogue for the way in which labour was deliberately deskilled in order to exert management control by adherents of the Taylorist school of management (Kanigel, 1997). In essence, as soon as pre-eminence of either skill or system knowledge is relinquished in any process, so control of the process by the executor is lost. It is at this point that architectural design control in particular can be rapidly lost. In general terms it is the increase in the number of technologically advanced firms, with its attendant loss of design control, which presents the most difficult challenge for architects in the future.

12.4 Causes of increased levels of sub-contracting

Since the turn of the 19th century, many factors have caused an increasingly rapid shift from site production to site assembly of an enormous variety of components many of which are made in factory conditions. Componentisation and further technological progress thus becomes an increasingly important concept that needs to be addressed by architects. As the number of components increases and technology changes, there is an increasing demand for the knowledge of specialists. Complex sub-assemblies and systems can now be delivered to site pre-assembled for 'bolt on' inclusion in the construction process, rather than bespoke assembly *in situ*.

Examples of such complex systems in common usage today are modular shower/ toilet units for inclusion in developments such as hotels, etc. These units offer significant benefits for the construction process in terms of build quality and system performance since they are pre-assembled in controlled factory environments. However, such modular construction techniques can be perceived as being an inhibition of design freedom from the point of view of design professionals. In the UK there is a particular institutionalised bias associated with modular construction techniques. In the 1950s, the pre-fabricated house building systems became synonymous with shoddy, poor quality, living spaces. Subsequently, the 'system-build' techniques of the 1960s and 1970s received equally poor reputations. However clichéd, the pervasive view of system-build construction is that of anodyne, anonymous tower blocks whose main contribution to society and architecture is in their creation of high-rise ghettos. However, these approaches to construction are largely considered to be prototypical of modern modular systems.

12.5 Appointment and management of sub-contractors

Sub-contractors may be nominated, where work is of a specialist nature and where the architect desires greater control. Alternatively, it may be domestic when appointed by the contractor or named when the architect wishes to restrict the contractor's choice of suppliers. The expectation is that the contractor, in conjunction with the project stakeholders, will appoint firms who are financially sound and technically competent, as performance of the sub-contractor is critical to project success. Unfortunately this expectation is not always realised. Sub-contracting is highly diverse, fragmented, specialised. Specialisation, in particular, has a revolutionary effect upon the way in which the construction process must be managed. Today, for a construction project to be created, all of the required knowledge must be brought together to consider the problem. As the use of components increases, complexity of the component manufacturing and component design process becomes part of the problem of managing the construction process. Detailed design becomes increasingly more complex with each interaction between components, as components cannot be readily altered on site.

To be successful, the project's design leadership and management should focus on operative efficiency giving overall due consideration to the organisational complexity of the whole process. Ideally, the design team must take account of all inputs into the scheme, including manufacturing schedules, logistical limitations, handling needs and assembly processes. A comprehensive approach to design and co-ordination is a prerequisite to the efficient engagement of specialist contractors on any project. Cognisance of the industry's workload diversification by type, size, function, form and method of production, materials used, and execution of the works, equally predicates the requirement for many different trades and specialists. Effective construction is hinged, therefore, upon designing and implementing an integrated and systematic project organisation. With this in mind, we shall now examine the findings of a case study from South Africa based on the development of a new conference and hotel complex in Cape Town.

12.6 Case study: Cape Town International Convention Centre project (CTICC)

12.6.1 Background

In 1999 the Western Cape Provincial Government, the Cape Metropolitan Council, the City of Cape Town and Business Cape joined forces to develop a truly world-class convention centre on a 6.1-hectare site on Cape Town's northern foreshore. To this end, they formed the Cape Town International Convention Centre Company (Pty) Ltd (CONVENCO). CONVENCO was thus tasked to develop an international-standard, multi-purpose conference, convention and exhibition centre (www.capetownconvention.co.za) which, hitherto, was a missing piece of tourism and business infrastructure in the Western Cape.

The CTICC is a development of massive importance to the economic growth of the region and the country. It has been estimated that the centre will create both directly and indirectly 47,000 jobs over the next ten years, as well as contribute R25 billion to South Africa's GDP within that period. Leading hoteliers, ArabellaSheraton, and managers, RAI Group (of Amsterdam), were chosen to run the completed facility following a comprehensive international selection process involving bids from 11 international companies. The project is now complete and hand-over of keys to the operators for final commissioning was made in April 2003. CTICC will bring to bear the RAI Group's extensive international experience in all facets of the facility's operation. The centre boasts of the largest and most advanced equipped kitchen in the Western Cape; the largest dining facility in Cape Town and a highly advanced building management system operating the entire building.

Figure 12.1: 3D model of the Cape Town international convention centre

3D Birds-eye view

1	Auditorium	20	Jasminum and Strelitzia restaurants
2	Ballroom	28	ArabellaSheraton Grand Hotel
3	Boardroom	29	Canal head & ferry terminal
4, 6, 10, 11	Meeting rooms	30	Convention Square & Main entrance
5, 7, 9	Meeting suites	33	Convenience store, Business Centre & Coffee shop
8	Auditorium 1	34	Main foyer
12	Roof Terrace room	36	Marshalling yard
13	Exhibition Hall 1A	37	Gallery walkway
14	Exhibition Hall 1B	38	Marimba à la carte restaurant
15	Exhibition Hall 2	39	Auditorium foyer
16	Exhibition Hall 3	40	Management offices
17	Exhibition Hall 4	41	Lounge
18	Registration foyer		
19	Clivia, Jasminum and Strelitzia conservatories		

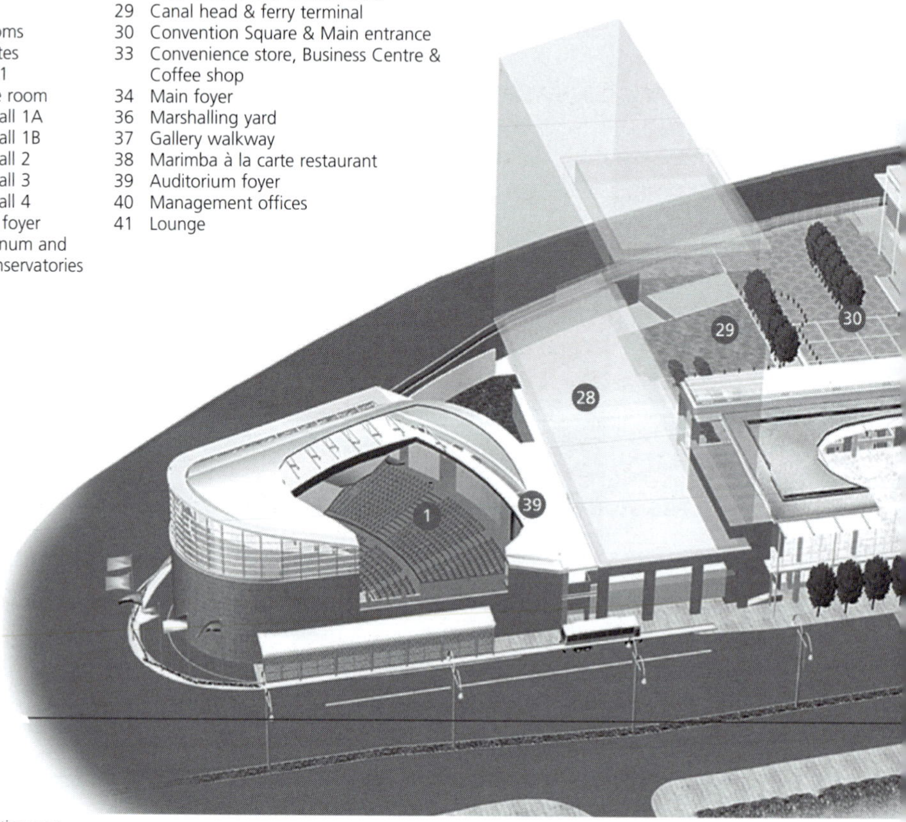

Source: www.capetownconvention.co.za

12.6.2 Project description

CTICC is a world-class undertaking, providing 25,000 m² of space featuring high levels of quality, and exceptional interior and exterior design elements. The project comprises the development of a multi-purpose conference, convention and exhibition centre. It is a three-storey building including numerous facilities, such as an integrated deluxe hotel, dedicated column-free exhibition space, and extensive banqueting and conference facilities. Such an ambitious project required meticulous design of auditoriums, ballrooms, meeting suites, breakout blocks and exhibition halls. CTICC aims to provide a landmark feature at the city/waterfront gateway, and has an impressive domed external appearance with numerous glazed concourses and incorporating internal landscaped areas. Figure 12.1 depicts a schematic of

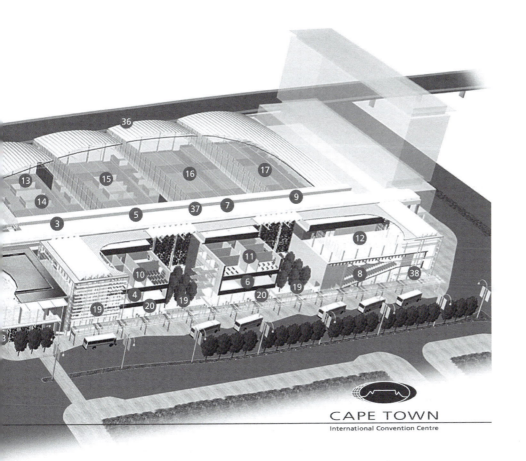

CAPE TOWN
International Convention Centre

the overall CTICC development. The CTICC was designed by an internationally experienced, professional team of design engineering and operational experts, consisting of both local and foreign joint venture partnerships. The centre has been meticulously designed with absolute respect for the end-user and with the most modern amenities and technology as mandatory ingredients. The centre provides flexibility without compromise, with all facilities accommodated under a single roof. CTICC focuses on flexibility throughout the development, which in turn means that a conference organiser does not need to weigh value against facilities, catering against accommodation or environment against practicality since CTICC has it all.

Key elements in the development include:

- Dedicated state-of-the-art 10,000 m² exhibition and trade show space on the ground floor. The exhibition space is column-free, rectangular, with heights from 10–16 m, with power, water and data communications every 4.5 m throughout the hall and a floor load of up to 30 kN/m². This space can accommodate 10,000 delegates in plenary session or can be configured into five separate venues for smaller exhibitions, banquets or conferencing.

- Accommodation includes two raked fixed seating auditoria for 1,500 and 600 people. A further 33 breakout rooms are provided, of which 20 can be reconfigured to different sizes according to need.

- High specification 500-room ArabellaSheraton Hotel is integrated into CTICC.

- Highly advanced kitchen facilities ensure superb banqueting facilities at the CTICC with separation of traffic flow allowing access to all banqueting venues in the centre without interfering with the delegates.

Overall, CTICC is a substantial building, consuming 32,000 m³ of concrete, 3.2 million bricks, 3,000 tons of structural steel and 26,000 m² of roof sheeting. The centre used the services of over 200 sub-contractors, making time, quality, cost, value and design management a real challenge for the project management team. There are three distinct sections within CTICC, namely:

Section 1

- An auditorium seating 1,500 people;

- A hotel;

- The auditorium entrance and foyer.

Section 2

- The convention square;

- A water-borne transport terminal;

- A banqueting area with enclosed bridge connecting sections 1 and 3;
- An administration block.

Section 3

- An auditorium seating 600 people;
- A meeting room accommodating 300 people;
- 10,000 m^2 of exhibition space;
- 20 breakaway rooms;
- A number of bars, a restaurant and coffee shop area;
- The convention foyer;
- A concourse area.

12.6.3 Project team for the construction phase of the CTICC

The design for the convention centre was won in a proposal-call process that was open to professional teams electing to submit proposals for the design and management of the project. Widespread consultation with various stakeholder groups led to further positive input into the design. Each discipline was made up of a number of professional organisations working as single entities for the purposes of contractual arrangements (i.e. as either a consortium, a joint venture or some other form of association). The two main appointments were the project manager and the design architect. Foreshore Architects was named as the joint venture responsible for developing the total design concept, this is an association of various architectural practices including:

- Revel Fox and Partners (architects and planners);
- Van der Merwe Miszewski Architects;
- Lucien le Grange Architects and Urban Planners;
- Stauch Vorster Architects;
- Magqwaka Associates, Architects.

WBHO/Rainbow Construction Cape was named as principal construction developer. The construction phase of the project, which commenced in February 2001, involved the engagement and management of over 200 sub-contractors most of them working in consortia, associations and joint ventures. Consequently, the management and direction of these 200 sub-contractors became a key aspect for the successful delivery of the CTICC, and indeed a critical aspect of the project from the point of view of the architect.

12.6.4   Procurement management strategy

Before examining the role of the sub-contractor management in the successful completion of CTICC, it is essential to understand the socio-political situation within post-apartheid South Africa. CTICC was built in South Africa's Cape metropolis at a time when the country and its construction industry are going through significant restructuring (Dept. of Public Works White Paper, 1999). Top of the list of the South African Government's Reconstruction and Development Programme (RDP) is provision of infrastructure designed to bring relief to people in the form of jobs and economic business development. Expansion of business, the government contends, would increase potential for investment for small, medium and emerging contractors (particularly those representing affirmative business enterprises [ABEs] and previously disadvantaged individuals [PDIs]). PDIs are a key aspect of this situation since they were often long-term unemployed and/or unskilled workers from the townships selected as a means to expand economic activity without particular reference to the skills of the individuals. On-the-job training therefore became an inherent component of the development of all ABEs employed on the CTICC.

Essentially, the RDP policy framework requires that the development of the construction industry must respond to the broad social and economic imperatives of the country. These include sustainable employment creation, affirmative action, active promotion of small, medium and emerging enterprises (SMEEs). The vision is for a construction industry policy and strategy that promotes stability, fosters economic growth and international competitiveness. Furthermore, that the policy should create sustainable employment, which should simultaneously address historic imbalances in employment opportunity as it generates new capacity for economic development. In this regard government is willing to promote appropriate and innovative public/private sector partnerships, which build on the strengths of respective sectors to promote investment in the delivery of infrastructure.

In terms of project and sub-contractor management this strategy created a nightmare situation on site. The PDI selected to work on the site often had literally no construction experience; ABEs had neither skilled manpower nor access to capital since, in essence, they were largely start-up enterprises. SMEEs were inexperienced, lacked managerial and marketing ability and, similarly, had very limited finance. Moreover, the very nature of the construction industry is well known to be high-risk, to both the client and the contractor. Consequently, the potential for disaster was very high, both at a macro, policy making level and at the micro, start-up company level. So how then were the problems addressed in the delivery of the CTICC?

CONVENCO, in conjunction with Foreshore Architects and the other leading members of the project team, formulated an ingenious solution to the management nightmare. Firstly, the project total cost was divided equally between the construction team and the project design and management consultancy team. Then, on the design and project management side, an impressive team comprising of leading local and international consultants was put in place. The design architects' consortium, Foreshore Architects; development manager, CONVENCO Ltd; project managers' consortium, Foreshore Project Managers and principal construction developer joint venture, WBHO/Rainbow Construction Cape, led the team.

At the outset, and in line with the RDP previously mentioned, CONVENCO adopted a human resource development and empowerment policy framework, which is based on principles for empowerment within the context of the procurement process. This framework covered the implementation of empowerment targets, the implementation of empowerment protocols and a targeted procurement management system (TPMS) to monitor, audit and report procurement activity on site. In general terms, the framework is aimed at:

- Ensuring that PDIs and ABEs are afforded opportunities;
- Allowing PDIs and ABEs opportunity to compete for work through association with traditional contractors;
- Ensuring that the process of awarding work is objective and fair;
- Ensuring that CONVENCO's consultants, professionals, contractors, suppliers and manufacturers comply with certain minimum industry standards, while complying with company policy requirements;
- Auditing compliance in terms of its empowerment targets.

In accordance with SunWest's Targeted Access Programme (TAP), submitted as part of its bid for the Cape Metropolis casino licence, CONVENCO's empowerment benefits were directly applied to the ABEs, SMEEs, PDIs (and PDI students) and, finally, the highly, culturally significant need to employ women and women-owned businesses.

12.6.5 Management of sub-contractors at the CTICC project

The procurement of sub-contractors was in line with the targeted procurement policy. Up to well over 200 sub-contractors participated in the project. To ensure equity, targeted contract procurement goals were established. To ensure that the choice, performance, workmanship, health and safety issues, sub-contractor design, manufacturing and installation were all properly managed and co-ordinated, a targeted procurement strategy, support and management system was put in place. This strategy worked wonders in the empowerment and procurement of sub-contractors. The challenges and successes in the management of sub-contractors are described below.

12.6.6 Challenges and successes in the management of sub-contractors at the CTICC

CONVENCO was created to be an equal opportunity, affirmative action employer within the South African context. As such, CONVENCO declared an empowerment procurement policy that offered opportunities to Western Cape organisations and previously disadvantaged individuals, enterprises and industries. All of the participants in the project therefore had to alter their standard methods of working in order to accommodate the strategic goals of CONVENCO. No least did this apply to Foreshore Architects, the scheme design consortium. Some of the challenges and successes on the project were as follows:

Choice of sub-contractors

Strict criteria were set up to properly assess the sub-contractors' capability. Adjudication provisions included *inter alia* that the following criteria be assessed as part of the pre-qualification to tender process:

- Proven track record;

- Specialist construction experience on similar works;

- Appropriate management skills;

- Necessary quality and quantity of resources;

- Adequate financial ability;

- Adequate construction plant;

- Appropriate empowerment.

Appropriate empowerment meant that an ABE or PDI was given an opportunity to benefit from the empowerment process, i.e. an ABE or PDI was identified, allocated a set target according to pre-qualification criteria, given the necessary tender advice at the desk, provided with linkages for financial support and then had their key performance indicators (KPIs) monitored throughout the project by the TPMS system, flagging non-compliance. This meant that Foreshore Architects had to be proactive and deliver to sub-contractors design expertise up-front to assist in their completion of the project. This tends to fly in the face of the normal methods of interfacing with sub-contractors. Normally, particularly with sub-contractor designed elements, there is an expectation of just leaving them to get on with the job and dealing with specific design detailing problems as they arise. Particularly, these problems tend to be with regard to how specific details of a sub-contractor designed element interfaces with the overall scheme concept. This traditional way of thinking could be considered to be 'management by exception', i.e. deal with it when it goes wrong. However, the 'new' way of dealing with sub-contractors was actually to provide extensive amounts of advice and additional detailing up-front. Where possible this was achieved by providing a fully completed design to the sub-contractor at the start. When this, for reasons of programme, was not possible, then Foreshore Architects worked very closely with sub-contractors *in situ* to develop workable solutions.

The project also maintained, through Convenco Empowerment Consultants, a database of all local firms that had met the preconditions of affirmative action and could therefore be used on site. This database was accessible to all members of the core design team. This accessibility meant that as packages were let out to tender as the project developed, Foreshore Architects knew very quickly which sub-contractor was to be selected and could therefore provide all the up-to-date drawings and information very rapidly to the necessary companies. Once again, the rapid up-front provision of information was found to be particularly advantageous since sub-contractors arriving on site were much more up to speed on the nature and scope of the project than they might normally have been.

Concurrent engineering

The development of CTICC saw a real effort to integrate activities more effectively using a concurrent engineering (CE) approach to project development. CE is defined as:

> A systematic approach to the integrated, concurrent design of products and related processes, including manufacture and support. [It] is intended to cause developers, from the outset to consider all elements of the product life cycle from conception through disposal, including quality, cost, schedule and user requirements' (Winner *et al*, 1988).

Whilst not explicitly thought of as a CE approach by Convenco and Foreshore Architects, in essence, the principles of CE were very closely adhered to. Indeed, a precondition of winning any of the major contracts on the project was that the contractor maintained an office in the main management block close to the CTICC site as a means of enhancing and facilitating communication. This is a classic feature of CE known as 'Genba Genbatsu', which is a Japanese concept meaning 'actual time, actual place'. The idea being that it is much easier to solve a problem if you are at the site of the problem and can see the physical context that the problem exists in, rather than trying to interpret from either drawings or photographs. Current best practice tends to highlight the use of telepresence (for further information on telepresence in construction see www.caber.org.uk) using digital video cameras and other visual media. However, the experience of the CTICC is that the best and most effective type of telepresence is to actually be on the site!

Consequently, the physical co-location of the design team with the site became probably one of the most successful elements of CE at work within the project, occupying as it did a single floor of an office complex 50 m from the main construction site. This meant that Foreshore Architects were consistently on site all of the time – as one sub-contractor noted the 'ever present architect' was a substantial help in delivering the sub-contract on time. The presence of the architects so close to the project created tremendous synergy and time savings as problems from the site were able to be dealt with almost immediately – usually through a rapid on-site inspection within a very short period of time from the problem being raised. This was found to be massively advantageous compared to the traditional 'technical query' route, which is as standard in South Africa as it is in the UK. Foreshore Architects were much more able to make timely decisions, whilst simultaneously retaining a greater degree of design control than might normally be expected on a project with significant sub-contractor designed elements.

Information technology

Foreshore Architects were instrumental in the use and updating of the aforementioned sub-contractor database. The availability of this database in conjunction with an all-informed Intranet for the project significantly increased the ability of the design team to turn around problems as they arose. The particular benefit of the Intranet came in the enhancement of decision making with regard to sub-contractor procurement. The most appropriate contractors were identified immediately without the need to invite tenders since they had already pre-registered their interest in participating in the project. This significantly reduced the transaction costs (i.e. the search costs) of finding a suitable sub-contractor. This is a worldwide problem since the costs in terms of time and money of reviewing tenders are substantial. The use of the Intranet and databases held for the project was very beneficial therefore to Foreshore Architects and the project team as a whole. The system significantly benefited the sub-contractors also since it provided them with a fast-track through the tendering process for any of the smaller minor contracts that arise through the gestation period of any project. Foreshore Architects particularly contributed through the regular updating of the projects' requirements for technical expertise and system performance, which meant that sub-contractors could be up or downgraded for certain types of contract on an on-going basis.

Time, cost and quality performance of sub-contractors

Performance was achieved through strict work breakdown, which ensured that each sub-contactor only performed their part of the 'pie' but while working as a conduit in the supply chain. The partnering arrangement was driven down the supply chain to give sub-contractors a feeling of ownership of their part of the pie. A particularly innovative feature of the project was how the ethos of private public partnership was driven down the supply chain through formation of joint ventures between established contractors and ABEs or PDIs. These joint ventures were encouraged as a way of ensuring performance on the part of ABEs and PDIs. It should not be inferred that the ABE or PDI participants were in some way inferior to other potential bidders for contracts. Indeed, the performance of all participants has been seen to be excellent. However, the political and social imperative for this project was that it should be a success in all dimensions. To this end, Foreshore Architects along with all the other design team members had to be much more proactive and collegiate in their approach to dealing with sub-contractors. Sub-contractors were not appointed with the aim of devolving risk to organisations often unable to handle such exposure. On the contrary, the project organisation and management focused on the need for mutual support of each other's activities in the successful delivery of the common aim. This can be seen as a positive expression of corporate and project culture, which is not often duplicated in the adversarial atmosphere of the UK industry in particular.

The role of the architect in achieving this very positive aim was through the provision of information at the earliest time possible. Furthermore, the architect had a regular on-site supervisory role in the assessment of quality at the very lowest level within the project. To this end, the architectural input was always physically available and ever present on-site, rather than the traditional tendency for architects to be physically remote. This was a conscious effort to facilitate team working. Interestingly, in spite of going against the 'normally' expected role of the architect, in many ways this is a step forwards into the past, with the architect being much more closely linked to the way in which, and the quality of, the work being conducted on site. By adopting such an approach to assisting both ABEs and PDIs it was simultaneously possible for the architectural team to retain a much higher degree of design control than may have been anticipated with a similar design and contract elsewhere.

Design manufacturability and assembly

The architects worked hard to facilitate the rapid construction of the project by designing the building for ease of construction. Where possible the structure was designed for modularity, with significant elements of the structure designed specifically to be assembled off-site and brought in. Therefore, in order to speed up construction, all main beams were precast. However, for the 12,000 m^2 suspended parking deck designed for bridge loading (10 t point load), Foreshore Architects argued for a more cost effective *in situ* solution to the originally proposed precast deck. The structural steelwork was contracted out to four suppliers instead of one to ensure supplies kept pace with construction. Moreover, because time was lost during hotel negotiations, the only way to achieve the objective was to come back from foundations at a level of minus 8 m below sea level back to plus 4 m, which is the general ground level, with 12 m long columns, leaving out the basement floors. The tower block was constructed on the 12 m columns going conventionally from there upward. Overall, every effort was made to facilitate ease of construction but, for obvious reasons, on occasion there were instances where compromise had to be struck between ease of assembly, and the costs and practicalities associated with pre-assembly methods.

12.6.7 Conclusions – lessons to be learned from the CTICC

Today, construction is so technologically advanced that no construction firm can or even wishes to conduct the building process in its entirety. As construction technology continues to advance so does the requirement to sub-contract specialist work and trades to those who specialise in the most appropriate discipline at a lower cost than a non-specialist. Such an approach usually provides an achievable solution (on the basis of previous experience and expertise), in less time and to better quality and value. Indeed, most projects today will have even up to 90 percent of their work delivered by sub-contractors with the main contractor only playing a management role. Causes of increased levels of sub-contracting have been seen to be; technological progress leading to greater specialisation, promotion of an enterprise based culture centred on individual initiative and drive towards self employment and specialisation, and the effects of employment taxes on firms.

The effectiveness of both the explicit policies and those techniques such as concurrent engineering principles that were adopted almost by accident have been demonstrated by the significant time and cost savings achieved by the design team under the auspices of the Foreshore Architects. In general, project excellence was achieved through paying careful attention to the effective and value driven selection of sub-contractors. Happily for the CTICC project, the value driven selection of suppliers was not compromised through the requirement to adopt policies to enhance participation by PDIs and ABEs. Whether in Southern Africa or in Northern Europe, value driven sub-contractor selection can be hugely effective.

Once sub-contractors have been appointed, it is essential for any project team to put in place the policies and infrastructure necessary to facilitate the effective working of the design and delivery teams. This can be seen to be highly effective in that the single common office space allowed the physical co-location of team members close to the site and thus in a better position to be able to influence operational activities. This deliberate policy of co-locating the team meant that the architects in particular had a much more 'hands on' way of doing business than in many similar sites worldwide. The concurrent engineering approach used, with its multi-disciplinary approach to problem solving, cut down the time normally taken using the iterative problem solving methods of traditional procurement and design. This resulted in the more effective inclusion of sub-contractors in the definition of, and solution to, problems as they occurred. Particularly important in this context was the need to design for effective construction from the outset, whilst not compromising the architectural integrity of the CTICC scheme. On the basis of the CTICC case study, the CE approach to sub-contractor management should be considered as a means of project management by both architects and project stakeholders.

Underpinning the two main themes of value based sub-contractor selection working within a CE framework is the provision of an effective IT infrastructure and relevant protocols for its efficient utilisation. IT infrastructure and software were significant items of investment for the CTICC project and procedures for handling such technologies had to be sufficiently robust and transparent to enable a CE philosophy. Probably the most important aspect of IT implementation for architects in the UK to consider is that if a value base of sub-contractors is created the integrity of that list has to be maintained, otherwise the effectiveness of such an approved sub-contractor list in saving time in selecting contractors is lost. Much collectively is made of the need to implement IT systems, however the example of the CTICC has indicated that the technological advancement of the database itself, or indeed any accompanying software, is not significantly important. What is most important is a willingness to use and give access to information for as broad a spectrum of stakeholders and sub-contractors as possible. The effectiveness of the approaches adopted, highlighted by the project being delivered within programmed time and budget, demonstrated the epithet quite clearly that 'Knowledge is the only factor of production not subject to diminishing returns'.

Numerous further examples of good practice in the management of sub-contractors came about within the context of CTICC, but that would require much more space than has been allocated in this publication. The unique situation of CTICC means that, in certain dimensions, the case study discussed in this chapter provides relatively limited utility in informing architects and construction practitioners around the world. However, there is much that can be culled from the South African experience that can be used to inform the way in which projects are managed in a UK context. Without doubt, wherever a project is undertaken around the world, effective management of sub-contractors remains an absolute prerequisite for project success.

References

Banwell, H., 'The placing and management of contracts for building and civil engineering work', Report: Ministry of Public Buildings and Works, HMSO (1964).

Department of Public Works (DPW) White Paper, 'Creating an enabling environment for reconstruction, growth and development in the construction industry', Gazette No. 20095, Vol. 407, May, 1999, Pretoria.

Egan, J., 'Rethinking construction', Report of the Construction Task Force on the Scope for Improving Quality and Efficiency of UK Construction, Department of the Environment, Transport and the Regions (DETR) (1998).

Emmerson, H., 'Survey of problems before the construction industries', Report of the Ministry of Works, HMSO (1962).

Kanigel, R., *The One Best Way: Frederick Winslow Taylor and the Enigma of Efficiency*, Viking Press (1997).

Latham, M., 'Constructing the Team', Joint Review of Procurement and Contractual Arrangements in the United Kingdom Construction Industry, Final Report, HMSO (1994).

Murray, M. and Langford, D., *Construction Reports 1944–98*, Blackwell, Oxford (2003).

Winner, R. L., Pennell, J. P., Bertrand, H. E. *et al*, 'The Role of Concurrent Engineering in Weapon System Acquisition', Institute for Defence Analysis, IDA Report R-338, Alexandria VA. (1988).

Acknowledgements

The authors would like to sincerely thank the following people who made significant contributions in helping shape this chapter:

Ms Anya Van der Merwe, Van der Merwe Miszewski Architects (working as Foreshore Architects)

Ms Christine Fife, Convenco Empowerment Joint venture Consultants

Mr Terence Smith, Convenco Empowerment Joint venture Consultants

Convenco and their website www.capetownconvention.co.za

Coping with change and improvement – a simplified guide

Steve McCabe, Faculty of the Built Environment, University of Central England, Birmingham, UK

13.1 Introduction

Apparently, the Gucci family motto goes as follows:

> Quality is remembered long after price is forgotten.

This is undoubtedly true. Much as we all like to purchase what seems to be a bargain, the things that perform least well are those we tend to be most happy to tell others about. As a test, think about something (or someone) that has given reliable service. Now think of alternatives that are not so good. Which would you prefer?

The answer tells you all you need to know about the principle of quality and excellence. Those products, services or people we use in which we have confidence in terms of reliability and performance are ones that, if necessary, for which we would pay extra. The next questions are: 'What is it that they do to ensure they provide a "quality" product or service, and what can all of us learn (the fundamental principle of benchmarking) so that we can achieve similar results and confidence in those customers who purchase/consume our products or services?'. This chapter will, with some examples, provide an overview of the principles of quality improvement, excellence and benchmarking. The text may act as a catalyst for reflection within your architectural practice but perhaps, more importantly, should encourage deeper analysis of the architect's role in the construction supply chain.

13.1.1 The principle of quality

Some believe that the word quality has, in the last 20 years, become somewhat over-used. Many other quality-associated words have entered the lexicon of managers; 'culture', 'improvement', 'excellence', 'benchmark' and, the increasingly ubiquitous, 'world-class' being among them. What quality means is a debate that has raged for many years. Indeed, in the construction industry we have seen an evolution from the prescriptive adoption of 'quality assurance' certification in the 1980s and 1990s (i.e. BS 5750, ISO 9000 series) to the performance specifications of the post-Egan industry (key performance indicators). The earlier formalised systems may have helped to standardise parts of the construction process, but no doubt some architects (and contractors) will have secured 'quality assurance' certification as part of a marketing strategy. Anecdotal evidence would suggest that too many construction organisations have paid 'lip-service' to quality assurance and the rhetoric in many annual reports does not sit easy with an industry that continues to provide a service/product that often fails to fulfil the clients'/users' expectations.

Organisations that have been successful in recent years are frequently found to be those that have dedicated effort to ensure that what they produce is perceived as being not just good value or that it matches expectations, but that it surpasses what was hoped for. What such organisations have found is that developing an obsession with quality is something that has the dual effect of being good for the client and good for the organisation. Because organisations are made up of people, quality works best when those involved in day-to-day tasks are genuinely engaged and, crucially, become passionate about searching for ways to improve the overall service or product that the client receives. Given that the design and construction of a building involves multiple organisations, this cultural transformation is often perceived as difficult. Creating and maintaining a 'passion' for quality in construction has been notoriously problematic. The extended supply chain of designers, contractors, sub-contractors and suppliers creates an extensive barrier to a common goal attitude. However, the intention of this section is to describe how your organisation can consider the ways that it may be possible to engage in improvement in the design processes that you utilise. The knowledge gained from such a process could usefully be fed into the construction process within any project.

13.1.2 Some relevant stories

Despite the fact that we live in a world that appears obsessed by science and the desire to use its principles to solve all our problems, the reality is that it is people who cause most problems and, of course, they who ultimately solve them. In this section there are three tales which show that the 'human element' is an essential part of improvement. Firstly, there is my experience as a young engineer being encouraged to cover up faults. Secondly, there is the experience of a friend who works in car production. Thirdly, an adapted tale suggests that those who design should consider what it is they really do and how it will be used on site.

A personal experience

I remember being on site in the late 1970s as a naïve engineer and was setting out when I discovered an inconsistency in the drawings with the drainage. I talked to the foreman about what he thought I should do. His reply went something like this:

> Well, you could ring up the architect and get it sorted out by them. Trouble is, we'll all stand around waiting which will cost the contractor big time. Alternatively, you could use your initiative and do what fits in and tell them what you've done afterwards. You could, though, just do what it takes and keep your mouth shut. No one will be any the wiser.

'Wouldn't that be wrong and mean that the drawings were not "as built"', I asked. His reply was, to say the least, honest:

> That's the way this industry works. The drawings are there for guidance only. If we expected them to be right we'd never get anything built.

The car worker's story

Someone I know works for one of the well known car manufacturers in the Midlands area and describes his experience in the last 20 years:

> It used to be that we were obsessed by production. We didn't care what happened as long as the track kept rolling. If there was a problem, everyone kept quiet. If we were lucky, it wouldn't be noticed until something went wrong in use and the dealer had to sort it out. The trouble was, buyers started to ask themselves: 'Why should I put up with this?'. And when they realised there were alternatives, especially from Japan, they showed what they thought of our models.

> These days, if someone knows there's a problem, they are encouraged to stop the track. We'll get the engineers or designers down to sort it. We have learned that it's far more damaging and expensive to allow our product to leave the factory than to solve the problems as we find them.

The novice designer

I remember reading an account of a young designer talking to an older more experienced colleague.[1] As the story goes, the younger person is keen to be seen to be doing his job. Accordingly, he draws in a way that is almost unthinking. Noticing this, the older person suggests that in order to become a competent designer it is necessary to do more than demonstrate an ability to work rapidly. The older designer went on to explain that every line on a drawing has a meaning and will cause an action to occur with consequential cost. More important, it was stressed, was the need to carefully consider the range of alternatives that might satisfy the design needs. Having done so, the designer's role is to select the one that is the most efficient method of construction in terms of time, cost and quality. Such knowledge, the older designer advised, came by understanding the technology and people involved in the process. After considering this advice for a couple of moments the young designer started rubbing out what had been drawn.

13.1.3 *Moving on from past mistakes: learning from others*

The stories, above, all suggest that problems are well known but, crucially, eradicating them is 'too much trouble'. Going back to things that 'are quality', we all know that feeling of something that has gone wrong or does not work. To put it plainly, we feel annoyed and, as we often find, getting even minor problems fixed takes up valuable time and effort. The thing is, how do clients of construction feel when what they receive is late, over budget and still has problems?

We all know that construction is never easy. There is increasing pressure to cut both capital and whole life costs whilst offering 'best value' to clients. Regular build clients (i.e. UK supermarket chains) are also seeking shorter contract programmes. Now, according to reports such as 'Rethinking Construction' (Construction Task Force, 1998) and 'Accelerating Change' (Strategic Forum for Construction, 2002), clients believe that as well as wanting construction to produce cheaper and faster products the quality of what they receive is to be significantly improved. However, such reports also make explicit the responsibility of clients to engage in best value rather than lowest bid procurement practice.

A common complaint is that there is no fun in construction any more. Whilst we can feel that the pressures are undoubtedly greater, it is important to realise that construction is not alone. Take automotive production, for instance. In that industry there has been increasing pressure in terms of cost, time and quality. Anyone who bought a car in the 1970s[2] will tell you that things have definitely changed for the better. As British car manufacturers discovered, customers found that there were alternative cars – usually Japanese – which were often not only cheaper and delivered on time but also performed better in terms of breakdowns and performance. Those in car production will often testify that what they produced was, to quote one, 'not terribly good'. There is an adage that is often used to describe the experiences of those who became aware of the potential threat that Japanese alternatives made:

   Get better or get beaten

Therefore, as many construction clients typically ask: 'If other industries can change, why can't you?'. This is the fundamental principle of a technique known as 'benchmarking' (which is fully described in a subsequent section).

What is important is that what other industries – like car manufacture – have so successfully applied, can be used in construction. Most particularly, the design process can benefit from rethinking its processes and the way that its 'product' can be improved so as to benefit the total process and, therefore, what the client receives.

The remainder of this chapter will describe what the principles of improvement are and how, using established tools and techniques, it is possible to create the conditions for similar change to occur in any organisation that carries out design. Prior to doing so, it is worth describing the historical origins of how and why the quality revolution occurred and what impact it has for organisations that want to become more 'customer-focused'.

13.2 **The quality revolution**

The history of quality (particularly that involving post second world war Japanese producers of electronic and automotive products), demonstrates that dedication to improvement can transform the ability of manufacturers of what had previously been perceived as shoddy and cheap products into what are now accepted as being the standard of excellence which others must emulate. As you have probably discovered, products that are regarded as being 'the best' can often attract premium prices. Clearly, dedication to improvement pays.

So, how did the Japanese do it? The answer is effectively to concentrate on two aspects that any organisation is involved in:

1 To continuously search for incremental improvement in every part of the process of creating the product or service;

2 To dedicate time, effort and resources to ensure that those people involved in every process are seen as valued and, significantly, that they are actively encouraged to contribute to the search for improvement.

This approach has been generically called 'Total Quality Management' (TQM) and is the way that an organisation manages its resources to ensure that every process (defined as being the way that inputs are transformed into outputs) and sub-processes are carried out in a way that is 'value-adding'. What this means is that every aspect of what is done to complete day-to-day operations or tasks is analysed in order to look for ways in which the objective might be completed more effectively and with less potential for wasted time, effort or resource. Thus, TQM has clear parallels with the current interest in 'lean' construction. It challenges project teams to explore what value means to a client. Zairi (1996) explains what TQM involves:

> Total quality management recognises contributions from all employees and ensures that people are aligned towards the same ultimate goal, that of meeting customer satisfaction.

In order to achieve this it is essential that the following conditions exist:

- Customer satisfaction becomes the number one priority of the organisation.

- Every person in the organisation (and those that supply from outside) see the value of dedication to the pursuit of continuous improvement in satisfaction levels of customers.

- Rather than seeing any production process as being a number of isolated steps, it is seen in its entirety (the basis for 'Total' in TQM) and, crucially, that they are mutually interdependent upon one another.

13.2.1 The value of improvement

The producers of products that are accepted as being of high quality discover that the extra effort that is dedicated to improvement is worthwhile. As Dr Deming[3] suggested, any production process is an activity that can be constantly improved and there are four major steps which should always be borne in mind: Plan; Do; Check; Action.

Figure 13.1: The Deming Cycle

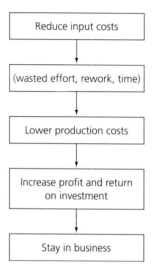

Therefore, he advised, before doing anything, it is necessary to consider how the various parts of the production process fit together. He stressed that every person, if encouraged to do so, would be able to suggest better ways. Additionally, by using simple statistical methods they could measure the improvement that resulted from any alterations. What he believed would result, has been called the 'Deming Cycle' (Figure 13.1).

As well as concentrating on techniques to improve production, he explained, it was essential that more effort should be dedicated to discovering what customers want. Indeed, as he is said to regularly quote, 'Customers are the most important part of the production process'. Accordingly, by improving what you produce, and making it more innovative (think of how miniaturisation has been used in electronic products), you not only stay in business but, significantly, can increase market share.[4] Therefore, investing effort in improvement is worthwhile. The question is: 'How can you do it?'.

13.2.2 Getting started: getting people involved

Achieving high quality does not happen immediately. A cursory inspection of any high quality product will usually reveal that it has attributes such as robustness, attractiveness or elegance, ease of operation and – something that Japanese manufacturers paid a great deal of attention to – reliability. In particular, the design of such products is carried out in a way that ensures the product can be both easily produced and, most especially, any potential problems have been anticipated and eliminated. Undoubtedly, whilst the so-called 'end-customer' is vital in terms of designing to match expectations, it becomes crucial to ensure that every part of the production process is analysed and that the principle of the internal customer assumes great importance. What this means is described by McNair and Leibfried (1992):

> The starting point in achieving excellence is the customer. Whether external or internal to the organisation, the customer sets the expectations for performance and is the ultimate judge of its quality [. . .] A customer is anyone who has a *stake* or interest, in the on-going operations of the company.

In any process, such as the design and construction of a building, there are a number of stages that must be completed. Whilst it seems sensible that each of these stages is independent of each other, the reality is that they are, in fact, *interdependent*. Therefore, if a problem occurs at one stage and is unresolved, it will be passed onto the next stage. So, what becomes crucial is to get people who are involved in each stage to see what they do as being important because, regardless of the size of input, it will become part of the total process. This sometimes means that cultural change is required and that teambuilding is necessary (see below).

The objective of getting people to reconsider their input as part of the total process is fivefold:

1 Create a sense of what is called 'process-orientated thinking';

2 Constantly search for improvement by the use of problem-solving techniques;

3 Understand that integrating activities carried out at each stage will lead to enhanced relationships;

4 Give greater sense of customer focus;

5 Develop a sense of positive change and make employees feel valued.

The first of these, 'process-orientated thinking', is the way that it is aimed at ensuring the explicit link between what is carried out (process) and the results that will ultimately be enjoyed by the customer. So, instead of merely accepting the argument that 'it's always been done like that', the counter-argument is 'can it be done better by doing it differently?'. This could be considered problematic for construction project teams who do not regularly conduct post-project appraisals. One may envisage that the strategic partnering relationships that are developing between architects and clients/ contractors/consultants are facilitating such learning.

Example 1

On one job I came across, there were a number of particular details that had been designed which were awkward to get at. Those carrying out the work complained that when they produced full-sized drawings, this added to problems. The designer noticed this and talked to the foreman who suggested that if the details were A4 sized they could be attached to a clipboard which would lessen the difficulty.

As the person relating this story explained, it required no extra effort on the part of the designer and ensured that those on site perceived that their difficulties had been acknowledged; something that had not been the case before.

The use of problem-solving techniques is important because this reinforces the importance of improvement in processes. Part of the change is to get those involved to admit that problems do occur (not always easy!), to consider what the consequences are, and to search for ways to reduce and, ultimately, eliminate their cause.

Example 2

On another job the person made responsible for distributing drawings was very demoralised by the complaints that he was not able to get them to the right people on time. When asked, he reluctantly admitted that those complaining may be right but that he was too busy trying to keep on top of the job to consider change.

With the help of someone trained in problem solving, he analysed who received what and what was the level of importance attached to their receiving particular information. As he discovered, some people did not need to receive all drawings and did not need them daily. By reorganising the distribution system, he was then able to focus his efforts on making sure that the drawings arrived with the intended recipients more efficiently. As a direct consequence the complaints stopped and the person involved instead received plaudits. This was good for the organisation and good for the individual; he was motivated to attempt problem solving more widely.

In any process there will usually be a number of different people or departments who receive the output from the preceding stage. Their ability to produce their optimal results (which can be passed onto the subsequent stage), will be determined by what they have received. For example, everyone has come across examples in construction of how information is received that is either incomplete or incorrect. The former means that time and effort must be wasted on getting complete information. In the latter, it is possible that this information is used, the result of which is an avoidable mistake that has to be put right later; again, incurring wasted cost.

Those with a stake in the overall process will include every person and department whose survival depends on the end customer continuing to consume the product or service. Improvement, as experienced by end customers, is dependent upon all those who have a stake (the internal customers), dedicating themselves to ensuring they co-operate with each other and that relationships are enhanced.

What is described in this section is frequently referred to as being the philosophy that constitutes what is commonly known as TQM (Total Quality Management).

This is, essentially, an approach that focuses on improving all aspects in which an organisation is involved. The most crucial part of improvement is getting those people who carry out day-to-day tasks to be willing to commit themselves to being involved in searching for ways to improve what they do and to implement solutions that are devised. This leads to a need to address the culture that exists – the beliefs that are accepted as to what the organisation stands for – and attempt to encourage a change in attitudes to where excellence is the accepted standard.

13.2.3   *What is organisational culture?*

The word 'culture' is one that has become as commonplace in management as has 'quality'. Indeed, many argue that they can be seen to be directly related to one another; a point that is made below. Accepted definitions of what constitutes culture are made difficult by the tremendous variety that exist.[5] Some are:

> The culture of the [organisation] is its customary and traditional way of thinking and of doing things, which is shared to a greater or lesser degree by all its members, and which new members must learn, and at least partially accept, in order to be accepted into service... (Jaques, 1952).

> Culture refers to the underlying values, beliefs and principles that serve as a foundation for an organization's management system as well as the set of management practices and behaviours that both exemplify and reinforce those basic principles (Dennison, 1990).

Perhaps this definition is more useful by virtue of its simplicity:

> Culture is '*how things are done around here*'. It is what is typical of the organisation, the habits, the prevailing attitudes, the grown-up pattern of accepted and expected behaviour (Drennan, 1992).

The issue of organisational culture is viewed as being important precisely because of the way that many commentators have identified it as being a key element that has led to the success that so called 'excellent' organisations have achieved. As Tom Peters and Robert Waterman state in their best-selling book, *In Search of Excellence* (1982):

> Without exception, the dominance and coherence of culture proved to be an essential quality of the excellent companies. Moreover, the stronger the culture and the more it was directed toward the marketplace, the less need there was for policy manuals, organization charts, or detailed procedures and rules.

The message here is that if you have a culture that is customer-focused, you do not need to force people to follow rules and regulations. Rather, people do whatever is necessary because, and to borrow from Drennan, 'that is the way things happen around here'. Experience will have taught us what a good organisation that provides very good (indeed, excellent) service and products is like: polite and helpful staff;

commitment to delivery at the time agreed; methods by which, should something go wrong, there is an attempt to limit damage (and, usually, profuse apology and, possibly, compensation). Contrast that with the opposite. We have all experienced it: surly and unsympathetic staff; lack of concern for how much we have been inconvenienced; as for apologies and any compensation, forget it! What is surprising is how the latter type of organisations appear oblivious to the fact that disgruntled customers will not only avoid using them again, but also will tell everyone they know to do likewise. The former, however, we will happily both reuse and recommend.

Therefore having staff who are willing, committed to the principles of TQM and, most especially, customer care, is vital. The thing is, even though most people when asked will agree that *they* know how things should be done, but, typically, will suggest that no one ever asked them or will tell you that senior management do not seem to be prepared to provide the sort of leadership required. Consequently, it is the responsibility of senior managers who want their organisation and, of course, employees to be committed to the principle of customer-focus and TQM, to provide the right sort of leadership to achieve this.

13.2.4 Leadership – the key ingredient of culture change

Some argue that change only occurs when an organisation is facing crisis. An example might be loss of a vital order to a competitor. This will cause a great deal of anguish and searching for why this happened. There are many examples of organisations that have reacted to such a crisis and, having survived in the short-term, have redefined their processes to be more able to match future customer expectations. However, this is not to be advised. Rather, organisations should initiate the desire to improve in order to avoid crisis; prevention being better than cure. The trouble is, even though people will agree that improvement is important, they often cite any number of reasons why they believe change cannot happen immediately:

- 'We're too busy';

- 'It'll cost too much';

- 'The client probably won't notice any difference'.

Therefore, it will be necessary for those who are leading the initiative to change to do some work on convincing others that it is essential to do things differently. This is a task that may be delegated to those who are sometimes referred to as 'quality champions' or 'change agents'. However, even though such people sometimes emerge during the process of creating change, it is more likely that they will have been appointed by those who, in theory, are in the best position to see the virtues of change and, more importantly, possess sufficient influence to convince others. This needs leadership and means that senior managers must be prepared to demonstrate personal commitment. According to John Oakland (1999), who is one of the most pre-eminent authors on TQM, senior managers should do five things to demonstrate effective leadership:

1 Develop a clear statement on the purpose that the organisation seeks to serve (the mission statement) and which is unambiguous in the desire to achieve improvement.

2 Formulate a strategy that supports this mission.

3 Identify the critical success factors and core processes (see section on benchmarking below).

4 Carefully consider the existing organisational structure and be prepared to alter.

5 Empower people to give them the power to make changes that they believe are important to allow them to do their job better.

In addition, as part of a process of improvement, senior managers should, in order to act as role models, do the following:

- Visit excellent organisations to see how their counterparts carry out their duties.

- Talk to clients on a more regular basis to find out what they really want from your organisation.

- Using typical Tom Peter's vernacular, to carry out 'management by walking about', i.e. go out and talk to staff who carry out day-to-day operations more regularly.

- To become actively involved in training and educating staff in how to use quality tools to produce improvement.

- Be prepared to encourage staff to openly discuss problems/deficiencies that currently exist in the organisation.

- Set up forums and social events to celebrate achievement of success.

- Constantly ask the question: 'How can I, as part of the senior management team, do more to assist my staff to achieve their best'.

This is not an exhaustive list. However, it is absolutely essential to stress the need for improvement to be seen as something that is never-ending. Thus, no senior managers in any organisation should ever allow themselves to believe that once 'enough has been done to get things going', they can leave it to others. Just as destructive, would be the decision, because of limited budgets, to decide that after a certain period improvement will end. For this reason, organisational improvement must be seen as never-ending. To do otherwise, risks becoming complacent and, therefore, being overtaken by competitors.

Of course, senior managers cannot do everything. In providing the lead, they should expect, and have confidence in, the ability of others to follow and play their part in dedication to improvement and customer-focus.

13.2.5 *People and the Importance of teams in cultural change and improvement*

John Oakland, in his book *Total Organizational Excellence – achieving world-class performance* (1999), believes that an essential part of organisational improvement is the need to encourage teamworking. As he explains:

> Barriers are often created by 'silo management', in which departments are treated like containers which are separate from one another. The customers are not interested in departments – they stand on the outside of the organization and see slices of it – they see the **processes** [his bold]. It is necessary to build teams and improve communications around the processes.

Oakland provides the following reasons why the use of teams will prove to be superior to individuals working on their own:

- A greater number of issues can be dealt with.

- Problems that are too complex for one person to cope with can be tackled.

- There will be a sharing of expertise and knowledge.

- The fact that others share their concerns will mean that the perception of isolation will be reduced.

- Co-ordination of effort will result in anticipation of potential problems.

- Conflicts which arise between departments and inter-organisational groups as a result of misunderstanding or interpretation of requirements are likely to be reduced.

- Implementation of solutions to problems will have consensus; the chances of success are therefore increased.

In addition to this list, there is a belief that by using teamwork the following things will occur:

- People will be more committed to the principle of TQM.

- It is likely that the needs of customers will be understood.

- There will be greater understanding between managers and workers (who co-operate in teams) about the decisions taken and their impact on the business.

- Morale will increase among employees if success is achieved in organisational goals.

- Improvement will become an accepted part of the culture of the organisation.

As you may have heard, the word 'team' can be considered to be an acronym for:

Together Each Achieves More

Teamwork, therefore, is an essential part of TQM and improvement. Without it, people will continue to do things in the same way they always have. Given this essential ingredient in the improvement process, we may ask: 'Are construction projects designed and built by teams or groups?'. Few projects would appear to achieve the benefits derived from the potential synergy. Understandably, the inter-organisational and inter-disciplinary nature of construction does present additional hurdles compared to the manufacturing industry. Time will tell as to what impact such 'Egan' enablers (i.e. supply-chain management, concurrent construction and co-located teams) will have on developing cultural alignment in construction teams.

A personal observation of culture change in a design-orientated organisation

One company in which I carried out research was dedicated to the principles of TQM and improvement. Their reputation for producing innovative designs was very good (including much of the systems used for either production or merely to ensure efficient operation). The trouble was, many of the problems occurred when the designs had to be used by site personnel. It was obvious, get the site staff to talk to the designers. Trouble was, until someone who was dedicated to the role of improvement was appointed, and could get this to happen, there had always been a traditional reluctance for site and head office people (where design was carried out), to attempt to understand each other.

As the person appointed to manage the cultural change explained:

> People are very happy to remain in their day-to-day roles. They see problems as being the fault of someone else. The real challenge here was to get everyone to see what they were involved in as being a total process, and that all that counted was the building they received. If that building leaks or there is a 'teething' problem with the services, they don't care which department caused it; they simply think, 'Right, next time I want another building, I won't use them again'. It's as simple as that. Getting that change in perception and attitude is the biggest change I've had to tackle. Once that is sorted, it's amazing how many problems have been identified by site staff that can be eradicated by more thoughtful design. It saves money, it avoids delay and it means we are less likely to have dissatisfied clients.

13.3 Learning from others – benchmarking as a tool for improvement

Benchmarking has various definitions but, crucially, it is based upon the principle that if an organisation wishes to improve, a good way to do this would be to compare itself to others who are acknowledged as being very good (or better still, excellent). Whilst there are many ways to judge others, the main thing that excellent organisations can be seen to be committed to is customer service. As will be described below, the model that clients are increasingly using to select organisations to carry out construction work, The EFQM Excellence Model, places a very large amount of emphasis on the way that customer service is managed.

What is important in benchmarking?

1 Knowing what you currently do – this involves people accurately defining the processes (in which *inputs* are turned into *outputs*) that they carry out.

2 Best way to show a process is by means of a diagram (use a flowchart).

3 Identify the *critical success factors* which are aspects of performance or quality of what the organisation produces that can be measured (quantifiably) to show that definitive improvement is taking place.

4 Look for the parts of the process that cause problems to occur – consider what are the origin of these.

5 Find a process that has similarity to that which you want to improve and learn what is done to ensure better assurance of customer satisfaction (can be another part of the organisation, a competitor or something entirely different).

6 Consider what you have learned from looking at others' processes (how they do things, organise, lead and motivate people) and how, by adopting a similar approach, your processes would benefit.

7 Implement change and monitor change in measurable output – if positive, continue and try other alterations to process(es), if not, consider alternative solutions.

Keys to success in benchmarking

1 Should be simple – complexity causes confusion.

2 Involve those involved in day-to-day tasks – they know what happens, know what works and are likely to know what will possibly improve.

3 Repeat, involve those in day-to-day tasks – if they do not feel they were adequately consulted or involved, they will be less likely to support the changes in processes.

4 Make sure that you can measure the critical success factors properly and that these are appropriate to the type of product or service being offered – do not be afraid to ask your customers what makes them delighted with what they receive (satisfaction is believed to be too passive a word).

5 Managers to provide leadership in terms of support, inspiration and resources and, importantly, to avoid blame if things do not work out and praise as success occurs.

6 Remember that success does breed success and, therefore, attempt small-scale initiatives rather than trying to change everything at once.

7 Constantly try to find new processes to benchmark in order not to lose momentum once benchmarking has commenced.

8 Always be on the lookout for opportunities to be able to analyse the processes of organisations that are regarded as, and can show measures of, producing best practice.

Figure 13.2: Quality management model

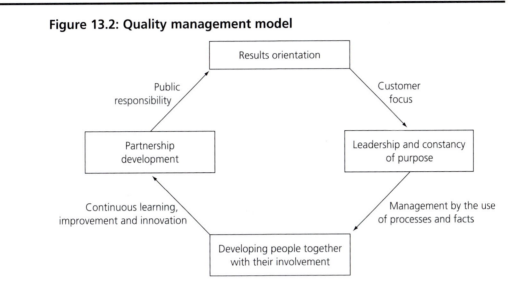

13.3.1 A ready made model for excellence

The EFQM (European Foundation for Quality Management) Excellence model is based upon the need for the management of any organisation to dedicate themselves to the task of encouraging and supporting all employees in the objective of excellence. There are eight fundamentals involved which are shown in the Figure 13.2.

The main purpose of using the Excellence Model is for an organisation to understand what it does and, by analysing how it achieves its objectives, to create organisational improvement. In particular, there are certain key concepts that the EFQM Excellence Model seeks to addresses. These are:

- Leadership and consistency of purpose;
- People development, involvement and satisfaction;
- Customer focus;
- Supplier partnerships;
- Processes and measurement;
- Continuous improvement and innovation;
- Public responsibility;
- Results orientation.

Figure 13.3 – the so-called 'Nine-box Model' – summarises the EFQM Excellence Model and is based upon a framework that consists of nine criteria (the relative worth of each is shown in brackets).

Figure 13.3: The EFQM Excellence Model

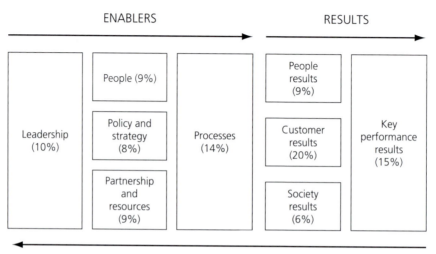

Advocates of this model claim that it applies to any organisation where the desire of senior management is to achieve the following:

- Increase the satisfaction of its customers;

- Motivate its employees;

- Ensure that its impact on society is enhanced.

The EFQM Excellence Model is based upon the principle that using self-assessment, any organisation should be able to achieve the four *results* criteria through the implementation of the five *enablers* criteria. Therefore, this model can be regarded as a vital part of benchmarking in order to achieve improvement. It will enable any organisation, regardless of what it seeks to achieve, to systematically review and measure its processes.

13.4 Conclusions

Architect: Part of a larger chain

So far, this chapter has largely dispensed anecdotes on how any 'one' organisation can engage in performance improvement through TQM and benchmarking principles. As previously noted, the construction industry is arguably more complex in nature compared to the industries in which these management theories were developed. The most important challenge for construction is surely to smooth the interdependencies that exist in the process that leads to customer satisfaction (delight). Faulty materials or bad workmanship easily removes excellence in design. Construction has played out this game for far too long and construction lawyers have 'cashed-in' at everyone's expense. The employment of new procurement ideology (design and build) or new professional roles (project managers) has not complemented construction's 'false' adoption of prescriptive quality assurance criteria. The industry has, by an large, failed to 'walk the talk'. The concept of the 'internal customer' has not received sufficient attention. Consider the often chaotic dissemination of vital project information between design and construction professionals for example. However, the current interest in the construction process, generated by Egan's 1998 report, does present the industry with a credible opportunity for radical continuous improvement. Despite critics arguing that 'the measuring of performance' is rather too 'new Labour' the focus on input–output is largely based on the principles of established management achievements obtained in other industries. Thus, the case for benchmarking is indeed justified. The task at hand for architects is to join the revolution and engage in the dissemination of best practice equally within their own profession and in the projects in which they have been commissioned.

So, what's stopping you?

Change is never easy. We often fear that by attempting to do things differently, we may make mistakes. Apparently, the psychologist Freud compared what he saw as the 'feeble-mindedness' of adults to the willingness of children to experiment and explore. Whilst no one would advocate that all established protocols be dispensed with, there are undoubtedly many opportunities that exist for you to attempt to create improvement in the way that your organisation carries out design work. The challenge is, of course, in creating the time and effort that will be required in the first instance to search for these opportunities.

Whilst some may want to argue that the changes clients increasingly desire are impossible, there is a belief that unless the whole of the chain involved in providing construction products co-operates and improves, many customers may look elsewhere. This is not intended to sound overly-pessimistic. Rather, there is evidence that some clients may look to manufacturing to provide cheaper, more reliable and higher quality components and, in some cases, buildings.

Therefore, improvement becomes not so much desirable, as more of an imperative. The principles that have been described here are not intended to be seen as difficult or threatening. Rather, they should be perceived as offering your organisation well-proven tools and techniques that can not only deliver improvement, but can motivate the people who work in your organisation. As you will find, highly motivated people do not need to be instructed in how to deliver excellent service, it comes naturally. So, be brave! Start considering improvement right away. That, arguably, is the hardest part of the improvement process. Once you have started, you will find that it is not just never-ending, but extremely rewarding.

References

Construction Industry Task Force, *Rethinking Construction*, Department of the Environment, Transport and the Regions, London (1998).

Dennison, D., *Corporate Culture and Organizational Effectiveness*, John Wiley, New York (1990) p. 2.

Drennan, D., *Transforming Company Culture*, McGraw-Hill (1992) p. 3.

Egan, J., 'Rethinking construction', Report of the Construction Task Force on the Scope for Improving Quality and Efficiency of UK Construction, Department of the Environment, Transport and the Regions (DETR) (1998).

Jaques, E., *The Changing Culture of a Factory*, Dryden Press, New York (1952) p. 251.

McNair, C. J. and Leibfried, K. H. J., *Benchmarking, a tool for continuous improvement*, John Wiley and Son Inc., New York (1992).

Oakland, J. S., *Total Organizational Excellence, achieving world-class performance*, Butterworth-Heinemann, Oxford (1999) pp. 12–14, 17.

Peters T. and Waterman R., *In Search of Excellence; lessons from America's best run companies*, Harper and Row, New York (1982) p. 75.

Strategic Forum for Construction, *Accelerating Change*, Department of the Environment, Transport and the Regions (2002).

Zairi, M., *Benchmarking for Best Practice – continuous learning through sustainable innovation*, Butterworth-Heinemann, Oxford (1996).

Key Reading

CIRIA, *Benchmarking for Construction, a strategic review* (Special report 69), CIRIA, London (1998).

McCabe, S., *Quality Improvement Techniques in Construction*, Addison Wesley Longman (1998).

McCabe, S., *Benchmarking for Construction*, Blackwell Science, Oxford (2001).

Pickrell, S., Garnett N. and Baldwin J., *Measuring Up, A Practical guide to benchmarking in construction*, BRE, London (1997).

Endnotes

1 Adapted from original source in *Quality and Profit in Building Design*, edited by P. S. Brandon and J. A. Powell (1984), E&FN Spon, London.
2 I was the 'proud' owner of two Austin Allegros, both of which leaked water, had umpteen mechanical problems and suffered terribly from rust.
3 He was invited to advise senior managers on improved production techniques.
4 It has been shown that customers happily pay higher prices for high quality products.
5 As long ago as 1952, 164 definitions had been identified.

Health and Safety

14

John Smallwood, Department of Construction Management,
University of Port Elizabeth, South Africa, and
John Anderson, Construction Health and Safety Consultant, Chester, UK

14.1 Introduction

In the past, health and safety (H&S) matters on construction sites have been perceived as the contractors' 'problem'. However, research and experience have contributed to the realisation that clients, designers and other stakeholders influence H&S. Although H&S is often the difference between life and death on a project, and is a serious issue in the industry, ultimately H&S is a means to an end, namely optimum project performance and sustainable construction and development, as opposed to an end in itself – H&S on construction sites.

Levitt and Samelson (1993), Hinze (1997) and various other authors have documented and raised the level of awareness with respect to the influence of design on H&S. However, the International Labour Office (ILO) (1992) specifically states that designers should:

- Receive training in H&S;

- Integrate the H&S of construction workers into the design and planning process;

- Not include anything in a design which would necessitate the use of dangerous structural or other procedures or hazardous materials which could be avoided by design modifications or by substitute materials;

- Take into account the H&S of workers during subsequent maintenance.

However, the influence of design is not limited to design as a process. The design function often includes advising clients with respect to the type of procurement system and form of contract to be used, the pre-qualifying and selecting of a contractor, and the project duration. Designers can contribute to the process of partnering and can facilitate the pre-planning of H&S through completeness of design.

Furthermore, although clients often appoint designers or project managers to manage the design process and/or supervise the works on their behalf, the specific ILO recommendations relative to clients should be noted. These are that clients should:

- Co-ordinate or nominate a competent person to co-ordinate all activities relating to H&S;

- Inform all contractors of special risks to H&S of which they are, or should be, aware;

- Require contractors submitting tenders to make provision for H&S;

- Consider H&S requirements when estimating dates for stage and overall completion of the project.

This chapter primarily consists of seven sections:

1 An introduction, which introduces the terms and definitions;

2 The holistic influence of design;

3 The motivation for addressing H&S;

4 H&S legislation applicable to designers;

5 Impact of the Construction (Design and Management) (CDM) Regulations;

6 An overview of the role of clients and designers in H&S and the role of H&S in overall performance;

7 Conclusions.

It is not intended to provide a 'step-by-step' guide to H&S in terms of the RIBA Plan of Work or the CDM Regulations – space precludes both the former and the latter – but rather to sensitise designers with respect to the holistic role of H&S and to provide a synopsis of the implications of legislation for designers.

A range of terms and definitions will be used throughout the chapter, and are therefore defined to facilitate consensus and an understanding of the holistic role of H&S.

Health is defined as 'the degree of physiological and psychological well being of an individual', and *safety* as both 'the state of being safe: freedom from injury or danger' and 'the quality of insuring against hurt, injury, danger or risk' (Taylor *et al*, 1998). These definitions clearly indicate that H&S have both an occupational and a non-occupational dimension. Within the occupational context, *healthy* is defined as 'free from illness or injury attributable to occupational causes' and *safety* as 'free from any hazard'. Occupational health includes occupational hygiene, occupational medicine and biological monitoring (Republic of South Africa, 1993). *Injury* refers to 'damage to tissue resulting from acute exposure to physical and chemical agents', whereas *disease* is defined as 'a departure from a state of health usually recognised by a sequence of signs and symptoms, or a process, which disturbs the structure or functions of the body' (Slappendel, 1995). Hazards and risk are both important terms; *hazard* means 'something with the potential to cause harm (this includes articles, substances, plant or machines, methods of work, the working environment and other aspects of work organisation)', and *risk* means 'the likelihood of potential harm from a hazard being realised. The extent of the risk depends on (i) the likelihood of that harm occurring, (ii) the potential severity of that harm, i.e. of any resultant injury or adverse health effect, and (iii) the population which might be affected by the hazard, i.e. the number of people who might be exposed' (Health and Safety Commission, 2002). Furthermore, safety is predicated upon two activities, namely, *the measurement of risk* and *the value placed in the risk* – judgement. Judgement is of particular importance as a tunnel collapse on the Heathrow project was said to be impossible with the result that such a probability received no consideration at all. Incidents and accidents are further terms frequently used relative to H&S. *Accidents* are 'unplanned consequences of events, or a missing or inappropriate response' and 'any occurrence/ event arising out of, and in the course of, employment which results in personal or property damage' (Taylor *et al*, 1998). *Incidents* are similar, except that they do not result in personal damage in the form of an injury, or property damage – all accidents are incidents, but not all incidents are accidents. The issue being that there are many more incidents than accidents in construction, and that invariably an accident has been preceded by a number of incidents. Furthermore, the actual outcome of accidents is often fortuitous, and can be minor, major, or even catastrophic.

An integral aspect of H&S is that of *ergonomics*, which is defined as 'the scientific study of the physical relationship between people, the equipment they use and their working environments' (Bohle and Quinlan, 2000). Many ergonomists, within the context of occupational H&S, argue that ergonomics as a discipline encapsulates H&S, whereas some H&S practitioners argue that ergonomics is an aspect of H&S. Given that the brief for this chapter referred to H&S and that the authors deem H&S to include ergonomics, the approach to this chapter has been along these lines.

A further related aspect is that of health promotion within the occupational environ-ment, which according to Bohle and Quinlan (2000) entails a systematic attempt by management to offer programmes intended to encourage workers to make behavioural and lifestyle changes that are believed to be conducive to good health. Improvement of lifestyle can lower the risk of certain work place hazards, such as smoking and occupational respiratory disorders, drinking and workplace accidents, and poor fitness and musculoskeletal stress in lifting. The benefits of health promotion are well documented and include (Bagwell and Bush, 1999):

- Improved health and fitness;
- Reduced health care costs;
- Reduced absenteeism;
- Improved productivity;
- Increased job satisfaction;
- Enhanced self-responsibility.

14.2 The holistic influence of design

14.2.1 Introduction

Designers influence H&S, both directly and indirectly. Directly, as a result of design, supervisory and administrative interventions. Indirectly, as a result of type of procurement system used, pre-qualification, project time, partnering, and the facilitating of pre-planning (Smallwood, 2000).

14.2.2 Direct influence

Design interventions include: concept design, general design, selection of type of structural frame, site location, site coverage, details, method of fixing, and specification of materials and finishes (Smallwood, 2000). Co-ordination of design is a further design-related intervention, which may be undertaken by a designer or a project manager.

The concept design may imply a natural stone cladding, which could require work at elevated heights, possible handling of heavy panels, and work off tower scaffolds adjacent to public thoroughfares. Furthermore, such concept design may include over sailing sections, which would need to be clad, thus requiring both working at heights and overhead.

The general design may include projections on plan due to say balconies to a block of apartments, which during construction would mean increased edge protection and vigilance on the part of workers.

The selection of the type of structural frame has substantial implications – consider a structural steel (SS) frame, as opposed to a reinforced concrete (RC) frame. Both the SS and RC frames would require work at elevated heights. However, in the case of the SS frame, such work would be undertaken while attached to stanchions or working on narrow beams, and the use of a degree of body force. The RC frame would enable the greater percentage of such work to be undertaken on large areas of support work and off scaffold towers to columns. However, depending upon the support work and formwork system used, the erection and striking thereof could require substantial use of body force. A further aspect is the constituents of such a RC frame, namely formwork, reinforcement and concrete, and the implications thereof in terms of movement and housekeeping.

Site location has a range of implications. A central business district site will require access for the delivery of materials and plant – traffic safety. Such a site will also be passed by pedestrian and vehicular traffic. Consequently, designers should be conscious and mindful when selecting the type of structural frame and external fabric. An extreme international example is the aerial cableway station project atop Table Mountain, Cape Town, South Africa, which entailed exposure to high wind speeds while working on scaffolding. Ideally, the need to work off such scaffolding should have been limited through appropriate design.

Site coverage is important as it affects the available area for storage of materials. Limiting such an area has implications for housekeeping.

Detail and method of fixing may require: bending or twisting the back in an awkward way, working in awkward or cramped positions, reaching away from the body, reaching overhead, repetitive movements and use of body force.

Materials, in turn, may be heavy, or large, and present manual materials handling problems. They may also have sharp edges, or rough surfaces, or contain hazardous chemical substances.

Co-ordination of design is of particular importance due to the various implications of design for construction, such as the installation of a range of services in ceiling, roof spaces and ducts. Optimum co-ordination engenders ergonomics during both construction and maintenance.

A further role identified for designers is that of optimal interaction with clients, particularly at the design brief stage. This is the most crucial phase for the successful, healthy and safe completion of any project. Deviations from it at a later stage result in variation orders, which can be the catalyst that triggers a series of events from designer through to workers that culminate in an accident on site. Consequently, clients must know exactly what they require and develop a comprehensive brief for the design team (Jeffrey and Douglas, 1994).

Supervisory and administrative interventions include: reference to H&S upon site handover, and during site visits and inspections; inclusion of H&S as an agenda item during site meetings, and the requiring of H&S reporting by contractors.

14.2.3 Indirect influence

Procurement systems and related issues are important as they affect contractual relationships, the development of mutual goals, the allocation of risk and, ultimately, provide the framework within which projects are executed (Dreger, 1996). Evidence gathered suggests that incorrect choice and use of procurement systems has contributed to neglecting of H&S by project stakeholders. The traditional construction procurement system, for example, entails the evolution of a design by designers; the preparation of bills of quantities and related documentation; the engagement of a contractor through competitive bidding, invariably on the basis of price, which system does not always complement H&S. Rwelamila and Smallwood (1999) suggest that this could be due to the:

- Separation of the design and construction processes;
- Incompleteness of design upon both preparation of documentation and the commencement of construction;
- Engagement of contractors on the basis of price.

However, design and build overcomes some of the inherent problems presented by the use of the traditional construction procurement system, through the integration of the design and construction processes (Meere, 1990).

Competitive tendering can marginalise H&S in that contractors can find themselves in the iniquitous position that should they make the requisite allowances for H&S, they run the risk of losing a tender or negotiations to a less committed competitor. The inclusion of a provisional sum, or specific items for H&S, ensures that all contractors allocate an equitable amount of resources to H&S.

Contract documentation is important as it details the rights and obligations of the contracting parties. However, various international contracts require H&S specific interventions by clients, designers and contractors. Furthermore, due to client processes and/or commitment to H&S, clients may include project specific H&S requirements. In essence, contract documentation can engender commitment to H&S and focus thereon.

Project duration also impacts on H&S, as the duration may be incompatible with the nature and scope of the work to be executed safely. Hinze (1997) cites pressure to meet unrealistic deadlines as a common source of mental diversion, which diversion increases the susceptibility of injury. Pressure to meet deadlines can also engender omissions and ineffective interventions relative to H&S. Inappropriate project durations often result in the introduction of excessive resources into the work place, namely sub-contractors (SCs), plant and equipment, and materials.

Various authors advocate the pre-qualification of general contractors (GCs) and SCs on H&S by clients and GCs respectively. The purpose of pre-qualification in the H&S sense is to provide a standardised method for the selection of contractors on the basis of demonstrated safe work records, H&S commitment and knowledge, and the ability to work in a healthy and safe manner. Such pre-qualification enhances the likelihood that H&S conscious contractors are selected (Hinze, 1997).

Pre-planning H&S realises a structured approach to H&S related issues by both designers and contractors. Liska (1994) maintains that there are two parts to pre-planning: pre-project and pre-task, and that pre-planning provides the foundation for project H&S programmes. Pre-planning identifies all the ingredients of and resources required for the H&S programme to be effective and efficient. However, the design of a project is a great influence on determining the method of construction and the requisite H&S interventions. Consequently, sufficient design-related information needs to be available at pre-construction phase to facilitate budgeting for adequate resources.

14.3   The motivation for addressing H&S

The motivation for addressing H&S is multi-faceted; legislation being merely one motivator for the addressing thereof. The primary motivators are:

- Moral/religious;
- Ethics;
- Humanitarian;
- Respect for people;

- Sustainability;

- Customer service;

- International standards;

- Legislation;

- Cost of accidents;

- Risk management;

- Total quality management;

- Industry endeavours;

- Best practice.

Eckhardt (2001) says the 'golden rule', which establishes a moral level of care for others that we are responsible to provide, is a common theme in most, if not all, of the world's major religions. Consequently, all people should be conscious and mindful of the health and well being of each other, regardless of their stakeholder constituency.

Ethical business practice includes compliance with legislation. Given that values embrace ethics, the existence of H&S legislation amplifies the need for the inclusion of H&S as a value, and as a project parameter. The inclusion of H&S as a value, as opposed to a priority, is important as priorities change. The inclusion of H&S along with the traditional project parameters of cost, quality and time is important. Exclusion thereof creates the impression that H&S is less important, focus is on the traditional project parameters, and the potential synergy resulting from optimum H&S is not realised.

Flowing from the humanitarian motivation for H&S is the aspect of 'respect for people', one of three principles of *Rethinking Construction* initiated by the report of the Construction Task Force chaired by Sir John Egan in the United Kingdom in 1998 (Rethinking Construction Ltd, 2002). How does 'respect for people' manifest itself? Endeavours and interventions to engender and enhance 'respect for people' cited, include those relative to H&S, site conditions and welfare. However, appropriate planning such that people have the requisite skills, supervision, information, materials, plant and equipment, and time to undertake their work constitutes a further manifestation. This has major implications for all project stakeholders including clients, project managers and designers – clients influence time, and designers should evolve designs and details which complement construction ergonomics, and which are constructable and appropriate in terms of the level of skills in the industry.

Related to the humanitarian aspect is the issue of sustainability. Accidents can result in fatalities, injuries, disease, damage to materials, plant and equipment, all of which result in waste. Waste in solid and other forms impacts on the sustainability of the Earth as a result of the use of landfill sites, and the unnecessary consumption of non-renewable resources in the case of rework. Furthermore, fatalities and injuries marginalise the sustainability of the families of the deceased or injured, and in the case of the latter, the sustainability of the injured, particularly in the case of permanent disablement.

Designers are both suppliers and customers – suppliers in the sense that they provide designs and details to contractors and, indirectly, their workers. Consequently, they should not supply contractors with designs, details and specifications that require non-ergonomic work, unnecessary and/or undue exposure to hazardous processes and materials.

The ISO 9000 Quality Management System series and ISO 14001 Environmental Management System both require that issues pertaining to H&S be addressed. However, the existence of a system and procedures engender optimum H&S. Beside many design practices and contractors having acquired certification relative to one or both of such systems, there are many clients that have such certification, which in turn requires that their contractors and suppliers be managed in a manner appropriate to the relevant system(s).

The cost of accidents (CoA) is frequently cited as a major motivation for addressing H&S (Levitt and Samelson, 1993; Health and Safety Executive, 1995; Hinze, 1997). Research conducted in the USA and the UK indicates the total CoA to constitute 6.5 percent of the value of completed construction and approximately 8.5 percent of tender price respectively (The Business Roundtable, 1995; Anderson, 1997).

The need to reduce risk and increase certainty is a further motivator for H&S. During research conducted in South Africa, 96 percent of project managers (PMs) maintained that inadequate, or the lack of, H&S increased project risk (Smallwood, 1996). Inadequate, or the lack of, H&S results in variability of resource input and output, consequently, an increase in risk and also the probability of an accident. Given that risk is a function of probability and impact, and that the outcome of accidents is often fortuitous, the potential risks as a result of inadequate, or the lack of, H&S are substantial.

A further motivation for H&S is the synergy between H&S and the other project parameters of: cost, environment, productivity, quality and schedule – total quality management (TQM). The research conducted among PMs in South Africa investigated the impact of inadequate H&S on various project parameters – productivity (87.2 percent) and quality (80.8 percent) predominated, followed by cost (72.3 percent), client perception (68.1 percent), environment (66 percent) and schedule (57.4 percent) (Smallwood, 1996).

A range of UK industry wide endeavours have addressed H&S, and there are currently many underway. The 'Constructing the Team' report which resulted from the investigation of procurement and contractual arrangements in the UK construction industry led by Sir Michael Latham, highlights a number of aspects such as the degree of attention afforded to H&S by designers and established a target of a 30 percent improvement in productivity (Department of Environment, 1994). The 'Rethinking Construction' report which resulted from an investigation led by the Deputy Prime Minister, John Prescott, to determine the scope for improving the quality and efficiency of UK construction identified accidents as a key performance indicator and set a target of 20 percent reduction in the number of reportable accidents and a 10 percent increase in productivity and profitability (Department of Environment Transport & Regions, 1998). The 'Rethinking Construction' report proposed that a 'movement for change' be established in the industry to engender improvement. The *Movement for Innovation* (M4I) was established as a result thereof, the aims of which are to lead radical improvement in construction in terms of value for money, profitability, reliability and respect for people, through demonstration and dissemination of best practice and innovation – commitment to people being one of five drivers of change. Demonstration projects are intended to benchmark performance, set high standards in H&S and respect for people, and to disseminate the results of their work. According to Rethinking Construction Ltd demonstration projects are consistently shown to be safer sites, namely 25 percent safer than the industry at large (Rethinking Construction Ltd, 2002). However, it must be noted that this statement is based upon accident statistics, and that the absence of accidents does not mean that sites are necessarily safe, but rather that M4I sites have less accidents because they are better managed. The discussion document, *Revitalising Health and Safety in Construction*, provided an opportunity to assess where the industry is in terms of H&S, where the industry wants to be and how to get there. Both the role of clients and designers is addressed in detail (Health and Safety Executive, 2002).

14.4 H&S legislation applicable to designers practising in the UK

14.4.1 Legal background to the involvement of architects in construction industry H&S

In the UK the creation of criminal H&S legislation to protect persons at work extends back to the early 19th century, and it was in 1833 that the first four inspectors of factories were appointed with powers to enter premises to check on the legality of working conditions and to investigate accidents. It was not until 1937 that regulations were in place to protect those at work on construction sites, and the 1937 legislation – which was followed by further legislation in 1961 and 1966 – applied only to the 'employers of workmen'. The Robens Committee undertook a substantial review of all the UK H&S legislation in the early 1970s, which resulted in the creation of the Health and Safety at Work Act in 1974. Not all the recommendations of the Robens Committee were accepted by the then Government, but the new Act extended the duty of care for the health, safety and welfare of all persons at work to all employers whatever the work activity. Some six million people were suddenly brought within the scope of the H&S legislation, and that included duties on the self-employed.

Section 3 of this 1974 Act places duties on employers and the self-employed to persons other than their own employees:

> It shall be the duty of every employer to conduct his undertaking in such a way as to ensure, so far as is reasonably practicable, that persons not in his employment who may be affected thereby are not thereby exposed to risks to their health and safety.

> It shall be the duty of every self-employed person to conduct his undertaking in such a way as to ensure, so far as reasonably practicable, that he and other persons (not being his employees) who may be affected thereby are not thereby exposed to risks to their health and safety.

'Conducting an undertaking' is not defined in the Act, but the legal commentary in Redgrave's *Health and Safety* makes it clear that this phrase has been held by courts to include the provision of service and is not limited to the carrying on of an industrial undertaking or process (Ford and Brown, 2002). An architectural practice would be an 'undertaking', and the parts of Section 3 of the Act quoted above create an offence of absolute liability subject only to the defence of reasonably practicability. Other Acts may allow the defence of having 'exercised all due diligence to avoid the commission of the offence', but that is not permitted in this legislation. Although Section 6 of this Act places duties on 'any person who designs articles for use at work', the definition of 'article for use at work' relates to items of plant for use at work and components of these articles of plant. A building or structure is itself not an article for use at work – although, of course, there may be items of plant within the buildings.

The Health and Safety at Work Act was then, in effect, added to by the adoption by the UK of the 1989 European Union Framework Directive by means of the then Management of Health and Safety at Work Regulations, 1992, but the European Commission proceeded to draw up a further special Directive to address what they saw as the particular needs of the construction industry. This was the 1992 Temporary and Mobile Worksites Directive, and it is through this Directive that the first specific duties on designers of buildings or structures came into existence (European Commission, 1992). Prior to the drawing up of this Directive the European Commission commissioned some research into the industry, and the two findings of the research found their way into two of the Directive's preambles:

> Whereas unsatisfactory architectural and/or organisational options or poor planning of the works at the project preparation stage played a role in more than half of the occupational accidents occurring on construction sites in the Community.

> Whereas it is therefore necessary to improve the coordination between the various parties concerned at the project preparation stage and also when the work is being carried out.

At the time it was hotly disputed that shortcomings in the pre-construction stage could have played a role in over 50 percent of site accidents, and the hard evidence for this conclusion was not produced or investigated in detail within the UK. At the time the debate moved on to what the UK would write into the UK H&S legislation in terms of detail, and in particular what new criminal duties would be placed on designers. There were two sets of UK Regulations drawn up in response to the 1992 Directive – the Construction (Design and Management) Regulations, 1994, hereafter referred to as the CDM Regs, and the Construction (Health, Safety and Welfare) Regulations, 1996. Curiously, the words 'design' and 'designer' are not used in the Directive, but were both defined in the 1994 CDM Regs. Countries within the European Union are free to 'add' to the text of a Directive, but they must adopt the minimum requirements of any Directive. In the case of this Directive the Health and Safety Executive, in putting forward proposals for new Regulations, added quite a lot of new material to the Directive, particularly on the issues of competence and resources. After a much-extended public discussion period the CDM Regs were promulgated and specific duties on all 'designers' associated with 'construction work' were effective from March 1995. A breach of duty imposed by Regulation 13, the primary Regulation imposing duties on designers, does not confer a right of action in any civil proceedings.

14.5 The broad duties of designers and others under the CDM Regs

The broad thrust of the CDM Regs is quite clear, and that is that along with other Regulations it is intended to protect the H&S of people working in all forms of construction work, and to protect others who may possibly be affected by the work activities whatever they might be. It was intended to require a more systematic and effective management of projects from their concept to their completion, and part of this was by looking in a structured manner to the foreseeable hazards and risks at the design and planning stages. Another key element was to create an H&S co-ordinator at both the planning and construction stages whose work would be to co-ordinate the work of all parties to achieve the best possible levels of H&S performance. In the UK Regulations this was to create the new legal person of the 'planning supervisor' and the 'principal contractor'. New duties were also imposed for the first time on the 'client' for the works, defined as 'any person for whom the project is being carried out'. So, whereas the Health and Safety at Work Act placed duties on employers and the self-employed, these 1994 Regulations, applying only to construction work, created defined bodies of 'clients', 'designers', 'planning supervisors' and 'principal contractors', and each of these parties is required to work alongside one another to reduce risks and hazards, and to devise and implement safe systems of work to control the residual risks and hazards so as to ensure safety.

An approved code of practice was written, which has legal status, and guidance was also published aimed at designers, planning supervisors, clients and contractors. A research report commissioned by the HSE themselves showed that all was not well with the implementation of these Regulations, while there had been 'a greater awareness of H&S issues right across the construction industry', there had been substantial problems in implementation and a wide variation in practice in response to the Regulations and even 'misinterpretation' and excessive 'bureaucracy' (Health and Safety Executive (HSE), 1997). The main response of the HSE was to take soundings from industry and to revise and publish a new Approved Code of Practice and Guidance, which came into effect on 1 February, 2002. The Regulations themselves remain unchanged.

14.5.1 *The detailed duties of designers under the CDM Regs*

Before looking at the Regulation imposing duties and responsibilities on designers, it is important to look carefully at the legal definition of both 'design' and 'designer'.

For the purposes of these Regulations:

> *Design* in relation to a structure includes drawing, design details, specification and bill of quantities (including specification of articles or substances) in relation to a structure.

> *Designer* means any person who carries on a trade, business or other undertaking in connection with which a design relating to a structure or part of a structure is prepared.

Structure is also defined and means about everything the construction industry might build – including temporary works – and 'any fixed plant in respect of work which is installation, commissioning, de-commissioning, or dismantling and where such work involves the risk of a person falling more than two metres'. *Person* in these legal terms means an individual and/or a company or organisation. The duties applying to 'designers' do not rely on the fact of an appointment by, say, the client. Designers attract the duties under these Regulations by the nature of the work they actually undertake – principally the drawing and specification of a building or structure, or part of the building or structure. Clients who specify matters can, and probably will be, CDM 'designers' as are quantity surveyors who may draw up bills of quantities. Temporary works designers such as of scaffolds or of falsework are also CDM 'designers' and are subject to the same duties. Site contractors may also be CDM 'designers' if they specify materials or substances for either the permanent or temporary works.

Turning specifically to the principal Regulation on designers – this is Regulation 13. Some would say that this has the appearance of having been written by a committee. Readers are advised to look at the full text, but the key part is as follows:

> Every designer shall ensure that any design he prepares includes among the design considerations adequate regard to the need to avoid foreseeable risks to the health and safety of any person at work carrying out construction work or cleaning work in or on the structure at any time, or of any person who may be affected by the work of such a person at work.

Essentially, as part of the design considerations of each and every design, (and it is important to realise that 'design' in this context is what the Regulations define as 'design'), adequate regard should be taken to define, and where possible avoid by means of design choices, foreseeable risks during the construction works and other risks during the cleaning of the final end product. The considerations need to extend not only to those at work undertaking construction and cleaning but also any risks to others (which could mean anybody) 'who may be affected by the work of such person at work'. An obvious example is, say, a shopping centre with, say, a glass atrium. The designer (as defined in these Regulations) has to consider risks to the H&S of those constructing the design; the risks to those involved in the cleaning of the finished design, and the risk to other persons who might be in any danger while the cleaning process is underway. The designers' duties in regard to foreseeable risks are limited 'to the extent that it is reasonable to expect the designer to address them at the time the design is prepared'. This Regulation also requires that the design 'include adequate information about any aspect of the project or structure or materials of the structure which might affect the health or safety of any person . . .'. Following from this a number of questions might arise, including:

How soon in my design process do I have to start considering H&S issues?

The way the law is worded means that as soon as any 'drawing' is prepared, then the duties on the producer of that drawing become 'alive', and whatever other design considerations are in being at that moment in time, then health and safety has to be part of these considerations. The Guidance to the CDM Regs is explicit in that it states 'it is vital to address health and safety at the very start'. It does not depend on such matters as the existence of a client; on funds having been allocated; on planning permission having been obtained; or on other appointments having been made.

What do I need to actually do, and do I need to keep a record of what I do?

The process of responding to the requirements of these Regulations should be to devise a systematic approach to ensure that at the various stages of the design development there is a way of identifying the hazards associated with the future construction and cleaning of the structure. The Regulations assume that either the designer has a sufficiently detailed knowledge or has direct access to such knowledge. Knowledge of alternative means of construction may be needed. Having identified hazards and the possible risks that could arise from them, the designer has to consider what risks can actually be eliminated via design choices. The duty is to do so if such elimination or avoidance is possible, and this may mean challenging past ways of doing things. Residual risks will be left, and the designer should consider the possible nature of risk controls, and at the end of the design process provide information, and, if appropriate, advice and guidance to others. Curiously, there is no legal duty to record the findings of this process, but the HSE guidance says 'if these decisions are not recorded it will be more difficult for designers to demonstrate that they have exercised reasonable professional judgement in their compliance with the CDM Regulations'. Many design practices record their procedures and findings in a 'design risk assessment' and perhaps by also compiling a 'risk register'. Knowledgeable clients may require designers to follow their particular systematic process.

What do I not have to do?

Although the CDM Regs have been in place since 1995, there is still a degree of misunderstanding and misinterpretation of the Regulations, and the only way of avoiding wasted time and effort is to study both the text of the Regulations and the new Approved Code of Practice and Guidance. Approved Code of Practice is essential reading in that it 'fleshes out' the practical requirements of the text of the legislation. The 2002 Code contains a section on 'Designers', but it would be a mistake to assume that all you need to know is within this section, but it is the essential starting point. As well as the eight pages of description of what designers have to do, the text lists certain things that designers are not required to do under the Regulations, and these include the specification of construction methods (except in special cases where the design requires a particular approach for safety reasons); the exercising of any H&S management function over the contractor; and the reporting to the client or anyone else of the contractor's site H&S performance.

Can I be required to undertake duties and responsibilities for health and safety not set out in the CDM Regs?

Designers must undertake all the duties and responsibilities set out in the Regulations. However, construction clients may, for example, ask designers to undertake additional H&S roles or activities but these would be set out in the civil contractual arrangements. The criminal legal requirements of the H&S legislation cannot be 're-allocated', 'passed on' or 'shared' via any civil contract to any other party.

How am I supposed to relate to other parties with regard to H&S?

The essence of the Regulations is to encourage the coming together of all parties to any construction project to co-operate and communicate with each other in order to achieve the best H&S performance. There are requirements for the designer to inform the client on their H&S duties, and for designers to co-operate with the planning supervisor. The law is a bit curious in that it requires the planning supervisor to ensure that the designers have complied with their Regulation 13 duties, and this is the case even if the designer is not available to discuss the issues. The planning supervisor has no power under the CDM Regs to give directions to any designer, but co-operation and flow of information is essential if the intentions of the Regulations are to be met. Mechanisms commonly employed include the planning supervisor being present at design team meetings and at any joint meetings where designs are formally reviewed. The planning supervisor has a duty to ensure co-operation between designers, and should be looked upon as a probable source of H&S information and guidance.

What should I do if an inspector calls?

At the present time – mid 2003 – the HSE is visiting design offices throughout the UK to see and understand how designers are reacting to their duties under the CDM Regs. Although the HSE has produced some separate specific guidance for designers, it is likely that they might be looking at three issues. The first of these is what system is in place within the design practice to address the requirements of the CDM Regs, i.e. what are the general instructions to staff on this issue? How are health and safety issues in design to be tackled and recorded? A second key point is what training and guidance have individual designers received? How is their work in these issues assessed or judged in terms of completeness and quality? A third key point might be – what and where are the outputs from the system, and do they address the issues that really matter? The more the outputs wander off from the business of accident prevention the less effective the whole process will be. If an inspector calls, he or she is an instant accessible resource, who should be pressed for advice on improvements that can be made to a practice's systems, competence and outputs.

Are all these H&S considerations worth the time and effort involved?

The only purpose of any H&S legislation is the prevention of accidents and cases of ill health in the industry. There can be no 'balance sheet' approach because although one might count up the cost of compliance, there is no way that the time and effort involved can be directly linked to the numbers of lives that were 'saved' as a result of the expenditure of that resource. Accidents arise on site as a result of exposure to risk, and the less the risks are on site the less the likelihood of accidents and ill health. The absence of accidents does not necessarily mean that all work activities are healthy and safe. The real 'cost' of avoiding accidents is eternal vigilance.

14.5.2 Impact of the CDM Regs

It is a requirement of Article 14 of the Directive that 'Member States shall report to the Commission every four years on the practical implementation of the provision of the Directive'. These reports are sent from the HSE to the European Commission but have been given no publicity in this country. The general feeling is that the Regulations and their supporting documentation have not been as effective as was hoped in terms of the ultimate aim of reducing construction industry accidents. Some argue that this is not the fault of the Regulations themselves, but the way in which the implementation of these legal requirements has taken place. Others point to the actual, often-complex, wording of the Regulations and what some consider the birth of a new professional in the form of the planning supervisor, which disperses the ownership of this subject away from traditional parties to construction projects. Extensive CDM training has been held throughout the industry yet the number of accidents has not reduced. The HSE and many others are looking towards the education of future construction industry professionals as a way to long-term gains, and the Health and Safety Executive and Commission made a commitment in June 2000 that they 'will act to ensure that safety-critical professionals such as architects and engineers receive adequate education in risk management to be delivered through a programme of direct approaches to relevant higher and further education institutions and professional institutions' (Health and Safety Commission, 2000). HSE's own research, subsequent to their June 2000 commitment, has demonstrated that changing the nature of professionals' education in this field is not easily achieved (Health and Safety Executive, 2001).

Yet it is perhaps unfair to 'blame' the Regulations as they lie within the perspective of many other Regulations that apply to construction work, and all these requirements lie within a complex, diverse and changing civil contractual environment with its own objectives and pressures. Rather than blame the pre-construction design industry for contributing to over 50 percent of the accidents on site, it would help greatly for those who could to assemble and publish a volume of 'best practice' information – help and practical guidance for all to learn from.

14.6 An overview of the role of clients and designers in H&S and the role of H&S in overall performance

Thus far, this chapter has addressed the influence of design on H&S, the motivation for addressing H&S, legislation applicable to designers, and the perceived impact of the CDM Regs on H&S to-date. However, given that this is a chapter in an architectural handbook of construction management, it is necessary that an overview of the holistic role of clients and designers in H&S and the role of H&S in overall industry performance be provided – Figure 14.1 does so in the form of causal loop analysis. For reasons of brevity and legibility the role of contractors has been excluded – with the exception of government and contractor commitment, which has been included in the left-hand ellipse to indicate the relationship between these two stakeholders and clients and designers. The right-hand ellipse indicates the impact of lack of/insufficient client/designer commitment to H&S on H&S/overall performance. Conversely, the left-hand ellipse indicates the impact of client/designer awareness/acknowledgement (and government/contractor) on H&S and, ultimately, overall performance and cost.

The right-hand ellipse is addressed first. Lack of/insufficient client/designer commitment to H&S results in inappropriate design/details/specification/poor constructability and inappropriate procurement/conditions of contract, which both result in poor ergonomics and contribute to the existence of hazards and risk. Poor ergonomics contributes to hazards and risk, results in strains, which in turn results in both absenteeism and ill

Figure 14.1: The holistic role of clients and designers in H&S and the role of H&S in overall performance

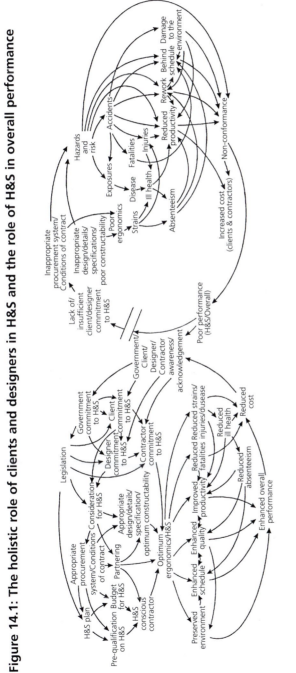

health, and ill health in absenteeism. Hazards and risk contribute to the probability of exposures and accidents. Exposures can result in disease and, consequently, ill health and, in turn, absenteeism. Absenteeism can result in reduced productivity, rework and falling behind schedule due to the absence of key crewmembers. Accidents, the outcome of which is largely fortuitous, can result in any, all, or a combination of the following: fatalities, injuries, reduced productivity as a result of work stoppages, rework as a result of damage to completed work, or work in progress, falling behind schedule as a result of work stoppages, and damage to the environment. A further consideration is the negative effects that reduced productivity, rework, falling behind schedule, and damage to the environment have on each other. Accidents also constitute a non-conformance, which would not be favourably viewed by many clients. Injuries may require first aid, or medical aid by a medical practitioner, and may result in temporary or permanent disablement. Although hazards and risk may not result in exposures or accidents, due to the consequential lack of optimum H&S, they can result in any, all, or a combination of the following: reduced productivity, rework and falling behind schedule. In essence, hazards and risk contribute to and constitute non-conformance. Although reduced productivity constitutes a non-conformance, it along with other non-conformances contributes to increased cost and, ultimately, poor performance overall.

More importantly, the left-hand ellipse indicates that the only way to break the cycle represented by the right-hand ellipse, represented by the break in the arrow between poor performance (H&S/Overall) and lack of/insufficient client/designer commitment to H&S, is for government, clients, designers and contractors to become aware through education and training, and acknowledge that the lack of such commitment contributes to poor performance (H&S/Overall).

Awareness and acknowledgement of the role and importance of client/designer commitment to H&S, are a prerequisite for commitment and change. Such awareness and acknowledgement engenders and/or reinforces government, client, designer and contractor commitment to H&S. Legislation is a result of government commitment to H&S which, in turn, engenders consideration for H&S in general, and both client and designer commitment to H&S. Legislation requires the development of an H&S plan at pre-tender and contract phase. Consideration for H&S increases the likelihood of the selection of an appropriate procurement system/conditions of contract, and appropriate design/details/specification/optimum constructability. The selection of an appropriate procurement system/conditions of contract should engender an appropriate design/details/specification/optimum constructability, a H&S plan, budgeting for H&S and partnering. Pre-qualification on H&S and budgeting for H&S should engender the engagement of a H&S conscious contractor. Partnering engenders appropriate design/details/specification/optimum constructability as a result of multi-stakeholder contributions, H&S conscious contracting, and optimum ergonomics/engenders all, any, or a combination of the following: reduced injuries/disease, reduced fatalities, improved productivity, enhanced quality, enhanced schedule and preserved environment which, ultimately, result in enhanced overall performance and reduced cost. A further benefit is the synergy between preserved environment, enhanced schedule, enhanced quality and improved productivity. Reduced fatalities result in improved productivity and reduced cost. Reduced injuries/disease result in improved productivity, reduced absenteeism, reduced ill health and reduced cost. Reduced ill health results in improved productivity and reduced absenteeism which, in turn, results in improved productivity, enhanced quality and enhanced schedule. The ellipse cycle should be perpetuated as a result of the reinforcement of government/client/designer/contractor/awareness/ acknowledgement resulting from enhanced overall performance and reduced cost.

14.7 Conclusions

Optimising H&S performance reduces the exposure of persons and the environment to risk and complements many other project goals. Thus effective management, and specifically H&S management, is a means to various desirable outcomes and not just the prevention of fatalities, injuries and/or ill health. The appropriate consideration of H&S issues is a must for clients and designers, and the best results are achieved through optimum co-operation between all the stakeholders on a project through processes such as partnering: working in isolation to achieve 'compliance' is never going to achieve the full intention of legislation.

Furthermore, there are a number of prerequisites for appropriate consideration of H&S. Firstly, a commitment to H&S by the architectural design profession. However, a prerequisite for commitment is awareness. Further, architectural designers need to be empowered to consider H&S issues. Given that education is a prerequisite for awareness and the need for empowerment, there needs to be comprehensive inclusion of H&S and risk management education in architectural and other designer tertiary programmes to provide the catalyst for the requisite paradigm shift. Secondly, the realisation and acknowledgement that H&S is a means to an end – optimum project performance and sustainable construction and development – as opposed to an end in itself – H&S on construction sites.

References

Anderson, J., 'The problems with construction', *The Safety and Health Practitioner,* May, 1997, pp. 29–30.
Bagwell, M. M. and Bush, H. A., 'Health Conception and Health Promotion in Blue Collar Workers: Program planning issues', *AAOHN Journal*, Vol. 47, No. 11, 1999, pp. 512–18.
Bohle, P. and Quinlan, M., *Managing Occupational Health and Safety, A Multi-disciplinary Approach*, 2nd edn, Macmillan Publishers Australia Pty Ltd., South Yarra (2000).

Department of the Environment, Transport and Regions, 'Rethinking Construction', DETR (1998).

Department of the Environment, 'Constructing the Team', DoE, HMSO (1994).

Dreger, G. T., 'Sustainable development in construction: Management strategy for success', *Proc. of the 1996 CIB W89 Beijing Intl Conf. Construction Modernization and Education*, China Architecture and Building Press, 1996. CD Rom file: //D1/papers/160-169/1633/163. htm.

Eckhardt, R. E., 'The Moral Duty to Provide for Workplace Safety', *Professional Safety*, Aug., 2001, pp. 36–8.

European Commission, 'Temporary or Mobile Construction Sites Directive', Council Directive 92/57/EEC of the 24 June 1992, Luxembourg.

Ford, M. and Brown, E., in Redgrave's *Health and Safety*, 4th edn, Butterworths (2002).

Health and Safety Commission, *Revitalising health and safety – a Strategy Statement*, HSE Books (2000).

Health and Safety Commission, *Managing Health and Safety in Construction: Construction (Design and Management) Regulations 1994 Approved Code of Practice*, HSE Books (2002).

Health and Safety Executive, *The costs to the British Economy of work accidents and work-related ill health*, HSE Books (1995).

Health and Safety Executive, 'Evaluation of the Construction (Design and Management) Regulations 1994', HSE Research Report 158/1997, HSE Books (1997).

Health and Safety Executive, 'Identification and management of risk in undergraduate construction courses', HSE Research Report 392/2001, HSE Books (2001).

Health and Safety Executive, 'Revitalising Health and Safety in Construction', HSE London (2002).

Hinze, J. W., *Construction Safety*, Prentice Hall Inc., New Jersey (1997).

International Labour Office, *Safety and health in construction*, ILO, Geneva (1992).

Jeffrey, J. and Douglas, I., 'Performance of the UK Construction Industry', *Proc. of the 5th Annual Rinker Intl Conf. focusing on Construction Safety and Loss Control*, University of Florida, Gainesville (eds R. Issa, R. J. Coble and B. R. Elliott) 1994, pp. 233–53.

Levitt, R. E. and Samelson, N .M., *Construction Safety Management*, 2nd edn, John Wiley and Sons, Inc. New York (1993).

Liska, P., 'Zero injury techniques', *Proc. of the 5th Annual Rinker Intl Conf. focusing on Construction Safety and Loss Control*, University of Florida, Gainesville (eds R. Issa, R. J. Coble and B. R. Elliott) 1994, pp. 293–303.

Meere, R., 'Building can seriously damage your health', *Chartered Builder*, Dec., 1990, pp. 8–9.

Republic of South Africa, 'Occupational Health and Safety Act: No. 85 of 1993', *Government Gazette No. 14918*, Pretoria (1993).

Rethinking Construction Ltd., *Rethinking Construction: 2002*, Rethinking Construction Ltd. (2002).

Rwelamila, P. D. and Smallwood, J. J., 'Appropriate project procurement systems for hybrid TQM', *Proc. of the 2nd Intl Conf. of CIB Working Commission W99 Implementation of Safety and Health on Construction Site, Honolulu, Hawaii*, Balkema, Rotterdam (eds A. Singh, J. W. Hinze and R. J. Coble), 1999, pp. 87–94.

Slappendel, C., *Health and Safety in New Zealand Workplaces*, The Dunmore Press Ltd, Palmerston North (1995).

Smallwood, J .J., 'The role of project managers in occupational health and safety', *Proc. of the 1st Intl Conf. of CIB Working Commission W99 Implementation of Safety and Health on Construction Sites, Lisbon, Portugal*, Balkema, Rotterdam (eds L. A. Dias and R. J. Coble) 1996, pp. 227–36.

Smallwood, J.J., 'The holistic influence of design on construction health and safety (H&S): General contractor (GC) perceptions', *Proc. of the Designing for Safety and Health Conf. London*, European Construction Institute, Loughborough (ed. A. G. F. Gibb), 2000, pp. 27–35.

Taylor, G., Easter, K. and Hegney, R., *Enhancing Safety, An Australian Workplace Primer*, 2nd edn, Training Publications, Perth (1998).

The Business Roundtable, *Improving Construction Safety Performance*, The Business Roundtable, New York (1995).

Key Reading

Bohle, P. and Quinlan, M., *Managing Occupational Health and Safety, A Multi-disciplinary Approach*, 2nd edn, Macmillan Publishers Australia Pty Ltd., South Yarra (2000).

Health and Safety Commission, *Managing Health and Safety in Construction: Construction (Design and Management) Regulations 1994 Approved Code of Practice*, HSE Books (2002).

Post Project Evaluation

Closing out a project **15**

Richard Fellows, Department of Real Estate and Construction,
University of Hong Kong, and
Alex Amato, Department of Architecture, University of Hong Kong, Hong Kong

15.1 Introduction

It may be argued that successfully closing out a project commences at project inception, if not conception; that is because what the project is intended to achieve, in terms of its functional, in-use performance must be determined and articulated at the very early stages to provide focus for the numerous, subsequent design, evaluation and production activities. In practice, closing out operations revolve around determining that the project about to be (or which has just been) handed over to the client (employer) for beneficial occupation and use conforms to the various 'benchmarks' specified for its performance. Traditionally, and most commonly, such specifications occur as product specifications and similar performance requirements (target minima). Those targets, in the typology of time, cost and quality standards and measures, represent the culmination of design activities of determining client (project commissioners') desires (objectives and requirements) and parameters through the briefing processes and coupling those with realisability (constructability) considerations to yield, in essence, a performance specification which is progressively converted through interpretations and translation decisions into the product specification form.

In developing and, at closing out, examining the realisation of the project against the specifications, it may be helpful to consider the usual means by which the (main) participants on a project are brought into working association with each other. Most commonly, the means focus on price competition with the lowest bidder securing the work – as under the Code of Procedure for Single Stage Selective Tendering (NJCC, 1996) – with a similar situation prevailing for design consultants following the required abolition of mandatory fee scales. Despite heightening awareness of the interrelated importance for performance of the three overall performance criteria, remaining emphasis on price competition tends to lead participants' business-oriented operating requirements into conflict, if only via their profit-seeking motive. The upshot is that clients and designers may regard the targets stipulated (in the contract documents, etc.) as minima whilst constructors regard them as absolutes to be achieved but not exceeded (except for 'marketing purposes').

Hence the necessity to ensure that criteria for compliance are adequate, achievable and clear, and that evaluation of compliance is vested in an expert. Usually, such vesting is in the project architect who, it is acknowledged, operates as an independent professional under a contract for services with the client. In instances of serious disagreement between participants over compliance, the recourse is to arbitration – both under standard forms of contract (e.g. JCT 98) and the UK's Arbitration Act, 1996.

15.2 Case study – church refurbishment and meeting rooms extension

The case study discusses the closing out of a small project (approx. £500,000) in the home counties for the refurbishment of an existing church, constructed in the 1950s, to provide improved day and artificial lighting, to improve the thermal comfort of the parishioners by the provision of thermal insulation and a new heating system, and generally to overhaul the fabric and improve the church visually. The works also included provision of a small complex of two meeting rooms, an office and store cupboard, two rooms for church purposes, a kitchen and a WC, with a small landscaped garden connected to the larger of the meeting rooms by means of large, glazed sliding doors.

Initial trial excavations established that the existing foundations for the church would make the construction of the adjoining meeting room complex very difficult if built traditionally. An extremely lightweight steel solution was developed that required reasonably lengthy discussion and aesthetic design development with the planning authorities. Although the project was within a conservation area and the proposed cladding materials – bright green, 'crinkly tin' cladding – were not in any way traditional, the local planning authorities were remarkably supportive, which was a very welcome, if an unusual experience (yes, there are enlightened planners out there!).

The project, thus, duly passed through all its regulatory requirements, negotiations with adjoining owners, client approval stages, etc. The outcome was a small single storey building with a copper roof, bright green metal cladding and extensive areas of glazing at roof level to allow light into the church and the back of the meeting rooms. The building was in no way typical and greatly contrasted with the soft red brick and flint of the surrounding conservation area.

The atypical construction, for what was, essentially, a relatively small building contract, was an immediate concern in terms of overall budget and cost control. Therefore, it was decided that the procurement strategy should involve specialist sub-contractors in the design and value engineering of each of the critical packages. Hence, the building was designed in detail, engineered structurally, the mechanical and electrical engineering scheme developed in detail – all of which enabled the following specialist sub-contracts to be tendered well before the main contract:

- Structural and architectural steel;
- Wall cladding, roof and floor decking;
- Mechanical and electrical engineering package;
- Specialist dry lining;
- The glazing package;
- Furniture and special timber cladding.

After the tenders were returned, the lowest tendering sub-contractors for each package contributed to the process of value engineering and design development. This process continued until the budget and key design issues were resolved and it was only after this stage that the main contract was tendered with the specialists eventually being adopted as nominated sub-contractors to the main contractor.

To complicate matters, the client organisation was, effectively, a multi-headed hydra, split between parish and diocese and then split again into many factions in the parish. All consultants' appointments, for instance, were made to the diocese, as was the main contract (for financial reasons). However, the real client, in terms of being the eventual building users, were the parish as they were instrumental in the instigation of the project and all the key decisions in the design development including the eventual funding of the project. Within the parish, a building committee was established with some members taking more interest than others. This split arrangement between diocese and parish required collateral warranties to be signed by the consultants that established responsibility between the parish and their consultants and, in due course, one was established between the main contractor and the parish. In the consultants' collateral warranties however, a caveat was added to the effect that the collateral warranty could not be further assigned to any future purchaser of the church and that the building's function could not be changed. Infringement of these requirements would invalidate the collateral warranty agreements.

Finally, the project was ready to commence. The last complication was a planning requirement to deal with the archaeology of the site as it was located within the boundaries of an ancient Anglo-Saxon settlement. Archaeologists were appointed on a watching brief, ready to spring into action should anything emerge during site excavation required for foundations, drainage, etc. Almost immediately after site clearance, graves, approximately 150 years old, were located under the existing sacristy extension when it was demolished. The archaeologists swung into action and further findings of graves were predicted. Moreover, some of the pad foundations were to be located at depths of up to 3.5 m with the likelihood that, at these depths, truly ancient remains would be unearthed with the potential for delaying the contract considerably.

The resolution was a swift change of foundation design to a shallow, raft type slab – and it is worth remarking that this was possible only because of the lightweight construction of the main building. Even though this eventuality could not have been foreseen it did partly vindicate the design decision to adopt the lightweight method of construction. Although shallow, raft slab foundation type is usually more expensive, as it uses very much more material, there were practical and financial advantages that, to some extent, offset the additional cost of the raft. The excavation process was rather delicate, to say the least, with small pads being located at rather considerable depths and the contractor was rather nervous about the practicality of digging these. The archaeologists were very pleased also not to have any destructive excavation go through the deeper Anglo-Saxon strata and were content to have the graves, and any potential further remains in deeper strata, covered by the concrete slab of the raft, effectively sealing them in position for future generations. Finally, the adoption of a raft reduced the extent of excavation to less than 400 mm adjacent to the site boundaries, which simplified the 'Party Wall/Boundary' procedures considerably.

The second and third unfortunate developments were insolvencies of two of the specialist sub-contractors. The first was the M&E sub-contractor who had, fortunately, not really commenced on site. Although an alternative price was quickly sought from the second lowest M&E sub-contract tender, the situation was resolved by an employee of the original sub-contractor taking over the sub-contract for the same contract sum, resulting in very little time lost.

What dealt the main body blow to the project, and which, potentially, could have frustrated it entirely, was the insolvency of the steel fabricator and, although an alternative sub-contractor was found relatively quickly, the consequence was considerable delay and additional cost to the contract.

15.2.1 Practical completion

Although it is more usual for a project to be handed over at a single instance, most construction contract forms permit handing over in parts or in stages/sections. Partial handing over occurs for the convenience of the parties on the particular occasion, whereas sectional completion is envisaged from the outset and so target dates for completion of each of the sections identified are noted in the contract (see, e.g. JCT 98; clause 18 and the sectional completion supplement).

Most construction contracts place an overriding obligation upon the contractor to carry out the works regularly and diligently, and to complete them by the Date for Completion (JCT 98; clause 1.3; date inserted in the Appendix). That date relates to practical completion (usually referred to as 'substantial completion' in civil engineering contracts) although several important contractual obligations remain, notably the prompt making good of any defects as listed by the architect within 14 days from the end of the defects liability period (DLP; otherwise called the maintenance period – usually of six months' duration from the date of practical completion).

Unfortunately, JCT 98 (like its predecessors) does not define practical completion (see clause 17). Reference to case precedents, industry practice and the legal doctrine of substantial completion indicates that practical completion occurs when the project (whole or part) may be regarded as (functionally) complete for all practical purposes. Thus, some minor defects may be present and some items of work may remain to be completed but such items do not materially detract from the functioning of the building. The decision as to when the project is practically complete is the architects and, to a significant extent, is a matter of opinion rather than of 'fact'. Thus, in order to avoid dispute, common procedures have been developed to smooth the process.

For practical completion to be achieved under clause 17 of JCT 98, three things must have occurred:

1 The architect is of the opinion that the works are practically complete.

2 The contractor has complied sufficiently with clause 6A.4 – i.e. has provided adequate information for the health and safety file to the planning supervisor to comply with the requirements of 14(d), (4) and (f) of the CDM Regulations.

3 The contractor has provided adequate drawings, etc. to the employer regarding any performance specified work.

(Clearly, the judgement of the architect is fundamental to the issue of the certificate of practical completion.)

The procedures include incorporating objective measures of performance in the specification (e.g. compressive strength tests of concrete cubes) – compliance with which may be checked as the work progresses. For more subjective assessments (e.g. paint colours), specification charts may be used and 'trial panels' of fair-face brickwork, plastering, etc. can be produced on-site as the benchmark for compliance – naturally it is important that such panels are produced under realistic working conditions, the standard is agreed and the panels protected and preserved. Clearly, the underpinning notion is to eliminate subjectivity as far as possible from compliance decisions (both statements of requirements and testing) and to maximise objectivity by referencing to independent, widely-accepted standards (BSs, codes of practice, etc.).

However, even extensive use of independent, objective standards will, itself, be unlikely to eliminate differences of perspectives on compliance. Hence, a procedure of 'building acceptance' may be advisable through progressive joint inspections, discussions and negotiation. The result is the common approach of 'incremental completion' whereby small parts of a project are agreed to have achieved practical completion and are secured by the contractor, who retains responsibility for them, until the project (in whole, part or section) achieves formal practical completion via the architect's certificate.

JCT 98, clause 42, concerns 'performance specified work', and is work which the contractor must design and execute on the basis of a performance specification provided by the employer. (Here, the architect has authority to approve methods proposed for executing the work and the contractor must provide drawings, maintenance requirements details, etc. of such work prior to achieving practical completion.)

Despite endeavours to increase objectivity in determining compliance with specification (both product and performance), the issue of procedures in instances of non-compliance remains. JCT 98 addresses that matter in clause 8 under which the architect may order opening up of works for inspection/testing. The historic approach of 'if there is compliance, the employer pays; if non-compliance, the contractor pays' has been modified under clause 8.4.4 by the incorporation of a code of practice for testing. That code seeks to demonstrate the extent of reasonableness for testing where some items in a sample drawn from a large population have failed (e.g. a project of 500 flats, each with a balcony, where, in a sample of 20 balconies tested, one has failed – how many more should be tested and how should that further sampling for testing be done?).

The achievement of practical completion has a number of very important consequences for all the project participants. Amongst the consequences, the most significant are:

- The employer takes possession of the works.

- The employer assumes responsibility for insuring the project (and for frost damage to the works).

- The defects liability period begins.

- The next interim certificate must include release of the first moiety (half) of retention held in respect of the works which have achieved practical completion (subject to clause 35.17 concerning possible early releases of retention to nominated sub-contractors).

- The contractor's (potential) liability for liquidated and ascertained damages for delay ceases.

It is important that the architect ensures that the employer is aware of the consequences of practical completion of the works and is advised in due time so that the employer can make adequate arrangements for the changes (notably effecting the necessary insurances).

15.2.2 Practical completion of the project

As previously mentioned, there were a number of unavoidable reasons that delayed the progress of the works and so practical completion was considerably later than anticipated by the original contract programme. In this case, the client took over the refurbished church some weeks before the meeting rooms' complex was finished sufficiently for practical completion to be considered. The client used the church for Sunday services only during this period and this enabled a considerable number of minor, yet important, work items to be completed within the church during normal working hours, including Saturdays. Meanwhile, work progressed on the meeting rooms until some weeks later when they were sufficiently complete for practical completion to be considered.

A certificate of practical completion was, eventually, issued with a list of minor incomplete works as an addendum and with the proviso that these outstanding items would be dealt with as quickly as possible. One particular item, the timber front entrance door, was noted as being likely to fail due to excessive warping and subsequently did. It was replaced by the contractor without arguments during the course of the year leading up to the end of the defects liability period.

The next nine months, during which the contractor completed the outstanding items, was a difficult period. From the client's perspective, the building was over budget, late, unfinished and, moreover, was not performing as expected in minor respects and one serious respect – acoustically. From the contractor's perspective, they had performed in an extremely co-operative and non-claims conscious manner considering all the difficulties that had emerged as paramount, while being held to an extremely parsimonious final account. The contractor completed all the unfinished minor items in a reasonably diligent manner and delivered a building to the specification of exceptional value. From the consultants' perspective, especially the architects, they had produced a building to the agreed design, being duly diligent of all the unforeseen circumstances, and managed to deliver to the client a building that still represented very good value, while averting (by a willingness to undertake a considerable amount of additional work without additional fees) the nightmare scenario of a terminated contract with a partly complete building.

Over this 12-month defects liability period, these conflicting views were resolved by an acceptance by all the parties of their respective concerns with a considerable effort by all to maintain the spirit of reasonableness that was present throughout the contract. Many of the initial behavioural faults of the building were due to the client body not really understanding how the building could be operated and there followed a real learning process when an effective building operation client committee came into being. Operating systems of large sliding doors, heating, lighting and audio systems were explained again and again, often to several groups of different people. Moreover, remedial works were carried out by the contractor at little or no additional expense. Gradually, the client body took on responsibility and a sense of ownership of their building.

Slow but steady progress was made to finalise all the outstanding minor works, while the client came to accept, although, perhaps, grudgingly, the acoustic limitations of the open plan and lightweight design of the building. In fact, the more professional members of the client body always understood that the design of the building was a compromise between providing additional daylighting (the original church was very dark and gloomy) and, effectively, providing an absolute acoustic separation between the church and the meeting rooms. Indeed, these same professional members of the parish committee were the more active ones during the entire design development process and reminded the others that the architect had gone to considerable lengths to 'walk the committee', in detail and on several occasions, through the entire project, pointing out that the expected level of acoustic separation would only be about equivalent to the separation that had existed previously between the un-refurbished church and the demolished old sacristy.

Gradually, the client body overcame their initial misgivings, learned to operate and manage their new building and refurbished church with some enjoyment and satisfaction. The contractor had, by the end of this period, agreed the final account and dealt with almost all of the outstanding works items. That occurred, almost exclusively, because, by this time, the 12-month defects liability period was coming to an end and two further events had complicated matters.

15.2.3 *Defects liability period (DLP)*

Normally, the duration of the DLP is six months for building projects but 12 months (maintenance period) for civil engineering. Commonly, governments require a 12-month DLP and, especially during economic recessions, there is a tendency to extend the DLP. The purpose of the DLP is to provide a time for latent defects to appear so that they can be remedied promptly (that includes any damage due to frost which occurred before the date of practical completion).

Contracts (notably, JCT 98) commonly refer to defects, shrinkages and other faults which appear during the DLP and which are due to materials or workmanship that do not accord with the contract and any damage due to frost which occurred prior to practical completion to be the subject matter for making good. Although no patent defects should be apparent for practical completion to be certified, in practice that will be the case only rarely – if ever – but such patent defects must be minor (as noted above). Clearly, shrinkages may occur (progressively) over time and so their inclusion for DLP action is appropriate. Frost damage must be caused by frost which occurred before practical completion (rather than the resulting damage or its appearance). The 'catch-all' of 'other faults' can be regarded as a 'safety net' to ensure all items of non-compliance with the specified works may be remedied under these contractual provisions.

However, the operation of the DLP provisions does not guarantee that each and every 'defect' will be detected and made good. Design defects outside of 'performance specified work' are excluded; latent defects which cannot be detected during the DLP naturally fall outside the scope of the contract and, therefore, must be dealt with under collaborative/marketing arrangements or via statute, notably the Latent Damage Act, 1986, or Common Law. Here, attention should also be given to the terms of the Limitation Acts and to legal relationships between potential 'plaintiff' and 'defendant' concerning the nature of damage (and claim), whether under the law of contract or tort and the presence of any collateral contracts/warranties (see below). Finally, any defects which are not listed by the architect on the schedule of defects or appropriate architect's instructions fall outside the scope of the DLP contractual provisions.

In detecting and listing defects, etc. for making good and in, subsequently, certifying the making good, provided the architect has acted with the required level of skill and care and executed the terms of engagement, there should be no liability on the architect for any defects, etc. undetected.

Under JCT 98, the architect may notify the contractor of defects, etc. to be made good in two ways. The main method is to list all the defects in the schedule of defects which must be delivered to the contractor as an AI within 14 days of the end of the DLP. As only one schedule of defects may be produced for a project, it is advisable for the architect to prepare it at the end of the DLP to ensure that all detectable defects are included. Normally, the contractor bears all costs of making good of defects, which must be done within a reasonable time of receiving the schedule.

The second method in which the architect can require the contractor to make good defects is by issuing an AI. However, such AIs are issued usually in respect of more serious defects that require prompt making good – otherwise, occupation of the premises would be disrupted frequently. Further, such AIs cannot be issued after 14 days from the end of the DLP.

Once the architect is satisfied that the contractor has made good all the defects, then the certificate of completion of making good defects must be issued. That certificate is a prerequisite for the issue of the final certificate.

JCT 98, clause 30.8.1, notes the timing for the issue of the final certificate; that gives prima facie indication that, normally, a reasonable time in which the contractor should remedy defects is within two (calendar) months of the end of the DLP.

15.2.4 *Final certificate (and final account)*

The architect is required (clause 30.8.1) to issue the final certificate for the project within two (calendar) months from the latest of:

- The end of the DLP;

- The date of issuing the certificate of making good defects;

- The sending to the contractor of ascertainment of loss/expense due to delay and the final account statement (as per clauses 30.6.1.2.1 and 30.6.1.2.2).

Such final certificate must state:

- The total of any advance payments to the contractor and the amounts stated as due in interim certificates (i.e. the total amounts already certified as due to the contractor).

- The total of the contract sum adjusted in accordance with the contract (i.e. the total of the final account for the project).

- To what the final contract sum relates and how it has been calculated.

Then, the final certificate must note any balance due either from the employer to the contractor or vice-versa.

The employer must inform the contractor of the amount to be paid, how the amount has been determined and how the payment will be effected within five days of the date of issue of the final certificate. The balance must be paid within 28 days from the date of issue of the final certificate. Normally, the balance will be the amount stated in the final certificate; the provisions just noted are to enable the employer to vary such amount – as in the case of any outstanding liquidated and ascertained damages. Any late payment attracts interest at 5 percent above the Bank of England's then current base rate.

JCT 98, clause 30.6, gives details of how the final contract sum is to be calculated – either by the architect or, more commonly, by the quantity surveyor (QS). In order to determine the final contract sum, the contractor must provide all necessary documents (to the architect or QS, as appropriate) within six months of the date of practical completion. The architect, or QS, has three months from receipt of those documents to prepare the final account (see JCT 98, clause 30.6.1.2).

Essentially, the final account is prepared by adjusting the (initial) contract sum for changes as per the contract, notably Prime Cost Sums, provisional sums, variations, fluctuations and various types of claims for loss/expense. That is because JCT 98, in common with most standard forms of building contract, is a lump sum contract. However, most civil engineering contracts are measure and value (remeasurement) contracts and, therefore, the final account is prepared by measuring all work as executed and valuing it at 'bill rates' plus adjustments as per the contract for claims, fluctuations, etc.

In the absence of fraud(!) and excepting any items subject to adjudication, arbitration or litigation being commenced within 28 days of the date of the final certificate (clauses 30.9.2 and 30.9.3), the final certificate has the following main effects that:

1 Any items required to be to the satisfaction of the architect are so;

2 All computations leading to the final account sum accord with the terms of the contract – except for errors of inclusion/exclusion and arithmetic errors;

3 All extensions of time (under clause 25) have been given appropriately;

4 All claims for direct loss/expense due to delays, under clause 26, are completely settled by the amounts included in the final account.

The scope of item 1, above, is reinforced by clause 30.10 which specifies that the final certificate (and, indeed, any other certificate) does not provide conclusive evidence of works, materials, etc. being in accordance with the contract, save regarding instances where the opinion of the architect is the criterion for compliance. Thus, where objective tests, etc. are specified in the contract for performance of items of the works, then it is the results of those tests which provide evidence of compliance with the contract, rather than the final certificate.

15.2.5 End of defects liability period

The contractor's organisation had gone through a fairly extensive restructuring process but, not entirely because of it, all the contractor's personnel who had worked on the project, from the site foreman to the contracts manager to the director in charge, had left the company. Another contracts manager was put in charge of dealing with the small number of outstanding items but he too left after a relatively short period. Additionally, the second steelwork sub-contractor went into liquidation, leaving two of the outstanding items unfinished.

The defects liability period came to an end and joint inspection with the contractor and client, although still hypercritical, revealed a very small number of defects – shrinkage cracks and doors that had fallen slightly on their hinges. The extent of the defects was extremely small and these were promptly dealt with, after which an inspection was carried out to confirm that each item of the defects liability had been made good.

Just one item of work remained outstanding; this was from the steel sub-contractor's items which was, perhaps, not surprising – involving as it did the complex fabrication of a specialist light fitting in steel, glass and timber. The making good defects certificate was issued but with this as an outstanding item attached. Eventually, the architect had to track down an equivalent fabricator as this was in the client's best overall interests and the quickest method of resolving matters. Additional drawings were issued and fabrication of the light fitting commenced. In due course, the light fitting was tested and fixed on site. The last item was finally complete and the contract was finalised with the prompt issue of the final certificate.

15.2.6 *After the final certificate*

Subject to the provisions regarding adjudication, etc., once the final certificate has been issued, the contract has been brought to an end through performance by the parties and their 'agents'. Hence, such completion of obligations under the contract means that any problems which emerge later must be resolved through extra-contractual mechanisms – whether relational ('marketing' incentive) or at law. In litigation, limitation provisions restrict the period within which an action must be commenced to (usually) 3 years (personal injuries, etc.), 6 years (simple contract) or 12 years (contract as a deed) with time commencing when the 'cause of action accrues' (the damage first occurs or should be discoverable; see also Latent Damage Act, 1986). Outside of contract, legal action may occur under Tort (in which the possible actions may be more restricted than at contract) where the limitation periods usually are 3 years (personal injury, etc.) or 6 years. To take effect, limitation must be pleaded as a defence. Naturally, in relational considerations limitation (as such) does not apply!

Despite changes to limitation provisions following major cases (notably, difficult to detect latent defects) many constraints remain – especially involving preclusion of claims for pure economic loss under Tort. Thus, much attention has been devoted to devising mechanisms by which parties may obtain more extensive protection of their interests in projects via recourse to project participants. In the post final certificate phase, that attention has revolved around extended insurance in mainland Europe and collateral warranties in UK, USA and elsewhere. Further, in the UK, the Contracts (Rights of Third Parties) Act, 1999, applies to all contracts entered into after 11 May, 2000.

The US president, Harry S. Truman, had a sign on his desk in the oval office which read 'the buck stops here', indicating his apparent acceptance of ultimate responsibility – at least, in the USA! Unfortunately, the approach adopted by many participants to construction projects is more akin to 'the buck starts here' indicating a desire to be 'teflon-coated' through blaming others (any/all) for problems and rarely, if ever, accepting responsibility. In consequence of this widespread approach, the construction industry is believed to have a 'blaming/responsibility avoiding' culture for both design and construction activities. The situation is exacerbated by the high incidence of bankruptcies and liquidations (often accompanied by the rapid re-emergence of firms, etc. in amended guises!).

The issues, noted above, have two main consequences for the post final certificate period – statutory provisions and 'collateral warranties'. S1(1) of the Civil Liability (Construction) Act, 1978, states that, '...any person liable in respect of any damage suffered by another person may recover contribution from another person liable in respect of the same damage'. The intent of such legislation is twofold – (i) to ensure adequate compensation to a plaintiff; (ii) to enable defendants to recover an appropriate share of compensation from others who are liable for causing the harm to the plaintiff. Given that the major concern is to compensate the plaintiff, the defendants incur joint and several liability – hence, the provisions to enable recovery of contribution(s) from other liable parties (who were not cited in the initial action to be defendants) who still exist (in a legal sense – consider liquidation effects here!). For latent defects on construction projects, such provisions are relevant to defects caused partly by design and partly by construction – in such cases, consultant designer(s), main contractor, sub-contractors and suppliers may all have contributed (independently) to the defect and, so, be joint and severally liable.

A response to the joint and several liability has been for project participants to endeavour to insert clauses into contracts (including collateral warranties) which are known as 'net contribution clauses'. Under such clauses, the warrantor limits their liability to the amount it would be just and reasonable for that party to pay on the basis that all other participants have similar terms in their contracts (and remain in existence) i.e. the limit is the warrantor's contribution to the damage/compensation (maintaining joint but removing several liability/compensation).

Of course, in seeking to limit liability by a contractual term, parties must comply with the provisions of the Unfair Contract Terms Act, 1977 – notably S2(2) under which such terms must satisfy the requirement of reasonableness. The person seeking to rely on the limiting term incurs the burden to prove that the term is reasonable – timing, notice, content, etc., bearing in mind the nature of the parties (e.g. as in a 'consumer contract').

Collateral warranties have become widespread in construction, especially since high profile cases demonstrated that pure economic loss is unrecoverable in Tort. Essentially, collateral warranties establish a contractual link between the parties (which, otherwise, would have been reliant on Tort) and, therefore, via the terms of such warranties, may extend liabilities. Commonly, a collateral warranty is an agreement (often in a standard form document) whereby a consultant, contractor or sub-contractor warrants, usually to a financier, buyer or tenant of a project, that it has complied (and, through extended undertaking to make good any latent defects for a prescribed period) with the terms of engagement, main contract or sub-contract.

An important feature of most collateral warranties is assignment, especially where the intended beneficiaries are tenants, purchasers or re-financiers. The usual case of standard form warranties is for a prescribed number of such assignments to be allowed.

However, under Common Law, following *Shanklin Pier Ltd*. v. *Detel Products Ltd*. (1951) [1(1951) 2KB 854], the courts may imply a collateral warranty to give 'business efficacy' to the relationship between the parties – such as where a client relies on a representation (say, of fitness for purpose, durability, design) given by a supplier or sub-contractor.

A further development of 'consumer protection' legislation is the Contracts (Rights of Third Parties) Act, 1999. Under that Act (S1), a third party (i.e. someone other than one of the contracting parties; hence, someone who is not privy to the contract) may enforce the terms of the contract in their own right provided either the contract so provides (expressly) or, if the contract term(s) in question purport (imply) to confer a benefit on such a third party. The section applies unless either there is an express term in the contract excluding such third party rights (subject to reasonableness as per the Unfair Contract Terms Act, 1977) or unless a contrary intention is clear from proper construction of the contract (i.e. such an exclusion will be implied).

If a contract contains no express provisions regarding rights of third parties (as is common in construction standard forms) there is likely to be doubt about which terms give what rights to which (actual/potential) third parties! A complex situation in construction, especially speculative developments, where so many third parties are likely to be involved and affected. Hence, it is hardly surprising that bodies which produce standard contracts have responded by developing standard clauses that endeavour to exclude the application of the Act.

15.2.7 *Conclusion – project assessment*

The entire project could be considered as one of the more ill-fated contracts and bears testament to the difficulty of trying to produce small buildings that are in any way different and not constructed traditionally. The reliance on fairly sophisticated construction methods for small projects must be regarded as problematic and there are a number of reasons for this. One of these is the inevitable reliance on specialist sub-contractors. Mostly, such firms are organised to undertake much larger contracts and this then means that any small project is not considered with anywhere near the same importance as the larger projects that are being dealt with by the company at the same time. Sometimes it was very difficult to even get two specialist sub-contractors to return a tender price. Nevertheless it is difficult, looking back, to see how the progress of the project could have been handled differently or the design changed radically.

What is remarkable though, apart from the project's history of receiving one blow after another, is that, at every turn of events, when matters could have led to a breakdown of communications and eventual recourse to arbitration or litigation, the major participants seemed able to listen to the other's point of view and try to accommodate those views. At no stage did anybody say 'no' and compromises were always found, if accepted grudgingly and often with great inward frustration. Slowly but surely then must be better than dispute and, overall, all the participants realised this and that their best interests were served by this course of action through which all disputes were finally resolved fairly. Fairly, though, does not necessarily equate with happily, but fairness must be the primary basis for the successful completion of any contract.

References

Arbitration Act 1996, HMSO.
Civil Liability (Construction) Act 1978, HMSO.
Contracts (Rights of Third Parties) Act 1999, HMSO.
Joint Contracts Tribunal (JCT), *Standard Form of Building Contract, Private Edition, with Quantities*, RIBA Publications (1998).
Latent Damage Act 1986, HMSO.
National Joint Consultative Committee for Building (NJCC), *Code of Procedure for Single Stage Selective Tendering*, RIBA Publications (1996).
Shanklin Pier Ltd. v. *Detel Products Ltd.* (1951) 2KB 854.
Unfair Contract Terms Act 1977, HMSO.

Key Reading

Aqua Group, *Pre contract Practice and Contract Administration for the building team*, Blackwell Science, Oxford (2003).
Fellows, R. F. and Fenn, P., *Standard Form of Building Contract*, 1998 edn: a commentary for students and practitioners, Palgrave (2001).

Knowledge management: post project reviews **16**

Charles Egbu, School of the Built and Natural Environment,
Glasgow Caledonian University, UK, and
John Easton (Senior architect in commercial private practice), Glasgow, UK

16.1   Introduction

Modern organisations in the construction industry have to react fast and be flexible to deal with innovative and multi-disciplinary challenges. Increasing complexity of project work, as a result of a growing number of technical and social relationships and interfaces to be considered, gives higher value to existing knowledge in order to deal with complexity and to increase efficiency. Projects, therefore, have to adapt knowledge and experiences from the daily work of an organisation and from former projects. Members of the project team can be the main carriers of knowledge and experiences from daily work; they bring this input into the team (Egbu, 2001; 2002). Organising by projects is on a strong increase, because projects are seen to be learning-intensive organisational (albeit 'temporary organisations') forms; where the knowledge of individuals and teams can be harnessed for the good of the project; and at the same time allow for lessons to be learned for the benefit of future projects.

The construction industry could be termed as a knowledge-based industry, and construction organisations as knowledge-intensive organisations, involving several project teams working together in order to achieve the required client's objectives within the given time frame and other resource limits (Egbu and Gorse, 2002). Each project team utilises the tacit and explicit knowledge of 'knowledge-intensive workers' (Nonaka and Takeuchi, 1995; Egbu and Botterill, 2001). Many disciplines are involved in construction projects, where the interaction of various stakeholders with different cognitive levels, experiences and skills promotes the preparation of project deliverables within pressured deadlines. The above description assumes that project outcomes are milestones in a knowledge-management activity and the various deliverables are just knowledge exploitations in meaningful formats (Pemberton and Stonehouse, 2000). It can therefore be conceptualised that project deliverables consist of knowledge-artefacts integration through a social communication process. The dimension of learning is of critical importance in this regard. The exploration of knowledge promotes the realisation of reusable knowledge artefact. In this context, past experiences, expertise, proficiency, competence – skills and capabilities – and embedded knowledge of all kinds are examples of resources that in their integration promote the meaningful constructing structure element of knowledge. The iterative process of building experiences (and dynamic capabilities) and capacities for effective actions requires an 'infrastructure' where an organisation gains wisdom from participation in projects.

A variety of mechanisms have been put forward to prevent the loss of knowledge and experiences from project to project and from project to organisational base

(Gulliver, 1987; Kumar, 1990; Collier *et al*, 1996; Cross and Baird, 2000). However, only a few organisations systematically identify and transfer valuable knowledge from project to project or from project to organisational base. It would seem that most construction organisations and project teams are not able to evaluate projects and learn from them. Weiser and Morrison (1998) note that 'project information is rarely captured, retained, or indexed so that people external to the project can retrieve and apply it to future tasks'. Kumar (1990) also informs us that 'evaluation is performed only on a small fraction of projects, the purpose of evaluation does not seem to be provision of improvements in development or project management practices'. A broad range of reasons have been offered as to why organisations and project teams do not evaluate and learn from projects. These reasons include organisational, technical, methodical issues as well as social problems to be addressed and discussed (Boddie, 1987; Abdel-Hamid and Madnick, 1990).

An important consequence of not reviewing a finished project is that the actions and decisions that caused the problems and errors may be repeated. Reviewing projects should prevent 're-inventing the wheel' and repeat mistakes. Indeed, this is an important benefit of effective knowledge management. Knowledge management, from a project management context, can be viewed as the process by which knowledge relevant to a project is identified, created, acquired, captured, codified, stored, disseminated (shared/ transferred), implemented (adapting, transforming, synthesis) and its impact measured for the benefit of the current and future project(s); and for organisations involved with the project. Project knowledge is a complex concept which consists of information and skills acquired through experience: truth and belief, perspectives and judgements, expectations and methodologies. It exists in individuals, groups, routines, in various forms. A knowledge-management approach could be employed in effective project review, especially post project review. Such an approach should take a holistic and balanced perspective in dealing with the people, technological and other resource issues that could be involved.

16.2 Case studies

Case study 1: The preservation of valuable relationships

Client and project: A UK based manufacturer, international distributor and franchiser commissions the construction of new world headquarters and central manufacturing facilities.

Project manager and contract administrator: An officer of the local enterprise company, who is largely an absentee from the project. Steps in occasionally, usually at the wrong time or too late, and otherwise signs the certificates that the quantity surveyor (QS) prepares for him. Given the shortcoming of his own performance he bizarrely decides to chair a post completion review.

The design and construction team: All major names, a management contractor and work package contractors, architect, QS, C&S engineers, M&E engineers, and a landscape architect (the latter a sub-consultant to the architect). All bar the QS and the project manager (PM) are novated to the contractor.

The scenario: The project goes very badly. Completes late and over budget. The post completion review was definitely needed, but was instituted for the wrong reasons. A witch-hunt by the PM on behalf of the client.

The review: The contractor employed the design team. Numerous and costly contract claims were still outstanding at the time of the review. As a consequence, no one felt free to speak openly at the review. The proceedings could have been bitter and acrimonious or a superficial waste of time. They were the latter. The summary report promised by the PM was never issued.

The outcome: The client was streetwise and a very skilled negotiator, and eventually settled the final account at an amount substantially below the claimed amount. The project team felt hard done by, but had learned valuable lessons even if they were not shared (indeed, it was many years before the contractor and architect repaired their relationship and worked together again). While the architects did not gain much from the formal review, they already knew enough to institute significant organisational changes as a consequence of their experience. These became core procedures that in time led to ISO 9001 quality assurance.

Case study 2: The distraction of mutual self-congratulation

Client and project: A major UK insurance company wanting to fit out offices in a large new shell and core city centre development.

Project manager and contract administrator: Led and administered by the architect. There was no consultant project manager.

The design and construction team: All major names, a management contractor and work package contractors, architect, QS, M&E engineers, and C&S engineers (the latter a sub-consultant to the architect). An executive architect had prepared the initial design intent earlier. All of the consultants were hand picked by the client and joint architects. The management contractor was hand picked without competition, on the understanding that a named manager known to the architects would lead the construction team. The works contractors were in turn all hand picked by the contractor without agreed contract sums. All accounting was open book, based on agreed rates.

The scenario: The 12 week £4.2 m project finished exactly on time and on budget. All of the participants were delighted with the experience and the outcome.

The review: A post completion review was held in a spirit of mutual self-congratulation. As a result few probing questions were asked and many of the valuable experiences were not properly understood, passed on, or repeated. No record of the review was made.

The outcome: The project participant had understood instinctively that a special procurement method was needed, based on key personal skills rather than on cost (although the cost turned out to be no higher than normal). Although this approach is suited to only a few projects, the lack of any analysis of its merits and potential future uses meant that, tragically, it has never been repeated.

16.3 Post project reviews: definition and purpose

The post project review process may be known by other names such as 'Lessons Learned', 'Project Completion Review', 'Post Project Appraisal', 'Post Implementation Evaluation' and 'Project Post-mortem'. Basically, it is a process which consists of activities performed by a project team (and major stakeholders) at the end of the project's life-cycle or the end of significant phases of work to gather information (and knowledge) on what worked well and what did not, so that future projects can benefit from that learning. For some organisations, this process might be employed some time well after the project has been completed if the organisation so wishes or deems it useful. The outcomes of project reviews can help participants make the right decisions and plans so that the next project runs better (Busby, 1999; Kotnour, 1999). It can also help clear up misunderstandings and other issues. Winston Churchill said that the further we look back, the better we can see ahead. This is the motivating force behind conducting a project retrospective. If we do not want to repeat the same mistakes and repeat unprofitable experiences, let history be our guide to tomorrow. But we must learn and move on; and our learning needs to be 'conditioned' and purposeful.

16.4 Barriers to capturing Information and knowledge for post project reviews

For most projects, normal project work is being pressed by time and budget restrictions. Other necessary work after the end of the project, such as capturing project information and experiences are often dropped because of time resources. Similarly, members of the team are often needed for other following projects and their new team leaders will 'pull' to get them into the team as soon as possible. The implication of this is that most project teams are being dissolved gradually without the chance for all team members to systematically 'work together' and document the knowledge and experiences. Teamwork in this respect is vital (Egbu and Gorse, 2002). Perhaps, this is why some take the view that knowledge and experiences should be captured and documented during, rather than at the end of, the project. This is where effective knowledge-management practices are vital. It is important that the acquired knowledge and experiences are identified, prepared and distributed through specific actions to bridge the boundaries between one project and another.

Another barrier is the considerable individual and social barriers which exist in articulating and documenting individual knowledge and experiences (Disterer,

2001). A substantial body of academic research into organisational learning and case examples from the construction industry exist, much of which confirms the reluctance of organisations and project teams to examine objectively their performance. Chris Argyris (1991) noted that whenever a manager's performance comes under scrutiny, the individual begins to be embarrassed, threatened and, because they are often 'well paid', guilty.

> Far from being a catalyst for real change, such feelings cause most to react defensively. So, when their learning strategies go wrong, they become defensive, screen out criticism and put the 'blame' on anyone and everyone but themselves. In short their inability to learn shuts down precisely at the moment they need it the most.

Project analysis of failures and mistakes would be very valuable but, too often, an open and constructive atmosphere to articulate and analyse errors is missing. This point is put succinctly by Boddie (1987), using a football metaphor as he noted 'the post-mortem experience is much like a losing football team watching a game film. It's not comfortable, but if the team pays attention to its mistakes, it can perform better the next time it plays'. Because it is not comfortable, members of the project team avoid admitting mistakes, they are scared of the negative effects of them. It is important therefore that a working and conducive atmosphere, which allows open and constructive discussions, is provided by management and by the leaders conducting the post project review.

16.5 Processes and scope of post project reviews – applying knowledge-management principles

It is often said that one of the main reasons why organisations and project teams apply knowledge-management principles in what they do is to be able to transfer tacit knowledge into explicit knowledge so that this knowledge is better captured, documented and can be disseminated widely to many for the benefit of the organisation, current and future projects (Egbu, 2002).

It is important to have a process and structure for the post project review. Evidence from some successful reviews indicates that at least a six-stage activity profile is useful. This is depicted, albeit simplistically and linearly, in Figure 16.1. It is important that the process to be used for the review is defined, and so is the need to establish how the data, information and knowledge are to be captured. The lessons learned need to be distributed and made available to all in a suitable format.

As part of the need to have a structured and effective approach to conducting the post project review, it is important to consider the roles of those who are to participate in the reviews. Where post project review meetings are to be conducted, the roles played by the facilitator or moderator, the post project review leader and the team responsible for making sure that lessons learned are operationalised, in the form of action plans and guidelines to lead to improvements in future projects,

Figure 16.1: A six-stage activity profile for post project review

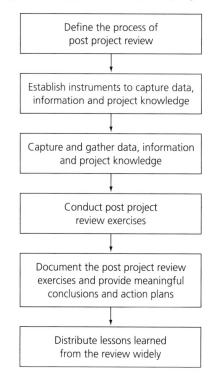

Table 16.1: Key roles in a post project review

Roles/Titles	Role definition
Facilitator or moderator	A person who facilitates, organises and oversees post project review meetings.
Leader of post project review/project	A person who represents the project overall. This could be the project manager or a key person who participated in the project .
Participant to post project review	A person who provides input (information, knowledge and experience) to the post project review, based on his or her experiences with the project or its results.
Scribe	A person who captures and gathers information, experiences and knowledge from participants and presents this in the final post project review report.
Project and process improvement teams	Responsible for making sure that lessons learned are operationalised in the form of action plans and guidelines to lead to improvements in future projects.

are important. Table 16.1 provides the key roles and their definitions in a post project review.

16.6 Some practical advice to help conduct meaningful project reviews

Experiences gained from successful post project reviews would indicate that there are some practical steps that need to be considered in conducting meaningful reviews. These can be documented under eight main stages.

The involvement of all members of the project team, stakeholders and contributors

Although it may not be possible to bring together everyone on the project to participate in the post project review, where possible as many team members should participate. The review would benefit from a rich source of project information, knowledge and lessons learned that is likely to be obtained from the many rather than a few people who were involved in a completed project. Post project review meetings are a good start. It is useful that this is planned for, and participants are communicated to, when this is to take place. Enough time should be set aside for this and for people to reflect on their experiences. The good, bad and ugly aspects of the project need to be uncovered. It is important, however, to start off with more general issues; and the successful points from the project, before the negative points are raised and discussed. It is equally important to have a template or form that allows information from post project review meetings to be effectively documented. A good technique, that is also useful to help identify major issues, is to do something like voting. Each participant puts up items that can fall into categories of 'what went well', 'what needed improvements' and 'what went wrong'. This makes every participant feel that their views are being considered. It also helps to provide a complete view of the many problems and issues encountered in the project.

Document the post project review in writing

It is important that the post project review is documented in writing. This is important to creating an explicit, deliverable post project review. Experiences and knowledge gained through the project become even more explicit if someone files the outcome of the review exercise in an easily shareable format and location. For smaller projects, this can be created in a simple text document. For larger projects, a more structured approach and template could be used and documented using HTML. The document can then be published on an Intranet (Egbu and Botterill, 2002), allowing anyone interested to have access to it. In this way, it is possible to provide links to additional resources such as design documents schedule and archived files. In addition, it is possible to create a collection of lessons learned or project post-mortems over time, with links between related sections of different documents. By documenting the post project review in this way, explicit project knowledge becomes tacit again if new project managers and team members diligently access the database of existing project knowledge before they finalise their project plans. This is an important aspect of the knowledge-management principle – the transformation of knowledge and its exploitation for the benefit of projects and organisations.

Start off with a project overview

It is advisable to start the post project review with an overview of the project, incorporating the design overview, estimated budget, project start and finish dates. Also, make a note of the purpose of the project, the client/customers and other important general project information. This is useful in giving a context to the project review.

Document the quantifiable details of the project

More details of the project should be documented. This should include the project time and budget estimates as well as the true outcomes (actuals). Document the main requirements of the client/customer or end user (as applicable). Note (together with detailed contact addresses where appropriate) which procurement strategies, project methodology, and key stakeholders and project partners were involved in the project. Also, document the roles and contributions of the project partners.

Note the successes from the project – document what went right

It is important to document the main things that went right during the project. At least ten main things that went well should be documented. It is important that carefully worded questions are put in place to allow this information to be collected. See Table 16.2 for a template of selected questions and key post project review issues, albeit not exhaustive, which could be used. Each project team will need to develop a template of questions and key issues to enable them to elicit appropriate project information and knowledge so as to capture the relevant lessons learned.

Note the failures from the project – document what went wrong

Similar to what went right in the project, it is important to document what went wrong. It is important to document at least ten main things that turned out worse than expected. Also, list the main difficulties encountered and compile a detailed list of the project's shortcomings. It is important that the questions (e.g. see Table 16.2) to elicit such information are carefully worded and presented to the participants of a post project review in a constructive way to encourage participation.

An assessment of the project risk management approach

Success or failure is often seen as a measurement of how effective the risks on the project were managed. It is important to document, as much as possible, all the main risks encountered and how effectively they were managed. Also, note

Table 16.2: A template of selected issues and questions to examine key project performance for post project reviews

- For the project, identify at least the ten key things that were done right and were continued throughout the project.
- For the project, identify at least ten key things that were done wrong and needed to have been improved during the project.
- Ascertain what unusual environmental influences (which might have either favourably affected or not the project) should be kept in mind when examining the performance of the project.
- Consider the risk management that was done for the project. For which identified risks were you unsuccessful, and why? What unidentified risks surfaced as problems or crisis? How could these have been mitigated or avoided?
- Ascertain the extent to which the project methodology was successfully employed in the project (including the frequency and efficacy of regular team status meetings, technical and design meetings, and milestone reviews).
- Ascertain the extent to which the project team was satisfied with the project result.
- Were the intended goals and visions of the client and other project stakeholders made clear to you? If not, was it due to a lack of understanding on your part or that of the client/stakeholders?
- Ascertain the extent to which the project team was satisfied with the way the project was carried out/performed (the process).
- Ascertain the extent to which senior management was satisfied with the project result and project process.
- Ascertain the extent to which the project met the cost, time, project quality, project benefit goals and other planned outcomes.
- Identify the organisations (project participants, professionals, consultants, contractors and sub-contractors) and the extent to which they performed their roles in the project (the successful and less successful episodes).
- Was the project leader available when you needed help?
- Was your work (contribution to the project) conducted in an atmosphere of anticipated success or pressure to meet deadlines at all costs?

the risk management plans that were rolled-out during the project and how effective they were. It is important to pay due cognisance as to how the lessons learned on risk management could be improved upon for the benefit of future projects.

Document conclusions and take meaningful actions

The essence of an effective post project review is to learn from the project for the benefit of future projects. It is important, therefore, to document meaningful conclusions from such a review. The conclusions should provide an opportunity to establish what the project team should start doing, keep doing and stop doing. The whole post project review exercise would be a waste of time if the information documented from such an exercise is archived and forgotten about. The final step should be the development of an action plan that can be applied to the next or future project(s). It is important therefore to specify and document new guidelines to follow in the future. This would also allow any project checklist to be updated or refined taking into account lessons learned from the post project review.

Although exercises conducted during such reviews provide valuable feedback, an effective methodology, in which continuous project-phase reviews are conducted and documented during the life of a project, should be encouraged. Standard project methodologies, such as Projects in Controlled Environments (PRinCE 2: Bradley, 1997), allow this process to be conducted. Corporate and non-standard project methodologies should endeavour to encourage this process, and build it in as part of the project methodology. These regular reviews, when effectively planned and documented, should serve as an important and factual source of information for use in post project reviews.

16.7 Conclusions

The post project review process consists of activities performed by a project team at the end of the project life-cycle, or at the end of significant phases of work, to capture information and knowledge on what went well and not so well, so that future projects can benefit from that learning. Post project reviews are a valuable way for teams to prevent 're-inventing the wheel', reduce mistakes and improve their performance and skills. They also offer opportunities for continuous improvements and improve team morale. It is important to engage as many participants and stakeholders as possible in the post project review and to ensure that they all understand that it is not a time for assigning blame or making personal attacks. Therefore, a working and conducive atmosphere, which allows open and constructive discussions, must be provided by management and by the leaders conducting such reviews.

The principles of knowledge management can contribute to successful post project reviews in a host of ways. For example, it would allow effective documentation of project experiences which represent methods, outline precise problems, describe successful solutions, mention persons to turn to and external experts, plus descriptions of successful co-operations and their success factors. In addition, effective knowledge management would lead to strategies that allow tacit knowledge from team members to be transformed into explicit knowledge, which can be documented and shared to all that need it.

Although recognising the importance of post project reviews, there is evidence to suggest that only a few organisations and project teams manage systematically to identify valuable knowledge from project to following project. The main reasons offered for this being organisational, technical, methodological issues and social problems. A sound project management methodology should be able to build in regular reviews of project phases. These reviews, during the life of the project, should be documented. They should serve as an important source of information for use in post project reviews. Construction organisations and project teams need to do more to provide the relevant resources, especially in terms of time and commitment, which this important aspect of project management activity deserves.

References

Abdel-Hamid, T. K. and Madnick, S. E., 'The elusive silver lining: how we fail to learn from software development failures', *Sloan Management Review*, Vol. 32, No. 3, 1990, pp. 39–48.

Argyris, C., 'Teaching smart people how to learn', *Harvard Business Review*, May–June, 1991, pp. 99–109.

Boddie, J., 'The project post-mortem', *Computerworld*, 7 Dec., 1987, p. 7.

Bradley, K., *Understanding PRINCE 2*, published by SPOCE Project Management Ltd, Poole, Dorset (1997).

Busby, J. S., 'An assessment of post-project reviews', *Project Management Journal*, Vol. 30, No. 3. Sep., 1999, pp. 23–29.

Collier, B., DeMarco, T. and Fearey, P., 'A defined process for project post-mortem review', *IEEE Software*, Vol. 13, No. 4, 1996, pp. 65–72.

Cross, R. and Baird, L., 'Technology is not enough: improving performance by building organisational memory', *Sloan Management Review*, Vol. 41, No. 2, 2000, pp. 69–78.

Disterer, G., 'Individual and social barriers to knowledge transfer', in R. H. Sprague (ed.), *Proc. of 34th Hawaii Intl Conf. on System Sciences*, IEEE, Los Alamitos, CA, USA, 2001, pp. 1–7.

Egbu, C. O., 'Knowledge Management and HRM: The role of the project manager', *Proc. of PMI Europe 2001 – A Project Management Odyssey*, 6–7 June 2001, Café Royal, London.

Egbu, C. O., 'Knowledge management, intellectual capital and innovation: Their association benefits and challenges for construction organisations', *10th Intl Symp. – Construction Innovation and Global Competitiveness, CIB W55/W65*, 9–13 Sep., 2002, Cincinnati, Ohio, USA; Vol. 1, 2002, pp. 57–70.

Egbu, C. and Botterill, K., 'Knowledge management and intellectual capital: Benefits for project based industries', *Proc. of the RICS Foundation – Construction and Building Research Conf. (COBRA)*, Glasgow Caledonian University, 3–5 Sep., J. Kelly and K. Hunter (eds) Vol. 2, 2001, pp. 414– 22.

Egbu, C. O. and Botterill, K., 'Information Technologies for Knowledge Management: Their Usage and Effectiveness', *Journal of Information Technology in Construction*, Vol. 7, 2002, pp. 125–37.

Egbu, C. and Gorse, C., *'Teamwork', Project Management Pathways – The Essential Handbook for Project and Programme Managers*, published by the Association for Project Management (APM), Chapter 71:1–71:16 (2002).

Gulliver, F. R., 'Post project appraisal pay', *Harvard Business Review*, Vol. 77, No. 2, 1987, pp. 106–16.

Kotnour, T., 'A learning framework for project management', *Project Management Journal*, Vol. 30, No. 2, June, 1999, pp. 32–38.

Kumar, K., 'Post implementation evaluation of computer-based information systems: current practices', *Communications of the ACM*, Vol. 33, No. 2, 1990, pp. 203–12.

Nonaka, I. and Takeuchi, H., *The knowledge-creating company: How Japanese Companies Create Dynamics of Innovation*, Oxford University Press, New York, USA (1995).

Pemberton, J. and Stonehouse, G., 'Organisational learning and knowledge assets. An essential partnership', *The Learning Organisation*, Vol. 7, No. 4, 2000, pp. 184–94.

Weiser, M. and Morrison, J., 'Project memory: information management for project teams', *Journal of Management Information Systems*, Vol. 14, No. 4, 1998, pp. 149–66.

Key Reading

Busby, J. S., 'An assessment of post-project reviews', *Project Management Journal*, Vol. 30, No. 3. Sep., 1999, pp. 23–29.

Collier, B., DeMarco, T. and Fearey, P., 'A defined process for project post-mortem review', *IEEE Software*, Vol. 13, No. 4, 1996, pp. 65–72.

Egbu, C. and Gorse, C., 'Teamwork', *Project Management Pathways – The Essential Handbook for Project and Programme Managers*, published by the Association for Project Management (APM), Chapter 71:1–71:16 (2002).

Facilities Management

Concepts in facilities management

17

Danny Shiem-shin Then, Department of Building Services Engineering, Hong Kong Polytechnic University, Hong Kong

17.1 Introduction

In a recent high profile launch, the British Institute of Facilities Management (BIFM) published a document entitled, *Looking to the Future: Re-thinking Facilities Management* (2003). In the document, BIFM states that 'Facilities Management has come of age' ... 'our vision for Facilities Management to become widely recognised as a strategic business discipline' and asserts itself as 'one of the fastest growing professional organisations in the UK with over 8,000 individual and 240 corporate members...'. The same document also laments that '10 years on... there is still much ambiguity about what FM is and what value it offers'.

As a young discipline which is still evolving, facilities management (FM) has reached a stage of development that apart from debates of its content and future direction (Spedding and Holmes, 1994; Then, 1994, 2003; Nutt and Mclennan, 2000; BIFM, 2003); issues of its unique professionalism (Grimshaw, 2002) and the need for its own philosophy (Cairns, 2003) have began to surface. It is a healthy sign that facilities management is beginning to be seen as more than just about buildings and surroundings and activities within buildings, but about the effective management of an essential business resource to achieve corporate objectives.

This short chapter on concepts in facilities management is an attempt to map the multi-dimensional roles that facilities management has added value to in a business context and summarises some of the more obvious concepts that have driven facilities management practice since its appearance in the early 1980s.

Feedback on how operational facilities actually perform has been a problem for architects, as designers of the built environment. The separation of the design, construction and operation stages over the life-cycle of a building is often cited as the prime reason for this deficiency. The growing acceptance of the facilities manager as the custodian of 'working buildings' offers an opportunity of closing the feedback loop as detailed by the RIBA Plan of Work. The relationship between architects and FM professionals is bounded, when viewed from a context of performance evaluation. FM is involved in the longest phase of the asset life-cycle of buildings. The development of information systems (CAFM) that integrate graphics, text and extensive database capabilities has led to better data capture, analysis and trending of occupancy costs, as well as benchmarking across organisations. The availability of performance-in-use data provides for user evaluation, and assessment and validation of assumptions made at the briefing and design stages.

The chapter also considers areas of activities where architects and FM professionals can work together to optimise facilities solutions to meet business challenges.

17.2 Scoping the content and context of facilities management

An appropriate preamble to any discussion of facilities management (FM) is to define FM. In this respect there are numerous definitions, some of which are listed in Table 17.1 (see under section 17.3 on professional core competency). In summary, the various definitions seem to be converging in a consensus that FM is not only about buildings, but also about the people that occupy the spaces within the buildings, the processes they are supporting; all operating within known (hopefully) constraints of available resources and the prevailing corporate culture. The operative word in FM for making space (the unit of analysis for buildings), people, processes and politics to work in harmony is 'management' – often an intangible that defies clear-cut definition given the varying context in different organisational settings.

The approach taken here is to illustrate the potential content of FM as justification as to why management is critical in FM practice and that an FM structure within an organisation setting must be driven by clear strategic direction with demonstrable deliverables in terms of physical settings and service levels. Figure 17.1 provides a platform for abstracting key concepts from literature and practice that then forms the basis for discussion and a speculative interim conclusion.

The growing body of academic literature and publication on the nature of FM practice (e.g. Nutt, 1999; McGregor and Then, 1999; Atkin and Brookes, 2000; Green and Price, 2000; Grimshaw and Cairns, 2000; Best, Langston and De Valence, 2003) has done little to dispel the impression that there is still diversity in FM practice and that FM, in whatever guise, will continue to grow. The term 'FM' is now recognised in all five continents. As noted by Grimshaw (2002): 'In many ways it is the tension between these different but overlapping positions that provides the dynamics for the onward development of FM . . .'. These 'different but overlapping positions' are clearly illustrated in Figure 17.1 where the relative pulls of focus in relation to *investment*, *space*, *asset* and *people* are often apparent in the crafting of facilities solutions to meet ever changing business demands.

In a scan of literature on what drives value added in FM, there have been several conceptual models that are built on the nature of relationships between a business, its people, the nature of their work and the physical assets (space) that are needed to support the production processes.

Pioneering work by Duffy (1983) highlighted the importance of technology and how they impact on the design of the future workplace. This was followed by exploring the relationships between physical space and organisation change, physical space and human productivity and advocating how design of offices can be used to leverage organisation change (Duffy and Tanis, 1993; Becker and Steele, 1995). These early studies concentrated mainly on the workplace dimension of FM (space planning and management) with a focus on office design and space configurations. FM is seen as a vector for change by adding value and minimising cost (Duffy, Liang

Figure 17.1: Scoping the content of facilities management

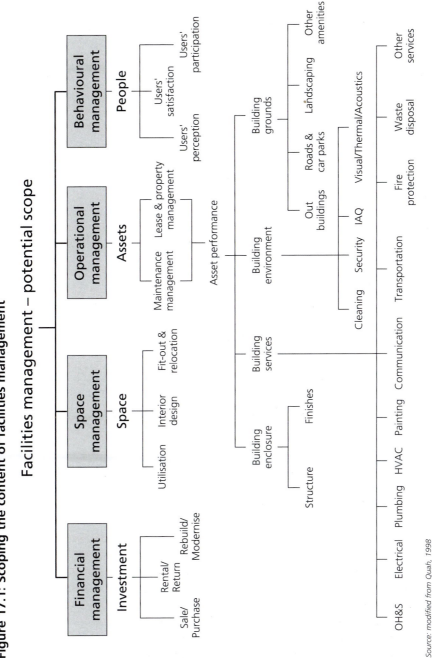

Facilities management – potential scope

Source: modified from Quah, 1998

and Crisp, 1993) where facilities managers must strive to assume the mantle of leader of the workplace.

Becker (1990), in suggesting a definition for FM, places organisational effectiveness as the key goal.

> Facility management is responsible for co-ordinating all efforts related to planning, designing, and managing buildings and their systems, equipment and furniture to enhance the organisation's ability to compete successfully in a rapidly changing world.

Becker's definition contains three key concepts central to the management of operational facilities as a business resource: namely, FM is a co-ordinating function pertaining to the planning, design and management of an organisation's physical resources; FM has a co-ordinating planning role over the life-cycle of the operational building, and FM must operate within a strategic framework to integrate operational decisions in order to achieve organisational effectiveness. He sees the evolution of facilities organisation moving along a 'trajectory of change' within a dynamic business environment. In responding to the demands for organisational change, facilities organisations must strive to be proactive and strategic (i.e. an 'elastic' facility organisation).

Then (1996) adopted an economic resource view of FM by considering the forces of demand and supply in the derivation of facilities solutions. Figure 17.2 illustrates how FM can play a key role in resolving the constant tensions between demand and supply

Figure 17.2: Reconciling supply and demand to create an enabling workplace environment

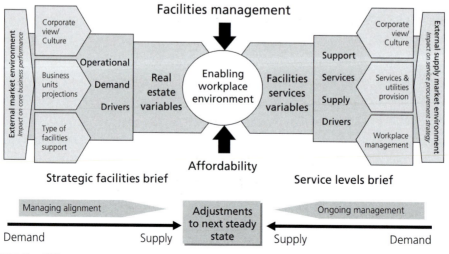

Source: Then, 1996

by skilfully managing information flow from the business domain, and applying building and operational knowledge to provide continuously appropriate facilities solutions to meet business requirements. The emphasis (in the figure) on 'adjustment to the next steady state' recognises the volatile environment of the business world in which facilities managers must operate as proactive agents for change. The context of the different focuses of 'management alignment' and 'on-going management' within the respective domains of the strategic facilities brief (SFB) and service levels brief (SLB) is important, as both the SFB and SLB are driven by different sets of factors that are embedded within the constraints of the corporate culture in which they must operate. The 'enabling workplace environment' is seen as the product of reconciliation of real estate variables on the demand side and facilities services variables on the supply side.

The primary driver of demand management of the real estate resource is meeting business objectives through economic space utilisation. The practice of resource management requires a composite approach to resource management in which the various disciplines within the business are employed. This view regards functional space as the outcome of the synergy of three basic organisational resources – *people*, *property* and *technology*. In the context of the operations of each business, understanding the role of buildings and how they can be deployed effectively is the essence of what facilities management is about. It is essential for businesses to realise that buildings are necessary not for their own sake, but as *supporting resources* through the provision of workspaces to accommodate business processes. And, in so doing, to provide appropriate workplaces at which the people in the business can perform their tasks to the best of their abilities. Figure 17.3 illustrates the positioning of buildings in the context of business.

Figure 17.3: The position of buildings as a business resource

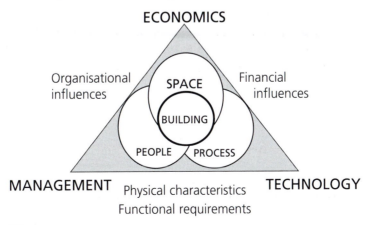

Source: Then, 1994

Figure 17.4: Four generic trails to the future

Facilities resource management

	Financial resource trail	Business
	Human resource trail	People
Four trails	Physical resource trail	Property
	Knowledge resource trail	Knowledge

Source: Nutt, 2000

Nutt (2000) also advocates that '... overall, the primary function of FM is resource management, at strategic and operational level of support'. Within the resource management context, the supporting role of FM is seen as the most singularly significant factor that distinguishes it from business and operational management. Taking a strategic view, Nutt explores this wide-ranging support role of FM by considering four basic 'trails' to the future. These trails correspond to the generic types of resources that are central to the FM function: the management of financial resources (Business), human resources (People), physical resources (Property), and the management of the informational resources (Knowledge) as illustrated in Figure 17.4.

> It (FM) impacts on the financial issues of facility investment, asset value, and operational costs and benefits; and the physical issues of space, structure, technology and maintenance. But most significantly, it covers the management structures that link knowledge and experience across these financial, human and physical areas of concern (Nutt, 2000).

Commenting on Nutt's four-trails model, Grimshaw (2002) observes that the relationships between the four foci of business infrastructure are changing:

> Whilst business and knowledge have been elevated to a global level, people and physical facilities have not – they remain in their national context and in a much weaker position. The relationship between a business, its people and its physical assets has fundamentally changed – this is the real context of FM development.

Grimshaw extends on Nutt's model by using it as a framework for evaluating the issues in the tensions that occur at the six interfaces between the four trails (Figure 17.5). In addition, he asserts that it is the management of these interfaces to ensure that the tensions are creative rather than destructive that defines the challenge FM faces now and in the future.

Figure 17.5: The resource model of strategic FM

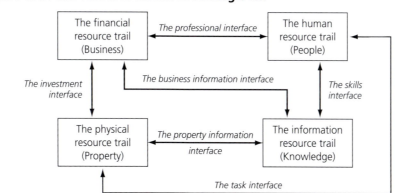

Source: Nutt, 2000, with Grimshaw's interface added

From the above brief review of the potential content and context of FM, it is clear that effective FM depends not just on knowledge and systems, but on the professionalism and management abilities of the people who work in the field.

In discussing the nature of FM's professional credentials, Grimshaw (2002) argues that the professional core of FM lies in the interface between business and people, i.e. the 'professional interface' in Figure 17.5. In the context of FM, the focus of the 'business trail' is property as a capital investment and how to manage the asset to ensure that the return on investment (ROI) reflects the risks involved. In recent years, global business is spending a growing proportion of investment capital on electronic infrastructure rather than physical infrastructure. In addition, there is a significant trend towards outsourcing support services and even core functions, and a growth in flexible working arrangements. This has led Duffy (2000) to caution that FM practice is in danger of being pushed into a cost control and outsourcing function in order to reduce servicing costs for the asset and to increase the ROI. The focus of the 'people trail' is how to ensure the effective deployment of people as a business resource in a rapidly changing business context. The rapid pace of progressive technological developments (especially in the IT and telecommunication fields) in recent years is transforming the traditional nature of work and workplaces for the employees. In a recent report by Gartner Research and MIT on workplace futures, *Agile Workplace* (2002) predicts that in the next five years changes to the workplace will be driven by the need to be more flexible, more people centric and more responsive. The workplace will transform from a 'collection of properties to a network of place and electronic connections'.

Grimshaw (2002) has argued that:

> The ethical basis for FM to claim professional status is based on the impact that the physical environment of work has on individuals.... The linking of FM and stakeholder needs reinforces the message that the impact of IT that is driving

both the 'business trail' and the 'people trail' has much wider social and economic connotations for the people in the workplace.

The FM profession is developing at a time of rapid change in all the areas that define its practice. The landscape for FM is also increasingly global in context rather than national, given trends in 'total outsourcing' of physical portfolio and services delivery by large public sector authorities and major international corporations. In short, in its continued evolution, FM must embrace change and allow diversity in the way it defines and manages practice.

17.3 An emerging consensus of 'the professional core' for FM

The debate on whether FM has claimed the mantle of being a true profession or discipline with its unique core knowledge base will no doubt continue. It is perhaps worth taking a look at how 'the professional core' of FM has evolved in the eyes of three national institutions of facility or facilities management; the North American International Facility Management Association (IFMA), the British Institute of Facilities Management (BIFM) and the Facility Management Association of Australia (FMA Australia).

Table 17.1 lists the professional core competency of FM as advocated by three national institutions in relation to their respective assessment of professional memberships.

From Table 17.1, we can summarise the role of facilities management as comprising of the following:

- It is a supporting management function to the core business.

- It concentrates on the area of interface between physical workplace and people.

- It is about managing change.

- It requires a multi-skill approach.

- It is about the pursuit of quality – in planning, design, provision and management of buildings as operational facilities, and in how they are managed over time.

- Its goal is organisational effectiveness.

Facilities Management is about:

- Understanding the business;

- Planning and providing for the business;

- Managing the facility as an asset resource over its functional life-cycle;

- Managing the facility as functional enablers to support human resource and production processes within affordable occupancy costs;

Table 17.1: Professional core competency for FM

International Facility Management Association	British Institute of Facilities Management	Facility Management Association, Australia
'The practice of co-ordinating the physical workplace with the people and work of an organisation. It integrates the principles of business administration, architecture and the behavioural and engineering sciences.'	'The integration of multi-disciplinary activities within the built environment and the management of their impact upon people and the workplace.'	'A business practice that optimises people, process, assets and the work environment to support the delivery of an organisation's business objectives.'
Core functions	**Core competences**	**Competency standards**
Facility Function – professional practice	Understanding business organisation	Use organisational understanding to manage facilities
Human & Environmental factors	Managing people	Develop strategic facility response
Planning & Project Management	Managing premises	Manage risk
Finance	Managing services	Manage facility portfolio
Operations & Maintenance	Managing the working environment	Improve facility performance
Real Estate	Managing resources	Manage the delivery of services
Communication		Manage projects
Quality Management & Assessment Procedures – Research & Analytical Methods		Management financial performance
Integrative & Problem-solving Skills		Arrange and implement procurement/sourcing
		Facilitate communication
		Manage workplace relationships
		Manage change
Focus	**Focus**	**Focus**
Co-ordinating management function	Multi-disciplinary activities	Driven by business objectives
It concentrates on the area of interface between physical workplace and people	Relationship between built environment and workplace	Co-ordinating management function
It requires a multi-skill approach	Relationship between people and the workplace	Supporting business function

- Managing change;

- Being visible;

- Being professional.

If we accept the above propositions as valid outcomes for the continued development of FM, it will be appropriate to develop a conceptual model that encapsulates the

Figure 17.6: Facilities management – main components

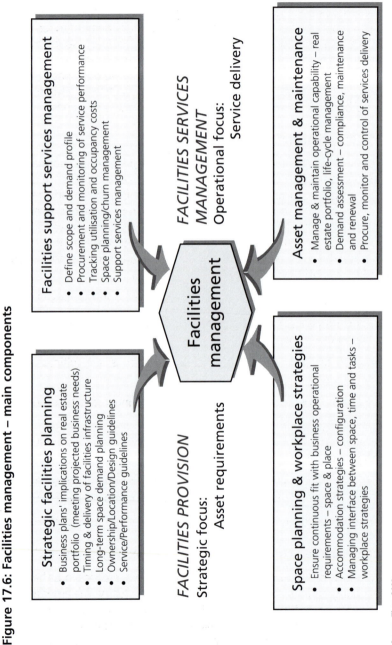

Facilities support services management
- Define scope and demand profile
- Procurement and monitoring of service performance
- Tracking utilisation and occupancy costs
- Space planning/churn management
- Support services management

FACILITIES SERVICES MANAGEMENT
Operational focus:
Service delivery

Asset management & maintenance
- Manage & maintain operational capability – real estate portfolio, life-cycle management
- Demand assessment – compliance, maintenance and renewal
- Procure, monitor and control of services delivery

Strategic facilities planning
- Business plans' implications on real estate portfolio (meeting projected business needs)
- Timing & delivery of facilities infrastructure
- Long-term space demand planning
- Ownership/Location/Design guidelines
- Service/Performance guidelines

FACILITIES PROVISION
Strategic focus:
Asset requirements

Space planning & workplace strategies
- Ensure continuous fit with business operational requirements – space & place
- Accommodation strategies – configuration
- Managing interface between space, time and tasks – workplace strategies

Facilities management

Source: Then, 2003

'professional core competency' as advocated by the above national FM professional bodies.

Figure 17.6 proposes a model that sees FM's involvement spanning from *facilities provision* (strategic components) to *facilities service management* (operational components). The four components of *strategic facilities planning, space planning and workplace strategies, facilities support services management,* and *asset management and maintenance,* reflect the broad, but interrelated resources base (investments, space, assets and people – Figure 17.1) that the practice of FM must manage effectively to bring about an optimum solution to business demands.

17.4 Key concepts underlying FM practice

The above review of the evolution of FM provides a platform to speculate on some key concepts underlying FM embryonic 'theory' and maturing practice outcomes as 'a strategic business discipline – a discipline which is seen to add real value to organisations, not just a range of non-core activities to be managed as economically as possible' (BIFM, 2003). The following listing of 'key concepts' owe their origins to many writers and practitioners of FM since its appearance in the early 1980s. Although not exhaustive, some of them are cited earlier in this brief chapter and under References and Key Reading.

- FM must ensure that facilities strategy is a key element in business planning.

- As a support function, FM support needs are driven by the nature of the business and its operational requirements.

- Definition of facilities needs and service standards are ultimately strategic considerations.

- Procurement of support infrastructure and services must match corporate culture and risk preference.

- The management of FM delivery demands specific but related competences – need for intelligent client role.

- FM support strategy is about matching supply to demand – ultimately, a demand (operational requirements) and supply (procurement and delivery) issue.

- An integrated approach is the only solution to meeting business challenges.

17.5 Implications on interactions between facilities managers and architects

The above review of FM development over the last two decades must be seen in the context of changes in the construction and property industry. The emergence of new innovative procurement methods (e.g. PFI and PPP) have brought about changes in the traditional roles of the financing, design, construction and property management of building portfolios in both the private and public sectors. These changes can be partly attributed to a greater understanding and awareness of the role of physical assets within the overall business delivery processes. The growing acceptance that an optimum facility solution must be a by-product of the considerations of the business operational needs (for space), the users (people) of the facility in performing their work tasks, and the necessary support infrastructure (technology and support services) to carry out their tasks efficiently and effectively, has had the impact of promoting the integrative nature of managing business resources.

The integrated components of FM as illustrated in Figure 17.6 point to a need to understand the business needs for space (demand) as the driver of facility provision (supply) – the start of the building development cycle. The use of new procurement methods has led to the integration of design-build-operate necessitating a partnership approach between professions and taking a whole-life view of buildings as durable assets.

Facilities management has grown from managing and maintaining corporate property (operational buildings) with a deliberate slant towards meeting stakeholders' expectations. The FM focus on supporting business delivery has led to an increasing involvement in strategic facility planning where the need to align *demand* for functional space by effective management of current *supply* (real estate portfolio) is now seen as prudent business resource management.

Architects claim that they are at the forefront of designing the built environment with their professional expertise in the field of building design and construction of new buildings, the reuse of existing building and spaces. If architects are to continue to help businesses, they must endeavour to create environments which are pleasing and functional for the people who work and do business within them. There are a number of 'crossover' opportunities where the particular competences of the architect and facilities manager can be complementary or mutually beneficial in providing appropriate facilities solutions to business challenges. (See www.careersinarchitecture.net).

Facilities managers, by virtue of their role in ensuring the smooth operation of business delivery, must have an intimate knowledge of business processes to be supported and operational requirements. Architects, on their part, can tap into this corporate knowledge, when working in collaboration with facilities managers.

Taking Figure 17.6 as a reference of the potential scope of facilities management, it is not difficult to come to the conclusion that the architect's contribution is likely to fall within the strategic components of *facilities provision*. Both *strategic facilities planning* and *space planning and workplace strategies* rely on design competences in the crafting of design solutions to meet business requirements for functional and flexible spaces. The outcomes of the architects' design solutions are reflected in form and feel of the operational facilities which, in turn, form the basis for the facilities management delivery processes in facilities support services and asset maintenance management within the business setting.

There will always be overlap of activities between the numerous 'professions' that service the property and construction industry. Market forces will ultimately decide which individual or combination of services can offer the optimum facility solution(s) to meet clients' demand. The architects' roles can be all embracing – from briefing and design, from project management, from site selection to completion. The growth of the FM profession is another evolution to meet market demand for better delivery and on-going management of operational facilities. Architects must and will similarly evolve to meet demands for new specialised services. This has been reflected in terms of demand for better briefing to better capture the realities of the business need for basic shelter, image and location, and corporate culture reinforcement in workplace design (e.g. Duffy, 2000; Blyth and Worthington, 2001). More recently, the design of innovative workplace environments to cater for the diversity of work and workplaces as a result of the rapid information technology development has spawned specialists in workplace strategies, and space planning and management (e.g. Duffy, Liang and Crisp, 1993; Marmot and Eley, 2000). These are clear signs that traditional professions will and must respond to, to meet market demand for new services.

Three areas of activities fall within the competences and training of architects that will potentially add value to businesses when considering facility issues:

1 Strategic and project briefing;

2 Workplace strategies and workspace design;

3 Users' evaluation for feedback.

17.6 Conclusions

Facilities management will continue to evolve to meet business demand for efficient and effective facilities and services support. The role of the facilities professional will expand to embrace strategic facilities planning, audit and review, at the corporate portfolio end; management of operational services and service providers of bundled services on behalf of clients, at the delivery end.

The underlying concepts influencing the practice of FM will shift over time (e.g. from cost reduction/cost optimisation to facilities value added; from adversarial to partnering relationships; from single service to bundle services procurement; from prescriptive specification to defined service levels, etc.), but the principles governing facilities provision and service delivery will remain largely unchanged (corporate alignment at portfolio level, service quality comes at a price; contracts and culture make for lasting relationships in service delivery; communication is key in client–service provider relationships). Sustainable FM outcomes can only happen when users' expectations are managed within constraints of what is affordable. Architects can play a constructive role within the facilities provision domain of facilities management through evaluation of strategic options in supporting business needs for facility infrastructure that are appropriate, cost effective, flexible and affordable.

References

Atkin, B. and Brookes, A., *Total Facilities Management*, Blackwell Science (2000).

Becker, F., *The Total Workplace – Facilities Management and the Elastic Organisation*, Van Nostrand Reinhold (1990) pp. 6–7.

Becker, F. and Steele, F., *Workplace by Design: Mapping the high-performance workscape*, Jossey-Bass, San Francisco (1995).

Best, R., Langston, C. and De Valence, G., *Workplace Strategies and Facilities Management: Building in Value*, Butterworth-Heinemann (2003).

BIFM, *Re-thinking Facilities Management – Looking to the future*, British Institute of Facilities Management (2003).

Blyth, A. and Worthington, J., *Managing the Brief for Better Design*, Spon Press, London and New York (2001).

Cairns, G., 'Seeking a facilities management philosophy for the changing workplace', *Facilities*, Vol. 21, Nos 5/6, 2003, pp. 95–105.

Duffy, F., ORBIT Study, London, DEGW, 1983.

Duffy, F., 'Design and Facilities Management in a time of change', *Facilities*, Vol. 18, Nos 10/11/12, 2000, pp. 371–75.

Duffy, F. and Tanis, J., 'A vision of the new workplace. Site Selection', *Industrial Development Section*, Apr. 1993, Vol. 162, No. 2, pp. 427–32.

Duffy, F., Liang, A. and Crisp, V., *The Responsible Workplace – The redesign of work and offices*, Butterworth Architecture in association with *Estate Gazette* (1993) p. 14.

Gartner Research and Massachusetts Institute of Technology, *Agile Workplace* (2002).

Green, A. and Price, I. 'Whither FM? A Dephi study of the Profession and the Industry', *Facilities*, Vol. 18. Nos 7/8, 2000, pp. 281–92.

Grimshaw, B., 'FM: Exploring the Professional Interface', in (eds) J. Hinks, S. Buchanan and D. Then, *Proc. of CIBW70 2002 Glasgow Symp. – Extending the Global Knowledge Base in Facilities and Asset Management*. pp. 3–13, CIB Publication No. 277 (2002).

Grimshaw, B. and Cairns, G., 'Chasing the Mirage: managing facilities in a changing world', *Facilities*, Vol. 18, Nos 10/11/12, 2000.

McGregor, W. and Then, D., *Facilities Management and the Business of Space*, Arnold (1999). Reprint under Butterworth-Heinemann (2001).

Marmot, A. and Eley, J., *Office Space Planning – Designing for tomorrow's workplace*, McGraw-Hill (2000).

Nutt, B., 'Linking FM Practice and Research', *Facilities*, Vol. 17, Nos 1/2, 1999.

Nutt, B., 'Four competing futures for facility management', *Facilities*, Vol. 18, Nos 3/4, 2000, pp. 124–32.

Nutt, B. and McLennan, P. (eds) *Facility Management – risks & opportunities*, Blackwell Science (2000) p. 1.

Quah, L. K. (ed), *Proc. of CIB W70 Symp. on Management, Maintenance and Modernisation of Building Facilities – The Way Ahead into the Millennium*, 18–20 Nov. 1998, Singapore, McGraw-Hill (1998) pp. xv.

Spedding, A. and Holmes, R. 'Facilities Management', Chapter 1 in A. Spedding (ed) *The CIOB Handbook of Facilities Management*, Longman Scientific & Technical (1994) pp. 1–8.

Then, Shiem-shin, D., 'Integrated Resources Management Structure for Facilities Provision and Management', *ASCE Journal of Performance of Constructed Facilities*, Vol. 17, No. 1, Feb. 2003, pp. 34–42.

Then, S. S., 'Facilities Management – The Relationship between Business and Property', *Proc. of Joint EuroFM/IFMA Conf. – Facility Management European Opportunities*, Brussels, 8–10 May 1994, pp. 253–62.

Then, S. S. (1996) in W. McGregor and D. Shiem-shin Then, *Facilities Management and the Business of Space*, Arnold (1999) pp. 144–45.

Key Reading

Alexander, K. (ed.), *Facilities Management – Theory and Practice*, E&FN Spon, New York (1996).

Atkin, B. and Brookes, A., *Total Facilities Management*, Blackwell Science (2000).

Barrett, P. and Baldry, D., *Facilities Management –Towards Best Practice*, 2nd edn, Blackwell Science (2003).

McGregor, W. and Then, S. S., *Facilities Management and the Business of Space*, Arnold (1999). Reprint under Butterworth-Heinemann (2001).

Facilities management in a PFI environment

Margaret Nelson, Centre for Facilities Management, School of Construction and Property Management, University of Salford, Manchester, UK

18.1 Introduction

Public Private Partnerships (PPP) refer to any collaboration between public bodies and private companies created for the provision of services. They are not specifically for the exclusive provision of capital assets such as buildings, and may result in the provision of services to meet user requirements that do not require a construction or building project. Unlike privatisation, PPP is more like a merger, with both sides sharing the risks and, hopefully, the benefits of the project. The UK Government sees PPP as a way of doing business more efficiently and making best use of the available skills in the public and private sectors to deliver better services.

Public Private Partnerships may take many forms, for example Prime Contracting, strategic partnerships or joint ventures with the private sector, not-for-profit Public Interest Companies, wider markets initiative, NHS LIFT, ProCure 21 and Public Finance Initiative (PFI).

Prime contracting[1] is primarily used by the Ministry of Defence (MoD) to procure physical assets. There are three main types of Prime Contracts: Regional, Capital Stand Alone and Functional. The prime contractor has an overall single-point responsibility for the management and delivery of a project, or an integrated estate service covering the provision of new assets to a pre-agreed value and/or type and maintenance of the existing infrastructure. They are also responsible for co-ordinating and integrating the activities of the pre-appointed supply chain to meet service delivery specification efficiently, economically, innovatively and on time.

Strategic partnerships or flexible joint ventures between the public and private sectors have been used to deliver some local government back office functions such as IT and payroll services. In the wider markets initiative such as the canal network and the MoD's marketing of irreducible spare capacity, the private sector extracts value from existing public assets.

Not-for-profits organisations, such as Housing Associations and the newly proposed NHS (National Health Service) Foundation hospitals, run public services independently of government, but are owned by local communities, not shareholders. Foundation Hospital Trusts will be allowed to borrow from the private sector; but will be restricted by an independent regulator; and borrowing will count against departmental spending limits.

NHS Lift creates a vehicle with public and private capital to improve primary care and community-based facilities and services; and to help 'batch' facilities for improvements in inner city areas, particularly health action zones.[2] It aims to procure and supply capital investment needs for public bodies and other health care providers delivering health or health related services to the public, enabling local authorities to undertake and be responsible for many health related functions.[3]

ProCure 21 is a public/private partnering arrangement set up by the NHS to deliver better quality healthcare buildings and improved value for money. It aims to develop long-term framework agreements with private sector suppliers who will deliver better value for money and a better service for patients.

The Public Finance Initiative (PFI) is the most developed and most widely used of all PPP models.[4] Launched in 1992 in a bid to encourage private capital investment in public sector projects, PFI like other PPPs procures a service rather than the underlying asset. Although PFIs have primarily focused on the acquisition of new facilities, service-only PFI contracts do exist; for example, the supply of catering services to schools in the London Borough of Lewisham. The basic justification for adoption of PFI includes in addition to financial incentives, greater certainty of delivery, higher quality outputs, focus on core business, and exploitation of private sector skills.[5]

The government's procurement on all public procurement of goods and services is based on the concept of best value for money; defined by the Treasury as 'the optimum combination of whole life cost and quality (or fitness for purpose) to meet the user's requirement'. The emphasis on whole life costs means that the public sector contracting authorities are required to take account of all aspects of cost, including running and disposal costs, as well as the initial purchase price of an asset.

In the past two decades, capital investment in public services reduced from 5 percent to 1 percent of national income, leaving the UK bottom of the EU in terms of public investment (The Guardian, 1 Oct., 2002). Between 1997 when the Labour Government came into power and 2001, PFI comprised 9 percent of total publicly sponsored gross capital spending. The 2002 Budget, however, forecasted that its share would fall as conventionally financed capital spending increased (Maltby, 2002). PFI spending is expected to peak at just over £3.5 billion in 2003/4, and fall to just under £3 billion by 2005/6.[6] Capital expenditure forms on average just 22 percent of the total cost of PFI projects[7] with the balance being the long-term cost of providing support services.

Various government organisations have adopted PFI as a means of raising capital investment. The MoD PFI programme includes the provision of accommodation, training, equipment, logistics, communications and utilities. Evaluation of completed projects shows that on average PFI has worked out 10 percent[8] cheaper than the cost of delivering services in-house using the public sector comparator (PSC).[9] This has represented a challenge to in-house facilities management for treasury-funded projects.

Facilities Management (FM) has been variously defined as:

The development, co-ordination and control of the non-core specialist services necessary for an organisation to successfully achieve its principal objectives (US Library of Congress, 1989).

The process by which an organisation delivers and sustains support services in a quality environment to meet strategic needs (Alexander, 1996).

FM in PFI terms represents the long-term cost of providing support services, which makes up 78 percent of the costs of a project. In the healthcare sector, which this chapter focuses on, in the early 1990s, the NHS capital stock was valued at £25 billion with investments of £400 million in new hospital schemes and £500 million on maintenance (Audit Commission, 1991). In May 1997, the Labour Government inherited an NHS with dilapidated facilities; having one-third of its hospitals built before 1945 and 10 percent in the 19th century or before (The Guardian, 1 Oct., 2002). It also inherited a backlog maintenance bill in the National Health Service amounting to £2.5 billion.

As provision of an improved NHS system was on the Labour party's political manifesto, PFI was embraced as the solution to the refurbishment of existing and provision of new healthcare facilities promised at the elections.

We are building a 21st century NHS which is fast, fair and convenient for patients. People expect first-class hospital facilities, which meet the needs of patients and their families. . . . Our ten year programme of modernisation includes the biggest ever hospital building programme in the history of the National Health Service. The Private Finance Initiative is a vital element in renewing the fabric of the NHS (Alan Milburn, 1999).[10]

PFI has been seen as the primary means of providing new hospital buildings since the National Health Service (Private Finance) Act 1997 received Royal Assent. Since then, 31 major hospital developments worth over £3.1 billion compared to six publicly-funded schemes worth nearly £220 million have been authorised. This represents approximately £700 million in capital costs and £2.4 billion in FM costs. Nineteen PFI schemes have so far been completed with a capital value of £1.4 billion, and another six have reached financial close with work started on-site at a capital value of £1.1 billion.[11]

One of the primary reasons for the popularity of PFI is the perception that using the PSC, PFI projects offer better value for money and cost savings. However, compared to the 10 percent average savings achieved by the MoD, evaluation of two completed NHS PFI projects, Dartford & Gravesham and West Middlesex, by the National Audit Office (NAO) shows average savings of 3 and 4 percent respectively.

Whole life costing is an essential aspect of PFI. The financial and risk implications of getting it wrong to both the authorising body and the supplying consortium known as the Special Purpose Vehicle (SPV) are enormous. The government believes that good design can deliver whole life and environmental benefits. The Inland Revenue, for example, specified in its PFI, a requirement that all the bidders must comply with the Inland Revenue Green Guide. This included a building that was naturally ventilated (i.e. no air conditioning), lighting that switched itself off when people left, gas-fired heating with individual thermostatically controlled radiators, double glazing, building materials from sustainable sources and building management systems that monitored the use of resources.[12]

Sustainability and green issues are also to be emphasised in PFI projects. The policy and regulatory framework for the environment are intended to help achieve the government's objective of a more sustainable environment, and are likely to be toughened over time. In some cases, this might involve change of law provisions within the signed PPP contract.

The Green Paper, Public Private Partnerships (2002), recommends that bidders should consider the following issues in developing a PPP proposal:

- Minimising waste;
- Reducing whole life costs without compromising user comfort;
- Enhancing service delivery;
- Promoting wider social and environmental benefits;
- Encouraging in-built flexibility.

To achieve this requires supply chain integration. PFI is an ideal vehicle to enable supply chain integration and collaborative working. The majority of the private sector interest was initially made up of construction companies, reinforcing the emphasis on 'bricks and mortar' (Boyle and Harrison, 2000) rather than services. However, the market has witnessed a shift not only in the composition of the SPV, but also in the repackaging of construction companies as FM organisations, with a marked shift in the proportion income from FM.

FM's role in the PFI process spans the whole process. In fact, FM is the only discipline that is a part of the project from inception through contract management to expiration, reversion and eventual disposal of the facility or service. FM has a role in the identification of business needs, advising on space and accessibility issues, use of materials and value management, risk assessment and whole life costing. However, although experience shows they contribute to some of the process, the SPVs rarely work together as an integrated team. This is made even more compelling when insurance claims feedback have shown that (Bicknell, 2003):

- 40% of building defects are design related;
- 40% are construction related; and
- 20% are due to component failure.

The transfer of FM staff under Transfer of Undertakings (Protection of Employment) Regulations (TUPE) has also been an issue of great contention under PFI. In the NHS, unions have successfully campaigned for their non-managerial members to opt out of the TUPE transfer. Non-managerial employees have the option to remain NHS staff and be 'seconded' to the private consortium supplying PFI services. Managerial employees are, however, required to transfer under TUPE.

These issues all combine to make the PFI a major issue of discussion in the public healthcare sector. Like it or hate it, PFI has provided urgently needed new and refurbished facilities for the NHS, at a rate at which the government could not adequately provide within the same time-scales. FM has had to adjust to the changing structures and roles, and witnessed the growth of a crop of new expertise in PFI project and contract management.

18.2 The PFI procurement process

PFI is governed by strict procurement rules. Previous issues considered by NHS Trusts developing PFI projects included the procurement process and output specifications (Nelson, 2001). These have since been addressed by a review of the procurement process, and the development of standard output specifications for several service lines.

Whereas the RIBA Plan of Work[13] has 11 stages, the PFI procurement process (NHS Executive, 1999) incorporates 15 stages (Table 18.1). Although some similarities exist between the two processes, the PFI procurement process has some unique characteristics including the use of OJEC (Official Journal of the European Communities) rather than standard JCT (Joint Contracts Tribunal) contracts, refinement of the appraisal after selection of bidders, detailed output specification at the final evaluation stage, and contract management.

At the initial appraisal and bidders pre-qualification stages, outline proposals and output specifications are developed. This is in contrast to the RIBA Plan of Work where final proposals are defined before going out to tender. The government maintains that all output specifications, irrespective of the form of procurement adopted, should be output or outcome based, unless exceptional reasons can be demonstrated to the contrary.

It is further suggested that output specifications should be left as open as possible whilst ensuring that they accurately describe the outcome required, as unnecessary detail tends to inhibit innovation and result in extra costs. There, however, needs to be a compromise between openness and a lack of minimum standards across the board. To this end a list of standard output specifications was drawn up for the NHS in the following services, which may be customised from Trust to Trust.

- General;
- Estates;
- Ground and gardens;
- Pest control;

Table 18.1: Comparison of RIBA Plan of Work and PFI process

Step	RIBA Plan of Work	PFI process
1(A)	Appraisal	Establish the business need
2(B)	Strategic brief	Appraise the options
3(C)	Outline proposals	Business care
4(D)	Detailed proposals	Developing the team
5(E)	Final proposals	Deciding tactics
6(F)	Production information	Publish OJEC
7(G)	Tender documents	Bidders pre-qualification
8(H)	Tender action	Selection of bidders
9(J)	Mobilisation	Refine the appraisal
10(K)	Construction to practical completion	Negotiate
11(L)	After practical completion	Evaluation of bids
12		Final evaluation
13		Contract award
14		Contract management
15		Post project evaluation

- Utilities management;
- Portering, including post and mortuary duties;
- Residential accommodation;
- Materials management;
- Car parking;
- Helpdesk;
- Domestic;
- Security;
- Catering;
- Reception.

Output specifications are currently being developed for the following services:

- Linen;

- Day nursery;

- Medical equipment;

- Waste management;

- Sterile services.

Whereas the RIBA Plan of Work ends on commissioning (after practical completion), the PFI process incorporates the management of the PFI contract over its life.[14] The PFI contract management kicks in at financial close, and a key measure of success is when a satisfactory level of services is delivered on an on-going basis once construction is complete. Two key areas are monitored, and the proposed arrangements should be set out in the Invitation to Negotiate (ITN). These are:

1 The period up to completion of commissioning of the new PFI facility including the phased hand over of any services to the private sector operator;

2 The operational phase of the contract.

18.3 FM role in the PFI environment

As stated earlier, FM represents the largest proportion of the value of the PFI contract. The role of the facility manager cannot therefore be overemphasised in this process. FM has a role a role to play from the establishment of the business need through to reversion, and eventual disposal. Typically in NHS PFI projects, the Trust's chief executive officer (CEO) is the project owner. The role most commonly taken up by the facilities director is that of project director. The project director not only sits on the project board,[15] but is also responsible for (NHS Executive, 2003):

- Developing the business case, output specifications, evaluation criteria, project plan and budget for the development;

- Ensuring adequate communications on all aspects of the project (both internal and external);

- Ensuring the project and contracts are completed and implemented through a managed process;

- Ensuring the post project evaluation of the scheme.

The project director is also a member of the project team made up of representatives of each service department, finance, advisers and consultants, the NHS Executive's Public Finance Unit and the Treasury taskforce where appropriate. FM also has a role to play as representatives of the commissioning health trust, who make up part of the project team responsible for:

- Defining the project brief and formulating departmental output specifications;

- Consulting with users on the project brief;

- Monitoring to ensure that the output specification is delivered;
- Establishing and managing the evaluation team.

The NHS PFI process is defined under four broad stages (NHS Executive, 1999) related to the 15 stages of the PFI process (Table 18.1) earlier described. These are:

- Stage 1 – Establish the strategic context and make the case for change. This represents the selection and preparation of schemes up to the Invitation to Tender stage.

- Stages 2 & 3 – Identify the preferred option and prepare an Outline Business Case; assess and plan the preferred option in detail, and prepare a Full Business Case. These represent the procurement process from OJEC to contract award.

- Stage 4 – Manage the project through implementation and evaluation to ensure that the outputs are delivered. This represents activities post contract award including the final phase of contract management and project evaluation.

18.3.1 FM role in Stage 1

Although the NHS has stated that the Health Improvement Programme will be the means by which the need for change is identified for future PFI projects, FM has a role in identifying the requirement for refurbishment, adaptation or provision of new facilities, or the identification of new services to meet the changing needs of the healthcare organisation. This includes the provision of state-of-the-art medical facilities and equipment. FM has the capability of working proactively in identifying not just current healthcare requirements, but future service requirements as well. FM needs to be aware of healthcare policies and local and national requirements, as well as technology trends which influence the mode of delivery of medical services.

FM is best placed to appraise the options available to the Trust. Best practice FM should be able to identify which option provides best value, and make decisions backed by facts. The business case for PFI has to be prepared to justify this procurement method in place of Treasury funding. In developing the business case, risk assessments need to be undertaken for the various options available. FM is experienced in undertaking business risk assessment relating to facilities and so is best placed to undertake this role.

Developing the team is a responsibility of the project director. FM, traditionally, has undertaken a co-ordinating role in ensuring delivery of managed services to an organisation. Team development should not just be seen as an exercise in project management, but as a means of managing the FM value chain (Nelson and Sarshar, 2003).

FM can also contribute to strategic planning of the contract management at this early stage to ensure proper monitoring of the delivery to specification over the contract term. This is critical to the effective management and monitoring of the PFI contract, and needs to be incorporated at the development and negotiation stages of the PFI project to ensure that best value is achieved throughout the term of the contract.

FM is the resource base for the data required in putting together a business case for the PFI project. The quality of the FM data would greatly influence the quality of the business case and the achievement of value for money. It is worthwhile remembering that the PFI project need not necessarily include the provision of new facilities, but is actually about the delivery of serviced facilities for the use of the NHS Trust. Therefore, the PSC is not strictly limited to the procurement of new buildings but can be used to compare the cost of traditional procurement strategies for services against procurement through PFI. The PFI contract usually includes the transfer of the provision of existing services as well as a property interest to the SPV for a fixed term contract.

18.3.2 FM role in Stages 2 & 3

PFI creates an opportunity for supply chain integration and collaborative working. The FM role as a team member on the client side during these stages is invaluable. However, there is also a major role for FM on the supplier side as part of the SPV. On the client side, FM has a role to play in the design of the new facility and/or clarification of the service requirements, integration of new facilities into existing operations, commissioning, transfer of existing staff and risk assessment.

FM has a role in capturing the Trust's business requirements to be fed into the business cases and output specifications. It should be involved in the negotiation stages to develop and refine the details of the PFI project. The development of an effective performance measurement and monitoring system is crucial to achieving best value. Key Performance Indicators (KPIs) linked to the Trust's business strategy are developed at this time. Space planning and utilisation skills are required at this stage to create a facility to meet the needs of the Trust.

FM is also involved in the human resource issue relating to the transfer of its existing staff over to the SPV as part of the PFI process under TUPE. Negotiations with unions and the SPV, as well as communication with staff, are very important roles in a PFI project.

On the supplier side, FM has a role to play in driving the integration of the supply chain, and supply chain management. As on the client side, FM is responsible for the data required for the development of the service specification in the PFI bid. It also has a role as part of the design team using expertise in space planning and utilisation, as well as capturing user requirements.

The development of service delivery strategies as well as performance measurement systems to ensure delivery to the Trust's KPIs, are part of the FM role. Strategies are not static and would need to be innovative and flexible to ensure continuous improvement in the standards of services provided.

18.3.3 FM role in Stage 4

PFI contract management involves three stages: procurement, development and delivery. Procurement and development have been addressed in the three previous stages. The management of the delivery process on the client side involves an auditing role, risk management, and contract and performance monitoring. FM plays a role in the commissioning process to ensure a smooth transition to service delivery by the SPV.

The Trust's FM is responsible for monitoring the provision of contracted services, including the availability of facilities and performance, to ensure that they conform with contractual specifications. Facilities managers also manage the payment mechanism system, and are responsible for contract variations and negotiations. FM monitors compliance not only with the terms of the contract, but also Health & Safety and other legislation, and the SPVs' quality management systems.

On the supplier side, it involves a spectrum of activities including service delivery, performance measurement, innovation and continuous improvement. It is an opportunity for the SPV to work collaboratively as an integrated FM team.

The FM role in post project evaluation on both the client and supplier sides is to conduct an objective review of the project processes and feed-forward to future projects. Lessons must be learnt through each process which should inform best practice FM.

Throughout all four stages, FM on both client and supplier sides has a responsibility for risk management. This includes:

- Identification;
- Evaluation;
- Measurement;
- Control;
- Management;
- Business continuity planning;
- Monitoring.

18.4 FM role post PFI

One area that is often ignored at the earlier stages of the PFI process is what happens after the expiration of the contract. Reversion of the PFI interest to the Trust after the expiration of the contract term is a very important issue, which FM needs to address proactively. In the planning and development stages of the project, it is important to ensure that decisions are made not only on the standards of maintenance of the facilities required from the SPV, but also on the condition of the property at the expiration of the contract, bearing in mind that PFI contracts are for 25–30 year terms.

FM also plays a role in the assessment of options as the contract draws to its natural conclusion depending on the contract terms. It is responsible for compliance with the hand-back procedures set out in the contract, which may involve surveys prior to expiry. FM will also be responsible for verifying the assessment of the value of the asset at the end of the contract.

18.5 Case studies

The three NHS PFI case studies described below focus on procurement issues. The first two, Dartford & Gravesham NHS Trust and West Middlesex University Hospital NHS Trust, have been audited by the NAO, and found to provide marginal cost savings compared to traditional procurement routes. The third case study, The Cumberland Infirmary, Carlisle, was the first PFI hospital scheme completed, and was lauded in terms of completion of construction ahead of schedule and on budget.

18.5.1 *Dartford & Gravesham NHS Trust (Select Committee on Public Accounts, 7 April, 2000)*

- In July 1997, the NHS Trust let a 60-year contract to Pentland, a private sector consortium, for the first major hospital contract under the Private Finance Initiative.

- Estimated value of £177 million (in 1996 values) over the first 25 years that the hospital is in use, after which the Trust may terminate the contract without penalty if it decides to close the hospital.

- The Health Authority hoped that the new hospital scheme would be 'revenue neutral'. However, a failure to detect significant errors in the public sector comparator led to £12 million less in savings than originally anticipated, and extra funding of over £4 million per annum is now required to enable the Trust to meet its commitments under the contract, which will run for at least 25 years.

- Provided a new hospital to replace services previously provided on three sites in need of major maintenance.

- Provided an opportunity for the Trust to concentrate on delivering clinical services rather than building maintenance and support services.

Lessons learnt

- Trusts and Health Authorities should agree at the outset likely funding limits for the project.

- Trusts should conduct a rigorous review of the expected costs and benefits of the proposed PFI project with the conventionally financed alternative before taking key decisions.

- Trusts should have regard to overall value for money in selecting final bidders, not just price, and bidders' willingness to comply with the bidding requirements.

- The NHS Executive may wish to consider the scope and benefits of commissioning certain advice centrally on common issues to help reduce costs; and benchmarking advisers' costs with those incurred on other PFI projects.

- The Trust did not quantify the full effects of changes in contract terms and of the sensitivity of the deal to changes in key assumptions.

- The Trust did not assess the effect of significantly higher and lower usage levels on its costs when comparing the PFI option with traditional procurement.

18.5.2   *West Middlesex NHS Trust (House of Commons, 21 Nov., 2002)*

- In January 2001, the Trust let a 35-year PFI contract to Bywest, a private sector consortium, with possibility to extend the contract term to 60 years.

- Estimated net present value of unitary payments of some £125 million.

- The contract requires Bywest to redevelop the Trust's site at Isleworth, West London, and provide on-going maintenance and facilities services.

- The Trust has sought to manage the risks of a PFI contract by building into the contract some flexibility and arrangements to test that any contract variations add value for money.

Lessons learnt

- Lessons learnt from the Trust's first abortive attempts at PFI were helpful during the second attempt.

- Identified need to:

  - develop a strong project team with key decision makers involved;

  - involve key stakeholders in order to ensure buy-in to the project;

  - make the role of advisers clearer and regularly monitor their costs.

- The Trust reviewed the experience of the first wave of PFI hospital projects and issued new guidance to address many of the issues raised by the NAO and the Committee of Public Accounts in their reports on Dartford & Gravesham.

- The Trust also made use of new standard NHS PFI contracts to speed up the process.

- The Trust obtained confirmation in writing from Bywest (preferred bidder) during negotiations to hold the contract price for seven months, and remain committed to the same timetable.

18.5.3 Cumberland Hospital

- First PFI major district general hospital to be completed in the UK.

- Financed by the first 30-year PFI bond worth £75.8 million, and the first bond deal in the National Health Service.

- Preferred bidder was Health Management Carlisle, made up of AMEC and Building & Property Group.[16]

- Interservefm provided all non-clinical services in the old hospital and will continue to provide non-clinical support services to the hospital over 45 years with an option to review at 30 years. Services to be provided include estates management, domestic staff and portering, utilities, catering, laundry, telecommunications, reception, security, engineering maintenance, and clinical and non-clinical functions and waste disposal.

Lessons learnt

- Despite opening on budget and ahead of schedule, the Cumberland Infirmary has faced significant problems.[17] This includes reports of:
  - blocked sewerage pipes which spewed out waste into sinks;
  - flooding in the maternity unit;
  - overheating in the atrium;
  - a patient injured after falling in the hospital's revolving door.

- Many patients have complained about the atrium – a centrepiece of the hospital. On one occasion, temperatures reached 110 °F in the hospital.

- There were also basic design faults, such as disabled services being placed at the back of the hospital away from the car park. A new one was built, but the door to the unit was not suitable for disabled use.

18.6 Best practice FM in PFI

The three case studies identify that progress has been made in PFI procurement with knowledge transfer. Risks associated with contract variations for example, which were not considered at Dartford & Gravesham were addressed in the West Middlesex PFI project. The contribution of FM to the design and co-ordination of the project, as well as the inclusion of key stakeholders in the process, was also identified at West Middlesex. Clearly, FM has a responsibility not only in identifying and specifying the client's requirements, but also in delivering to meet these requirements.

The focus of audits and research studies so far, however, has been on the financial aspects of the PFI scheme. The seminal report of the Commission on Public Private Partnerships,[18] *Building Better Partnerships*, found that although the PFI had delivered improvements in value for money in prisons and roads, the benefits of school and hospital PFIs were less clear cut.[19] This is significant as it relates to the nature of the PFI schemes. School and hospital PFIs are peculiar in the sense that only facilities and ancillary services are transferred to the private sector. The core business itself is not transferred, which offers limited opportunities to demonstrate value for money as the private consortium is only given control over ancillary staff (e.g. cleaners and porters), whilst core staff (e.g. doctors and nurses) remain in the public sector. This represents a challenge to FM to demonstrate added value to the Trust. This need not only be financial, but may be related to the image or reputation of the Trust, flexibility and adaptability to changing requirements, and increased productivity for Trust staff.

Although the advice from the office of the Deputy Prime Minister is to always focus on value for money and not the lowest cost, evidence from the audited PFI cases shows that the lowest cost bids were accepted. Value for money is to be assessed on a need to sustain levels over the life of the project. Surveys by the Committee of Public Accounts have shown that 23 percent of government authorities considered that there had been a decline in the value for money derived from their PFI projects after the contract had been let. In the Dartford case study, we see errors in calculating the PSC eroding £12 million off the savings from the project after the contract was let. This calls for a need to revise the use of the PSC in determining value for money.

FM's role in determining value for money could create a challenge to PFI to look beyond creating financial savings, to being more innovative. It has already been demonstrated that with the right strategies in place, cost savings could be achieved in non-PFI service contracts over a period of time. At Hairmyres Hospital, for example, through the establishment and implementation of clear FM procedures, cost savings of an estimated £1,769,000 in five years were identified linked to contract renewal.

The need to shift towards outcome focused management of PFI contracts in order to meet the government's public service agreement (PSA) targets has also been identified. The government has a clear objective for the current period that 67 percent of PSA targets are outcome targets, with only 14 percent and 8 percent respectively representing process and output targets. This represents a major change from 51 percent process and 27 percent outcome targets for the period up to July 2000.[20] To achieve this, FM input into the contract development is crucial. There is also a requirement for a clear definition of outcome-based contracts as opposed to output-based.

Evidence suggests, though, that some Trusts have looked beyond financial concerns and recognised that the provision of healthcare within PFI will require specific skills and expertise which are not compatible with the traditional NHS administration and management structure. At Hairmyres NHS Trust, FM services are based on output specifications and promote the use of generic workers. The generic team approach through multi-skilling has been developed to maximise operational efficiency. This merging of cultures has ensured that FM staff have become fully integrated members of ward and departmental teams (Centre for Facilities Management, 1997).

These are, however, not being reflected in the management of PFI contracts which are still entirely dependent on the development, monitoring and measurement of suppliers performance through the key performance indicators (KPIs) and service level agreements (SLA) agreed at the start of the project. There lies a challenge to FM to include flexibility in the use of KPIs and SLAs in PFI so as not to inhibit innovation and continuous improvement. The use of other performance measurement tools such as market testing, customer satisfaction surveys and benchmarking should also be encouraged.

An audit of the DSS PRIME project identified a number of areas in which the PFI contract had failed to demonstrate best practice (Centre for Facilities Management, 1998). These included:

- Under-development of the specification of requirements, expressed at a very general level of detail and not including specific performance requirements or criteria. The specification, therefore, provided an inadequate basis for the performance measurement system.

- This led to the performance requirements and performance criteria in the Invitation to Negotiate failing to provide an adequate performance framework. The system neither measured (facilities) performance nor service quality.

- The performance measurement system and associated payment regime was found to be unlikely to encourage innovation and outstanding performance.

Ensuring that the contracts provide sufficient flexibility to address future uncertainties in long-term healthcare is just one of the ways of sustaining a PFI scheme. PFI procures a service rather than the underlying asset, so PFI contracts go a step further than providing total facilities management (TFM) services under one packaged contract. It enables supply chain integration and collaborative working, as it requires a combined team effort from the initial stages. However the evidence so far suggests that, although teams are working more collaboratively as the same teams bid for more contracts, we are still a long way off from supply chain integration. Reasons for this have been identified as the arms-length approach to procurement, clients' conservatism and lack of procurement skills, and constraints from the PFI finance providers (Be, 2003).

Although PFI creates an opportunity for early collaboration and supply chain integration, the process itself could be an inhibitor, as the final bidder is not chosen until step

11 (Table 18.1). At this stage it is more difficult to involve the users in the briefing process. At the Cumberland Infirmary, Interservefm worked in collaboration with the Trust and AMEC, which allowed the provision of valuable, practical input to many aspects of the design, and the optimisation of operational efficiency between clinical and non-clinical functions. This multi-disciplinary teamwork was also credited with the delivery the UK's first PFI hospital on budget, and ahead of schedule.

Examples of best practice in partnering between the client organisation and supplier are more evident in the PFI provision of state-of-the-art custody centres, and provision and management of the custody function and facilities for Sussex Police (Mathews, 2002). It has been used as an opportunity to change and improve work processes. This has not been evident in the healthcare PFI sector, as the core business is not a part of the PFI contract.

Other examples of best practice PFI from other sectors includes the inclusion of clauses which state that the properties need to be returned in specific condition at the expiration of the contract in MoD PFI contracts.

The early pioneers for the PFI scheme helped to establish what the major issues were, and the support required by the Trusts to speed up an otherwise very lengthy process. The development and use of standard output specifications in PFI schemes have helped redress the problem of very long time-scales as evidenced at West Middlesex. In addition, the West Middlesex experience was to feed into the development of the standard NHS PFI contract.

> The new guidance will ensure new NHS building projects, funded through the PFI, represent the very best value for money for the taxpayer (Alan Milburn, 1999).[21]

The PFI guidance is based on best practice and lessons learnt as a result of project evaluation from large and small-scale PFI schemes that have been successfully completed. It must be noted, however, that these standard output specifications and the NHS contract are not limited to PFI schemes only, but can also be applied to in-house and outsourced provision of support services, demonstrating best practice in this area.

A major source of constraint to best practice in this sector is the fact that PFI contracts are not purchased centrally but by individual Trusts as clients. Standardised contracts and output specifications also need to be customised to each Trust's needs and relevancy. Success also depends on the skills and experience of the PFI team in each Trust. Best practice can be adopted from the ProCure 21 initiative,[22] where project directors are specifically trained for the job, and respective trusts can employ them as required from a bank of skilled specialists. There now exists a crop of experienced NHS PFI project directors, mostly former FM directors, who are employed by Trusts undertaking PFI schemes as external consultants to inform the process and contribute their experience to the new schemes.

It has been suggested that long-term planning is difficult in the health service because healthcare and the local demography keep changing over time. The intelligence to make long-term decisions, which may affect the optimum type and location of facilities that are required, lies beyond the hospital or Trust boundaries. Some of the knowledge may reside within the Trust but NHS Estates, as well as the NHS Executive and the Department of Health, would also keep some of this intelligence. Ideally representatives of these bodies should also be involved in the PFI scheme from the very early stages, and FM could play a co-ordinating role in the collation of intelligence from all these sources. This would reduce the risks of Trusts being locked into long-term contracts for buildings and services that may no longer be needed in the same format or capacity in the future. This is very important, as termination of PFI contracts can be very expensive.

Presently, examples of risks transferred on to the private sector include:

- Construction design (except changes due to external NHS requirements);

- Meeting specified performance standards and operating cost risk;

- Non-NHS specific regulatory/legislative changes.

However, the following risks are not being transferred due to the retention of core services by the Trusts:

- Clinical service provision;

- Change in Trust requirements;

- NHS specific regulatory/legislative changes.

As PFI contracts usually encompass a combination of construction works and services, construction works and supplies, or supplies and services, it is not immediately obvious which regulations should govern PFI procurements. There is a very important role for FM to play in ensuring that all relevant legislation is complied with to avoid potentially serious regulatory breaches and mitigate risks. Just as important is the ability to ensure that the contract arrangements will encourage a cyclical process of continuous improvement of the quality of the buildings and working environment, service quality and process quality.

The DSS PRIME project example given also highlighted the risks associated with the under-development of the 'intelligent client' role which needs to be taken on board in the health sector. It was identified that there was an inadequate basis for managing quality, value and risk; and the processes for aligning facilities to the business needs, and the client and contractors responsibilities were unclear. The need to share risks and create opportunities for innovation and quality improvement were also emphasised.

Another risk faced by PFI schemes was in terms of the transfer of public sector FM staff to the preferred bidder under TUPE. At Cumberland Infirmary, for example, over 326 members of staff were transferred to Interservefm Ltd under TUPE regulations. At Dartford & Gravesham, there was some disagreement between the Trust and the preferred bidder, Pentland, as to whether Trust staff who have transferred to Pentland have retained their rights to certain early retirement benefits. Although under TUPE transferred staff are offered comparable pension terms by their new employer at both primary and subsequent contracting rounds, it was not clearly defined in the Dartford & Gravesham case.

Changes to TUPE regulations relating to the transfer of NHS staff have been successfully argued for by the unions. Under this revised regulation, rather then transferring to the new supplier, non-managerial FM staff (e.g. portering, catering, domestics, laundry services and security staff) retain all their NHS employment terms, but will be managed by the private sector 'Retention of Employment' Model.[23] This represents a legal secondment to the private sector partner. Formal guidance is currently being developed.

Environmental and sustainability issues also need to be addressed. Examples from the current PFI project at Barts and The London NHS Trust include the need to modernise listed buildings, and the management of the largest NHS PFI to-date with a PSC of £620 million. This raises two issues: sustainability and the capability of the FM market to deliver the requirements.

In terms of sustainability, the Office of the Deputy Prime Minister has emphasised the need for green issues to be taken into cognisance in PFI projects. This would suggest whole life value[24] assessments of PFI schemes to replace the current practice of whole life costing. This becomes even more important with the removal of the Crown exemption previously granted to NHS Trusts in terms of environment legislation, which carries a risk to be managed by FM.

The capability of FM to deliver to large PFI contracts also needs to be addressed. In addition to the Barts' programme, in London alone, the University College London Hospitals also have a £422 million PFI project in development. The PFI market has recently witnessed the withdrawal of large FM organisations due to losses incurred in PFI bidding. As projects grow larger, the risks associated with failure to win contracts also increase to suppliers, as does the benefits to be derived. On the client side, the risks associated with failure to develop the right contract have been identified and addressed through the continued engagement of the Trust's facilities staff in the process (Wright, 2003).

18.7 Conclusion

Best practice FM in PFI has been difficult to define in the health sector. Although a large number of NHS PFI schemes have now been completed, very little documented evidence is available to show the true picture of value for money provided to the Trusts. One of the major arguments for choosing PFI schemes over a conventional procurement method is the cost saving associated with PFI. To-date only two completed schemes have been audited by the NAO, which do not clearly demonstrate the case for value for money in NHS procurement, which the government has been campaigning under. In each case cost savings were found to have been minimal. However, it has been demonstrated that more recent NHS PFI schemes have taken on board lessons learnt from earlier schemes. Evaluation, feedback and feed-forward are seen to be essential for best practice.

The main focus of PFI in the health sector so far has been on financial aspects. It has been demonstrated that there is danger attached to the use of the PSC in making PFI decisions, and the fact that capital values shown are estimates. This was demonstrated in the Dartford & Gravesham PFI where not only were cost savings overestimated, but also the annual charge was underestimated. It highlights the need for a better system of deriving cost estimates and a need to revise the use of the PSC in determining value for money. It also highlights that FM has a major role to play in this area in creating a reliable facility database, and benchmarking. It must be noted that the costs associated with the scheme are also very high, and may reduce the overall cost savings to be achieved by going through this route.

FM has a role to play in establishing a clear and concise statement of output requirements including the values and evaluation criteria to be employed, and whole life value assessments. Contract management needs to shift towards outcome-based specifications, rather than SLAs. The development of standard output specifications for NHS PFIs has been seen to considerably speed up the PFI process, and enabled a better definition of Trust requirements.

Performance measurement is based on availability and service levels, rather than innovation, continuous improvement and flexibility to meet changing Trust requirements. The need to build in the capacity for flexibility both into the use of the facility and the contract cannot be overemphasised. The risks of being tied into a long-term contract should also be carefully assessed before commitment to projects. Dartford & Gravesham provide an example where the effect of significantly higher and lower usage levels on its costs was not assessed when comparing the PFI option with traditional procurement. As such, the Trust is committed to paying for availability of the facilities over the first 25 years of the contract, whether or not it is suitable for their needs or requirements.

Knowledge transfer has been adopted, with both individual Trusts and the regulating agencies learning from past mistakes. How well these lessons have been implemented is, however, the subject of more research.

The NHS has led the way in terms of the 'soft' side of PFI, people issues. The issue of morale amongst NHS staff had reached levels of such importance that the unions successfully campaigned for an adjustment to the TUPE regulations specifically for non-managerial NHS employees. Early PFI schemes raised issues such as whether

Trust employees who have transferred to the private sector consortium have retained their rights to certain early retirement benefits. Although assurances have been made for earlier PFI schemes that any employee who becomes entitled to these benefits will receive them, it was not enough to win the trust of the staff.

Although the opportunities for supply chain integration and collaboration are high in PFI schemes, it has not been explored to its full potential. Some evidence of part collaboration between suppliers within the consortium, as well as supplier and client, are available. There has also been evidence of user involvement in the development of PFI schemes. We are, however, still a way from full integration and partnership in the schemes. The jury is still out, as well, on whether PFI has demonstrated its value added to the NHS so far, or, as suggested, is seen merely as the creation of a few white elephants.

References

Alexander, K. (ed.), *Facilities Management – Theory and Practice*, E&FN Spon, New York (1996).

Audit Commission, 'NHS Estate Management and Property Maintenance', Audit Commission (1991).

Be, (2003) 'Improving PFI through collaborative working', a Be (Built environment) task group report for consultation.

Bicknell, C., 'An integral part of PFI', *Public Service Review: PFI/PPP*, 2003, www.publicservice.co.uk

Boyle, S. and Harrison, A., 'Private Finance and Service Development', in J. Appleby and A. Harrison (eds), *Health Care UK*, Summer, King's Fund (2000).

Centre for Facilities Management, 'A business approach to facilities management', Health Facilities Note 17 (1997).

Centre for Facilities Management, 'Value for money study: DSS PRIME project', Final Report, Commissioned by the National Audit Office (1998).

Green Paper, Public Private Partnerships (2002), Published by the Office of Government Commerce, the Office of the Deputy Prime Minister, the Department for Transport and the Department for the Environment, Food and Rural Affairs.

House of Commons, 'The PFI Contract for the Redevelopment of West Middlesex University Hospital', HC 49 Session 2002–2003: 21 Nov., 2002.

Maltby, P., 'What is the PFI?', Institute of Public Policy Research (2002), www.ippr.org.uk

Mathews, B., 'Opportunity to Innovate', *Public Service Review: Central Government*, Spring, 2002, www.publicservice.co.uk

Nelson, M., 'PFI issues in the NHS', internal report and presentation to NHS Estates, University of Salford (2001).

Nelson, M. and Sarshar, M., 'Supply, Demand or Value Chain Management – The FM Dilemma', in *Proc. of the 3rd Intl Post-Graduate Conf.*, Lisbon, Portugal, Apr. 2003.

NHS Executive, 'Public Private Partnerships in the National Health Service: The Private Finance Initiative, Good Practice Section 2: The PFI Procurement Process' (1999).

NHS Executive, 'Public Private Partnerships in the National Health Service: The Private Finance Initiative, Good Practice Overview', Dec. 1999.

NHS Executive, 'Public Private Partnerships in the National Health Service: The Private Finance Initiative, Good Practice Section 1: The Selection and Preparation of Schemes', (Revised version), Apr. 2003.

'Select Committee on Public Accounts', The PFI contract for the new Dartford & Gravesham Hospital, Twelfth report, 7 Apr., 2000.

The Guardian, 1 Oct., 2002, 'The PFI needs a review', society.guardian.co.uk

US Library of Congress (1989), in T. Mole and F. Taylor (eds) *Facility Management: Evolution or Revolution* (1992), in P. Barrett (ed.) *Facilities Management – Research Directions*, Surveyors Holdings Ltd, London (1993).

Wright, A., 'NHS healthcare for the future', *Public Service Review: PFI Journal*, Summer, 2003, www.publicservice.co.uk

Key Reading

Alexander, K. (ed.) *Facilities Management – Theory and Practice*, E&FN Spon, New York (1996).

Barrett P. (ed.) *Facilities Management – Research Directions*, Surveyors Holdings Ltd, London (1993).

Barrett, P. and Baldry, D., *Facilities Management – Towards Best Practice*, Blackwell Science, Oxford (2002).

Holti, R., Nicolini, D. and Smalley, M., *The handbook of supply chain management: The Essentials, Building Down Barriers*, CIRIA and the Tavistock Institute (2000).

Useful Websites

Be (Collaborating for the Built Environment), www.beonline.co.uk

Centre for Facilities Management (CFM), www.cfm.salford.ac.uk

Department of Health, www.doh.gov.uk

HM Treasury, www.hm-treasury.gov.uk

Institute for Public Policy Research, www.ippr.org.uk

National Audit Office (NAO), www.nao.gov.uk

NHS Executive, www.doh.gov.uk/nhs/

Office of Government Commerce, www.ogc.gov.uk

Office of the Deputy Prime Minister, www.odpm.gov.uk

The PFI Network (pfi.ogc.gov.uk). Developed by the Office of Government Commerce's Private Finance Unit to provide one-stop access to comprehensive information about PFI.

The British Library (www.bl.uk). For links to material regarding Public Private Partnership (PPP) initiatives in the United Kingdom's health services.

www.publicservice.co.uk

Endnotes

1 Smart Construction, www.mod.uk
2 Dig that debate, www.hsj.co.uk
3 NHS Lift – Overview, www.4ps.co.uk
4 Procurement guidance No: 5, www.ogc.gov.uk
5 Jeremy Colman, Assistant Auditor General, 'Mumbo jumbo . . . and other pitfalls', presentation at the Second Annual National Audit Office PFI/PPP Conf., London, 19 June, 2003.
6 'Private finance spending to fall', news.bbc.co.uk, 17 Oct., 2002.
7 'Private finance and investment: General Questions and answer briefing', www.doh. gov.uk
8 'Public Private Partnerships in the MoD', www.mod.uk/business/
9 Public sector comparator estimates the costs of a 'traditional' procurement. However the National Audit Office (NAO) discovered inconsistencies in the comparator, which they revised in the course of their reporting on PFI projects.
10 'New PFI manual to ensure best value for tax payers' Press Release 15 Dec., 1999, www.doh.gov.uk
11 'Major capital schemes approved to go ahead since May 1997 (England)', www.doh. gov.uk
12 Ibid.
13 *The Architects Plan of Work*, RIBA Enterprises, 2000.
14 Usually 25–30 years, but examples exist of 20 to 60 year contracts. Sixty-year contracts usually have a break clause after the first 25 years.
15 Project board comprises project owner, project director, non-executive directors, and representatives from senior clinical staff, commissioners, estates, IT, finance and personnel.
16 Now known as Interservefm.
17 'Hospital on the sick list?', news.bbc.co.uk, 3 Sep., 2001.
18 The commission is made up of representatives of the private, public, voluntary and trade union sectors.
19 'IPPR (Institute of Public Policy Research) calls for an end to PFI fundamentalism', Press Release 26 Sep., 2002, www.ippr.org.uk
20 HM Treasury, Outcome Focused Management in the United Kingdom, General Expenditure Policy.
21 'New PFI manual to ensure best value for tax payers' Press Release 15 Dec., 1999, www.doh.gov.uk
22 www.nhs-procure21.gov.uk
23 Private Finance and Investment, www.doh.gov.uk/pfi/
24 Whole life value assessments include an assessment of the financial and sustainability costs of the project.

Conclusion

The future role of architects in the building process 19

Michael Murray and David Langford, Department of Architecture and Building Science, University of Strathclyde, Glasgow, UK

19.1 Through the looking glass

Consistent with the ending of a book, it is valuable to take a very brief look back at the recent changes that have taken place in the world of architectural practice. We shall look back, but not stare, for it is a well-documented history that has been more appropriately discussed by architects rather than construction managers. Essentially, the critique has sought to answer what appears to be relatively simple questions – what is architecture and what do architects do? Moreover, why has the role of the architect been marginalised? These fundamental questions have been reiterated over the past two decades and with much heated debate, often relished with religious zeal. The debate has been partly characterised by a blinkered dichotomy within some architectural schools that either views architecture as a profession or considers its worthiness as a discipline that does not necessarily lead to employment as a practising architect. However, RIBA's (1999a) response to the Egan (1998) report clearly notes the importance of the former: 'we cannot respond to the challenge of "Rethinking Construction" unless we see ourselves unequivocally as part of the production process of building'. Interestingly, Richard Saxon (2003) former chairman of the Building Design Partnership and current chair of Collaboration for the Built Environment (Be) has recently argued that those architects who are interested in the building process tend to leave the profession. He cites Skanska's Keith Clarke and Mace's Bob White as two examples.

This handbook has been written for architects in practice and the art–science dichotomy, which is often the focus of those who wish to philosophise over architecture, has taken a back seat. Architecture in this world means, amongst other competing roles, developing a clear brief, preparing designs that take account of both capital and whole life costs and co-ordination of design and production information.[1]

19.2 Architects as project managers

This heading may well be a scenario of the cart before the horse if we consider the architect's historic role as contract administrator. However, the rise of construction management and then project management as recognised disciplines in the construction process has accelerated the decline in the architect's role. Indeed, Chappell and Willis (2000) note that although the architect is still usually the lead consultant and contract administrator, it is no longer a foregone conclusion. The 'on-site' role of a construction manager or project manager may well be determined by the conditions of engagement and these, in turn, are likely to have been derived from guidance given by the Chartered Institute of Building (CIOB) or the Association of Project

Managers (APM) for example. This relatively new breed of construction professional is often criticised for adding no new value to the construction process and, typically, construction managers are often likened to information processors who stand in the void between architect and constructor. As the chairman of Alsop Architects argues: 'I don't see the point in their [project managers] existence. Twenty years ago they weren't around and we [architects] took on the responsibility' (Alsop, 2001). However, Chappell and Willis (2000) argue that as architects traditionally hold such 'responsibility' (contract administrator in regard to the building contract) it can be complemented with training in project management techniques. Moreover, they do warn architects to be wary of accepting the role of project manager and, in particular, note that the terms 'project manager', 'lead consultant' and 'contract administrator' contain a mixture of the woolly and legally specific.

RIBA are, however, encouraging members to gain formal project management qualifications and the RIBA Certificate in Project Management is closely mapped to the current APM Body of Knowledge. Entry to study for this qualification is available to architects who have seven years experience including Part III whereupon formal examinations and syndicate working complete the assessment criteria. Fast-track intensive courses for the APM Professional Qualification in Project Management (APMP) and the RIBA Certificate in Project Management can be undertaken through the accredited course run by JC Consultancy (www.jc-consultancy.com). This course has been running since 2000 and to-date 63 RIBA members have successfully completed the course. Further evidence of RIBA's support for architects as project managers can be seen through its Linked Societies initiative. These independent, self-governing associations have close collaborative links to RIBA and one such group, Architects for Project Management (A4PM), was established in 1999. A4PM is recognised by RIBA as a source of project management interest and expertise.

19.3 Integrated project teams

The Association of Consultant Architects (ACA) has played a significant role in encouraging architects to fully participate in construction project teams and to develop collaborative working practices. Their Project Partnering Contract 2000 (Mosey, 2000) is intended to pioneer new working relationships between the client, professional team, contractor and specialists through an integrated project process. The philosophy behind the contract adopts the recommendations made in the Latham (1994) and Egan (1998) reports. Essentially, this means an end to the 'win–lose' project culture whereby a team-based multi-party approach is developed through an integrated design/supply/construction process. Indeed, architects, with their pivotal position in the construction process, have a big contribution to make to the development of partnering (RIBA, 2000).

Contract documents such as the PPC2000 will not in themselves 'restructure' the architect's role in the construction industry. RIBA have for many years encouraged architectural schools to develop collaborative student learning with other professions. The need for young architects to understand the operations of the building industry and co-operate in interdisciplinary project work is a key issue if progress is to be made and indeed RIBA argue that these issues should be 'fundamental not peripheral to an architect's education' (RIBA, 1999b). However, at a strategic level it has been argued that the government continue to thwart integration of design and construction by its sponsorship. Construction is sponsored by the Department of Trade and Industry and architecture by the Department for Culture, Media and Sport (Watts, 2003).

An essential part of developing closer working relationships in project teams will require architects to manage the whole design process.[2] The technological drift of an architects design responsibility to specialist sub-contractors is often characterised by 'fuzzy' responsibility and incomplete design detailing. Such a predicament is however being resolved in new innovative partnering projects such as the Ministry of Defence's Building Down Barriers projects. This initiative involved the restructuring of the project team and the use of a Prime Contract with similar conditions to that of the PPC2000. The design and construction of the two army facilities relied on truly collaborative integration between the design team, contractors and specialist sub-contractor.[3] These pilot projects seem to encapsulate the desire by RIBA to enforce greater understanding with regards to specialists: 'we need to recognise that [they] are the most undervalued part of the industry' (RIBA, 1999a).

This type of collaborative practice is also being undertaken in projects procured by clients such as the NHS Estates (ProCure 21 initiative). However, for architectural practices classified as SMEs (two-thirds of RIBA members work in practices of fewer than ten staff) this evolution may be somewhat elusive. Anecdotal evidence suggests that the majority of contracts undertaken by small architectural practices continue to be characterised by what could be termed 'JCT contract' behaviour where conflict and blame allocation continue to drain wasteful energy from the construction process. Contradictorily, there is evidence of small architectural practices involved with clients seeking to employ innovative procurement practices. The dissemination of knowledge from this type of progress is perhaps hampered by the relatively non-prestigious nature of everyday projects and the perceived need by practices to use such knowledge as competitive advantage. However, clients such as the UK supermarkets now require their framework-contracting organisation to engage in continuous learning vis-a-vis sharing best practice and this model is likely to gain wider acceptance throughout the industry. Architectural practices who were competitors may well become accomplices, albeit in a semi cartel type industry structure. This is already noticeable in the world of SME contracting where work becomes harder to find for those organisations not linked through strategic partnerships. This is the 'Eganised' prescription for consolidation within the construction industry. The Small Practice committee at the RIBA has identified this problem:

Sole practitioners and smaller practices are increasingly marginalised as government and major clients take routes such as PFI and inappropriate framework agreements, which tend to favour corporate consultants (RIBA, 2003).

As the growth of these 'new' professions mirrored the use of alternative procurement routes in the 1980s–1990s (moving from traditional, to management, to design and build) then so has the current re-engagement of architects. The Private Finance Initiative (PFI) has provided the playing field for enhanced teamwork with other construction professionals and for the restructuring of architectural practice itself. As Andrew Lowe, director of Architecture PLB, a medium-sized practice involved in PFI Schools notes:

> You're not on the other side of the table any more; you've got to work as a team. We've learned a lot from contractors, which has fed into our work. We've undergone a cultural change (Building, 2003).

An opposing view to the benefits derived in this procurement revolution is expressed by architect Gus Alexander (2001):

> The current funding mantra of try a new procurement system every five minutes, spearheaded by bean-counters and the Egan brigade, means novice clients are being encouraged to enter into novel forms of procurement where the traditional role of the architect, their principle adviser, has been sidelined as part of an inappropriate efficiency drive.

19.4 Engaging in cultural change

In 1999 RIBA produced *Constructive Change* (www.architecture.com) containing proposals for action in response to 'Rethinking Construction'. A year later a leaflet, *Architects and the Changing Construction Industry*, explaining how the industry can change for the better, and what architects can do about it, was sent to all members. Further evidence of the need for evolution in an architects role was emphasised at the 2002 RIBA conference. Paul Hyett argued that the profession was not in a good shape to cope with the demands placed upon architects. It was suggested that a mismatch had occurred between what clients wanted and what architects were able to give them (Building, 2003).

The outward perspective noted above has also been complemented with a less complementary introspective review of the architectural profession. A research exercise jointly funded by RIBA and the University of the West of England resulted in the report, 'Why Do Women Leave Architecture?' (see Graft-Johnson et al, 2003). The employment of white males dominate architecture like all other construction professions, however the report revealed that discrimination against women in architectural practices is too common an occurrence. In particular, the survey of 170 women architects revealed a culture within practices where workaholism, low and unequal pay, and macho and sexist behaviour towards female colleagues are contributory factors in resignations. Notably, the RIBA response to the report makes special note that many of the factors that lead to architects leaving the profession apply equally to men. Clearly, the challenge for RIBA and their members is one of public relations. The commitment shown to diversity and equal opportunity will ensure a continued supply of bright school-leavers applying to study architecture.[4]

Returning to the outward perspective, RIBA have made a strong case on behalf of their members by stating that 'any rethinking of the construction process must involve placing a high value on design' (RIBA, 2000). For example, architects can play a significant role in the Movement for Innovation (M4I) Demonstration project programme, and the Construction Best Practice Programme (CBPP) would like to see greater participation from architects. As of June 2003 the initiative included 134 active and 240 completed projects. Each project must demonstrate innovation and so far this has mainly concerned aspects of partnering, supply chain integration, respect for people and value management (Constructing Excellence, 2003).

19.5 Breaking down stereotypical barriers

If progress is to be made in assembling truly integrated project teams then the institutionalised stereotypical views held by far too many construction professionals require attention. The social class system (considering occupational prestige) that positions architects alongside doctors, solicitors and the upper middle class professional elite is to a large extent alive and well in UK society. Engineers are seen as socially inferior to architects despite the existence of world-class interdisciplinary practices such as Arup and WS Atkins. Contractors are better known as builders and are exposed by the media as socially inferior and this is played out by continual reference to cowboy practice.

The stereotypical descriptions held by a sizeable portion of the general public are also prevalent within the construction process. It could be argued that the relative lack in role and responsibility definition in the majority of projects manifests itself in the professionals also adopting such perspectives. One prescription for smoothing out such misunderstanding would be for greater transparency between the professions and with clients. The interdisciplinary schooling of young architects with other construction professionals, called on by RIBA for well over a decade, is of course intended to improve this matter. However, it is argued here that this process has been largely ineffective and has been spoiled by political game-playing undertaken by 'architectural academics'. A more radical reform, unpalatable to many readers, would see architects taking the initiative by returning to the ethos that was echoed by the likes of John Ruskin (1867). The teaching of space, urban planning and architectural history would be complemented by an equal time devoted to building design engineering. This should involve architects taking placement within the contracting side of the industry and would echo Ruskin's philosophy:

... be part of my scheme of physical education that every youth in the state – from the Kings' son downwards should learn to do something finely and thoroughly with his hand; so as to let him know what touch meant and what craftsmanship meant. Let him once learn to take a straight shaving off a plank, or draw a fine curve without faltering or lay a brick level in its mortar and he has learned a multitude of other matters which no lips of man could ever teach him.

The concluding remarks at the end of this handbook have been deliberately left to architects rather than construction managers. The RIBA (2000) report asks: 'Will architects be expelled from the Garden of Egan?' It is recommended that members should view the 1998 'Rethinking Construction' report as a catalyst for continuous improvement and, in particular, set the tone for the radical change called for in the report:

It is up to us to promote, inspire and take part vigorously in that change. The alternative is to be left beached.

References

Alexander, G., 'Procure for all ills', *Building*, 12 Oct., 2001, p. 33.

Alsop, W., 'No Beauty in Industry; Project Managers have lack of vision says the chairman of Alsop Architects', *Contract Journal*, 19 Dec., 2001, p. 5.

Building, 'Architects in Crisis', *Building*, 4 July, 2003, pp. 32–41.

Chappell, D., and Willis, A., *The Architect in Practice*, 8th edn, Blackwell Publishing, Oxford (2000).

Constructing Excellence, 'Rethinking Construction', Demonstrations Report, July 2003.

Egan, J., 'Rethinking Construction', Report of the Construction Task Force on the Scope for Improving Quality and Efficiency in UK Construction, Department of the Environment, Transport and the Regions (DETR) (1998).

Graft-Johnson, A., Manley, S. and Greed, C., *Why Do Women leave Architecture?*, Research Project funded by the RIBA and match funded by the University of the West of England, RIBA Publications (2003).

Latham, M., 'Constructing the Team', Joint Review of Procurement and Contractual Arrangements in the United Kingdom Construction Industry, Final Report, HMSO (1994).

Mosey, D., 'PPC 2000', ACA Standard Form of Contract for Project Partnering, Association of Consultant Architects (2000).

RIBA, 'Proposals from the RIBA Practice Committee for Sustained Action in Response to the Rethinking Construction', RIBA Practice Service (1999a).

RIBA, 'Architectural Education for the 21st Century', RIBA Education Centre (1999b).

RIBA, 'Architects and the Changing Construction Industry', Report enclosed in the July 2000 Issue of the *RIBA Journal*, taken from Debate/Constructive Change at www.architecture.com, 29 July, 2003.

RIBA, Small Practice page, taken from www.riba.org

Ruskin, J., *The Seven Lamps of Architecture*, Dover Publishing, New York (1867).

Saxon, R., Richard Saxon, in *Building*, 10 Jan., 2003, pp. 32–33.

Watts, G., 'Architecture professionals need to raise their game – or face permanent relegation in the project team', *Building*, 4 July, 2003, p. 37.

Endnotes

1 This is opposed to what Richard Saxon refers to as 'academic architecture' whereby he argues that many architects are retreating from reality and are not able to fulfil their role in the construction team.

2 Read the book written by architects Cornick, T. and Mather, J., *Construction Project Teams: Making Them Work Profitably*, Thomas Telford (1999).

3 See Holti, R., Hicolini, D. and Smalley, M. (2000) 'The Handbook of Supply Chain Management', CIRIA Report C546; Nicolini, D., Tomkins, C., Holti, R. *et al*, 'Can Target Costing and Whole Life Costing be Applied in the Construction Industry?: Evidence from Two Case Studies', *British Journal of Management*, Vol. 11, No. 4, 2000, pp. 303–24; Nicolini, D., Holti, R. and Smalley, M., 'Integrating Project Activities: The Theory and Practice of Managing the Supply Chain Through Clusters', *Construction Management and Economics*, Vol. 19, 2001, pp. 37–47.

4 For further information on employment practice see the M4I Respect for People Working Group Report (2000), 'A Commitment to People "Our Biggest Asset"', DETR, London.

Index

Index

Index

Index